SERVICE WITH
THE SIGNAL CORPS

SERVICE WITH
THE SIGNAL CORPS

THE CIVIL WAR MEMOIR OF
CAPTAIN LOUIS R. FORTESCUE

Edited by J. Gregory Acken

VOICES OF THE CIVIL WAR,

Michael P. Gray, Series Editor

The University of Tennessee Press / Knoxville

The Voices of the Civil War series makes available a variety of primary source materials that illuminate issues on the battlefield, the home front, and the western front, as well as other aspects of this historic era. The series contextualizes the personal accounts within the framework of the latest scholarship and expands established knowledge by offering new perspectives, new materials, and new voices.

Frontispiece. Louis R. Fortescue, photographed in 1865. Courtesy of The Civil War Museum of Philadelphia and The Heritage Center of The Union League of Philadelphia.

The paper in this book meets the requirements of American National Standards Institute / National Information Standards Organization specification Z39.48–1992 (Permanence of Paper). It contains 30 percent post-consumer waste and is certified by the Forest Stewardship Council.

Library of Congress Cataloging-in-Publication Data

Fortescue, Louis R., 1838-1915.
Service with the Signal Corps : the Civil War memoir of Captain Louis R. Fortescue / edited by J. Gregory Acken. — First edition.
    pages cm. — (Voices of the Civil War)
Includes bibliographical references and index.
ISBN 978-1-62190-125-9 (hardcover)
1. Fortescue, Louis R., 1838-1915. 2. United States. Army. Signal Corps—Biography. 3. United States—History—Civil War, 1861-1865—Personal narratives. 4. United States—History—Civil War, 1861-1865—Communications. I. Acken, J. Gregory, editor. II. Title.
E608.F59 2015
973.7'8092—dc23
[B]
2014040809

CONTENTS

ILLUSTRATIONS

Figures

Maps

FOREWORD

P hiladelphia's Rittenhouse Square draws in both tourists and locals for its pristine gardens and idyllic sculptures, serving as a peaceful retreat in bustling Center City. Near this attraction, but tucked away off Pine Street, stood one of oldest and undervalued Civil War institutions in the country. Founded by veterans in the Military Order of the Loyal Legion of the United States in 1888, the Civil War Library and Museum of Philadelphia was a historical treasure trove, where its visitors might see an eclectic mix of artifacts from uniforms, daguerreotypes, or weapons of common contemporaries, to pieces from more prominent figures, such as a presentation sword once owned by Ulysses S. Grant, a death mask of Abraham Lincoln, or the head mount of General George Gordon Meade's horse. A Civil War roundtable met there for many years, appropriately named after Meade's mare, "Old Baldy." This red-brick repository held more than the material culture of the conflict, before it finally closed its doors due to a lack of funding and its inconspicuous location in the backdrop of other destinations. It also contained a large collection of diaries, letters, and memoirs from those who were directly or indirectly involved in the struggle. Among them, buried within its holdings, were five bound cloth memoirs written by Louis R. Fortescue, who entered the war as common soldier, but left it with an uncommon occupation, making his work an extremely rare find.

Fortescue, a Philadelphian, first enlisted in a Pennsylvania regiment but his eventual fate was to become a specialized soldier in the newly formed Signal Corps. The twenty-three-year-old had to prepare for a duty that was unlike any he had undergone with the volunteers—and in command of his training and tutelage was the visionary Dr. Albert Myer. Albert Myer's progressive contributions would go well beyond the Civil War, but the conflict did serve as a platform for him in introducing an innovative language in warfare; under proper conditions, Myer's system let army personnel "speak" to one another from far-off distances, but in silence. While in medical school, Myer blended his labors in the telegraph industry with his graduate studies among the hearing impaired. Not only did telegraphy provide him with supplement pay for schooling, it made him think deeply about applying his new medium to benefit people who were not deaf—which eventually included the Union army. The Civil War catapulted Myer into prominence, becoming known as the "father of the Signal Corps," but the results of his dissertation on deaf communication helped him also move to other fields during Reconstruction, as he also revolutionized the study of meteorology with pioneering work on storm warnings. Yet, that foundation came from his experiences at war, his system based on the utilization of flags or torches, depending on the time of day, weather conditions, and the environment. Civil War signal corpsmen were trained to be extremely conscious of these elements, and Myer recruited soldiers with unique abilities rather than from the rank and file. He preferred men that were well educated, had physical attributes with especially keen eyesight, and those that were self-reliant. In selecting his elite corps, Meyer had chosen a young Philadelphia lieutenant from the 29th Pennsylvania volunteers, who saw civil war through a very atypical perspective.

Fortescue served nearly two years in the Signal Corps. He seemed to have relished his service, demonstrated by his refusal of a promotion to become a captain in his old regiment, which would have included company command. Readers may see the many privileges afforded to signal corps duty and understand, as did Fortescue, why he preferred not to leave. Unlike the regulars, signalmen had certain freedoms not granted to others, and although their tasks were physically and mentally demanding, they had adventurous and exclusive access to command, from field to tent: high-ranking officers cherished their vital intelligence, so signalmen were generally provided a better standard of army living.

The Signal Corp soldiers' role involved making astute observations, positioning themselves properly, transcribing and conveying information, as well as reading the environment. Finding high elevations that might gain them the best areas to signal from was essential, and as a result, Fortescue's descriptions of the terrain are valuable. Moreover, and depending on the circumstances, communication could be transmitted for some twenty-five miles, a type of long distance antebellum sign language, carried out by flags or torches and integrated into numeric codes that were translated—small wonder the use of Morse code by telegraphers along with Myer's work with the deaf caused his system to evolve; abbreviated messages or phrases, also called wig wag, were then translated. Although some Union commanders did not fully embrace the Signal Corps early in the conflict, by war's end prominent commanders, such as George H. Thomas, William T. Sherman, and George A. Custer, wholeheartedly endorsed the system.

One might see why the system gained such acclaim, along with appreciating its complexities, as the reader rides with Fortescue through the Virginia and Maryland countryside as he dismounted and then took the heights for position to commence or receive communiqué. Fortescue wrote about aerial balloons, the intricacies of flags and flares, and special codes that were used so that signals were not stolen by their adversaries. Fortescue's descriptions of how he dealt with diverse environments is exceptional, as are other events as he moved among civilians and guerilla warriors, through camp temperance movements to religious services—including a "spiritual" dinner with O. O. Howard. The operations of the Confederate Signal Corps are also touched upon; it had great success at First Bull Run, as one of Myer's former students signed on with the Confederacy. The list of engagements that Fortescue either was involved in or observed is impressive: he saw action at Cedar Mountain, Second Bull Run, Antietam, Fredericksburg, Chancellorsville, and Gettysburg. Readers will find the subject's poignant impressions of Antietam's Bloody Lane, as well as Ambrose Burnside's ignominious assaults at Fredericksburg—where Fortescue saw it unfold from atop a nearby cupola, eventually facing enemy fire himself. His observations from Chancellorsville are highlighted, and an indifferent Fortescue referred to Stonewall Jackson as an "over-rated flanker." Gettysburg is especially elaborated upon, as Fortescue watched the battle unfold from a nearby mountaintop, although his panoramic view left him behind enemy lines, which ultimately led to his capture. The Pennsylvanian, apprehended near the border of his native state, spent the rest of his service imprisoned in the South.

Editor J. Gregory Acken doggedly pursued his subject, going through the laborious process of piecing together the memoirs left in Philadelphia and in other archives in the South. Acken clarifies Fortescue's infrequent miscues and also meticulously adds where his subject detracts, giving much needed commentary to fully uncover any complexities and correct miscalculations that came with Fortescue's assessments. The editor has combined other primary accounts (including a diary and letters) into this important single volume—which is well written by Fortescue and enhanced by the editor. This work is ground breaking since no contemporary scholarly account of a Civil War signalman exists.

In addition to its rarity, *Service with The Signal Corps* speaks to new trends in the profession and will hopefully assist future scholarship. As environmental history continues to flourish in Civil War historiography, this work's strength lies in providing insightful observations from elevated positions. Consequently, readers gain a better understanding of the landscape of battle from this signal corps officer. Moreover, this volume is useful in explaining another recently emerging theme in the field, namely, studies that emphasize aftermath of battle, referencing the destruction of war not only on people, but also to animals, infrastructure, and countryside. Finally, an overarching theme of the Signal Corps and its creation is an insightful addition to disability history. The very genesis of the corps was founded by helping the deaf, and this work will hopefully inspire more work on the "challenged" and their relation to our foremost national conflict. More than two million soldiers fought for the Union during the Civil War—only three thousand served in the Signal Corps. As the editor of The Voices of the Civil War series, I am proud to introduce the first contemporary account of a Signal corpsmen, and I congratulate J. Gregory Acken on his rare find and his outstanding editorial work.

Michael P. Gray
East Stroudsburg University of Pennsylvania

ACKNOWLEDGMENTS

I began working on the Fortescue memoir in the late 1990s and had much of the editorial content completed by 2004, but due to professional and personal considerations, I was unable to finish the project until just under a decade later. For that reason, I am certain I will inadvertently neglect to mention all of those who lent support in some fashion throughout the process. I beg forgiveness of those individuals.

I would like to thank the late Blake Magner, an author and Civil War cartographer. Blake had begun preliminary work on Fortescue in the early 1990s, but other interests intervened, and he graciously passed the project to me. For general encouragement during my time working on the manuscript, thanks are due to acquaintances, friends, and fellow former board members at the former Civil War Library and Museum (now known as the Civil War Museum of Philadelphia), including the late John Craft, Steven J. Wright, Mike Cavanaugh, Herb Kaufman, Nancy Caldwell (who also cheerfully typed several early versions of the manuscript for me), and Russ Pritchard Sr. Russ, the former director of the Civil War Library and Museum, alerted me to the uniqueness and historical value of Fortescue's writing. At The Foundations of the Union League of Philadelphia (which now houses the two-dimensional collection of the former Civil War Library and Museum), Executive Director John J. Meko Jr. and Archivist Theresa Altieri were gracious in helping me secure permission to publish the work, as was Sharon Smith, president of The Civil War Museum of Philadelphia.

Walt Mathers of the Signal Corps Association, 1860–1865 kindly shared copies of excerpts from Fortescue's record of signals in the National Archives. Anyone interested in understanding more about the role of the Signal Corps in the Civil War would profit by exploring the website of that organization (www.civilwarsignals.org). Al Conner of Stafford, Virginia, was helpful in locating key landmarks mentioned by Fortescue in the environs of Fredericksburg; Noel Harrison at Fredericksburg and Spotsylvania National Military Park shared both his expansive knowledge of wartime buildings and river crossings in the Fredericksburg/Chancellorsville area and copies of contemporary maps that proved immensely useful. Scott Hartwig of Gettysburg National Military Park was immensely helpful in identifying some obscure geographic features in the Gettysburg area. Michael Hillman of the Emmitsburg Historical Society shared a historic photograph of a house in that town that is important in telling Fortescue's story; John Allen Miller, also of the society, lent his expertise on matters pertaining to Emmitsburg-area history. Marlea Leljedal of the Army Heritage and Education Center at the U.S. Army War College in Carlisle, Pennsylvania came to the rescue by expeditiously providing copies of photographs from their collection when other avenues had proven fruitless.

Richard N. Griffin, editor of a superb volume in the Voices of the Civil War series, provided advice and helped direct me to the good people at the University of Tennessee Press. Peter Carmichael, the former Voices series editor, received my initial submission with enthusiasm and passed me into the capable hands of Michael Gray, his successor as editor of the series, and Scot Danforth, director at the press. Scot has been a fountain of encouragement from our first contact, and I owe much to both him and Thomas Wells, also of the press, for their stewardship of the project. For constructive critical readings of the manuscript and meaningful suggestions to improve it, I am beholden to Gray and to Steven J. Rauch, U.S. Army Signal Corps historian. It has been a true pleasure to once again collaborate with George Skoch, who provided the comprehensive maps that grace the book.

I am indebted finally, but certainly most importantly, to my family, who put up with me shuttered in my office for extended periods of time. Brian, Will, Regina, Cameron, and most of all my wife Regina, thank you for your patience and understanding.

INTRODUCTION

s the Army of the Potomac marshaled its strength near Washington, D.C., during the winter of 1861–62, an artilleryman stationed with his battery at Poolesville, Maryland, was intrigued by the sight of a set of curious looking flags that moved almost unceasingly in the cupola of the town's courthouse. "To the men in the other arms of the service who saw this mysterious and almost continuous waving of flags," he later remembered, "it seemed as if every motion was fraught with some momentous import. 'What could it be all about?' they would ask one another. . . . To the best of my recollection, not an hour of daylight passed without more or less flag waving from that point."[1] What this man and thousands of other soldiers stationed in the environs of the capital who observed similar enigmatic activity emanating from the surrounding countryside witnessed were the nascent hours of an organization that would become known as the U.S. Army Signal Corps.

The concepts for military signaling that eventually led to the establishment of the Signal Corps as a permanent branch of service originated with a visionary pre–Civil War army surgeon, Albert J. Myer. A native of Buffalo, New York, Myer had been interested in signals and communications from an early age. Employed as a telegrapher prior to entering medical school, Myer's doctoral dissertation dealt with the development of a touch-based sign language—as opposed to the more widely utilized hand sign language—for the deaf.

During his time in the telegraph office, Myer had been enthralled by the ability of the telegraph line to transmit "every mental emotion" by the point and pause of sound and concluded he must develop a "system of sign writing" to benefit "those whom the Deity has seen fit to deprive the natural organ of speech." Myer proposed establishing a system of communicating by code using the tap of a finger on the hand or body of those without hearing or speech. Noting that traditional sign language attracted undue attention and might elicit unwanted sympathy from onlookers, Myer believed his system, which was based partly on the Bain telegraphic alphabet he employed in the telegraph office, would overcome the social stigma that sign language was thought to produce. "The deaf mute," he believed, "might almost cease to be an object of pity."[2] Expanding further upon the principle, Myer also believed that the hand, held in a fixed starting position over a table or other surface, could, when observed by the silent and mute, "tap" dots or dashes to form words. After the word had been spelled out in this manner, the hand would return to the fixed starting position, denoting either the end of a sentence or the beginning of a new word. Knowingly or unknowingly, Myer had begun to form the precepts that he eventually incorporated into his system of military signaling, where the signal apparatus commenced and concluded communication from a fixed position.

Entering the army in 1854 as an assistant surgeon, Myer transformed the principles of the sign language he had devised into a system of transmitting information utilizing a single flag (or torch for nighttime signaling) that would revolutionize military communications.

As Myer envisioned it, the flag and torch system (sometimes referred to as the "wigwag" system) could be utilized to communicate between disparate bodies of troops or seaborne vessels (ship to ship or ship to shore) at all hours, regardless of weather conditions. The equipment necessary to communicate would be easily carried and could be assembled and employed by a solitary signalman, meaning that as few as two men would be needed to transmit and receive signals.

In 1856, Myer submitted a plan for his signal system to Secretary of War Jefferson Davis, who felt the proposal lacked detail and rejected it. When Davis left office in 1859, an ally in Washington reintroduced Myer's plan to the War Department. Summoned to the Capitol to appear before an examining board headed by future Confederate general Robert E. Lee, Myer failed to secure the outright approval he had sought (the board thought the system would not work at distances greater than three miles) but was directed to more completely field test the process. Following successful trials at various locales along the East Coast throughout 1859, Davis's successor, John B. Floyd, recommended that a signal officer with the rank of major be appointed to the staff of the army, and on June 21, 1860, the bill approving the creation of the position was signed into law. Six days later, Albert J. Myer was appointed major and signal officer of the army.[3]

Not long after the outbreak of the Civil War, Myer was back in Washington, D.C., following a tour of duty in New Mexico. His signal system had performed well during the 1858–60 actions against the Navajos, and Myer immediately commenced the daunting task of implementing it throughout the volunteer Union army that was assembling. "The period of experimentation with and proving of his signals was over," wrote Myer's biographer regarding this time. "Now would come more rapidly and on a scale surely undreamed of the ultimate test of signal communications—their testing in combat, in one of the greatest wars of all time."[4]

Following the Union reverse at First Manassas (where the use of his signal system by a former subordinate had helped turn the tide of battle in favor of the South), Myer was posted to the staff of Maj. Gen. George B. McClellan, who soon assumed command of the Army of the Potomac. The need to effect communication among the divisions of the army stationed near Washington prompted Myer to issue a request in mid-August for forty officers and eighty enlisted men to be detailed for instruction in his signal code. Once trained, these recruits would man signal stations along the Potomac. The officers chosen, Myer directed, were to be "intelligent men of good education, possessing good eyesight, and persons in whom the regimental commanders have especial confidence."[5] Among the officers sent to Myer for instruction (and thus one of the first officers ever assigned to duty in the Signal Corps) was a twenty-three-year-old Philadelphian then serving as a first lieutenant in the Twenty-ninth Pennsylvania Volunteers, Louis R. Fortescue.

Like many of the soldiers sent to learn Myer's system of signals in the first months of the war, Fortescue believed his assignment was to be temporary. The colonel of his regiment, Fortescue recalled, understood "that

Albert J. Myer, founder of the U.S. Signal Corps, shown here after his promotion to brigadier general. Courtesy Library of Congress, Prints and Photographs Division.

we would be required, in connection with the four enlisted men we were to take, to master some code of signals necessary to his command, and would then be returned to our respective companies after an absence of possibly of a few weeks only." Happily for Fortescue, the detail was to become a permanent assignment, and he spent the next twenty-three months serving as an acting signal officer in the Department of the Shenandoah, the Army of Virginia, and the Army of the Potomac.

Very little is known of Fortescue's life prior to the war; the recollections he committed to paper deal only with his experiences from the days leading up to his enlistment in the Twenty-ninth Pennsylvania in late June 1861 to the end of the conflict. The level of education he attained prior to the war is not known, however, he notes while on campaign that he is reading novels by Dickens, Bulwer, and Eugène Sue and has interspersed comments from prominent poets in his memoir, leading to the belief that he had at minimum completed a high school–level course of study.

Motivated to serve by what he recalled as "President Lincoln's stirring proclamation calling the country to arms to maintain the honor, the integrity, and the existence of our National Union," and the insulting of the nation's flag "by Southern traitors who, upon their own soil, had openly and defiantly seized the Government property, made war upon those professing loyalty to the Union, and issued their mandates to the world declaring themselves henceforth an independent people," Fortescue helped recruit what would be formally organized as Company A of the Twenty-ninth Pennsylvania Volunteers. Mustered into service on June 29, 1861, the regiment encamped on the outskirts of Philadelphia for the next month and in early August was ordered to proceed to Sandy Hook, Maryland, opposite Harpers Ferry, Virginia, where it joined with several other regiments under the command of Gen. Nathaniel Banks.[6]

Fortescue spent a scant eight weeks serving with his regiment prior to his assignment as a signal officer, but his experiences during that time undoubtedly influenced his decision when faced with the choice of either remaining on detached signal service or returning to the Twenty-ninth Pennsylvania. He characterized as "principal ignoramuses" the major and lieutenant colonel of his regiment, which led him to wonder "what evil spirit ever inflicted these two consequential devotees of Mars upon us. . . . They possessed not a scintilla of military knowledge, were ignorant of the

English grammar, had no experience in the handling of men, and were rank cowards from their boots up."

To illustrate his point, Fortescue recalled an incident during drill from early in the regiment's service. The colonel of the Twenty-ninth (who unlike the other field officers, Fortescue believed was a capable leader) ordered the men to advance across the parade ground to a certain point, when they would be commanded to move by the right oblique, as if avoiding an imaginary obstacle. The lieutenant colonel, standing nearby observing the proceedings, perked up upon hearing this and, Fortescue remembered, "called out, 'Colonel, I will stand here in the field representing the obstacle.' 'Great Heavens!' shouted the colonel, 'how very appropriate,' to the extravagant delight of the entire regiment, who ever afterwards dubbed the offender 'Old Obstacle.'"

Throughout the balance of his service in the field, Fortescue would occasionally be stationed near his regiment, and it is apparent from the tone of his comments regarding its officers that he never regretted having left them to cast his lot with the Signal Corps.

Notwithstanding the uncertain future it offered many of the officers and men who joined it early in the war, signal service presented the opportunity for a range of experiences that could not have been realized had they remained in the infantry. Both commissioned and noncommissioned signalmen were mounted and had the ability to roam, oftentimes at will, upon the fringes of the army during active campaigns. Interaction with corps, division, and brigade commanders was frequent, while signal officers in the field were envied because they were thought to possess privileged information that even higher-ranking officers lacked.[7]

A signal detachment on active duty (sometimes referred to as a "set"— Fortescue spelled it "sett") was typically comprised of two officers and four enlisted flagmen, occasionally supplemented by a cook or servants. It was not uncommon—especially during periods of inaction—for these detachments to operate autonomously for lengthy periods of time, which was more than acceptable, according to accounts. "The lot of the signal officer was comparatively pleasant," remembered a New York captain. "His assignment gave him a latitude of freedom which many officers of higher grade did not enjoy. He was often located on stations far removed from the troops . . . as free and unrestrained as any fisherman's camp of the north woods in summer."[8] Fortescue certainly concurred, relishing, as he wrote soon after joining the Signal Corps, "having exchanged the stern discipline of regimental life for that of unrestricted special service."

Despite the benefits it offered, life as a signalman was not wholly idyllic. Separation from the bulk of the army they were attached to might have been amenable for signal detachments during an active campaign, but during winter quarters or other prolonged periods of inaction, tedium could easily set in. As isolated as they were at these times, surprise and capture were ever-present dangers, while pay was sporadic even during the best of times (though there would seem to have been little to spend hard currency on in the field). Active signaling between detachments was kept up at intervals around the clock, which, as Fortescue later explains, was a decided inconvenience on cold nights in the dead of winter. Reminiscent of the artillery arm of the service, promotion in the corps was rare, resulting in dissatisfaction among officers who might have fared better had they remained with their infantry regiments.[9] This fact aside, when Fortescue was offered the chance to return to the Twenty-ninth Pennsylvania with the increased rank of captain commanding his company, he declined the advancement because he was loath to forego the relative freedom that life as a signal officer afforded him.

~~~

The role of the Signal Corps was to observe, reconnoiter, and communicate. Signal detachments were to be located at prominent positions (ideally the highest elevations that could be found) around the terrain in which an army was operating and, through the use of signal flags and torches, transmit information between detachments of friendly troops (usually orders for movement or information on reinforcements) and communicate intelligence about their enemy's strength or movements. The nature of their work ensured that on many occasions, signalmen were the advance of the army. During an active battle, signalmen were posted at advantageous positions in and around the battlefield and would, when conditions permitted, gather and forward or relay information to brigade, corps, or army headquarters. At times, they were also called upon to act as forward observers, relating the results of artillery fire back to battery commanders. On occasion, when the need for concealment was paramount or adverse battlefield conditions such as powder smoke, atmospheric disturbances, or irregular terrain precluded signaling by flag, signal stations served as posts of observation and information was dispatched to authorities via mounted courier. It was also not uncommon for signal officers assigned to headquarters staff to be pressed into duty as temporary aides-de-camp during battle, as Fortescue would experience at Cedar Mountain in August 1862.

Signal stations were ideally located approximately eight miles apart, although when necessary and the atmosphere was clear, signals could be transmitted at distances of twenty-five miles or more.[10] At shorter distances (five miles or less), signals were read either with the naked eye or binoculars (referred to at the time as "marine glasses"), while telescopes, sometimes fastened to a tree or fixed upon a tripod, were used for reading communications sent over longer distances.[11]

The signal code conceived of and taught by Myer early in the war (which Fortescue explains further in the first chapter), known as the four-element code, was relatively easily learned and was comprised of the numbers 1, 2, 3 and 4, each of which was transmitted by moving the signal apparatus from side to side in a prescribed manner. (A wave of the signal apparatus from its upright starting position ninety degrees to the left and returning to vertical, for example, represents the number 1, while a similar movement to the right represents the number 2.) Different combinations of numbers represent various letters of the alphabet (an *A* was transmitted by signaling *11*), and words were formed by moving the flag or torch as dictated by the numerical code corresponding to the letter being transmitted. Frequently used words or short phrases—such as "Received," "All quiet," "Are you ready?" and "Did you understand?"—were assigned unique, shortened abbreviations. Messages, orders, and general communications that were to be sent were read aloud by the signal officer to the signalman on duty in coded (numerical) form, who would transmit them. Enlisted signalmen were not permitted to know either the signal code or the content of messages, but several of the more intelligent men became conversant in the code over time. Later in the war, when it became apparent that Confederate signalmen were reading their transmissions and were familiar with the cipher they were using,[12] cipher disks were introduced and the combinations used in conjunction with them were changed frequently to prevent further interceptions.

The signal flags most commonly used to send messages were four feet by four feet, usually attached to a twelve-foot wooden pole assembled in

A Federal signal station on Elk Mountain near Antietam, Maryland, after the September 1862 battle. Lt. Frederick Owen is seated with the telescope at left; Lt. Edwin C. Pierce is seated just above him with notebook in hand. The flagman at top holding the white background signal flag is unidentified; Pvt. Harrison W. Gardiner stands below the flagman; and Pvt. Robert J. Morgan stands at the right. Courtesy Library of Congress, Prints and Photographs Division.

sections. Dark flags (black or red) were to be used when signaling against light backgrounds, such as the sky, while white flags were used against dark backgrounds, such as woods or terrain. White flags were utilized more frequently than dark.[13]

Unfamiliarity with the advantages the signal system could offer meant that it was initially viewed with skepticism by field commanders. "None of the first detachments was received kindly," a prominent officer in the Signal Corps later recalled. "No one seemed to appreciate them. They were ridiculed and sneered at. Every article of equipage issued to them was done in a grudging manner, as if so much robbed from the hard-working soldier who did the fighting."[14] Fortescue encountered this attitude when he was assigned to duty under Ninth Corps commander Orlando Willcox before Fredericksburg in November 1862. After several days spent busily sending and receiving messages on behalf of the exacting general, Fortescue proudly reported that Willcox "could find no fault with the quality and importance of the work we performed, and later seemed really desirous of complimenting us on the rapidity with which the messages were transmitted."

Much of the reluctance to embrace the Signal Corps early in the conflict seems to have originated with high-ranking Regular Army officers. Maj. Gen. George B. McClellan, while complimenting the mission of the corps and the efforts of Myer, with whom he was friendly, recalled after the war that the officers serving under the major "were not trained as soldiers and therefore their judgment could not always be relied upon."[15] It should be noted though, as evidenced by a directive Myer himself issued to the officers of the Signal Corps during the Gettysburg Campaign, a full two years into the war, that McClellan's observations may not have been unfounded. He wrote:

> It having come to the knowledge of the Signal Officer
> of the Army that in some instances officers of the Signal
> Corps have transmitted information by signals of such
> a character as to produce alarm, uproar, and confusion
> among troops . . . which reports have often been without
> foundation . . . it is hereby ordered and enjoined that
> all signal officers shall be held fully responsible . . . for
> such stampede reports forwarded without foundation or
> forethought of this.

Under all circumstances must officers be fully cognizant of the responsibility resting upon them as proper and reliable sources of information or means of communications, such information being in most cases . . . the foundation of important movements or operations of the Army or Navy.[16]

While undoubtedly a cause for concern (nearly every signal officer who served in the Signal Corps during the war was from the volunteers), the idea that they might be perceived as undependable rankled the men who had dedicated their time in the service to signaling. Reflecting further on this preconception, one of the few Regular Army officers who served in the Signal Corps during the conflict recalled that McClellan's way of thinking

pervaded the army in the early part of the war, and may account for the timidity of the high authorities in recognizing the usefulness of the system, and explain why the early efforts of the Corps to take the high position it so obstinately worked for, and so firmly maintained before the war closed, were unsuccessful. The system was the invention of a doctor—a noncombatant—and the Corps was officered by lieutenants of volunteers without prestige. It was experimental, unknown to students of war. . . . The thought of detaching from the fighting forces of the army a number of officers and men to "flop flags," was not, at first, favorably considered. The allotment of money was made in the most penurious manner, and it required superhuman energy to obtain recognition for the Corps until the enemy had shown, by using signals at Bull Run, that it was prepared to adopt the system.[17]

Despite the fact that they struggled for the respect and recognition they thought they deserved, the men who served in the Signal Corps during the Civil War were proud to have been a part of it and considered themselves a breed apart from the balance of the army. "The officers composing the Signal Corps," wrote one of their number, "were, as a body, bright, active young men, fully alive to the possibilities of the corps, and always ready to do any work or take any risk that might be of service to the army. Indeed, many of them, with the reckless enthusiasm of youth, would incur greater risks than were necessary."[18]

That the signalmen were ultimately successful in establishing the worth of the Signal Corps and changing the attitude of officers who initially held misgivings about it is attested to in the accolades they collected as the conflict progressed. Writing from Chattanooga in late 1863, Maj. Gen. George H. Thomas avowed that "the value of the [signal] system has time and again been more closely demonstrated by the great amount of information of the movements of the enemy obtained and transmitted to headquarters by its aid, which could not have possibly been obtained by any other means, in time to have been of use." Ill-fated George Custer, writing from the Army of the Potomac at the same time, concurred: "Since I have become acquainted with the Signal Corps of this army, the information of the enemy obtained through its officers, and the rapid manner they have of transmitting intelligence by flag signals, has convinced me of the great value of this branch of the service during military operations in the field. An army can have no better outpost, from which to watch the movements of the enemy, than a signal station; and with a practised signal officer at such a position, no force can move without being detected." "In several instances," affirmed Maj. Gen. William T. Sherman in October 1864, "this Corps has transmitted orders and brought me information of the greatest importance that could not have reached me in any other way."[19]

~~~

Louis R. Fortescue's Civil War service, while not overly distinguished, was unquestionably unique. He experienced the conflict from several perspectives—infantry subaltern, signal officer, aide-de-camp (briefly), and prisoner of war—and took an active role in a number of important campaigns and battles. Following signal training in the late summer and fall of 1861 and a season of comparative inactivity during the winter of 1861–62, he was assigned to the Department of the Shenandoah, crossing the Potomac and moving south with the force under Nathaniel Banks in February 1862. Although present during the latter stages of the First Battle of Kernstown on March 23, 1862, he took no active role in the fight. Afterward, he and his fellow signalmen moved with Banks up the Shenandoah Valley, but Fortescue was taken ill before participating in any of the subsequent battles there during the spring of 1862.

Returning to active service in July 1862, he became a part of the Army of Virginia and was assigned to duty at Maj. Gen. John Pope's headquarters. He took part in the Battle of Cedar Mountain, and during the Second Manassas Campaign he served at both Banks's and Pope's headquarters. Following the Union defeat at Second Manassas and the assimilation of the Army of Virginia into the Army of the Potomac, Fortescue was posted at Harpers Ferry during the early phases of the Maryland Campaign (where his absence during a crucial period may have helped doom its garrison) and was on the battlefield to witness the horrors of Antietam. With the Army of the Potomac, he went on to participate in the Fredericksburg, Chancellorsville, and Gettysburg campaigns. Two days after the fighting ended at Gettysburg, Fortescue was taken prisoner and spent the next twenty months trying to survive the rigors of a succession of Southern prison camps, including Richmond's Libby Prison, the prison at Macon, Georgia, and the officers' prisons located at Charleston and Columbia, South Carolina.

Fortescue reveals much about himself during the course of his narrative, and to fully explore his outlook and attitudes in the introduction to his reminiscences would be redundant. However, in order to better understand his beliefs and appreciate what motivated him, it is not inappropriate—in the interest of providing context—to briefly examine his worldview and how it impacted both his wartime experiences and his resulting recounting of them.

Fortescue held strong opinions on many of the important issues of his time and holds nothing back in his memoir when expounding upon his beliefs. Politically, he was a pro-Lincoln Republican. He had little use for the Army of the Potomac's early commander, George B. McClellan, and disdained those who were cut from the same ideological cloth as "Little Mac." Unlike McClellan, who initially adopted a less hard line attitude toward the South, Fortescue advocated a vigorous, win-at-any-cost prosecution of the war and derided commanders who "placed safeguards around the property of Rebels and punished the weary and footsore soldier who helped himself to their fruit." Though not an avowed abolitionist, it is clear that he abhorred slavery. Like many volunteers, he despised the rigidity and formality he witnessed between the officers of the Regular Army and their men. By the standards of his time, he might have been considered enlightened or even progressive, however, he was not above using racial slurs to refer to African Americans he had interactions with, while a streak of nativism with which he was infused led to the expression on several occasions of prejudice against Jews and Irish Americans.

By the time Fortescue recorded his memoirs, some thirty years after the war, a wave of national conciliation between North and South had swept America, but Fortescue was unapologetically impervious to its effects. Indeed, a fitting subtitle for his memoir might be "An Unreconstructed Yankee." The roots of his lasting enmity toward the South, which undoubtedly, based on his writings, took hold and were nurtured during his early war service, were irrevocably deepened by his experiences in prison. Whether soldier or civilian, Fortescue could find nothing even faintly praiseworthy to say in his writings about pro-Confederate Southerners he encountered, and on occasion he would plumb the depths of hyperbole—and the limits of proper grammar—to convey the contempt he felt for them. A sampling from his diatribe against the citizens of Winchester, Virginia, in March 1862 ("lean, lank, sallow-pated and alcohol-drenched biliousites") or his ill-informed comment regarding the legendary Confederate general Stonewall Jackson ("an overrated flanker") are just several of many examples. Even with years of retrospection to temper his opinions, Fortescue was still unforgiving.

He rarely mentions his family in his writing, referring only twice to his younger brother, Joseph, who was captured while serving with the Seventy-third Pennsylvania Infantry in the Western theater and was held, ironically, in Richmond's Belle Isle prison at the same time Louis was incarcerated in nearby Libby Prison.

~~~

There is no shortage of reminiscences by veterans of the Civil War. Narratives and personal accounts written by infantrymen abound because the majority of Civil War personnel served as foot soldiers. Less common are reminiscences by members of the other combat arms—artillerymen, cavalrymen, marines, and sailors—because, as a matter of proportion, fewer personnel served in these disciplines. Accounts from what can be classified as the support arms—engineers, ordnance, provost marshal, quartermaster, medical services, and the Signal Corps—are rarer still. In relation to the U.S. Signal Corps, only a handful of firsthand accounts detailing the experiences of its personnel during the war have been published, and in each of these cases, the narratives have been limited to article-length accounts. It is estimated that nearly three thousand soldiers served with the U.S. Signal Corps during the war;[20] Fortescue's is the only book-length reminiscence by a member of the corps to have come to light.

The study of but a fraction of Civil War soldier's recollections reveals to the careful observer that the most determined adversary of truth and accuracy, in numerous instances, is time. Many of the most valuable personal accounts from the conflict were recorded while the events they relate were still fresh in the participant's mind, even though they may, due to ignorance, misinformation, or narrowness of experience, be inaccurate. These immediate recollections—imperfect though some may be—are typically uninfluenced by factors that tend to lessen the value of accounts written decades after the fact, factors such as the knowledge of their commanders or enemy's motives, the makeup or strength of forces opposing them, or the time-informed opinions of historians or fellow soldiers, to name several. Slightly less dependable (because they may be subjected to some of the same influences as immediate recollections) are reminiscences penned years after the conflict that are based on a contemporary diary or letters. Tending to be least reliable of all are firsthand accounts written either partially or wholly from memory many years after the war, which contain opinions based and conclusions formed on information that was unavailable to the writer when the events they describe occurred.

While it is unclear exactly when during the postwar years Fortescue composed his memoir (the typescript version upon which this work is based dates to the 1890s), it is evident that he based his writings on his contemporary diary entries and other personal wartime memoranda. Despite this, his work is not uninfluenced by three decades of hindsight, occasional factual errors, and, in several places, what seem to be deliberate misstatements. I have discovered three instances—one dealing with his role at the Battle of Chancellorsville, another describing the circumstances of his capture after Gettysburg, and a final one detailing a Fourth of July celebration in prison at Macon, Georgia, in 1864 (which is not included in the book)—where Fortescue's postwar version of his experiences is contradicted by both secondary evidence and, more tellingly, his contemporary diary entries. The discovery of even a single instance of untruthfulness in a personal reminiscence is alarming; uncovering multiple instances should rightly cast doubt on the veracity of the entire work. However, taking into consideration the breadth of Fortescue's recollections and weighing the fact that many of the numerous other personal incidents, anecdotes, and experiences he relates can, and have been, verified by the same methods used to uncover his few fabrications, his offenses are less serious than they appear, and are discussed in more complete detail as they occur within the narrative.

Although Fortescue may have filled several personal diaries, only one, covering the period from January 1863 to March 1865, has come to light. This small, well-worn volume, which is housed in the Southern Historical Collection at the Wilson Library of the University of North Carolina at Chapel Hill, is nearly illegible in places because Fortescue was compelled—due to his capture and imprisonment—to commit more than two years of experiences into a volume intended to accommodate a single year's worth. In many places, entries for 1864 and 1865 are written cross-wise over the corresponding dates for 1863. Given that Fortescue carried this book with him through two major campaigns and an almost two-year stint in five different prison camps, it is remarkable that it has survived at all. For several reasons, namely, the existing diary seems to pick up where a prior volume left off, the level of detail evident in his writings covering 1861–62, and he titled his finished memoir "War Diary of Louis R. Fortescue," it is almost certain that there was an additional diary (or diaries) covering his earlier war service, however, if it—or they—exist, I have been unable to find them.

A handwritten partial record of signals sent and received by him between November 10, 1861, and May 6, 1863, resides in the National Archives, and it is likely, based on references he makes to a number of these communications, that this record, like the aforementioned diary, was consulted when he wrote his account.[21]

Fortescue had the memoir upon which the current work is based typed, mimeographed, and bound into five cloth-covered volumes sometime near the end of the nineteenth century. The first three volumes cover the period from June 29, 1861, to July 18, 1863, and deal with Fortescue's service in the Twenty-ninth Pennsylvania and his time in the Signal Corps. Volumes 4 and 5, which cover the period from July 19, 1863, to April 15, 1865, are a re-counting of his experiences as a prisoner of war and are not included here. Each volume carries the title "War Diary" gold-stamped on the spine, while the title pages in each volume bear the heading "Diary of Army Service," followed by the dates corresponding with the events covered within. The covers of the volumes, each of which contains an average of 178 pages, are also embossed with the dates corresponding with the events contained within them. Fortescue had taken care to collect selected official papers, photographs, and various newspaper clippings and illustrations (some in his own hand) pertaining to his military service both during and after the war; these are bound into the pages of his memoir at appropriate points in the narrative. Fortescue's wartime recollections have been a part of the collection of the Civil War Library and Museum in Philadelphia (now known as the Civil War Museum of Philadelphia) since June 1923, when, according to bookplates fastened inside their covers, they were donated to the institution by a Miss Mary C. Longworth. How Longworth came into possession of the memoir and what her relationship was to Fortescue and his wife is unclear, as when Fortescue died in 1915, he was childless and was survived only by his widow, Mildred Maull Fortescue.

Editing Fortescue's manuscript proved challenging due to several factors, including his penchant for run-on sentences, a maddening tendency to alternate at will—many times within the body of a sentence or paragraph—between past and present tenses, an intermittent lack (and at times an excess) of punctuation, and the somewhat stilted, overly formal style of writing he utilized. In fashioning the work for publication, I have shortened some—though not all, as will be evident—of his lengthier sentences and have freely inserted punctuation and refashioned paragraphs according to modern standards in an effort to improve the flow of the text. In no instance have I altered or modified what Fortescue wrote in an effort to change the meaning of his recollections. As a result of the changes that were made, it was necessary on a number of occasions to insert a word or series of words into a sentence or paragraph to render it grammatically correct (or nearly so); in these cases the additional words are enclosed in brackets. Even with my changes, the reader will find that more than a few sentences remain grammatical anomalies, but I refrained from further adjustments for fear of altering the flavor of what Fortescue wrote.

At times, Fortescue related his experiences in random order. Based on the historical record, excerpts from his surviving 1863 diary and the recollections of fellow soldiers, I have placed these events in proper chronological order. Chapter introductions and detailed endnotes have been added to help the reader place Fortescue's experiences within the context of the war as a whole and provide avenues for more detailed research. Little effort has been made to identify the nonmilitary personnel Fortescue mentions in his writings. Lengthy recitations of mundane events not touching on Fortescue's military experience and other material that was deemed to be superfluous has been excluded.

~~~

Following his exchange from prison in March 1865, Fortescue returned to Philadelphia and began the process of putting his life back together. Initially employed as a clerk in the insurance business, he spent twenty-four years in private enterprise, working his way up to cashier of the Union Insurance Company. In 1889, he entered city government as chief clerk in the controller's department and was later appointed deputy city controller, a position of responsibility that carried with it the not-inconsequential annual salary of twenty-five hundred dollars. A disagreement with the city controller over a trivial matter led him to resign in 1909 at the age of seventy-one, and he appears to have spent the remaining six years of his life in retirement.[22]

Although he makes no mention of his future wife in his memoir (with the exception of his dedication of the work to her and several references interspersed in his diary), he married the aforementioned Mildred Adelaide Engle Maull in July 1866.

In January 1868, Pennsylvania governor and former major general John W. Geary, under whom Fortescue had served in late 1861, recommended him to the secretary of war for the brevet rank of major, citing his war service and his "sterling integrity and unblemished reputation." I have been unable to determine whether Fortescue ever officially received the brevet promotion, though in 1879 he was appointed aide-de-camp and signal officer with the rank of major in the Pennsylvania National Guard.[23]

Fortescue took an active role in a number of veteran's organizations in the years after the war. He joined the Pennsylvania Commandery of the

Military Order of the Loyal Legion of the United States in 1887 and served for a time as commander of Philadelphia's Post 2 of the Grand Army of the Republic (GAR). On at least one occasion, in 1884, he delivered a lecture on his prison experiences to his GAR comrades. He was a member of the Society of Ex-Prisoners of War (serving as vice president of the group in 1886), treasurer of the Survivor's Association of the Twenty-ninth Pennsylvania, and a member U.S. Veteran Signal Corps Association. In the latter organization, he served as chairman of the Executive Committee and on its Monument Committee. He was a member of the commission appointed by Pennsylvania governor Edwin S. Stuart charged with overseeing the construction of a memorial at Salisbury, North Carolina, dedicated to soldiers from Pennsylvania who had died in the prison camp there; in November 1910, he traveled to Salisbury for its dedication and during the ceremonies personally tendered the monument, on behalf of the commission, to the governor. A period photograph places him at the fiftieth anniversary commemoration of the Battle of Gettysburg in 1913.

Fortescue also actively corresponded with soldiers he had served with, made his personal papers available to the historian of the Signal Corps, and helped prepare the historical sketch of the Twenty-ninth Pennsylvania Regiment that was delivered at the dedication of their Gettysburg monument in 1889.[24]

A fondness for drawing he had developed to while away the wearisome hours in Libby Prison bore fruit in 1888, when a sketch he prepared showing a cross section of Libby and the escape route taken by the tunnel party in February 1864 was published in the March issue of the *Century Magazine*.

Fortescue died from what was described as acute indigestion in December 1915 at the age of seventy-seven. What he left us is a remarkably complete record of his Civil War service that fills a void in the historiography of the conflict. Fortescue stated in the preface to his memoir that he "faithfully endeavored to preserve for the pleasure and benefit of others this eventful period of his life." His undertaking, though unseen and little noticed for over a century, provides us with a glimpse of the most tumultuous era in the nation's history from a heretofore unseen perspective.

PREFACE

BY LOUIS R. FORTESCUE

A preface to a journal of daily jottings in the life of a soldier, during four years of calamitous civil war, is in my opinion superfluous for the reason that the title page conveys all that is necessary to express in advance.

Should, however, the volume be intended for publication it would seem requisite to address a few words to the stranger into whose possession it falls for perusal. But it so rarely happens that diaries drift beyond the control of those relatively near to the writer that nothing would be lost by the entire omission of a preface.

Every man can and should, though it may cost a little trouble, preserve for the pleasure or benefit of others the experience of eventful periods of his life, especially those which mark an army career. This I faithfully endeavored to do, with the single purpose in view that they might stand as a record in the years that were to follow.

Having, therefore, persevered in my resolve to note down all happenings, and briefly observed the unwritten law which prescribes the practice of a preface, I close this page by dedicating the contents, representing as they do the record of one whose aim was to perform his duty as he understood it, affectionately to those who during, and since those tumultuous times, were my most solicitous and appreciative listeners.

MY MOTHER AND MY WIFE.

CHAPTER 1

SIGNAL SERVICE ON THE UPPER POTOMAC

AUGUST 25–DECEMBER 31, 1861

T he Twenty-ninth Pennsylvania Volunteers had completed their organization in July 1861, and on August 3 the regiment was ordered to proceed
to Harpers Ferry, Virginia, to join the command of Maj. Gen. Nathaniel
Banks. Establishing camp in nearby Pleasant Valley, Maryland, on August 5,
Fortescue, like many of his comrades, could not help but reflect upon what lay
ahead. "I had entered upon a career that perhaps within a short time would
mark the end of all my earthly joys or vicissitudes of care," he recalled. "Should
I survive the conflict or share the fate of thousands now entering upon a course
of life from which they were never to emerge or to again see the forms of cherished ones at home?"

On August 25, while halted during a march near Buckeystown, Maryland, a request for officers to learn the signal code reached the camp of the Twenty-ninth. Fortescue and a fellow lieutenant were selected by their colonel to become versed in the intricacies of Maj. Albert J. Myer's system at an instructional camp set up at nearby Darnestown, Maryland.

After completing the course of study and successfully passing an exam given personally by Myer, Fortescue served briefly at signal stations near Darnestown and on Sugar Loaf Mountain (a commanding eminence several miles west of Hyattstown, Maryland) before being posted to Point of Rocks, Maryland, where he remained until February 1862.

With the exception of the Union defeat at Ball's Bluff, Virginia, on October 21 (which he witnessed from his lofty station on Sugar Loaf Mountain) and his first experience under fire, the majority of Fortescue's time spent along the river was uneventful. The familiar term frequently quoted in Northern newspapers at this time, "All quiet along the Potomac," originated with Fortescue and his fellow signalmen, who had little of note to report during the winter of 1861.[1]

. . . [*August 25, 1861.*] I little thought when resuming my place in line with the company this morning that this day's close would mark the end of my military career with the 29th Regiment, and that my future war services were to be cast in remote places from them.

At noon, while on the march, I was directed by the adjutant, W. H. Letford,[2] to report to the colonel at the head of the column for detail for special duty. [The colonel] imparted to me the information that an order had just been received to select two officers for signal service with instructions to report without delay at the headquarters of General Banks[3] at Hyattstown . . . adding that he had chosen Lieutenant Burr of Co. D[4] and myself from the fact that having known us both from boyhood, he felt assured that he could rely upon us to fittingly represent his regiment in our new sphere of duty. It was his impression, he said, that we would be required, in connection with the four enlisted men we were to take, to master some code of signals necessary to his command, and would then be returned to our respective companies after an absence of possibly of a few weeks only. Happily for us, he was unaware of the intentions of the Chief Signal Officer, Major Myer, to make the detail a permanent one, or perhaps we should not have been selected. After receiving a kindly admonition [from him], we arranged for our departure in the morning.

Monday, August 26, 1861. After a hasty meal of coffee and hard-tack I bid my company adieu, and with Ned Burr was off for Hyattstown. Being unencumbered with baggage because of the vague instructions and absence of means of transportation, we measured off the fifteen miles intervening at a lively gait, and in the early afternoon . . . presented ourselves at the tent of General Banks, whom we found to be, in this our first interview, a most pleasant and agreeable gentleman.

. . . After delivering to him our instructions, he inquired particularly after the health of our colonel, and was extremely solicitous of the condition of our regiment.

Nathaniel Prentiss Banks was commissioned at the breaking out of the war a Major General of Volunteers. Having no military training prior to that time, he was termed a political general and [was] presumably thus honored because of his success as a leader in the party then in ascendancy. . . .

His unassuming affability, always essential in successful politics, did not desert him as a military officer, and this trait, so readily distinguishable in the army, where martinets are as thick as flies in the summer, made him (although his achievements in battle were few), a prime favorite with all he commanded. This opinion, after a continuous service of more than a year at his headquarters, in which frequent pleasing intercourse was the rule, remained with me unchanged to the close [of the war], and I have naught but the most agreeable recollections of my connection with his administration.

Our interview ended, the general directed us to report to Lieutenant Leonard F. Hepburn of the 4th N.Y. Vols., (Scott's Life Guard), then detailed as Chief Signal Officer with this corps, whose quarters were on the opposite side of the road.[5] Here we were assigned a wall-tent with the request by Hepburn to make ourselves as comfortable as circumstances would permit until the arrival of the command nearer the Potomac, when he would impart to us a course of studies requisite to perfect us in the art of signaling.

On the following morning, August 27, we learned that our detachment from the regiment was to be a permanent one, and that our baggage, left with our companies, should have accompanied us. We were granted permission to return, and at 9 a.m., set out to find the regiment, then on the march towards Poolesville. At noon we reached Barnesville, a small village at the foot of Sugar Loaf Mountain, where Lieutenant Burr, who had been reinforced by an elder brother, and I procured dinner and a rough convey-ance for the modest sum of nine dollars to take us to Poolesville for the baggage and return. We accomplished [this] by evening, [and] persuaded a violent secesh gentleman, one Mr. Hays, to accommodate us with supper and a bed, and we retired considerably disjointed [by] the rude shaking-up experienced in the springless vehicle of the days' journey. We spent the next day after our arrival [back] at headquarters at Hyattstown in prepar-ing for a further march, and found our signal detachment augmented by an additional detail consisting of Lieutenants Stryker and Braine of the 9th N.Y., Shattuck and Cushing of the 12th Mass., and London and Harvey of the 2nd Penna. Reserves.[6]

Thursday, August 29, 1861. When we started on the march this morning we found it rather fatiguing and difficult work to maintain our place in the column considering the driving rain, deep mud, and terrible condition of the roads. . . . After wallowing all day through the Maryland mire ([which] is a thousand times worse than the ordinary dirt road to travel when joined with a multitude of men, horses, wagons, and artillery ahead, behind, and on both sides of you), we halted at night at Pleasant Hill, a euphonious and delightful cognomen for a settlement when the surroundings warrant it, but which in this case were decidedly the opposite, and on the carpetless parlor floor of a farm house we recruits of the Signal Corps made up couches for the night. General Banks was provided with a room overhead, which accounted for our not occupying it, and during the night [we] got a peep at the ludicrous figure of the general in a long night-shirt clambering over thickly recumbent forms to answer the call of his orderlies with dispatches.

In the morning we were off for Darnestown where a permanent camp of instruction in all of our important duties was to be established, and where we were to receive, after perfecting ourselves and passing a suc-cessful examination before the great mogul Major Myer, a complete outfit of signal equipments, including one of Uncle Samuel's best horses. This information nerved me to greater trials, in view of the parting admonition of our old colonel and the fact that he might have to pass judgment upon our efforts, and as we emerged from the sea of mud and came in sight of the promised rest I resolved to use my utmost endeavors to succeed in the task to which he had anxiously attached so much importance.

We arranged to study and practice in the basement schoolroom of a little church near by and to take our meals at the well-kept residence of

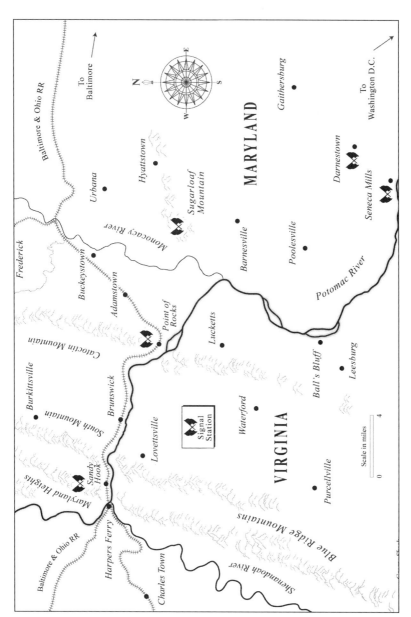

Signal stations along the Potomac, 1861–62.

another Mr. Hays, a relative of the chap at Barnesville, and like our former host, equally tainted with state's rights proclivities. We were then furnished by Hepburn with a code of signals to meditate over. These we were to commit to memory, after again subscribing to an oath (in addition to the one we had taken as soldiers) not to reveal to any person the signal instructions or matter emanating from the chief of the corps. This code might be likened, somewhat, to the Morse telegraph code, the alphabet of which was indicated by dots and dashes. Myer's alphabet was by the by the motion of the flag, right, left, and front, and consisted of five numerals, commencing at one and ending at five. . . . [Combinations of] four of these numerals

A group of Signal Corps officers and men, taken on Elk Mountain, Maryland, September or October 1862. Seated in front, left to right: a servant, Pvt. Robert J. Morgan, Lt. Frederick Owen, Lt. Aaron B. Jerome (holding telescope), another servant, and Lt. Edward C. Pierce. Pvt. Harrison W. Gardiner stands behind Lt. Jerome, facing right. The other soldiers are unidentified. Note the white background and red background signal flags held by the men. Courtesy Library of Congress, Prints and Photographs Division.

were used to represent the twenty-six letters of the alphabet, the fifth, or 5, being [used] to indicate the end of a word or message.

MYER'S CODE OF SIGNALS

A—11	H—231	O—14	V—2311
B—1423	I—2	P—2343	W—2234
C—234	J—2231	Q—2342	X—1431
D—111	K—1434	R—142	Y—222
E—23	L—114	S—143	Z—1111
F—1114	M—2314	T—1	&—2222
G—1142	N—22	U—223	

ing—1143; tion—2223; End of word—5; End of sentence—55; End of message—555; I see you—11–11–11–555; All right—11–11–11–5 and commence; Error in sending—143434; Repeat—234–234–234.

Here we have the alphabet ingeniously constructed out of four numerals, and to obviate any mistake of meaning by the officer reading it or misconstruction of a message, it will be observed that the [number] 1 in no instance follows 4, nor does 4 follow 2 or 4. The [number] 3 never follows 1, or does 3 follow 3. Neither does 1 follow 2, or 2 follow 1. In transmitting a message the flagman would stand directly facing the opposite station and [signal] the two even numbers, 2 or 4, [by a motion] to the right; the odd numbers, 1 and 3, to the left; and the 5 to the front. It should be borne in mind that the flagman, who was skillfully drilled in the work of swinging the flag or torch, was ignorant of their meaning, the officer never using the letter of the alphabet but the numeral when dictating a message to him.[7] This . . . [method] also prevented the disclosure of a message to unknown persons who might be standing near.

The detachments assigned to a station consisted of two officers and four flagmen. Each officer [was] supplied with a telescope and binocular or marine glass, and a kit of signal equipments [comprised of] flags, and torches. The former [was] carried by the officers with straps over the shoulders; the latter [was] distributed among the flagmen to facilitate ready transportation. All, of course, were mounted. The torch used at night was a copper tube about twelve inches long and about two inches in diameter, screwed to the end of a flag pole from which the flag had been removed. To obviate the confusion that would arise from the movements of a single torch at a great distance in the darkness, a second torch, somewhat larger, was placed at the feet of the man using the pole, thus enabling the officer receiving the message to distinctly decipher it. [By] keeping his eye directed at the foot torch, every movement of the swinging torch was clearly perceptible.

The distance at which signals could be read by day or night depended entirely upon the range of the telescope, provided no smoke or fog prevailed. The usual distance between stations was from five to fifteen miles, but messages of any number of words have been transmitted twenty, thirty, and forty miles; the latter distance when there was an absolutely clear atmosphere. The flags used were of three sizes—two, four, and six feet square; and were of three colors—white with square red centre, black with square white centre; and red with square white centre. The smaller ones were for short distances, often used while in the saddle; the larger for distances; [while] the medium size . . . [was used] most frequently. These were attached to a pole which could be adjusted to lengths of four, eight, or twelve feet. If the background was a dark one, as in a valley or in front of a piece of woods, the white flag was used. If upon an elevation with the sky beyond, a black or red flag was used, according to the distance.

A portion of the code which we studied as carefully as the alphabet, but which we discovered was somewhat cumbersome, was the making of numerals from 1 to 0, and by general consent the numbers of troops, etc., were spelled and abbreviated to a shorter combination than if the numerals had been used:

CODE INDICATING NUMERALS

1—14223	4—23114	7—22311
2—14234	5—22222	8—22342
3—22314	6—23111	9—22233
		0—11111

In calling a station, you were required to make the number indicating the initial letter of the name of the senior officer upon that station. Thus, when calling my station, the letter would be F, or 1114, made continually until seen by my man on duty at the glass, when my flag would respond 11–11–11–555, meaning, "Proceed, I see you." The opposite station would then reply 11–11–11–5, and then proceed with their message. At its conclusion I would acknowledge its receipt by 11–11–11–555, meaning, "I have it," and the station from which the message had been received would respond 11–11–11–555, indicating, "O.K., satisfactory." All words were abbreviated as much as possible, especially those of military significance, frequency making them readily recognizable. As an instance showing with what facility and readiness this admirable invention could be used, I have transmitted an ordinary sized message of some eight or ten lines twenty miles in ten minutes.

The theory was easily mastered in a few days, [but] the practice in the code, on the contrary, required more time inasmuch as we were expected to read promptly messages sent rapidly by the instructor with a small wand, and [which were] made by him in much quicker time than was required with the flag. We were soon, however, declared proficient, and about the 14th of September the major put in an appearance and the ordeal of examination was proceeded with. Academic training was not considered essential to capability by the major. The principal requirements were our proficiency in the signal code, then came a test in literature, the arts, our views of various authors of poetry and prose, our military knowledge (more especially that relating to our work as signal officers in which orthography played a prominent role), a slight dip into ancient history and Napoleonic campaigns, and lastly the elementary principles of arithmetic. [Following] . . . a thorough test of sight, [Major Myer] concluded his examination, and on the following day he returned to Washington, taking with him some of those who had been studying with Lieutenant Evan Thomas of the 4th U.S. Artillery[8] on Sugar Loaf Mountain. Of the class of fourteen officers but one was rejected, Lieutenant Cushing of the 12th Massachusetts, who returned to his company. [This was] an odd circumstance in view of my later experience with the troops from that state. My opinion, shared by many others, was that there was a superior order of intellect pervading their ranks that was not possessed by those from any other commonwealth.

The following officers remained under Lieutenant Hepburn to operate on the upper Potomac in the corps of General Banks: Lieutenant's

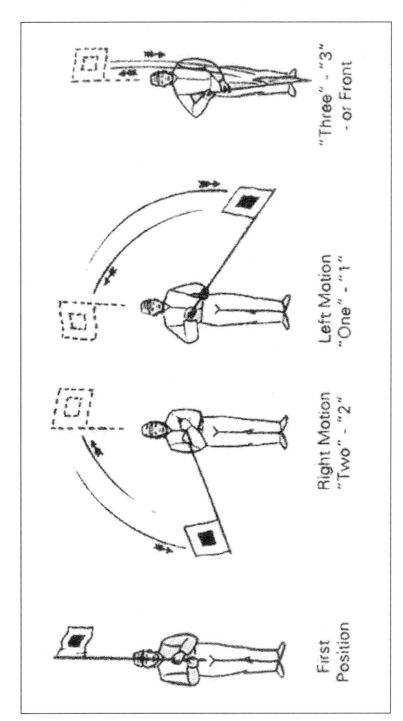

Signal method, showing the technique for signaling the numbers 1, 2, and 3; David L. Woods, A History of Tactical Communication Techniques (Orlando, Fla.: Martin–Marietta, 1965), plate V-6.

Rowley and Wicker of the 28th New York; Shattuck, 12th Massachusetts; Miner and Fralich of [the 34th] New York; Spencer and Larned of the 1st Minnesota; Hartshorne of the 1st Pennsylvania. Reserves; Byram, 27th Indiana; and Burr and myself, 29th Pennsylvania.[9] A station was established by Hepburn, Wicker and myself near Darnestown, and another in a large chestnut tree at Seneca Mills, on the banks of the Potomac, by Rowley and Shattuck. [They were] to communicate with Spencer and Larned at Poolesville (headquarters of General Stone),[10] [who in turn] communicated with Lieutenants Byram and Hartshorne on Sugar Loaf Mountain.

During my stay at the camp of instruction many pleasant hours were spent with the family of Mr. Hays, and frequently when the studies of the day were over, as a diversion, we journeyed to the respective regimental camps of the officers of our detail and enjoyed the evenings in games of whist or cribbage. Among those with whom I became the most intimate were the officers of Col. Donnelly's regiment, the 28th N.Y. Vols.; the 9th N.Y.S.M.; and Captain Best's Battery.[11] Of these, but few survived the war, nearly all being numbered with the slain heroes of our glorious cause. Of the thirty-three officers who entered the service with the 28th N.Y., but six remained when the end came.

At the station beyond Darnestown, in company with Hepburn and Wicker, I passed two enjoyable weeks, alternating the time between the flag and torch practice with the Seneca Mills station and visits to the camp of the 29th [Pennsylvania] regiment. It was while on duty here that the brigade composed principally of Philadelphians, under the command of Colonel E. D. Baker, joined the command of General Charles P. Stone near Poolesville, having marched from their old camping ground at Washington. Very many familiar faces greeted me in the 69th, 71st, 72nd, and 106th regiments as I watched them by the roadside pressing along.[12] Among others [I recognized was] Oliver Tack of the 71st, whom I had known well as [a] boy and man, trudging along with his usual captivating grace and dignity of personal bearing.[13] His inseparable companion, his violin, of which he was a practiced master, [was] under his arm, [he] having consigned his musket to the care of one of the teamsters for the trip. Poor Ollie! Cheerful, buoyant, and light-hearted, the pride of an aged mother and an affectionate sister, with no thought, perhaps, that the musical studies to which he had assiduously devoted his youth would, in a few days, be rudely closed, and his bullet-ridden form, among many others of the Ball's Bluff struggle, [would] find a resting place beneath the silent waters of the Potomac. Yet such was to be his fate. I never saw him again. "Requiescat in pace."

My flag practice being ended, and a much desired companion in the shape of an easy riding black horse [having been] assigned me, I made preparations, in compliance with Hepburn's orders, to assist Lieutenants Hartshorne and Byram in working the Sugar Loaf Mountain station, and to these officers I at once reported. I found the occupancy of this peak, for signal purposes, to be romantic in the extreme. It is doubtful whether a more delightful point, as a camp rendezvous, is to be found in either Maryland or Virginia. Its cone-shaped summit rises to some thirteen hundred feet above the level of the Potomac, and on three sides within two hundred feet of the top [it] presents an almost perpendicular height. The single road used for many years by the residents of Frederick City and farmers in the vicinity for excursion parties winds around it, shut in by a mass of tangled vine and briar until within hailing distance of the summit, when a precipitous climb compels the rider to dismount and ascend, leading the animal by the aid of the halter strap alone. Upon its table-like top the eye is enchanted with a view unfolded extending south into Virginia across the Catoctin range and Loudoun Valley. For

Sugar Loaf Mountain, Maryland, showing the portion of the mountain facing southwest. As Fortescue explained, a signal tower rose an additional thirty feet above the summit. Photograph by J. Gregory Acken, 2014.

many miles on either side stretch the well-tilled farms and luxuriant foliage of Maryland, [while] the broad and beautiful Potomac that divides these states is plainly discernible winding its way through the valleys until it meets the Shenandoah at Harpers Ferry, where it is lost to view behind the lofty Blue Ridge.[14]

It was our custom, on pleasant afternoons, to stretch ourselves upon a favorite grassy spot and watch, with telescope, the military maneuvers of the rebel troops stationed in Leesburg, Va., and when the air was heavy at night we would sit around our camp fire and distinctly trace our shadows outlined upon the clouds as they settled down upon [the mountain's] top and enveloped us in mist and spray. Upon the south side of its rocky peak we erected a tower some thirty feet high [so] that the view of the several stations communicating with us might not be obstructed by the branches of trees beyond our reach, and only those who had overcome their fear by a familiarity with its dizzy, precipitous cliffs could muster the requisite courage to swing a flag from its top.

> *"As some tall cliff that lifts its awful form,*
> *Swells from the vale, and midway leaves the storm*
> *Though round its breast the rolling clouds are spread,*
> *Eternal sunshine settles on its head."[15]*

In the high winds that prevailed during many nights of the winter of 1861 and '62, the old tower creaked and groaned as it swayed before the tempestuous elements, lending the deepest gloom to our airy habitation [which] penetrated the dense clouds far above the glimmer of the smoldering camp fires that dotted the banks of the river.

On the 21st of October occurred that colossal blunder by General Charles P. Stone at Ball's Bluff in which our forces suffered a most ignominious repulse, and caused the loss of many brave boys, including . . . that noblest Roman of all, acting brigadier general Edward D. Baker. General Stone's mistake was in permitting a portion of his troops to cross and be crushed by superior numbers of the enemy, although at that time [he was] in full possession of the necessary information giving him the strength of the rebel forces opposing him. As early as 7 o'clock on the morning of the 20th messages flagged to his headquarters at Poolesville reported the manifest intentions of the enemy at Leesburg. In their maneuvers they frequently changed position in such a manner as to indicate the arrival of reinforcements, and our messages reporting these facts were placed promptly in the hands of General Stone.

At 11 a.m. on the 21st, our troops, under General Stone's supervision (he remained on the north side), commenced crossing, the attacking party being under the command of Colonel Baker. Our brigade gained the opposite shore, using for the purpose two old flat boats, or scows, and upon landing formed line of battle and advanced . . . in the direction of Leesburg. When less than a quarter of a mile had been covered they were met by a murderous musketry fire from a force concealed behind rudely constructed breastworks of fence rails and corn stacks that commanded all the roads leading up from the river. Our little force contended nobly against these tremendous odds until between three and four o'clock, when a retreat was ordered to the river bank in the belief that General Stone had reinforced and intrenched to cover a retrograde movement. Almost immediately after giving the order to fall back, Colonel Baker fell mortally pierced in several places. His men rallied, however, and after securing his body, succeeded in bringing it off safely. Upon reaching the river bank and finding no reinforcements, the panic stricken mass rushed for the two boats, which were soon crowded and pushed into the stream. [A] shot from the rebel artillery . . . tore away the planks of one of the boats and it sunk with all on board. Those in the other boat were more fortunate and reached our side in safety, [with] but a corporal's guard, however, of the force that had crossed in the morning. . . .

Thus ended the fiasco at Ball's Bluff. Hundreds [were] killed or in the hands of the enemy, and another disaster, through rank incompetence or disloyalty of general officers, from McClellan down, [was] to be placed on the record of the soldiers hailing from the middle and New England states. General Stone was afterwards arrested and for some months imprisoned in Fort Lafayette, but it was conclusively shown at the time of his release . . . that the responsibility belonged, and should properly rest, on the shoulders of McClellan.[16] Colonel Baker's body was taken to Poolesville where it lay in state for two days, guarded by a detachment of his faithful followers, prior to its removal to Philadelphia. I had a view of his commanding features, which, although lacerated where the fatal bullet had entered his forehead, appeared unusually calm and placid in their repose upon the bed of the little cottage.

October 23, 1861. I accompanied a column of Banks's troops this a.m. moving down the river road to return to their old camps, and arrived at the Seneca Mills station about 5 p.m. Frequent loud and unwise expressions impressed me as I rode among them derogatory of Stone as a general officer, and [I heard] bitter unrestrained denunciations of those responsible for the recent calamity. They were, to all appearances, thoroughly disheartened, and launched their imprecations upon the head of General Stone, regardless of the peril in so disrespectfully referring to a superior officer. In the light of later truths, most of these insinuations against Stone were known to McClellan, and showed upon his part either a heartlessness in not protecting the former or else a fear that exposure of his own culpability in the disaster would disturb the equanimity of his reign as commander in chief, which he was currently reported to be inordinately elated over.

From Seneca Mills I turned my horse in the direction of Darnestown, and a few miles ride brought me to the old campgrounds of the 29th Regiment, and our late station. [It was] a deserted village, truly, and naught but the scattered debris remained of the scenes of activity of the week before. The close-fisted inhabitants, like vultures timidly awaiting the departure of intruders, had culled it over and left but the valueless remnants to the stray trooper who might chance to happen that way. Upon the ground of our former station I picketed my horse, and spreading my blankets, slept the sleep of the weary after the arduous labors of this ill-fated campaign.

In the morning, much refreshed by a breakfast at a neighboring farmhouse, I started again for my station on Sugar Loaf Mountain, and found there a message directing me to report at Poolesville to Lieutenants Cushing[17] and Thomas for duty in another quarter. Proceeding there I discovered that the officers of the several stations had received similar instructions . . . and were then reporting their arrival. It was a source of much gratification to meet personally in social intercourse those whom we had only conversed with by flag, and the opportunity was embraced to compare notes for future reference when we should again be separated on stations many miles apart. The only exception to perfect cheerfulness among those composing the gathering was the regret that poor Spencer had contracted a bad case of the measles and [was] unable to appreciate the reunion in the same spirit that we did.

Cushing had ordered a reassignment of the officers after furnishing each with a new set of equipments. The outpost station on Maryland Heights was given to Fralich and Wicker. Eleven miles east on the Catoctin Range, at Point of Rocks, to Harvey and myself. Sugar Loaf Mountain [was given] to Byram and Miner; Spencer and Larned [were] to remain at Poolesville; and Hartshorne [was] to join Rowley and Shattuck at Seneca Mills.[18] This made a continuous line of thirty-four miles under the immediate command of Lieutenant W. W. Rowley, 28th New York Vols.

That evening at six our party, consisting of Cushing, his brother of the 2nd Rhode Island Arty., Thomas, Fralich, Wicker, Harvey, and myself, set out for Point of Rocks, riding by way of the towpath of the Chesapeake and Ohio Canal, reaching our destination . . . at 10 p.m. Here we secured accommodations for the night at the St. Charles Hotel. The evening of our arrival, we were notified that in accordance with Major Myer's instructions, we would again undergo an examination before Lieutenants Rowley and Stryker as to our proficiency in the code. This test took place in one of the upper bed rooms of the St. Charles Hotel, and being found satisfactory to this board of officers, the line was formally pronounced open. . . .

October 29, 1861. Horses were saddled early and the rising sun found us, in company with Colonel Geary, wending our way up the stony slopes of the Catoctin. This station, the most important in my opinion of any constituting the upper Maryland line, was within the limits of the district commanded by Col. Geary.[19] His regiment, the 28th Pennsylvania, composed of fifteen companies, numbered at this time over fifteen hundred men, and was considered one of the finest that the Keystone State had contributed to the war. The men were mostly from the northern tier of counties, and in conjunction with the battery of six 10 Pounder Parrots under Capt. Joe Knap (manned entirely by men detailed from Geary's command),[20] rendered valuable aid in keeping this section free from armed rebels during the first year of the rebellion. At this time but six companies were encamped here as a reserve for the nine others who were doing picket duty from along the tow path at Noland's Ferry . . . to Dam No. 3, a distance of eighteen or twenty miles. . . .

The knowledge possessed by [Geary] of this section of Maryland and Virginia furnished him with superior qualifications as a commandant, and it was this knowledge, no doubt, that prompted the placing of him in command. Prior to the war, he had not only operated an iron furnace [here], but resided on the Virginia side, hence his familiarity with the sentiments of the natives and with every foot of the soil for many miles. He was evidently imbued with a true affection for the Union, notwithstanding his early political training as a Democrat, in which [party], as a partisan, he had held important offices by appointment of former Presidents. But his patriotism, like many war Democrats of the North, was beyond question, as evidenced by his early advocacy of the cause of the government, the adoption of a blue uniform, and prominence as a commander of a fine regiment. That he heartily despised secession I have abundant reasons for believing from the many conversations had with him, as well as from ocular proofs which convinced me of his utter disregard for the feelings of the residents here, nearly all of whom he knew to be traitors to the government. . . .

Lieutenant Harvey and I lived contentedly on our mountain retreat (agreeing on almost every question excepting that of politics), the reason being that to avoid dissension, I let him have his own way. In the matter of seniority I should have had command of the station, but he claimed the right, alleging that his commission was issued prior to mine. As he had conveniently sent the document to Philadelphia I did not insist upon its production, and [I] permitted him to assume charge rather than have a dispute over his pretended title.

As to politics, he was a dyed-in-the-wool Democrat. Being a native of the eastern shore of Virginia this was not difficult to account for, and when in some of his dissatisfied moods about the government's methods of conducting the war he launched forth into a panegyric of the good old Jeffersonian times, my Republican blood would be aroused, and the air would take on a cerulean tint with personal reflections until the flagman on duty at the glass would remind us of a call from an opposite station. This usually had the effect of restoring quiet in our otherwise agreeable family.

Our four flagmen were reinforced shortly after we became settled by a colored boy about fifteen years of age, the son of an old darkey named Hopkins who lived on the side of the mountain halfway between our rudely constructed tower on the summit and Geary's camp at the foot. This boy was said to be something of a cook, which Harvey and I greatly needed, so we employed him, his duty between [meal] times to feed and curry our horses. The flagmen, as is the custom with enlisted men, attended to these duties themselves.

It wasn't very long before our mess of two began to tire of the style of meals served up by our colored "Chef," whose range of palatable edibles was limited to fried eggs and corn pones, and whose frequent visits to his father's domicile were accompanied by a wealth of wholesome ham and similar stores from our larder for the old man's table. This we found too expensive for our moderate salaries, so making inquiry in the village among the few families living there, we decided to try boarding with a Marylander named Jim Bassant, whose wife, and daughter, Miss Fannie, seemed more inviting and congenial than the others. [As a result], our sable youth was relegated to the duty of caring for the horses only.[21]

We had a pleasant party at this house during our stay of five months. Some of the officers of the 28th Pennsylvania frequently took meals here, notably John P. Nicholson, Captain [Lansford W.] Chapman, and his brother, [Charles W.], a lieutenant, and the table was all that could be desired by soldiers in active service.[22] The wives of some of these [men] occasionally paid the camp a visit and made the house their rendezvous, and their presence contributed a great share to our enjoyment. As Harvey and I could not leave our station at the same time, except when the weather was bad, preventing signal operations, we arranged a plan by which each should go first to his meals in alternate weeks and return and relieve the other from duty for the same purpose.

Captain Chapman was a strong advocate of the temperance cause—being a man after Geary's own heart in his opposition to spirituous beverages—a feeling not shared, however, by the bulk of those doing duty under "Uncle Samuel." Geary and the captain, [who had] been appointed Provost Marshal, were persistent in their efforts to prevent anything of a stimulating kind [from] being sold in the neighborhood, and frequently caused much excitement by their raids upon the premises of supposed violators of the colonel's edict against the traffic.[23] They had long suspected our colored friend, the aged Hopkins, of furnishing whiskey to the privates of their command, but were unable to verify their suspicion. At last the secret leaked out and there was music by the band, some of the men giving it away when intoxicated. The captain threw out some decoys, who reported that the old man had a corn crib in the rear of his cabin where the boys were in the habit of leaving their canteens accompanied by a 25 cent piece. Upon returning later, they would find the canteens filled with a tolerable fair article of "commissary" which would be attended by the usual results—a high old time and neglect of duty. The old man was thereupon arrested and locked in the guard house for a short period, but upon promising to discontinue the practice was released. His experience in the guard

Capt. Lansford L. Chapman, Twenty-eighth Pennsylvania, Colonel Geary's temperance enforcer. Courtesy Civil War Collection, United States Army Heritage and Education Center, Military History Institute, Carlisle, Pennsylvania.

house, unpleasant as it was, soon wore off, and he was again caught at his whiskey tricks, whereupon the captain ordered the wife and daughter away from the vicinity. . . . The old man was again locked up, the boy left with us to take care of the horses, and a match [was] applied to the cabin and corn crib, [after which] naught remained but a few ashes to mark their former place of abode. I was informed by the officer in charge that when the boys were about removing the family preparatory to burning the place, the old woman protested and said "Dat she would call Captain Fortescue up on de mountain, who would not allow the fambly to be frowed out." [This] intimation [was] amusing to me, as well as to all the boys who knew me, when reflecting upon the ridiculous figure I should have cut in attempting to oppose the commands of an officer greatly my superior in rank, however much my sympathies may have been aroused in behalf of this unfortunate woman. The boy, Tom, and his black dog remained with us until the following Spring, some five months, when campaigning in the Valley near Winchester they disappeared, and we never saw them afterwards.

Captain Chapman, in the role of Provost Marshal, did not confine himself to colored culprits in the whiskey business, but extended his field of operations to more substantial dealers, and soon had within his toils the hotel proprietor at the Point, Mr. Berry, who, shielded by the fascinations of an attractive daughter, was supposed to be secure in his retreat. But the ruthless Geary was proof against the wiles of the maiden fair (a pronounced secessionist), and the contents of the barroom were rolled out on the sidewalk, the heads of the casks knocked in, and the liquor poured over the ties and tracks of the B&O Rail Road.

Chapman was [eventually] made lieutenant colonel of the 28th Pennsylvania. He was a brave soldier and distinguished himself on many fields of our war. At the Battle of Chancellorsville, while gallantly leading his men, he fell mortally wounded and expired upon the field. Before leaving the ground where they had been engaged, his men endeavored to find the body for proper burial, but were . . . unable to distinguish it from the large number that lay around. The regiment was afterwards sent to the Western army under General Sherman, and participated in its many engagements, accompanying that officer in his march through Georgia to the sea. Taking up its march through the Carolina's it again entered Virginia . . . after the surrender of the Rebel general Johnston, and was ordered to proceed to Washington to participate in the last Grand Review. On the way

. . . from Richmond it tramped over the same ground in the Wilderness where it had engaged in the deadly struggle of two years before, and there exposed lay the skeleton of the lost colonel. [It was] positively identified by the blouse that covered the bones, which, by its uncommon and peculiar pattern, always worn by him, was familiarly known to every member of his regiment. The bones were carefully placed in a box and later conveyed to his home at Mauch Chunk, Pennsylvania, where, in the churchyard, they were finally deposited. . . .[24]

One delightful Sunday afternoon . . . I was invited by Geary's regimental commissary sergeant [David B.] Hilt[25] and John P. Nicholson, quartermaster sergeant of the 28th Pennsylvania, to visit a young lady living near Adamstown, Maryland, about four miles from the Point of Rocks. Not wishing to take our horses on account of the probable lack of stabling accommodations, we secured a small hand-car on the B&O Railroad with the intention of working our way there through the aid of the handle bars. When about a mile out, [however], we were fortunate in meeting several track-walking contrabands going in the same direction whom we persuaded to get on and relieve us of this tiresome method of locomotion.

In due course . . . we reached the farm and after a formal introduction to the family, which consisted of [a] father, mother and daughter, proceeded to make ourselves agreeable until tea was ready. After enjoying sweet converse with the mother and daughter and a display of profundity with the old man in our knowledge of farming and agriculture in general (of course never touching on the subject of the war—a subject so near to us—from a lurking suspicion that it might clash with the family's views and interfere with the promised repast . . .), the welcome supper was announced. We joyously filed into the room where the spread was arrayed, and awaited the usual blessing from the paterfamilias. Before us we saw a table of delicacies properly disposed upon a snow white table cloth with appointments of glassware and silver of immaculate neatness, all of which accorded with the sublime simplicity and purity of the senior member of [our] trio, David Hilt, who had come prepared to make a capture of the youthful member of the family, and was, apparently, carrying his point with a high hand.

Alas, for the weakness and frailty of human kind a thrilling and unlooked for denouement was awaiting us, but then it is always the unexpected that happens. Hilt was accorded a seat at the head of the table opposite the master of the house, while John and I were seated at the side facing the mother and daughter. Directly behind Mr. H's chair . . . was a tall "Grandfather's clock" reaching nearly to the ceiling, upon the top of which was placed a stout hickory stick to steady or brace it against the ceiling. The repast was partly over and David, who had occupied the entire time with animated conversation interspersed with brilliant flashes of wit and scintillations of his mastery of the arts, literature and sciences, was in the glowing ardor of a well-rounded period when he tipped his chair back and touched the clock. This he should not have done, and would not [have] had he had a conception of the consequences. The clock yielded to the touch and unloosed the club standing on its top, which descended on a straight line to the crown of his bald head. Had it stopped there we might have in time assuaged the pain and mortification that David, by his imprudence, was now undergoing. But no, the curtain was not to drop until the finishing of the tableaux. The club bounded from his skull to the table, knocked down a pitcher of cream, and smashed into smithereens a large dish of preserved fruit, with lots of juice, that at once proceeded to spread itself over the surface as far as it could possibly reach.

The old lady and the daughter were terror-stricken. David held both sides of his head as if afraid it might fall apart, while John and I were absolutely speechless. The supper, however, was over. The wreck before us had dissipated all the bright anticipation our appetites had pictured, and between the mourning over lost glassware, ruined hopes, and the leveling of a knob about the size of a billiard ball on the top of Dave's head with camphor or something of that sort, we sneaked from the house and dolefully sought our way back on the hand car to the place of starting. Thus in an unguarded moment are the pre-eminently distinguished in captivating attainments, when nearing the very acme of bliss, ruthlessly flung from their high estate. . . .

With the advent of autumn came the fading glories of the summer beauty as viewed by us from our elevated home. The bleak and cheerless winter was indeed approaching, and to those who never braved its rigors under canvas or faced its searching discomforts as a soldier on the march or picket line, it presented terrors the snugly housed at home might well dread to encounter. Its influence was felt in the deprivation of nightly strolls by us to the face of the Catoctin, where overlooking the river we had frequently sought, with pipes and camp stools, its velvet-like grassy slope to enjoy the cool refreshing breezes that sweep the mountain tops. . . . I recall too, with pleasure, the many moonlight rides along the smooth and shaded paths of the canal and evenings spent with the officers of the picket posts. Or with that prince of good fellows, Dr. Sam Logan, assistant surgeon of the 28th,[26] in his improvised floating drug depository—a canal boat, nicely housed over—which enabled him to enjoy life very comfortably. In this he could float to any portion of the lengthy picket line and with his stock of hospital stores promptly minister to the needs of ailing veterans. But we had accepted the situation in true earnestness and whether in sunshine or in rain, whether warm or cold, [we] must endure the changing seasons as they come and go, forgetting the pleasures of peace until wars' bitter trials were ended.

Thanksgiving Day, November 25, 1861. The enemy's success at Ball's Bluff, instead of inciting them to further demonstrations along our line, seemed to have an opposite effect in settling them down to a quiet occupancy of the south side of the Potomac, content to remain passive as long as their territory was not encroached upon, but ever watchful to repel intrusion by the hateful "Yanks." This quiescent condition of affairs was unbroken until the day appointed by the President, via a Thanksgiving Proclamation, to offer up thanks for the Divine Blessings we had enjoyed. [In this], someone possessing the confidence of our worthy President might have suggested the interjection of one or two appropriate invocations to the all-wise Ruler [to the effect] that no more fakes in the guise of phenomenal strategists be drawn from the wheel of chance to lead the boys in blue to further disaster and defeat.

About 10 a.m. of this day, Tommy Armer, a telegraph operator detailed from Geary's regiment,[27] and me concluded to visit Sandy Hook, pay our respects to Major Hector Tyndale of the 28th in command there,[28] and devote the balance of the day to a ramble along the tow-path above [Harpers] Ferry. While conversing with some of the boys on picket, our attention was attracted to a squad of the enemy on the slope above the ruins of the burnt arsenal on the opposite side, who were hurriedly placing in position two pieces of artillery. Premising that their intentions were to send us a few compliments, we sprang into a rifle pit just as a screaming shell passed over and scattered its fragments against the rocks of the mountain towering above us. In a moment or two, another and still another of these howling iron messengers crashed into the rocks about the same place, sending fragments . . . in showers into the canal. . . . This performance was kept up until each rifle pit within a radius of a quarter of a mile had been saluted, but without doing injury to any of our men who remained under cover. The guns were then deliberately withdrawn, and all became serene again.

[The enemy] . . . had learned that one of our batteries . . . stationed on the bluffs of Maryland Heights had been withdrawn to another point, leaving the coast clear for a display of artillery practice on their part, without danger of interference from us as they were beyond the range of our riflemen. . . . To me this baptismal fire was quite a novel experience. It impressed me with the truth of the saying I had heard so repeatedly since entering the army; that the uproar of cannon created a terrifying and rattling influence upon the infantry soldier and cavalryman, but had little effect upon the artilleryman, who, being used to the large guns and their ammunition by daily handling, learned to regard its noisy pranks with a contemptuousness that disputed its claims as an engine of very great destructiveness. The uncommon apprehension of danger by the two former arms of service was due in a great measure, I fancy, to the inexperience of the volunteers, of which both branches were largely composed.

A charming view of the [surrounding] country is obtained from the station on Maryland Heights. The telescope takes in an area of nearly fifty miles and unfolds the numerous towns which dot the valley east of the North Mountain range. Winchester is the most distant, lying in one of its gaps, and is barely distinguishable except with a more powerful glass than we employ. Those clearly seen are Halltown, Charlestown, Martinsburg, Clarksville, Shepherdstown, Perryville, and Smithfield. The populace of these [towns] have gained much notoriety since the commencement of the war because of their extreme hatred of the Union forces, though frequently harboring rebel guerrillas, while professing friendship for us. Martinsburg might be excepted, however, from this list, containing as it did some adherents to the Union who courageously assisted, in diverse ways, our cause.[29] The others were filled with rabid traitors, in whom we entertained no particle of respect or confidence.

The little insignificant village of Charlestown was to us particularly obnoxious. Its disgustingly homely women were in the habit of closing their houses and exhibiting their true Southern politeness, whenever the boys in blue were around, by slyly, from half closed shutters, expectorating over them on the sidewalk.[30] It was here, upon a little knoll nearly opposite the Court House, that the martyred John Brown perished upon the scaffold.

Upon our first visit early in 1862, I entered the diminutive jail and inspected the cell where he passed tedious hours awaiting execution. A noble man and a noble purpose, though too hastily organized for an undertaking of such magnitude. But thanks to the Almighty Father, from that hour, "His soul went marching on!"

In the latter part of December we were subjected to another shaking up from an artillery fire at Point of Rocks, which, as usual, did little damage beyond frightening the residents nearly out of their wits, and caused their stampede, accompanied by all portable articles of value that happened to be within reach. The Rebs were inclined, on these semi-occasional visitations, to enact the cunning role by appearing at unfrequented places without warning. But their performance . . . was generally so stupidly amateurish that it excited the risibility's of the very mule teams at the amusing absence of execution done, and their hilarious though discordant "E-Haws" could be heard above the racket of the artillery and bursting shells. They thought to scare us this time by dragging a battery, during the night, to the top of the Catoctin on the Virginia side of the river, and were all ready at nine the following morning to start the ball.

Col. Geary happened to be absent at Frederick City that day, and the command of the post devolved upon Lieut. Col. DeKorponay of the 28th. [DeKorponay] was being visited by his wife and daughter, and feeling somewhat jubilant over his exalted position and the attendance of his guests, had indulged rather freely in Hostetter's Bitters, of which he was ardently fond. Becoming excited after the second or third discharge (which dropped a shell near his tent), he sprang out, and in his efforts to make his commands understood in broken German, got tangled up in a huge pair of Mexican spurs he had on, and was finally landed on the broad of his back with a badly lacerated ankle. Joe Knap quickly got his battery unlimbered and a very pretty artillery duel was indulged in, each [side] throwing about twenty-five shells. The Johnnies then concluded that they had had sufficient fun, and dragging their pieces out of the way, molested us no further.[31] It was ludicrous to see the number of bold citizens who had been taunting us with their rebellious sentiments fleeing to our station to seek the fancied protection our elevation afforded, only to find on their arrival more loose iron in the air than they had found down on the level. We had the call afterwards, getting back at them for hunting Yankee shelter from the missiles of their darlings in gray who seemed to have so little regard for the lives of their friends on our side of the river. Although we were almost daily in receipt of reports from reliable refugees or intelligent contrabands of threatened raids or attacks from the enemy encamped around Leesburg, this artillery demonstration was the only one that materialized during our stay here. But [it] had one very beneficial effect in that it increased the vigilance of the pickets marvelously, and moreover relieved the 28th regiment of the services of their bibulous lieutenant colonel, who was directly after forced to resign his commission, his exhibition in Geary's absence having so completely disgusted everybody that Geary dispensed with his presence by threatening a court martial.[32]

. . . [As Christmas approached, and] . . . now that I had exchanged the stern discipline of regimental life for that of unrestricted special service, no barrier presented itself to my joining the circle and partaking of the customary turkey-joint at home. Taking with me one of our copper torches that needed repairing and could only have the proper attention in Philadelphia, I made the journey, enjoyed the Christmas greeting and taste of the National Bird, had the necessary repairs made to the torch, and was back in time to witness an open air Christmas spectacle that helped to enliven those living within the camp lines of the 28th, and for whose benefit Lieutenants Tom Elliot and [Gilbert] Parker[33] had devoted some weeks of preparation. A large stage was erected in the centre of the ground and an attempt made at festooning from the limited evergreen at hand. The program of the afternoon was made up of the drama of the "Old Guard," and in the evening the burlesque of "Metamora"; the farce of the "Virginian Outwitted"; and a comic scene in a dentist's studio, both performances being interspersed with solos, duets, songs, and dances. The two gentlemen having the management of the entertainment were well adapted for the positions they were selected to fill, and succeeded, in spite of the many disadvantages they labored under regarding stage setting and costumes, in acquitting themselves in a very creditable manner.

CHAPTER 2

HARPERS FERRY, KERNSTOWN, AND THE SHENANDOAH VALLEY

JANUARY 1-APRIL 28, 1862

T he first two months of 1862 found Fortescue quietly manning his station at Point of Rocks, Maryland, but as winter drew to a close, active operations were imminent. Maj. Gen. George B. McClellan had decided to transfer the Army of the Potomac by sea to the tip of the Virginia Peninsula and advance westward against Richmond. To assuage President Lincoln's concern that his flanking move would leave Washington vulnerable, McClellan agreed to send Nathaniel Banks and his twenty-thousand-man division into the lower (northern) Shenandoah Valley to occupy Winchester, drive off Stonewall Jackson (something no Federal commander similarly tasked ever successfully accomplished), *and safeguard the vital Baltimore and Ohio Railroad line. Leaving an outpost behind in Winchester, Banks was then to move east through the Blue Ridge Mountains toward Manassas to aid in the defense of the capital.*

Fortescue and his fellow signalmen abandoned their stations in late February and joined the Federal column that was assembling to cross the Potomac at Harpers Ferry.

"Action keeps the soul in constant health, but idleness corrupts and rusts the soul."

If the author of this ancient truism had lived long enough, he might have been detailed for signal duty in the Union army under the indefatigable Major Myer, and then made the discovery that the extraordinary application to duty of some men is so pronounced that the health of those under them is in the greatest danger of injury from being forced to [over perform] their allotment. . . . [They might then] conclude that a little rustiness or inactivity might be more conducive to robustness and clearness of perception if practiced with discretion.

The major's anxiety to prove to the War Department the serviceability of his Signal Corps, and the valuable aid his code of signals were to the army and navy, led him into extravagances that at times threatened to involve him in ridicule, if not deprivation of extraordinary privileges. His principal indiscretion was a desire to supersede the telegraph as a means of communication. The Signal Corps [was intended] for observation and communication where the enemy's occupancy of the country prevented the use of the [telegraph] wire, and [this] was all that was contemplated in its establishment as an arm of the service. But no sooner was Myer's theory accepted and an act of Congress [establishing it] promulgated (the framing of which showed plainly his ear-marks), than his mind became engrossed with the formulation of plans to circumvent the [telegraph] wire, which, in its secrecy and absolute control of by the War Department. . . . Secretary of War Stanton valued too highly to suffer its displacement by the signal flag. The major, too, was an admirer of McClellan and a believer in his convictions politically, and through McClellan's prominence and friendship, endeavored to accomplish his object in defiance of Stanton, whom we are to believe abominated—with justness—McClellan and his clique of followers. So, from the moment that Stanton grasped the intentions of our chief, he seemed to relax his good opinion of Myer's creation and grow weary of our work, [regardless of] how industriously we strove to prove its usefulness or with what importance our reports of observations and movements were meant to impress him.[1]

This, in turn, was added fuel to the already persevering disposition of Myer, whose dignified manner, though of a gentlemanly quality to a certain extent, implied a desire . . . to disregard the growing displeasure of the war secretary, and his redoubled efforts to compel recognition naturally fell with greater force upon us. And so, he thought, as indolence degrades and idleness demoralizes, our indefatigable major concentrated his thoughts on how to keep his coterie of young men busily employed, even though in doing so their stock of endurance might be jeopardized. . . .

On many a night at twelve and three a.m. (the hours designated by him), I have taken my position at the telescope, made fixed and immovable in its place bearing upon the opposite station (with the searching winds howling through the apertures of the tower directly in the teeth, causing a chattering that required the utmost self-restraint to keep the eye upon the distant light and the mind upon the combinations being made), to be informed by the torch of a brother officer that all was serene in his vicinity and no signs of the enemy were visible. Remembering, however, that among the requirements of a soldier is a life of denial, and that obedience and submission to orders—however odious or unpleasant—are the characteristics of a true soldier, we accepted the assumption of our alert commandant that unceasing efforts on his part must eventually inspire confidence and esteem in his subordinates and overcome opposition brewing at the War Office.

Friday, February 6, 1862. Surely it can be said that treachery and cruelty are concomitants of civil war, examples of which are manifest daily in the acts of the arrogant and imperious followers of Jefferson Davis. The Rebellion has now been in existence but a few months, and yet [it is] sufficiently long to have developed, in all of their hideousness, many of the vilest acts of betrayal of friends and neighbors. . . . The intense hatred of the Southern people toward those living within the limits of the seceded states who are suspected of treasuring a love for the Old Flag grows in bitterness with each succeeding month, and curiously enough falls heaviest on those of the black race. It is not to be wondered then that they who are so persecuted should seek the protection of the Union Army, willingly risking the lash and fearful encounters with savage hounds in order to reach the promised shelter. That the escaping slave is thus encouraged (as a merciful liberation from the ownership of a brutal master) the South well knows, and . . . [will] thus resort to any act in return, no matter perfidious or treacherous, to repay the Boys in Blue for the deprivation of what they are pleased to call their chattels or property.

An exemplification of this occurred this morning at Harpers Ferry in the perpetration of a dastardly outrage resulting in the death of one of our men. About 10 a.m. our pickets observed a man on the Virginia side, partly concealed behind the first pier of the burned B & O R.R. bridge, waving a white flag for the evident purpose of seeking their assistance in crossing. Supposing from the appearance and actions of the man that he was a fugitive slave, a small boat was instantly manned by two of Geary's men [and] an army scout, who pulled for the opposite shore. When within fifty yards of the pier the man stepped out, the shore extending some distance beyond at low water, and taking deliberate aim fired, killing the scout. Before the piece could be reloaded our boys had rowed back out of harm, bringing the body of the scout with them.

Upon being informed of the affair, Geary ordered Major Tyndale across with three companies with instructions to burn all houses in the lower part of the Ferry affording protection to guerrillas or sharpshooters. The work was well accomplished; our boys, eager to avenge the death of the scout, responded with alacrity, and in a short time a line of fire and smoke marked the course of the Shenandoah and Potomac Rivers as far as the town extended on both fronts. No casualties occurred to our men, who returned with the information that the guerrilla who had so adroitly lured the boat across had blacked his face to more readily deceive the boys into making an attempt at another rescue.[2] Geary's retaliatory measure was prompt and complete, and tonight many a "Varginyah" gentleman is sitting in the cold ransacking his vocabulary of profane adjectives for something expressive to give vent to his garlic-burdened and whiskey-laden breath in denunciation of the incendiary inclined Yanks.

February 24, 1862. "Make preparations to move with troops, and report at Sandy Hook this p.m.," was the message flagged to us at noon today, and revealed the cause of the activity noticed this morning in Geary's camp, and camps further down the river. This is indeed important as it indicates that the commanding general, who has in some way succeeded to the title of the "Young Napoleon," has concluded to give the Johnnies a taste of Yankee strategy and powder. Before many hours are allowed to pass, we may be engaged in a lively tussle with the Graybacks and push them back again down the Valley, or in the end suffer the pangs of humiliation (as the boys did down at Edward's Ferry in October last) from incompetent generalship.

[We] reached the Hook in due time with our traps and found the 28th Regiment preparing to cross. Weather extremely boisterous, winds high, and many of Geary's regiment, who are uniformed in the regulation felt hat turned up at the side with feather, found themselves in a short time hatless, the river being dotted with their head gear from the pranks of the wind.

Harvey and I stopped for a while at the ancient hotel at Sandy Hook to get ourselves warmed up at its cozy and inviting old-fashioned parlor grate fire, and while tilted back in our chairs enjoying its cheerful glow and our briar root [pipes], we observed a cavalry soldier reading a book with feet resting on the fender. While thus engaged in conversation my attention was attracted by the effeminate appearance of the aforesaid cavalryman, whose profile was outlined clearly when turning from the heat of the grate. [This person] presently arose and withdrew, in company with the field officers of a Michigan cavalry regiment then passing the hotel. . . . As they mounted and rode away I made inquiry of the men, and was surprised to learn that the person referred to was a woman and the wife of a major of that regiment. She had donned the cavalry uniform to be near her husband, and had ridden by his side as his orderly ever since the departure of the regiment from Michigan for the front. Few would have noticed her sex while astride of a horse with the command, but her womanly walk and manners when dismounted made her easily recognizable and the subject of comment. What an unsuitable situation for a female. It requires the stuff of sterling womanhood to buoy up an existence beset by the thousand and one inconveniences, the hideousness of mutilated and shattered forms and the morbid mockery of plausible and mischievous natures.[3]

Sandy Hook presents quite an animated appearance compared with its usually dull condition. Each train arriving from below comes laden with troops who find quarters in the canal boats here, a number of which have apparently been concentrated for that purpose. A pontoon train is also here, and shortly after our arrival a boat was ordered across containing some members of the 28th Regiment, the intention being, presumably, to establish sufficient force opposite for the protection of the engineers in laying the pontoon bridge. Those having charge, however, were responsible for a most deplorable accident which happened to the first boat in permitting it to be overcrowded. Being taxed beyond its capacity it became incapable of management in the choppy water . . . , rapidly filled, and six men were drowned, all of Captain Tourison's Company P.[4] This unfortunate affair threw quite a damper over the whole command and halted for the nonce the efforts being made to effect a crossing during the prevalence of the windy weather. During the morning, however, the bridge was completed, and about 2 p.m. we were treated to a visit from General McClellan and staff. . . . After General Hamilton's brigade,[5] leading the van, went over, McClellan and his ponderous staff followed suit, and the march was taken up in turn by the various brigades. They filed around the main street to Bolivar Heights, where tents were pitched. General Sedgwick's division[6] was the outpost.

Notwithstanding the transfer of Banks's Corps and Sedgwick's division entire to the Virginia soil, and the establishment of a picket line on the day of our arrival just beyond Bolivar, there were no indications of a forward movement, when, on the third day after [the crossing], I received orders to accompany Geary's regiment to Loudoun Heights . . . for the purpose of keeping communications open between that command and headquarters in Bolivar. A few hours after found me across the Shenandoah and ascending Loudoun Heights, a most precipitous and rugged climb, [accompanied by] several companies of Michigan cavalry. My station was nicely situated in an opening among the timber, and communication with the headquarters station on Bolivar Heights all that could be desired. After an occupation of twenty four hours, I learned that Geary contemplated moving the following day south eastward in the direction of Leesburg, and that the cavalry command were to return to Bolivar. This rendered abortive the continuance of my station on Loudoun, and on reporting this fact to Lieutenant Rowley, I was directed to abandon the post and again report to the main column.

Once back in Bolivar, I made haste to secure a seat at the table of a family named Beal who had been recommended to me as still retaining a fondness for the Union, and possessing, moreover, the ability to provide a palatable meal for a moderate amount of Yankee money; two essentials calculated to entice the boy in blue having the wherewithal to indulge in luxuries. One or two meals sufficed to convince me of the fact that the representations as to the Beal family were correct in every particular, and that the reputation of their viands had attracted the notice of others beside myself. . . . Among the number were Colonel Kane and Major Devereux of the 69th Penna.[7] and their families, who availed themselves of the opportunity to enjoy well cooked meals with loyal Virginians.

March 5, 1862. Orders were received this evening for a forward movement in the morning. We are positively to move forward after a period of inactivity extending over a week. Here, in the country of the enemy, with a river in our rear made rapid and tumultuous from winter snows and thaws and spanned by but one frail pontoon bridge, an army that has been preparing for months starts forth impelled by the tone of impatience of the entire country at the long delay. Smarting under the caustic criticisms of the press, [it] actually halts within ten or fifteen miles of its winter quarters, goes into camp, and remains thus unemployed for one week. The secret of this, as I am informed, can be summed up in a very few words. We have an engineer officer for a commander who has a very super-sensitive nature. He has achieved a reputation as an exceptionally gifted organizer of armies, and has beguiled his time surrounding the Capital with earth-works, in which, it is alleged, a comparatively small force can resist the combined armies of the Confederacy, but otherwise he looms up as an exasperating procrastinator.

It is said that the fleet of canal boats we have left behind in the canal were collected there for the purpose of building a strong bridge in [place] of the pontoon boats now there, but if so I am at a loss to conceive how they were to be utilized as such. To attempt to get them out of the canal by cutting away the banks would drain the waters of the canal . . . and render the boats useless. It would [also] seem impossible . . . to take them apart and transfer them to the river, even if there were not very grave doubts as to the feasibility of the bridge remaining after completion.[8] It is also rumored that a larger body of troops were to join us from the neighborhood of Washington, but after the general's visit he countermanded the order and they did not start. Something is evidently wrong, and to a subordinate of my rank, it looks as if McClellan had some misgivings lest his plans result in a failure, in which case any excuse, however plausible, would be ridiculed [by], and disappointing to, the country.

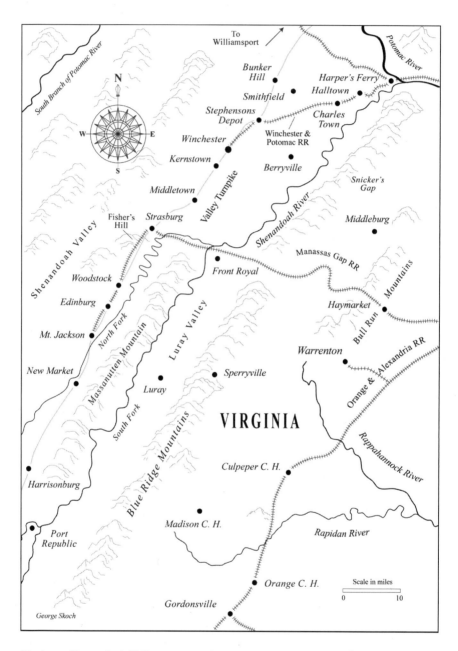

The lower Shenandoah Valley, 1862.

I am told that the President is hot, and as the shadows lengthen each day and no intimation of an advance reaches him, he grows restive and dejected, a condition in no way lessened by the unrestrained expression of indignation of those near him at the puerility of the general's explanations for his tardiness of movement. But the boys admire "Little Mac," as he is familiarly called, a feeling probably heightened by the subservient press, filled as they are with exciting expectations and flattery, and [they] believe that in time he will gratefully surprise the President by a crushing blow that will paralyze the rebellious hordes now seeking the nation's disruption. And in this the prayers of the nation are with them.

At an early hour we were on the road with the staff of General Banks, passing through Halltown and the still more infamous Charlestown. At noon a line was opened, by direction of the general, bringing his headquarters . . . at Charlestown, in communication with the Army of West Virginia, [under] General Shields,[9] then at Martinsburg. The following stations were now put in successful operation: Martinsburg, Lieutenant Fralich; North Mountain, Wicker; Smithfield, Halstead[10] and myself; two miles beyond, towards Charlestown, Pierce[11] and Miner; one mile further, same direction, Byram; at Charlestown, Rowley and Briggs.[12] Many important messages were transmitted over this line during its continuance, one of which, on the 11th, caused much excitement and filled the troops with glad expectations. It came by wire to Charlestown and thence by flag to the front, and read as follows:

Headquarters, Fairfax Seminary
To Major General Banks:

Manassas has been evacuated. Our cavalry occupied it last night
George B. McClellan
Maj. Genl.

At last a glimpse of sunshine has penetrated the gloom of the White House and the sleepless hours of our patient and much-maligned President will be fewer while resting in the inspired confidence of a leader of our armies whose proclaimed ambition has been that he might equal the men of that golden age who were all brave and war-like and, occasionally, successful in battle.

The morning of the 12th brought us still more refreshing news from the neighborhood of Winchester. The stay of the enemy in that Rebel stronghold had been sufficiently profitable, from a military standpoint, in the collection of supplies from the commissariat, and having absolutely sucked the orange dry, they have graciously left the parings for us. Their hurried retirement must have occasioned exceeding regret upon the part of the citizens old and young, especially the Southern wappy-jawed belles, judging by the contemptuous and frigid reception accorded our boys upon their entrance.

The message that contained the welcome intelligence came from Fralich, who had moved up from Martinsburg and joined the advance of the brigade at Bunker Hill:

Winchester, 9.50 a.m.
Official to Gen'l Banks, Charlestown

I occupied Winchester this a.m. at 7 o'clock. The Rebel force left yesterday at 5 o'clock. Their cavalry were only one hour ahead of us. Shall try and start the train of cars to Charlestown for stores tonight.
C. S. Hamilton
Brig. Genl.

Winchester was the extreme left flank of Manassas, and its evacuation compelled their retirement from it, although it is to be presumed that the proximity of Banks's column somewhat accelerated their departure. Upon receiving the above, I at once flagged it to Lieutenant Miner for transmittal to the general. After a lapse of some twenty minutes I was delighted to see the general and staff ride into the field toward my station in search of news. On nearing the glass where I sat, I observed that he showed signs of impatience or agitation. I promptly handed him my copy of the dispatch and received from him the following reply . . . which I immediately flagged to Bunker Hill:

Official to Genl. Hamilton, Winchester:

Your message is received. I congratulate you. Is other force needed immediately?
N. P. Banks
Maj. Genl.

An answer was soon received from Hamilton stating that his forces were adequate. The agitated manner exhibited by the general was explained to me about one hour after his departure, and reflected seriously upon the gentleman with whom I was associated, Halstead. . . . [While] I was receiving the message from Fralich announcing the evacuation of Winchester, Lieutenant Halstead stood by and took it down at my dictation. At its conclusion, Lieutenant Pierce, who had ridden up from the lower station and was seated on his horse behind me, inquired its purport. Halstead, being a practical joker, turned the paper over and wrote upon the back this bogus message from Hamilton:

"I attempted to occupy Winchester this morning. Was driven back by Rebel force. Their cavalry are now pressing me. Shall fall back and try to reach Charlestown tonight."

I was in entire ignorance of this idiotic performance of Halstead's, being seated with my eye at the glass engaged in acknowledging the receipt of the message. Pierce, who was of a practical turn and not easily dismayed by adverse report, failed to interrogate me, but coolly swallowing the bait, rode away. Had he met no one on his way to his post all would have been well, as Miner, his partner, had received the correct message from me in Pierce's absence. But unfortunately, he met General Banks and staff on the road and communicated to them the message Halstead had shown him, which caused a flutter among them and resulted in scattering the staff hurriedly off for reinforcements for Hamilton. The general had ridden rapidly forward to within a short distance of my station before observing my flag, and being anxious to hear further news at once came to inquire, and was handed the proper message by me.

His agitation after meeting Pierce can readily be imagined (although its full effect was well concealed from me), and in my unenlightened condition I shortly after read Pierce's flag desiring to know which was correct, that received by him from Halstead or the one flagged by me to Miner. This let the cat out of the bag, and Halstead, appalled at the thought of having created such dire commotion and trembling at the consequences, endeavored to frame a plausible excuse for his monkey tricks. But it fell upon ears deaf to his flow of eloquence entreating indulgence in acknowledging his error, and he awaited the summons of arrest that he felt would surely come from headquarters. He didn't have long to wait, and I was relieved of him, Harvey again taking his place with me. The matter was amicably adjusted later by Major Myer coming graciously to the aid of Halstead, whose pleadings for his own deplorable predicament, and for the sake of the reputation of our Corps, prevailed. Halstead . . . was kept upon the tenterhooks until the publication of the order restoring him to duty.

March 13, 1862. The possession of so valuable a point as Winchester and the consequent advance of our troops called for the abandonment of this line of signal stations, and at break of day we were packed up and off for Charlestown with orders to report at the earliest moment at Winchester. On our way [there] we stopped for the night at Berryville with a Quaker family, and indulged in an alleged rest on a made-up bed of downy feathers on the parlor floor. A most delightful snooze was anticipated from the appearance [of] the couch while preparing ourselves for the night, but it was deuced disappointing when reclining therein to find that the weight of the body sank through the fluffy down, and instead of blissful repose, we arose in the morning with aching bones. We could hardly credit it that the two lamb-like and painstaking Quaker ladies [of the house] had deprived us of so much needed sleep in revenge for our presuming to thrust ourselves upon their hospitality, yet it was unmistakably true. So, smothering our indignation . . . we retaliated by attacking in force their edibles, eating an inordinately large breakfast, which we were positively certain they did not enjoy.

While proceeding to Winchester this morning, we witnessed an exhilarating spectacle that truly exhibits the characteristics of the American volunteer in his adaptability to meet almost every known emergency. Within an incredibly short space of time, the disabled engines and cars left by the retreating Rebels near Winchester were put in running order by machinists and carpenters, and within twenty-four hours, engineers and firemen had them steaming to Charlestown for supplies for the troops. Thus all trades and occupations are readily furnished at a moment's notice from the ranks of Yankee regiments. . . .

In the afternoon, when nearing Winchester, we came upon the division of General Sedgwick halted on either side of the Pike for a rest. . . . Some of the boys of his Philadelphia Brigade, after enjoying a modicum of rest and desiring to give vent to the hate which still rankled with the bitterest intensity respecting the degree of generalship displayed at Ball's Bluff, had stuffed with hay a dilapidated and abandoned uniform, and bracing it up in the road, labeled it, "General Stone; behold the traitor."

As a relic of antiquity of the most advanced type Winchester takes the palm. I don't believe that the sight of a middle-aged resident of this place has been gladdened by the erection of a single new house . . . since his or her advent into the world, and even the oldest inhabitant may have but a dim recollection of any alteration, so obsolete does everything appear. Yet this is the promised land that we are struggling so hard and laying down so many lives to prevent a separation from. These purse-proud natives claim a higher civilization than all of the states combined, [and believe] that in the rich blood flowing in the veins of those who people the soil of the "Mother of our Presidents," there is, far and away, a quality superior to that which mantles in the cheek of the "Mudsill" who has invaded . . . the land of "Corn Pone" and "Hog and Hominy." If these lean, lank, sallow-pated and alcohol-drenched biliousites are the nobility upon which America leans for a place among nations, than indeed do we blush for our benighted land. The very embodiment of the sentiments of "States Rights Sovereignity" is exhibited in the epileptic specimens encountered on these sidewalks, and if we are to accept these recalcitrants as a sample of the haughty chivalry, then truly may it be affirmed that in contrasting them with the people of other lands, comparisons are odious.

I would not wish to detract [from] or underrate our own brave boys in alluding to the better showing of the foreigner in contrast with this so-called chivalry. Any regiment in this army may select its poorest company, and I will [compare] them against an equal number of these miserable abortions in cleanliness, energy, or politeness. Judged correctly, it would be the veriest absurdity to place any of our enthusiastic or vigorous young soldiers in the same class with this lazy element, whose only aim in life is the perpetuation of their oppressive politics, and the advancement of their tyrannous "slave oligarchy," [which is], briefly, the "Niggar" for work, and the corner grocery for the white man. Here, perched upon a barrel or box, [with] a hank of natural leaf for chewing purposes, a jack-knife and a pine sliver for whittling, with frequent opportunities for a guzzle of moonshine distillation and the discussion of political issues—regardless of the personality of the candidate so long as he is well grounded in the faith of property in man—we have a picture complete in every detail of the triumph of eternal happiness and contentment as evolved in the brain of the average Virginian.[13]

On the outskirts of this superannuated village our signal party halted and [we] made ourselves at home in one of the vacated houses of the southern nobility. [It was of] brick with broad piazzas and trailing vines indigenous to a milder climate than ours in Pennsylvania; in the rear were negro huts, barns, and sheds for fodder, poultry, and sheep, but which latter had long since been removed to fill the capacious maws of Southern soldiers, or hurried to a place of safety beyond the grasp of predatory Yanks. Negroes around in abundance, many no doubt raised from babyhood on the place, but unwilling to end their days there now, seeing that "Massa Linkum" had driven their owners away and had come to tote them to the promised land. Very little furniture was left in the domicile, and every piece was a relic of antiquity. Not a room with carpeted floor was to be seen, so we filled our tickings with hay and lay down regardless of the barren appearance; the shelter of a roof and our own sweet companionship amply compensating for the absence of civilized comforts.

Evidently, something is wrong, physically, with me. For the last twenty-four hours I have had a particularly enervating sensation that forebodes no good. I do not recall the same feeling at any period of my life, and yesterday afternoon, while chatting for a while with the many acquaintances I saw in the Philadelphia Brigade, I was more than persuaded to stop for the night at a farm house, fearing to rough it outside as I have been doing. This morning when I awoke I found myself greatly weakened by a profuse perspiration and in a condition that partly unfits me for the duties I am expected to perform. I verily believe that I have contracted a fever, and if so [I] may have to worry along in a meaningless sort of way without the ambition to keep up with the rest of the staff. How disappointing. After lying comparatively idle for months in fond expectation of active work in the campaigns of the spring, to be confronted at the very outset with a dread illness that promises to continue till the snow flies again, or to be left behind, even though it should mend me more rapidly, [are] debilitating thoughts that will keep the spirits in a depressed state for months.

On the following morning, Rowley ordered a line established to Snicker's Gap, distant about fifteen miles, to which Spencer was sent. I occupied the intervening post, but a persistently feverish sensation and attendant ills from night sweats deprived me of the pleasure and satisfaction I derived from the work of an important station in forwarding the results of observations, and almost made my very existence unbearable. The effort to keep up told upon me each day with increasing effect, and at the expiration of the third [day at this station], March 19, I flagged Rowley that my fatigue was so great that he must order me in for treatment, and in consequence, I returned to our quarters and remained quiet. Under the care of the headquarters surgeon I improved rapidly, and in a day or two began to feel like myself again.

[*Upon the Confederate withdrawal from Manassas, as Fortescue noted, Stonewall Jackson fell back from Winchester, covering the left flank of Joe Johnston's retreating army, and eventually halted some forty-five miles south near Mount Jackson. Jackson's mission, though, was to hold the Federals in the lower valley to prevent them from reinforcing McClellan. Nathaniel Banks, convinced that the now-distant Jackson no longer posed a threat, complied with his earlier orders and on March 21 began dispatching his forces east to Washington, leaving James Shields's ninety-five-hundred-man division at Winchester to defend the valley and protect the Baltimore and Ohio Railroad.*

Apprised of the movements of the Federals on the twenty-first, Jackson deduced that they were abandoning the valley, and in an effort to intercept them before they could consolidate with McClellan's army, he started back toward Winchester at dawn the next day, determined to stop them. The ensuing Battle of Kernstown was fought on March 23, and though minor in terms of casualties, it had far-reaching consequences for the Union war effort in the East.

Although he was present during the latter stages of the fight, Fortescue conveyed frustratingly little about his experiences during the action.]

March 22, 1862. In accordance with previous instructions, the troops composing Gen. Banks's old corps, consisting of Hamilton's, Williams's, and Abercrombie's brigades, took up the line of march early this morning for Centreville via Snicker's Gap.[14] General Banks himself preceded them by way of Harpers Ferry and Washington, his intention being to stop at the War Department before rejoining the division at its destination. This left, at Winchester, for the protection of the Valley, three brigades under Gen. Shields, commanded respectively by acting brigadier generals

Kimball, Tyler, and Sullivan.[15] [It was] a comparatively small force considering the area of country to watch.

About 4 p.m. the Rebels boldly made their appearance on the Strasburg Pike, with the evident purpose of again occupying Winchester. As afterwards developed, they were laboring under the impression that either our troops had left the place, or the force remaining [was] too insignificant to successfully cope with them. Their surprise was great, however, when they ran upon a large body of our pickets about one mile southwest of the town prepared to receive them. Their batteries took position and opened on the picket posts, followed in a short time by their cavalry, which began skirmishing with our infantry advance. The advance had, in an incredibly short period of time, double-quicked through the town and reached the outposts. On came our batteries thundering through the streets to the front, where our infantry were already forming line of battle. General Shields immediately took command of the first battery to arrive and started up an eminence to enfilade a Rebel battery which had opened rather lively on our lines. While placing it in position a shell from a Rebel gun burst near him, shattering his left arm near the shoulder, compelling him to retire from the field, and killing the driver on the lead horses of the gun near the general. Shields was carried to a house bleeding badly, and the command of the division devolved upon Colonel Nathan Kimball of the 14th Indiana, the next senior officer in rank. He at once proceeded to dispose the troops, as they arrived, to meet the assault which seemed imminent.

General Jackson, commanding the Rebel troops, soon perceived the folly of attempting the dislodgment of our forces before darkness set in . . . [and] he wisely concluded to partly withdraw his lines. At sundown, the firing ceased, with exception of a few desultory shots that could be heard among the pickets.

During a part of the evening the various commands of our division were busy getting in position for the attack on the coming morning, and then we all turned in, with the exception of those on picket, and were soon dreaming of the probable horrors that might be enacted when the early reveille should rouse the troops to arms.

March 23, Sabbath Day, and what a program had been outlined for this day designated as one of rest and prayer. Selected, too, by that miserable Rebel and traitor to his flag, "Stonewall" Jackson—so frequently paraded by his rebellious admirers as a devout Christian—to slaughter those whose efforts were directed towards the preservation of the government, a government which had charitably endowed him with a splendid military education. But, thank God!, if ever a blusterer's feathers were trimmed by brave Yankee soldiers, his were before he got through with this day's work.

I was sent early to Harpers Ferry by Lieutenant Rowley, who commanded our detachment, to get some packages from the Express office there, among which was one containing a remittance of $40 for myself from my uncle. . . . And after giving receipt for the various articles, [I] returned to Winchester, reaching there by the 12 o'clock noon train. I discovered upon my arrival that the battle had opened fiercely and that the citizens were in a high state of excitement from the fact that their houses were unceremoniously being converted into temporary hospitals, and they were [being] compelled to submit to other fancied indignities, such as waiting on wounded soldiers, a service very repugnant to the average Virginian of these parts.

At 11 a.m. the battle had commenced with slight skirmishing along the line and continued, gradually growing heavier until about 1:30 p.m., when the Rebels began to push matters by advancing their column and establishing it behind a stone wall that almost completely sheltered them from our shots. Colonel Kimball, whose towering form could be seen amidst the smoke and dust of the field, immediately ordered an advance of our line, which brought us within one hundred and fifty yards of theirs. This position was maintained until 4 o'clock, when a charge on the stone wall was ordered by the colonel. Cheerfully the order was obeyed by our men, who bounded forward with a yell, and for the space of ten minutes fought hand to hand with clubbed muskets for its possession. But the Rebels holding it could not withstand a shock as earnest and impetuous as this, and they fled precipitately, leaving our gallant boys the victors. Numerous assaults were made after this, both by the Rebels and our men . . . but our boys kept gaining ground until dark, when Mr. Jackson, thinking discretion the better part of valor, ordered a further retreat, leaving in our hands nearly all of his wounded, as well as some four hundred prisoners taken on the field.

Our loss was heavy. Out of three hundred men engaged in the 84th Pennsylvania, twenty-six were killed and eighty-three wounded. Colonel Murray fell leading this gallant regiment forward, and many other dashing officers were killed or wounded. The 5th and 8th Ohio shared the glory together with the 84th Penna. and 3rd Virginia (Federal), all suffering much. The total casualties on our side were some 500 killed and wounded.

The Rebel loss was 600 killed and wounded, together with [the aforementioned] prisoners.[16]

Our detachment of the Signal Corps, composed of Lieutenants Rowley, Wicker, Pierce, Shattuck, Miner, Fralich, Briggs, Halstead, and myself, were placed in prominent positions covering the field and the house in which General Shields was lying. From these stations, the various commands were kept informed of each other's movements. In General Orders issued afterwards, our Corps was highly complimented by General Banks and Col. Kimball for their efficient services.[17]

A statement went the rounds among some of our over-zealous newspaper correspondents, when reporting the battle, that a Rebel Irish battalion had refused to fire upon our men when ordered to do so. What grounds there may have been for the publication of this absurd rumor I am at a loss to imagine, as no single individual appeared to be able to substantiate it, and certainly the evidence was wanting that Irish troops had not fought as well for the Confederacy as they had for the Union. . . . I satisfied myself of the falsity of the statement that evening when encamped on the field among the wounded. Lying near the little camp fire around which we were sitting was a Rebel captain who appeared at intervals to be suffering very much. It was too dark to discern the cause of his trouble, but supposing that the stretcher bearers, who were searching for the wounded from among the dead, would soon remove him, we did not for a time heed his groans. We were finally drawn to him, [however,] by some profane remarks heard, and discovered that he was terribly wounded in the head. The ball had entered just at the corner of the left eyebrow and cut straight across, dropping the flesh, with both eyebrows, over his eyes. In his weak and semi-conscious condition, the blood had congealed and gave the appearance of both eyes being shot away. We started at once to look up a surgeon and stretcher bearer to have him attended to, but were surprised to hear him dissent to this to this proposition in a decidedly profane manner, cursing the Union cause and damning the Yankees who were responsible, he said, for his troubles. No consoling words . . . seemed to pacify him, and we were given to understand that he was an Irishman commanding an Irish battalion, adding that after his return he would make every Yankee son of a b——h he met suffer tenfold for the misery he was undergoing. He denounced everybody engaged in the Union cause in the bitterest terms, the intensity of his language far exceeding that of the native Southerners lying wounded around him. In his weak and helpless plight, however, he was unable to oppose the surgeons and their assistants, and they bore him off to a hospital for treatment.

I confess to a feeling of frigidity for him and his ilk, a feeling heartily shared by those of us who listened to his profane expressions of antipathy for the Union, when hearing a few days later that his wound had proven fatal. . . .[18]

[Although the Federals were victorious at Kernstown (they outnumbered the Confederates by nearly a three to one margin), the defeat of Jackson triggered a series of events that would render the battle a strategic victory for the Confederates. Jackson's aggression prevented Banks from reinforcing the capital, pulling him back to the Shenandoah Valley. Maj. Gen. Irvin McDowell's First Corps, which had been stationed at Fredericksburg ready to act in concert with McClellan's operations on the Peninsula, was several weeks later recalled by Lincoln to help in the defense of Washington, while another division that had been promised to McClellan was withdrawn and moved to western Virginia. Denying him these reinforcements, McClellan would later claim, "was a fatal error" that forced him to pursue a less audacious and ultimately unsuccessful campaign against Richmond.[19]

Once back at Winchester, Banks was urged by McClellan to press the retreating Jackson, yet he moved cautiously up the valley, convinced that he was faced by an equal number of Rebels.]

March 24, 1862. The station between General Shields' house and Colonel Kimball's headquarters had been temporarily abandoned last night, [and] I was again ordered this morning to resume it, it being on a small ridge near the battlefield of yesterday and [positioned to] communicate with Lieutenant Miner at Shields' house. The wounded occupant there was exceedingly anxious to be informed of every movement going on, and per consequence, Miner and myself had our hands full in keeping him supplied with details . . . concerning all operations in our front. Our column started this morning in pursuit of the enemy in the direction of Strasburg, and I was left undisturbed at my station on the ridge with instructions to look for a [signal] flag [accompanying] the advancing troops further down the Valley.

March 25, 1862. General Banks returned from Washington this morning, having in the meantime ordered his other division back to take part in the pursuit. Upon their arrival at noon I was ordered to call in Lieutenant Miner and rejoin the advance now nearing Strasburg. At 6 p.m. we reached Cedar Creek and found the bridge gone, its smoldering embers denoting the method of its recent destruction. A good ford just above, however, enabled the troops to cross without hindrance. At 9 p.m. we crossed, and while endeavoring to ascend the high bank opposite with our mules and wagon, the wagon accidentally tipped over, burying our sable driver, Jeff, beneath a perfect avalanche of valises, signal traps, and cooking utensils. He was soon extricated and the vehicle righted without much damage, and then owing to darkness a halt was decided upon until morning that other accidents of a like nature might be averted.

A few officers, including me, spent the night on the floor of a dilapidated looking cabin, the wretched owner of which—though evidently on the verge of starvation and betokening in looks and language the Southern ignoramus—evinced the usual inclination to try and impress us with his aristocratic Virginia ancestry. But the incompatibility between the prosperous planter of this commonwealth and the uncongenial landmark before us was so striking that to avoid another nauseous dose of Southern rot and balderdash (which was imminent), we gladly hunted up our blankets and turned in for the night. On awakening this morning we felt considerably refreshed, notwithstanding the very searching trial our anatomy had undergone on the cabin floor of this glittering sample of Virginia's First Families, and without waiting to settle our bills for his luxurious accommodations, or to even thank him for the privilege of stopping at his place . . . we were soon saddled up and on the march for Strasburg, entering that place about 10 a.m. Here a station was established, on a knoll east of the town, to which I was assigned, and communication at once opened with Lieutenant Fralich on a mountain in a southerly direction near Front Royal, and with Lieutenant Spencer, [who was] with the advance, on Round Top Mountain down the valley.

My station and that of Fralich's were important in that we were expected to exercise extreme vigilance respecting that portion of the country lying to the rear, over which General Banks's forces had traversed, and south, to the entrance of and up the Luray Valley, along which Jackson might be contemplating a flank movement.

The town of Strasburg, with its typical Southern aspect, contained prior to the war about five hundred inhabitants, and but for the rebellion would have, no doubt, soon increased in size, being one of the principal points on the Manassas Gap R.R. [and] the Shenandoah Valley R.R., partly completed but now abandoned. To the curse of slavery, however . . . is it indebted for the indifference and apathy of its people, whose neglected or deserted farms and devastated fields meet the eye on every side.

Just prior to receiving the order announcing the abandonment of this station, a regiment of cavalry was seen approaching from the direction of Winchester for the reinforcement of General Banks's column. I was impressed by the fine appearance they presented, both in men and horses, as the column moved at a slow trot around the base of the hill which I occupied, until its advance reached the west side, where it halted. In a few minutes an officer, accompanied by an orderly, rode up to my station. Informing me that he was Colonel Holliday commanding the First Vermont Cavalry[20]—ordered up to this department from Washington— he desired me to inform General Banks of his arrival at Strasburg, and to inquire what he should further do. I signaled the message to Spencer at Round Top Mountain, and while awaiting a reply occupied the time in conversing with the colonel and admiring the magnificent animal he rode, which, by the way, was a stallion, requiring a curb-bit with an iron ring encircling the jaw to control him, the first of the kind I had ever seen. The message from headquarters was soon [received], directing him to proceed with his regiment to the neighborhood of Woodstock, and upon his arrival report to General Banks for further orders. Upon receipt of this, the colonel descended the hill to the head of his regiment, and they were soon in motion going towards Woodstock.

On my way to the front that evening, an ambulance passed me in charge of a cavalry detachment, among whom I recognized the orderly who had accompanied Colonel Holliday to my station, and from whom I gleaned the particulars of a most deplorable event. It appeared that after leaving my station, the colonel had proceeded down the Valley Pike to a bridge spanning a small stream which crosses the road about one mile beyond Strasburg. Leaving the orderly, he rode down the hill and under the bridge, as was supposed for the purpose of giving his horse a drink at the stream. Presently hearing the report of a pistol, the orderly hurried to the colonel's side, and discovered that he had dismounted and shot himself in the head.

No motive could be assigned as a reason for the suicide, except a vague one that a lady was the probable cause.[21]

Universal regret was expressed at his sudden and untimely end, as much had been expected of him [by virtue of] his soldierly qualities as a cavalry officer having been tested in the Regular service, from which he had been detailed to command his regiment.

April 1, 1862. Fralich and I, in accordance with orders, moved forward and joined headquarters within five miles of Woodstock. Here the enemy had made a stand disputing our passage, but it was of so slight a character that our skirmishers soon brushed them aside, aided by a flanking column of our cavalry . . . and we soon took possession of this dreary, anti-diluvian looking place. In the short engagement just noted, the 29th Penna. lost two men by the bursting of one of the enemy's shells, and [they] were buried where they fell.[22]

On entering Woodstock, the officers of the Signal Corps singled out for their quarters the residence of one Mr. Ott, a Virginia leather dealer who, to use his own expression, was a thorough-going states rights man—a polite term for a Rebel. He was, of course, opposed to the war (that is to say a vigorous prosecution of it by the North), and wanted, like all of his kind, to be let alone. It was manifest to us that he was saturated with the sentiments of an out and out traitor, but just at this time, with so many Yanks around, considered it unhealthy to assert himself too loudly.

This fossilized specimen of ante-bellum times had two daughters whom he kept closely under lock and key during our stay here of several days, so apprehensive was he of the winning qualities of the blue-bellied Yankees, and imagined himself devilishly sly in thus hiding them away, although I presume it was with their sanction, considering their well-known spite-fulness towards everything savoring of Unionism. But the colored female help, those faithful friends of ours, gave the jig away. . . . With a view of humoring his belief in our ignorance, and of emphasizing our regrets at his being deprived of the pleasure of one or two daughters among his several children, we pretended to condole him at every opportunity about the masculinity of his household . . . [and] congratulated him on having such nice female help around him which might compensate for the ab-sence of girl members of his family, although a trifle dangerous when there were so many boys without sisters to guide them. He swallowed all of this, while chuckling to himself at his shrewdness in fooling the Yanks as to the hidden girls. And so we left him, making our stay just as lengthy as we possibly could, even to sending back for articles negligently supposed to have been left behind, keeping the old rooster and his darlings in a state of suspense until actually out of sight and hearing of this place. I suppose they had a hearty handshake all around after our departure at their imaginary deception and release from the thralldom of "those hateful men," but, as the poet hath said, "What fools these mortals be!"

On *April 3*, shortly after leaving Woodstock, I was ordered to take Lieutenant Miner and four men from the signal party and establish a station on Massanutten Mountain at a point about equidistant between Woodstock and Edenburg, which were about 10 miles apart. My instructions were to open communications with Lieutenant Briggs at the outpost in Edenburg and with General Banks's headquarters near Woodstock. To insure my safety, I had assigned to me, to guard the station, Co. B, 2nd Mass. Inf., Captain Williams,[23] and one company of the 1st Michigan Cavalry. At 10 a.m. my detachment reached the ford of the Shenandoah River . . . and to avoid getting the infantrymen wet—the water being waist deep—I directed the cavalry to cross and then dismount three men of each set of fours, and have the fourth man bring the led horses back for the use of the others, until all had crossed safely. The company of infantry were provided with three days rations. At the expiration of that time they were to return, and another company, provided for in a like manner, [would] succeed them, this plan being deemed preferable to retaining the first company and ferrying rations to them when needed. After a short march a favorable point on the mountain was selected, and the cavalry picketed the roads at the base, with the infantry placed at easy supporting distance.

From Massanutten Mountain could be seen the towns of Woodstock and Strasburg to the rear, and Edenburg and Mount Jackson in front, an area of some twenty-eight miles. Stonewall Jackson's forces lay at this time in the vicinity of Mount Jackson, [and] we had a good view of them and easily estimated their strength.

On the second day of our occupation I decided to visit the station at the outpost and confer with the officers there [so] that no mistake might occur when we forwarded them reports of the enemy's movements. Leaving Miner in charge, I crossed at the ford and reported to General Banks, at his headquarters, the position and probable strength of Jackson's army, and then rode to Edenburg. After making arrangements with Lieutenant Briggs, I sought out the location of my old company, A, of the 29th Pennsylvania, who were quartered in a little one story tailor store near the bank of the river.

The Shenandoah River, which tortuously winds its way down the Valley, intersects the turnpike at Edenburg, and is quite deep. Its width is about seventy-five or eighty feet, and prior to our arrival, was spanned by a bridge, the town being built up to and along the northern bank of the river. The rebels had burned the bridge behind them, however, and the 29th Pennsylvania were now on picket awaiting its reconstruction by the engineer corps. I was much pleased to greet the boys of Company A again after an absence of some weeks, and greatly enjoyed with them a soldier's dinner of bean soup, hard tack, and coffee. The captain, Samuel App,[24] true to his dignified instincts, had singled out two or three favorites with whom he was quartered in another house apart from the balance of the company, which had been left in charge of Lieutenant Wiggins.[25] Between these two detachments there seemed to be little intercourse; a state of affairs that continued and widened until a short time afterwards when this dishonest and supercilious package of arrogance (who had been honored by our company by a unanimous election to the office of captain, although a stranger to us), rendered the government the most important duty he ever owed it . . . by resigning his commission and going home.

April 6, 1862. The limit of time (three days) for which Co. B of the 2nd Mass. had been detailed having expired, Captain Williams began preparations this a.m. for leaving, and found the task most difficult, and, as afterwards proved, very distressful from the consequences of a terrible storm of snow and sleet that had prevailed the night before. The roads were almost impassable and the river had risen to a height that precluded all prospects of fording at the former place of crossing. I rode to the stream with the company, and with the captain's aid succeeded in finding a small boat, or scow, capable of carrying about six persons, which met the emergency—if exercised with care—very conveniently. Within half an hour all had been safely ferried across excepting the captain, two sergeants, and seven men, equal to two comfortable boat loads. While conversing with me about the detail to take his place, all those remaining, unobserved by the captain, got into the boat, pushed off, and were half way over before I called his attention to the jeopardy they were in from their crowded condition and the unsafe appearance they presented. The gunwale of the scow was scarcely two inches above the surface of the water, which was running, in its swollen state, very rapidly to a dam just below. He at once ran to the edge of the stream and expostulated with them against taking such desperate chances, cautioning them to remain very quiet. In a brief time they had reached to within ten feet of the opposite shore, the distance being not over fifty feet in all. Their apparent safety now made them reckless, and one of them, in attempting to rise, swamped the boat, which filled and instantly sank.

All sprang for the tall grass of the shore and succeeded in grasping it excepting the two sergeants, who, being heavily encumbered with two rifles each, which were swung across their backs, disappeared at once and were drowned. We ran to the dam and caught the boat, which, relieved of its load, rose to the surface and floated down, but the bodies of the sergeants were never seen again.[26] This calamity was to me saddening in the extreme in view of my warm personal regard for the captain, which had ripened with the many months of our association in the army, as well as from the fact that the lives of two of his best men had been lost on a special duty to which I had been partly responsible for their detail. I returned to the mountain, chilled to the bone and much depressed and exhausted by the exciting events of the morning, having remained at the river with the captain some three hours after the accident. He was loath to leave in the fruitless hope that his boys might yet be found.

Miner and I had arranged to take our meals at a farm house at the base of the mountain, and this evening, after the unfortunate episode just narrated, I was compelled to remain there, instead of spending the night at the summit, and nurse violently aggravated symptoms of the returning fever before alluded to. In the morning I awoke from a troubled sleep to find myself in a cold profuse perspiration, having suffered from another exhaustive night-sweat that knocked all ambition galley-west.

The family occupying the farm were excessively penurious, or else possessed of a determination, from hatred of the Northern soldier, to bleed his pocket book to its utmost limit. They had the assurance to charge us, for the most commonplace meals, rates equaling first class hotels, and upon remonstrating with the old lady against this absurdity and refusing to accede to her exorbitant demands, she indignantly declared that we had probably not taken into consideration the society of the family we were enjoying, which more than made up the difference between the cost of an ordinary meal, and that she expected us to pay her. The society [she referred to] consisted of the usual specimens of illiteracy met with in the South; an old man, a small boy, a frowsy unkempt girl, a hungry-looking canine, two cats, and the aforesaid ruler of the domicile, the old woman. It forces a smile to reflect upon the home comforts partaken of in their establishment, especially my last forty-eight hours with them. If sitting over a smoky wood fire in a cheerless, carpetless room, with chills, a feverish throbbing head, and absolutely no appetite can be likened to home comforts, of what then does full-fledged misery consist?

Virginia hospitality has become proverbial. That is, I find the proverb prevails to an immeasurable extent in Virginia, and you are surfeited by the natives with frequent references to this beautiful sentiment. In North Carolina, the native there rolls it as a sweet morsel under his tongue whenever the hospitality of North Carolina is referred to. The South Carolinian, too, feels that the hospitality of his state passeth all understanding, and so on throughout each Southern state. But the soldier boys have discovered that it exists in imagination only, and in comparison with the genuine hospitality of the Northern states, is a myth and deception that has been practiced upon the people of this country until its reiteration creates a nausea. To flatter a Virginian, call him hospitable. The significance of and importance of his having been born on the sacred soil of the "Old Dominion," (the assumed hospitality of which has been spread broadcast), puffs and swells him with inordinate vanity like the veriest gobbler. Yet this nicotine-freighted and gin-saturated model of Southern manhood will squeeze a greenback tighter and cling to it longer than the most inveterate money-seeking Hebrew in the land. But why dwell upon the virtues of these arrogant and so-called political dictators, these counterfeit dispensers of hospitality? In the language of our brave boys, "from all such frauds, good Lord deliver us."

That which I had been trying to make myself believe was only an incipient fever, to be counteracted with a little care, I found rapidly developing into a tangible attack of typhoid, and my powers of endurance—which had stood me so well through the many exposures to the elements during my life—were now deserting me. The setback I received from an extreme chill on the day of the accident to Captain Williams's company was so acute and penetrating that I was now fully persuaded that something must be speedily done, if at all, to resist the fever's gradually weakening influences.

The continued wet weather and melting snows kept the streams of the Valley at an abnormal height, making the crossing of the Shenandoah extremely troublesome. This, [coupled] with the disaster to Williams's men, probably discouraged the general and prompted him to withhold the anticipated guard which should have succeeded Company B of the 2nd Mass. We had to depend, therefore, entirely on the cavalry escort, and as this force was insufficient to afford me any protection at the farm during the day, I decided to remain on the mountain, excepting between 10 p.m. and daylight, and thus managed to keep up my sphere of duty alternating with Miner. There was, indeed, very little done at night, as our station was principally one of observation, and Miner was rarely disturbed after retiring until daylight brought me to the summit, at which time the operation of climbing fatigued me beyond measure.

There is no doubt that but for this station the Rebel artillery and sharpshooters would have annoyed the troops in and around Edenburg considerably, their movements being screened completely by the heavy timber on the opposite bank. But the reports we flagged of their doings kept our outposts and batterymen on the alert, and frustrated the schemes of the "Johnnies," who must have been amusingly nonplussed at the promptness with which their plans for surprising our boys were balked. . . .

An instance of this kind occurred while here that exhibited, in an admirable manner, the availability of the Signal Corps for observation purposes in a country as mountainous and undulating as the Shenandoah Valley. Just beyond Edenburg the turnpike makes a sharp turn to the right for a short distance, and then continues its usual course in a southwesterly direction. About one-fourth of a mile beyond this turn there is an old iron furnace, and between it and Edenburg the country is thickly wooded, obscuring the locality of the furnace entirely from view of our troops, but visible to us on the mountain, although distant [some] five miles, as the bird flies. About 10 a.m. on the third day after our occupation of the Massanutten we observed, with the aid of our telescopes, a section of a battery (two pieces), with caisson, in charge of an officer, slowly trotting up the pike in our direction. Upon reaching the furnace they turned in to their right, and passing beyond the piece of woods prepared to unlimber. Suspecting some deviltry, we at once signaled Lieutenant Briggs at Edenburg to notify Captain Best, commanding a battery of the 4th U.S. Artillery, to prepare for them, giving him their exact location. The intervening trees prevented our seeing Captain Best's position, but knowing him as an expert artillerist, we awaited further developments. In a few seconds a puff of smoke from a Rebel gun told us they had opened on our lines, and were no doubt chuckling at their slyness in getting the bulge on the Yankees. Scarcely had their smoke lifted, however, before we saw the smoke from one of our guns, and immediately a shell burst directly over their pieces. Again the reverberations were audible from their vicinity, and Best replied with two ringers. Still another from them, and Best this time gets in three, each one dropping, apparently, right among or around them. [This] reception was so warm it must certainly have exceeded their most sanguine expectations, for immediately after firing their third shot we had the pleasure of seeing them excitedly limber up and gallop out to the pike, down which they went "lickety-split" towards Mount Jackson. Captain Best, under our instruction, hurried them along with a few more shells from his 12 Pdr. Napoleons. . . .

April 11, 1862. Our advance moved this evening and came up with the Rebel rear guard early next morning near Mt. Jackson. We found, before striking them, that they had burned two foot bridges as well as railroad bridges, but luckily the absence of these did not materially impede our progress. We continued to drive them, and as our cavalry skirmishers entered Mt. Jackson, they discovered a squad of Johnnies just igniting a long foot bridge which spans the Shenandoah on the west side of the town. As the destruction of this would have greatly retarded our column, a charge was sounded and the incendiaries, [along with] a lieutenant and ten men, were gobbled, thus nicely baffling their designs. Two Rebel batteries (twelve pieces) were in position beyond the bridge and opened wrathfully on our lines. General Shields' division . . . formed on the right of the road, with General Williams, [commanding] Banks's old division, on the left. Preceded by skirmishers and with cavalry on the flanks, they moved quickly forward, and the brave Johnnies tarried not, but, very properly, limbered up their pieces and made tracks just as promptly as they had done at Kernstown.

No halt was ordered in Mt. Jackson, but the pursuit kept up to New Market, a few miles further, which we reached late in the afternoon. The Rebels continued their flight to the next town, Harrisonburg.

A portion of the Signal Corps, myself included, found excellent quarters at the house of a lukewarm secessionist near the upper end of the village where I was constrained, owing to my weak condition, to relinquish all active work. The family gave me some little attention, for which I was thankful, although I paid spot cash for all they did. They were very grateful for the coffee I furnished them, having been using for months a substitute entirely new to me, consisting of sweet potatoes cut in small cubes, browned over a hot fire, and then pounded fine and boiled. They tried to imagine that this counterfeit . . . tasted like the genuine article, but I was unable to perceive any similarity between the two. Neither was I slow to observe that their faith in this boasted substitute "for the drink that cheers but not inebriates," had a vanishing tendency after their re-introduction to the fragrant berry handled by our commissary.

On the 21st of April, our senior officer, Lieutenant Rowley, kindly endorsed and forwarded to General Banks for approval an application for my leave of absence for thirty days. The matter was referred to Medical Inspector King,[27] of his staff, who upon examination reported me as having symptoms of typhoid fever, and recommended my retirement for treatment. Upon this recommendation the general appended his signature, granting the request. The next important step was to get a conveyance of some kind wherewith to return to Winchester—a distance of some fifty miles—[because] in my enfeebled state . . . it was not possible for me to endure a ride in the saddle. I secured, with difficulty, an ancient and badly used up no-top buggy, and on the morning of the 23rd, in company with my man, Dick Powell,[28] bid good-bye to the boys and started in a driving snowstorm for Winchester. It was rather rough riding this, particularly to an invalid; the springs of the buggy having long since exhausted their vitality in transporting Virginia nabobs, but as I was well wrapped up in a blanket and fortified with a bottle of stimulating fluid from the surgeon's stores, I felt comparatively happy. . . .

There was some solicitude expressed by members of the staff concerning my escort of one man only, and the improbability of my getting through safely owing to the incursions in the Valley of Mosby's and White's guerrilla bands, who made frequent attacks on our wagon trains.[29] I was so anxious to find the needed rest though, [and this], together with a feeling of security in being accompanied by two heavily loaded navy revolvers and a carbine—which Dick was an expert in the use of—that I obstinately determined to take the chances of being intercepted. . . .

At noon we reached Woodstock, and to procure dinner for Dick I directed him to drive a short distance from the main road and make a test again of Valley hospitality at the residence of our former host, the leather dealer, Mr. Ott. Our appearance was such a surprise to the family . . . that when we jumped from the vehicle and walked in we discovered [that] the two daughters who had remained hidden in the top of the house during the first visit [were] now taking dinner the rest of the family. Dick and I pretended not to observe the embarrassment of those present. . . . But as soon as terms were agreed upon, we immediately sat down in front of the young ladies and fell to work upon the viands before us, although I think our abrupt appearance interfered greatly with the appetites of the household seated around. Not a word was spoken during the meal, but after Dick had had a perfect gorge (my appetite being limited), and [we] were about starting, I casually remarked to the old gentleman that I thought his family had somewhat increased since our first introduction to him. This suggestion seemed to tickle immensely the two female contrabands waiting on the table, but to our satirical sallies the old codger was as impervious as marble, never deigning to reply.

When Dick and I emerged from the lane leading from the Ott mansion to the main pike . . . the snow was still gently falling and a mist somewhat obscured the view on either side, shutting out entirely the mountain ranges that here so prominently mark the course of the Valley. Our horse had been fed and watered, and being a spirited animal was showing her mettle; the afternoon was slowly wearing away, and not an indication of living thing was visible. The path of the army could be traced, as those paths have been from time immemorial, by the absence of all farm stock or poultry, and by the complete obliteration of fencing indicating the limitation of each planter's estate.

Dick had filled his pipe while [we were] jogging along, and I had brought the nag down to a walk so that Dick might economize in the use of his matches, when glancing off in the direction of the Massanutten, I saw, to my amazement, eight or ten cavalrymen evidently waiting for someone. Their horses were clustered by the side of a road that apparently intersected ours about a quarter of a mile ahead. We were, at this moment, about to descend a depression on the pike which would shut us out from view of this squad, and to satisfy myself of their character, I had the horse reined in and [I] brought my marine glass to bear on them. Its power and accuracy at once convinced me that they were guerrillas. A moment's reflection assured me that we were not observed, and that we could make the junction of the two roads before being detected by them, if at all. . . . Hoping we would be able to escape their attention, we started at a lively gait down the hill. Scarcely had we gained the top of the rise—on a direct line with their road at the junction—when they observed us and instinctively put spurs to their horses in pursuit.

"Let her go, Dick," I shouted, and the whip fell on our animal, causing her to spring forward in a mad run. Ere many seconds had elapsed, I looked back and saw them just turning into the pike, their horses coming for all they were worth. It was now nip and tuck, for I verily believe our mare was holding her own, and if we could only make Strasburg, not over a mile ahead, I felt sure of ending this exciting and hazardous race. We kept up this breakneck speed until after rounding Fisher's Hill and approaching Strasburg, when I distinctly heard two shots and the whistling of bullets, which convinced me they must be gaining. . . . Taking the reins from Dick, he dropped on his knees in the buggy, facing to the rear, and gave them a well directed shot from the carbine. The distance between us now could not have been more than two hundred and fifty yards, within easy range of our breech-loading carbine, so putting in another cartridge while I was applying the whip, he again fired and gave a whooping yell as one of their horses plunged forward onto his knees and rolled over. This had no effect upon the others, who kept on until we had almost touched Strasburg; notwithstanding, Dick gave them two or three more shots, one of which we were sure was effective. To our surprise, a body of [our] cavalry, stopping temporarily in the village . . . came galloping to our assistance. We at once reined in our nearly exhausted mare, and with the cavalry gave them a volley from our revolvers, when they turned tail and got back as quickly as possible. The cavalry proved to be a squadron of a Michigan regiment, under whose protection we gave our winded mare a good chance to blow and a rubbing down. In an hour we were trotting away again in fine shape towards Winchester, profusely congratulating ourselves on our auspicious success in not only beating them in the race, but in the extraordinary good luck at meeting our boys at almost the very last moment.

At 6 p.m. I reached Winchester all right, and made for the boarding house of a Mrs. Jones on the main street, where I spent a most comfortable night in spite of the shaking up I underwent in the afternoon chase. In the morning, I sent Dick back with the buggy . . . with instructions to proceed to Strasburg, report himself to the officer commanding the cavalry, and request an escort as far as Woodstock, beyond [which] it was considered relatively safe. I learned later that Dick carried out the orders given to him and reported safely to Rowley at New Market that same evening. After parting with him, I secured a seat in the stage at the antiquated Taylor Hotel,[30] and at 8 a.m. was off for Frederick, Maryland, via Martinsburg and Hagerstown.

I partook of lunch at Martinsburg and proceeded to the river, crossing the Potomac on a flat-boat to Williamsport and from thence to Hagerstown, which I entered at dark. Instead of going direct to Baltimore by rail as contemplated, I was obliged to retrace my steps from Frederick to Point of Rocks, where I had left my trunk with the Bassant family at the commencement of the campaign. They were much pleased to welcome me again to their circle, but grieved at my forlorn and ill condition, and in parting (as a strong attachment had grown between us), I was assured of a cordial greeting if upon my convalescence the fortunes of war should chance to find me again in their vicinity. This sincerely refined and Christian family, to whom I have before referred, and with whom I had spent many pleasant hours, saw me depart with many misgivings as to my ultimate recovery. . . .

At noon of April 26, I took the train at the Point and reached Baltimore in the evening, stopping at the Eutaw House, the recognized Union hotel of that secession city. I remained here until Monday, April 28, when I decided I must start for home or seek medical assistance in a government hospital. As I was least desirous of risking the latter, I adopted the former and arrived in Philadelphia at 2 p.m., greatly fatigued and worn down from a persistent fever that increased with renewed force each day.

The intervening time between my arrival in Philadelphia and return must be briefly told. I sought Dr. Joseph Pancoast, and was advised to consult a neighboring physician, Dr. Thomas K. Reed, near our Queen Street residence, and [was told to] prepare for a case of typhoid and camp fever. I went to bed on May 1, under his care and that of a trained nurse, [and] remained there over two weeks, followed by a slow and tedious convalescence. My leave of absence was extended thirty days through a certificate furnished by Dr. Pancoast that I was still unfit for duty. Finally, I left home for Washington on the evening of July 15. I was notified just prior to starting that I had been promoted to the rank of captain of Co. A, 29th Regt., to date from July 11, 1862, a piece of good news that I was sure would give me quite a standing in our corps on rejoining them.

CHAPTER 3

CEDAR MOUNTAIN

JULY 17 - AUGUST 16, 1862

A fter two-and-a-half months of convalescence, Fortescue returned to duty and found that his signal detachment was now part of the newly formed Army of Virginia under Maj. Gen. John Pope.

Following the Federal defeats in the Shenandoah Valley during the spring and early summer of 1862, Pope, who had distinguished himself at Island No. 10, New Madrid, and Corinth earlier in the war, was chosen by Lincoln to unite the luckless forces serving under Banks, Fremont, and McDowell into a single army. His orders were to protect Washington, D.C., from attacks directed from Richmond, assure the safety of the Shenandoah Valley, and operate on the enemy's line of communications in the direction of Charlottesville and Gordonsville in hopes of drawing off a portion of the force that was confronting the Army of the Potomac near Richmond. By early July, Pope had consolidated most of his *command along the Rappahannock River and was soon probing south in the direction of Gordonsville.*

Meanwhile, George B. McClellan's Army of the Potomac had been forced to retreat to the James River south of Richmond after the Seven Days Battles, and Lee, confident that he could hold McClellan in place with only a portion of his force, sent Stonewall Jackson (who had joined him near Richmond from the Shenandoah in late June) back into the valley on July 13 to confront Pope. McClellan was soon ordered to transfer his army from the Virginia Peninsula to Fredericksburg, where it was to unite with Pope's command, while Pope, prior to moving toward Fredericksburg to join with McClellan's veterans, began to gather his forces in the vicinity of Culpeper.

On August 7, Jackson started north from Gordonsville, intent on attacking the first elements of Pope's force he could find, and on the sultry afternoon of August 9 encountered Banks's corps eight miles below Culpeper near Cedar Mountain.

July 17, 1862. Back in Warrenton, Va., and feeling tip-top. How strange it is that a man should be insufferably miserable in one locality, and yet miraculously improve in another? I came amply prepared with medicines from Dr. Pancoast to forestall any lingering traces of my late tie-up, but I am so braced up by the change from the city to open-air military duty that I have, literally, thrown the physic to the dogs. A heavy rain has fallen for two days and all the streams are swollen, compelling me to stay at the Warren Green Hotel, where the society of old associates compensates for the ennui that otherwise would be occasioned by detention in this ancient and wearisome-looking apology for a hotel. Our coterie of choice spirits is made up of Colonel Knipe of the 46th Pennsylvania., Major George W. Gile of the 88th Pennsylvania., John Reilly, Quartermaster Sergeant, 90th Pennsylvania., Lieutenant Will Augustine, 29th Pennsylvania., and many other shoulder-strapped gentry, who, like myself are corralled in Warrenton on account of impassable streams, [and] while away the time in swapping army experiences and singing popular songs. . . .[1]

On the morning of the 20th, three of us decided that an effort should be made to find the headquarters of the Army of Virginia, then known to be encamped in the vicinity of Sperryville, Va. A search was initiated for some mode of conveyance, for the use of which we knew a fabulous price would be demanded, but which, of course, would have to be submitted to. Having succeeded in our mission by prevailing upon an impecunious Warrentonian with his antique team to tote ourselves and valises, Captain Williams, 2nd Massachusetts, Will Augustine, and myself bid goodbye to our merry company and set out, taking a southwesterly course, crossing the Rappahannock near Waterloo at noon.

It gradually began to dawn upon us, after a couple of hours in this typical Virginia carry-all, that this style of riding was not conducive to comfort or calculated to rehabilitate the lost power of recently bed-fast fever patients, so having satisfied ourselves that the emaciated mules were in no condition to out-distance us, we alighted, preferring for the balance of the day to trudge behind and take the dust rather than be disjointed. We reached the camps [of the army] near Little Washington at dark.

Here a royal welcome greeted me and heartily glad was I to find myself, after so long an absence, again among the boys of our corps, whom I found in the midst of preparations for active campaign work, which promised, from the outlook, to be of some magnitude. I was a trifle nervous in the resumption of my signal duty, both at the glass and with the code, fearing that the recess had impaired my former mental vigor, but at the conclusion of the first day's operations it was fully manifest that my right hand had not forgotten its cunning in the intricacies of reading by flag or torch, and that I had fallen into the traces again as naturally as a young duckling takes to its watery element.

Now that I had settled down for at least twenty-four hours and was in such good physical condition, I began to feel an especial interest in the rumored early coming of our new commanding officer, Major General Pope. His successes in the Western armies had been heralded over the country, and had reached the ears of the soldiers of the Eastern armies long before it had been determined by the President to give him a trial in this section with a view of waking up some of the drowsy failures in command of us. General Pope personally assumed command of the Army of Virginia, a branch of the Army of the Potomac, during the latter part of July.[2] He had been in Washington for some days overseeing the minor details preparatory to taking the field in person, and while there directed the consolidation of his army, which was now comprised of three corps: the First, under General Franz Sigel, numbering 11,500 men; the Second, under General N. P. Banks, 18,000; and the Third, under General Irwin McDowell, 18,500 men.[3]

Whatever good opinion may have been entertained by the Eastern soldiers for General Pope prior to his coming was quickly dissipated upon the appearance among them of a lamentably weak General Order reflecting, by implication, upon the commander of the Army of the Potomac, McClellan, and as it [also] contained much that smacked of bravado, it was therefore less effective than if couched in language more moderate in tone. It read as follows:

Washington, July [14], 1862
To the Officers and Soldiers of the Army of Virginia:

By special assignment of the President of the United States, I have assumed command of this army. I have spent two weeks in learning your whereabouts, your condition, and your wants; in preparing you for active operations, and in placing you in positions from which you can act promptly and to the purpose. I have come to you from the West, where we have always seen the backs of our enemies, from an army whose business it has been to seek the adversary and to beat him when he was found. Whose policy has been attack and not defense. In but one instance has the enemy been able to place our Western armies in a defensive attitude. I presume that I have been called here to pursue the same system, and to lead you against the enemy. It is my purpose to do so and that speedily. I am sure you long for the opportunity to win the distinction you are capable of achieving. That opportunity I shall endeavor to give you. Meanwhile, I desire you to dismiss from your minds certain phrases I am sorry to find so much in vogue amongst you. I hear constantly of "taking strong positions and holding them," of "lines of retreat," and of "bases of supplies." Let us discard such ideas. The strongest position a soldier should desire to occupy is one from which he can most easily advance against the enemy. Let us study the probable lines of retreat of our opponents and leave our own to take care of themselves. Let us look before us and not behind. Success and glory are in the advance, disaster and shame lurk in the rear. Let us act on this understanding, and it is safe to predict that your banner shall be inscribed with many a glorious deed and that your names will be dear to your countrymen forever.

This address was the subject of much ill-advised comment and ridicule, prompted by the blind idolatry of the Army of the Potomac for McClellan, whose claims to military prominence had not been displayed except in the preliminary organization of that army and in the building of defenses around Washington, either of which could have been accomplished by scores of officers in his command.[4]

I confess to a feeling of aversion towards Pope from the start, due of course in a great measure to the above self-opinionated edict of his, pooh-poohed as it was by many of extended service, and intended for the ears of us striplings who had barely yet ripened into thinking voters. This impression was heightened by his coming, [which was] heralded with a most extravagant headquarters train and staff, exceeding that of McClellan. It surprised us to see an escort of a regiment of cavalry instead of a squadron, a train of one hundred wagons, two milch cows, a printing press for field orders, and French cooks for his cuisine. This display was in contradistinction to that published in his second general order, which affirmed that his "headquarters were in the saddle," and gave his enemies additional room for criticism.[5]

Never shall I forget the first meeting between he and Banks and the food for conversation it occasioned. Pope had just arrived from Warrenton, where he reviewed the corps of General McDowell, and as he rode across the field to the piece of woods where Banks's headquarters were situated, Banks and [his] staff emerged from their tents, uncovered, and advanced to meet him. Instead of dismounting and uncovering when he approached Banks—who was his superior officer, though nominally under him— Pope reined in his horse, reached over its neck, took the extended hand [of Banks] in a cold, formal manner, then wheeled about and rode away to select suitable ground for himself and staff, leaving Banks to return to his tent with scarcely so much as an inquiry after his health.[6] But time mollifies the passions and softens the asperity of men, and with all of General Pope's peculiarly inflated ideas of his own military aptitude, he possessed much merit and should have won [victories], and most certainly would have done so had the jealous adherents and political companions of McClellan permitted him. That General Pope, from experience as an old soldier and from former associations, knew better of the shallowness of some of these satraps than the volunteers who were spurred on to denounce him no one will deny. At all events, his predictions as to the brevity of the tenure of office of several of them were ultimately realized, and the country ere long saw them shelved to give room to officers who neither placed safeguards around the property of Rebels and punished the weary and footsore soldier who helped himself to the fruit, nor dictated lengthy letters to the President with a view of shaping his future policy and made his sleepy moments a hideous nightmare by persistently calling for reinforcements they had no use for, while conspicuously ignorant of the ability required to handle those already under them.

. . . While attached to this station, on the edge of a piece of woods some three hundred yards in the rear of General Pope's headquarters, the reckless use of a rifle came near winding up the earthly career of the writer. My telescope, bearing upon Culpeper Court House, was braced on forked boughs driven into the ground just in front of my tent. From my cot inside the tent, I could converse with the guard on duty, and when wanted could be seated in his place at the glass, ready to respond at a moment's notice. The days were sultry and feverish, and the tent walls [were] looped up from the ground to allow the free ingress of any stray breeze. . . . I was lying on my cot leisurely reading—in readiness to answer expected signals—and was listening to the reports of the rifles of those engaged in killing beeves for the troops . . . when my attention was attracted by a shout of alarm from a blacksmith whose forge was in the woods to the rear of our tents. Hastening out to learn the cause, I observed the man excitedly pointing to a huge black snake between he and I that, with reared head, was slowly moving towards my quarters, but which suddenly stopped upon hearing me call to my man at the glass. Quickly taking in the situation, my flagman ran to a point which with the blacksmith and myself formed a triangle, and with stout sticks hastily caught up, we closed in on his snakeship and soon laid him low.

Just before we made the attack, however, we were startled by the whiz of a bullet which passed through my tent and between us in the woods, but fortunately did no damage. Upon returning to the tent to investigate, I easily traced the course of the ball and found that it had come from the rifle of one of those engaged in killing beeves, and had passed through the tent diagonally across the cot from the foot to the relative situation of the shoulders, so that but for this reptile making its appearance when it did, I should have been lying in position to have received the shot upward through the body. The propitious circumstance of the coming of that snake, at what proved to be so critical a juncture in my existence, made me sincerely regret having been a party to its destruction, notwithstanding its repulsiveness and great length, which we ascertained upon measurement to be over six feet. . . . While reluctant to be the cause of distress in others, I was not to be deterred . . . from persuading General Banks to take cognizance of the unpardonable carelessness of his butchers (his tents being in an equally dangerous proximity from the firing). He ordered his commissary, Captain Murphy,[7] and his men before him and had them lectured roundly for their recklessness with the rifle while . . . in easy range of the camps of the troops.

The month of August had come and General Pope was beginning to feel more at home with his new assignment. The different corps had been reviewed by him, and the work of inspection by his trained staff completed. Additional manifestoes, in the guise of general orders, had been promulgated, and they indicated confidence, and to some extent, self-consciousness upon the part of the man controlling our destinies. While adding inspiration to many, they irritatingly became the butt of others instilled with "Little Mac-ism."

The messages flitting over our flag line were becoming more interesting and alarmingly frequent, keeping us diligently employed at the glass, and [we] impressed the new commandant most favorably with the energetic and efficient services of our detachment as a corps of observation. This was manifested by his frequent visits to our station [so] that he might be personally present to receive and further interrogate [us], through our informants, concerning the exact condition of the country in their immediate vicinity. Jackson's forces were reported by our Thoroughfare Mountain station, manned by Lieutenant Spencer, to be maneuvering in the neighborhood of Orange Court House, and we were hourly in expectance of an order to strike tents and move forward to engage this much overrated flanker. . . .

August 2nd, 1862. This morning at ten our corps took up the line of march in the direction of Culpeper Court House, not halting for the night until reaching the banks of the Hazel River at 5 p.m. Here I was assigned to the headquarters stations communicating as follows: to Butler Mountain, Lieutenant Halstead; to Red Oak Mountain, Lieutenant Miner; Culpeper Court House, Captain Ned Pierce; and from thence to Thoroughfare Mountain, Lieutenant Spencer. This line extended over forty miles and proved to be of incalculable importance to General Pope, so freely acknowledged by him in the faltering allusions made in his reports at the close of the campaign.[8]

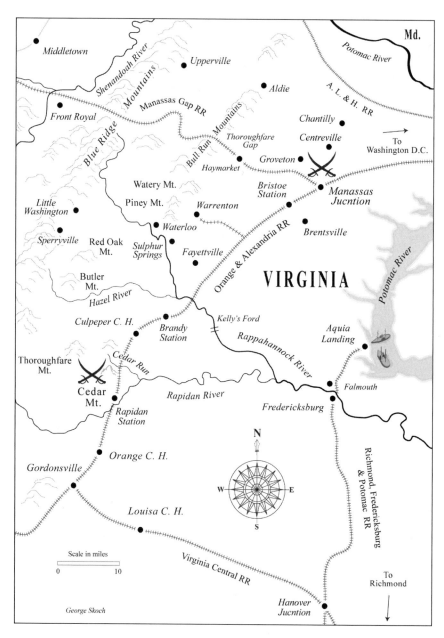

Cedar Mountain and Second Manassas, 1862.

The movement to Hazel River was undoubtedly hastened by the message from our Thoroughfare Mountain station which reported the enemy under Stonewall Jackson, [comprised of] Ewell, and—as afterwards was proven—A. P. Hill demonstrating heavily in the direction of Gordonsville.[9]

The view from this point was an extended one and enabled Spencer to observe, with the aid of his powerful glasses, the slightest indications of dust or signs denoting the presence or movements of troops, without regard to the size of the command. Spencer's vigilance as a signal officer had been the subject of much favorable comment. His ardor and enthusiasm in the success of our signal detachment was irrepressible although never immodestly exhibited. His courage and endurance was of the highest order, as exemplified by many others in the fine regiment from which he was detailed, the 1st Minnesota, and these sterling qualities led to his frequent selection for special or outpost duty, [which] usually called for extraordinary watchfulness to avoid surprise or capture.

When I reported for duty after my convalescence, I found him occupying Thoroughfare Mountain in the extreme advance, unmindful of the proximity of the foe, so that he was left, by them, unmolested. Here he remained until we were ordered to abandon the Hazel River camp and move to Culpeper Court House, which was within five days of the time we had pitched our tents there. It was just at this juncture that the enemy made the tempting discovery, by observing the flying torch in the darkness, that a Yankee Signal Officer was watching them, and [thought that] with a little tack on their part, his whole outfit could be gobbled.

But the wily Spencer was not to be so easily entrapped. He had his eye on every object for miles around, and when he saw a goodly-sized body of cavalry in the distance heading for the mountain, he instinctively smelt trouble and started to flag a notice to Culpeper of his peril. He had the message to General Pope partly underway when he found that to conclude it would materially lessen his chances of escape, so leaving the latter part untold he mounted his detachment and was off out of harm's way before the cavalry seeking him had begun to ascend the mountain.

The forced abandonment of this important outlook was very exasperating to General Pope, who depended greatly upon this superior point of elevation for prompt and accurate reports over that obtained from our reliable scouts, whose progress through the lines was ofttimes provokingly tedious. Hence, an order was immediately issued directing General Banks to detail a full regiment to march to Thoroughfare Mountain, taking with them a signal officer to replace Spencer, in the event of his not being found. Accordingly the 28th Pennsylvania was selected, [along] with Lieutenant Harvey and his flagmen, and in a short time they were on a rapid march for the point designated.

It required nearly a full day to reach the mountain, and when they got there, much to their surprise, there was Spencer in full blast again. It appeared that the cunning Spencer had ridden to a place of safety from which he could view, unobserved, the discomfited Johnnies in their fruitless search for him and their subsequent departure, and deeming it then safe had retraced his steps and opened the line, his flag being seen in operation by Harvey and the men of the 28th Penna. when nearing the Mountain. As they had been directed to stay and protect the station, the troops were disposed to meet and repel any further effort to dislodge the officers, [and] Harvey now joined Spencer and assisted him in the work of observation.[10]

Spencer's devotion to his duty and intense loyalty to our cause made it inevitable that the officer communicating with him should be constantly at the glass to receive minute descriptions of everything noticed within the range of his vision. His capacity for work was wonderful, neither sparing the opposite end of the line nor permitting those around him an idle moment; and in the long run he thereby profited much, as I personally know, from the lips of the man whose exuberant atmosphere Spencer reflected, Major Myer.[11]

General Pope, having become satisfied of the enemy's strength and their probable intentions, determined to meet them and prevent, if possible, their further advance towards the Potomac. With this end in view we reached Culpeper Court House on August 8 and found General McDowell's Corps passing through in a southerly direction. In anticipation of an attack upon McDowell's advance, Banks's Corps was ordered to remain within easy supporting distance. General Sigel, in the meantime, learning of the situation, promptly moved forward from the direction of Sperryville and was in Banks's rear, within three hours march of Culpeper, concentrating, through information furnished by the signal officers on Thoroughfare, Pope's entire army in Jackson's front before he was aware that we had a knowledge of his contemplated surprise and plan of attack.

A Mathew Brady image of the intrepid Lt. Joseph Spencer, shown here as a captain. "His courage and endurance was of the highest order." Courtesy Library of Congress, Prints and Photographs Division.

When halting at Culpeper I promptly sought the station of Captain Ned Pierce near the lower end of the Main Street, and arranged my traps in readiness for the morning's work. My experience and recollection of Pierce as an assistant and companion had been of an agreeable character, his sense of humor and natural flow of caustic wit made his society desirable and led me frequently to his quarters where a festive season was sure to be enjoyed. Like many of the clever New England boys who had donned the garb of blue, his introduction around the camp fire lent buoyancy to the conversation and an appreciative geniality in the companionship.

Pierce's every moment being occupied with Spencer, I decided to spend part of the night with him and help lighten the burden of hourly reading the Thoroughfare torch, the indefatigable Spencer insisting, from his knowledge of Pope's exacting disposition, that that gentleman demanded continuous doses as a salutary antidote against fault-finding, even though you had to awaken him to administer them.

The night was dark and heavy, scarcely a star being visible, and by ten o'clock all the troops, with the exception of the strong picket lines, had sought their blankets, many for the last time upon this earth. Naught disturbed the profound stillness but the chirping cricket or croaking tree-frog, yet far to the southwest, seemingly in the clouds, indifferent to the exposed situation and perils surrounding him, Spencer's light all the night long flashed its messages of the enemy's movements.[12] [This] required a mounted orderly constantly going and returning from our station to General Pope's headquarters. Many an eye, from a solitary picket post that night, watched that almost indiscernible glimmer and marveled at its import, few supposing that its flashes were directed towards our headquarters and not those of the Rebel "Stonewall."

THE BATTLE OF CEDAR MOUNTAIN

August 9, 1862. Shortly after daylight I reported to Lieutenant Rowley and was ordered with my men to proceed at once to Cedar Run, a small stream south of Culpeper. Taking my two flagmen I started for the front. A ride of six or seven miles brought me to Cedar Run, on the bank of which, seated under the wide spreading branches of a chestnut I found General Crawford[13] and staff, breakfasting on hard boiled eggs and hard tack, which they were washing down with copious gulps of black coffee from pint tin-dippers loaned them by some of the men. Their brigade was deployed through a piece of timber directly in front, supporting General Bayard's brigade of cavalry,[14] who were also deployed further to the front, their left extending to near the base of Cedar Mountain.

This mountain was a cone-shaped elevation of some six or eight hundred feet, and from the position where I found General Crawford at this time, [which was] near the main road crossing Cedar Run, [it] appeared to be distant about three miles to the south-east. There were no indications of troops on the mountain, which I scanned carefully with my glasses, nor at the base, although some were visible in the distance in front of our cavalry skirmish line, apparently maneuvering for position.

This was my first introduction to General Crawford, from whom I received, after reporting my instructions from General Pope, the somewhat curt response that I might take my station on a knoll to his right in front of a battery already unlimbered there, and report to him any messages received from Thoroughfare [Mountain] of the enemy's strength.

Brig. General S. B. W. Crawford, who in this campaign commanded a brigade in Banks's Corps, was commissioned as such by the President through a popularity gained in having been accidentally stationed in Fort Sumter with Major Robert Anderson when the first gun was fired at the commencement of the Rebellion. This appeared to be the sole ground of his promotion, the President, presumably, not desiring to single him out from a number of others there who were advanced on account of meritorious conduct during the attack on the Fort. His occupation then and prior to that time had been as an assistant surgeon, and it might be added that if his duties as such were no more successfully prosecuted than were those newer and more pretentious ones as brigade commander, they must have been of a quality that rated him among the very lowest in the scale of army "saw-bones." This dispenser of quinine, blue mass, and castor oil came to the corps much inflated by the addition of a star upon his shoulder, and with all the presumptuous and arrogant "caste" nonsense of the "Regulars," with whom he had been affiliated since his appointment to the medical staff of the army. Being accustomed to brow-beating and bulldozing the foreign element that made up the bulk of our soldier contingent before the opening of the war, he failed to realize the difference, so manifest, between those men and the volunteers now under him. [These men] though submitting to the inevitable, were plainly grieved and humiliated in not having a more capable and trained officer to command them.

I immediately made myself acquainted with the captain of the battery, who was awaiting orders to commence firing, and opened up with Spencer, posting my flagmen in front of the guns as the only available spot from which I could clearly flag that station. I soon had news of importance from there which I handed to Crawford, but with his accustomed iciness, or lack of "grey matter" to fathom information so weighty, it met with little or no consideration from him. At 11 o'clock he left to join his brigade in the woods, the hurried arrival of Banks's entire force, who were now pressing forward and forming line of battle, necessitating his departure.

It was becoming hourly more evident to me that a fierce engagement was pending. I could now distinctly discern, with the aid of my telescope, the placing of the enemy's artillery around the slopes of Cedar Mountain. One of our brigades, commanded by Colonel Gordon, 2nd Massachusetts,[15] had taken an extreme position in the woods on the right of Crawford, both of these commands partly facing the mountain. At the left of Crawford was Best's Battery of brass 12 pdr. Napoleons, and alongside of these on the knoll General Banks had taken his position to direct the movements.

Stretching out in front, forming almost a right angle to the two brigades mentioned, was Geary's Brigade in a cornfield, then General C. C. Augur's Division of two brigades, commanded by Generals Prince and Greene,[16] and in the rear of these troops were our long line of batteries, slightly elevated, principally 10 and 20 pdr. Parrott Rifles.

As I had rightly conjectured, the lull, which continued until about 2:30 p.m., was broken by the opening of the enemy's artillery on the mountain, their fire being directed along the line of infantry on our right. This opening was at once taken up by General Banks, who directed our guns to reply, and in a few seconds an artillery duel of great vigor was testing the nerves of the bravest soldiers.

The incessant discharges from the artillery soon filled the heated atmosphere with smoke so dense that Spencer's flag could scarcely be seen, [and] this, coupled with the terrific roar, made it most difficult for my voice to be heard by our flagmen when giving them the combinations to make, so that in half an hour we were forced to suspend and await the probable cessation of the firing. It was just at this moment that an orderly rode up and handed me an order from Lieutenant Rowley, our chief, directing me, in view of the difficulties met with, to abandon the station and in company with Lieutenant Miner, report to General Banks for duty as aides de camp upon his staff, his official family at this time being a trifle reduced in numbers. Sending my men with their signal equipments to the rear, I put spurs to my horse and in a few moments ascended to the top of the knoll, and saluting the general announced to him Rowley's instructions. I was at once recognized by his familiar salutation, and dropping behind him awaited developments, the action now assuming formidable proportions.[17]

A spirited cannonading was kept up for at least two hours during which time the infantry were forming preparatory to an advance. At 4 o'clock Major Perkins, staff officer and chief of artillery,[18] rode up to Banks and suggested to him the propriety of sending in the infantry, as the ammunition in the caissons was getting low from the unusually prolonged artillery fire. This suggestion was at once acted upon and the various aides, including myself, were directed to communicate the general's wishes to the division and brigade commanders, who advanced their lines and commenced firing.

One's sensations while sitting calmly in the saddle exposed to this hurricane of shot and shell cannot easily be portrayed. The strain upon the nerves would be lessened if only [one] could be kept upon the move, but the supreme test is in being compelled to await the pleasure of the general commanding, who, occupying a rise of ground from which he can view every portion of the theatre of action, invites by his prominence a concentrated fire which, while it may escape him, soon silences the weapons of war around him and changes the living organism into a mass of utter helplessness.

No words can depict the appalling destruction of life that took place during the last hour of that cannonading within a radius of fifty yards of the knoll on which General Banks placidly viewed the preparations for the impending struggle. Try as you will to still the throbbing heart the mind will dwell upon the shrieking shell as it passes beyond, or in its thundering roar when bursting overhead, and a man has to take a decidedly tight grip upon himself to overcome the impulse to seek shelter, especially when in the line of duty he must remain a passive witness of the terrible execution of both sides and immediately in his rear.

Instead of the long symmetrically dressed row of glistening bayonets our fancy pictures from the early school day histories, we see hurrying into line a thirsty, hungry, yelling, dust-stained body of combatants who, having just reached the ground where formation is intended, are met, near the head of the column, by a bursting shell that tears a horrible gap, and through the cloud of dust we see a confused mixture of men dropping and others painfully limping away vainly endeavoring to hold their gaping wounds together and stay the dripping blood.

While deeply absorbed in the scene depicted, a most depressing shriek at our backs causes me to turn, and I am an eye-witness to a scene so ghastly that I am almost unnerved by the sight. A shell has gone directly over our heads, apparently within a few feet, and yet we did not realize its nearness. It has struck one of the general's orderlies squarely in the chest, gone through him and carried away the tail and back-flanks of his horse, and bursting, tears almost to pieces three infantry soldiers coming up the rise directly behind.

This appalling spectacle of men instantly silenced by shell and shrapnel is followed by a warning voice alongside, informing me that my horse is struck and may fall with me. Quickly dismounting to investigate, I find it is the general's horse immediately in front, a trail of blood trickling down his hind leg showing where the rifle ball has cut a furrow along his flank and passed between the front legs of my horse without touching him. My neighbor saw the general's horse wince and bleed and concluded that the ball in its course had struck my horse in the chest. . . . Finding him all right I mount again, and turning to address a staff officer on my right, observe him change to a deathly pallor and quickly place his hand to his left shoulder. The constant sharp ping of the bullets around us assures me he has been struck, and I reach over to assist his swaying form to the ground in time to prevent a seeming collapse. A dismounted orderly then assisted him to the rear to a piece of woods, where many surgeons are operating upon the wounded.

It is said that General Banks—encouraged by the hesitation of Jackson, who was deceived as to the real numbers under Banks and continued the cannonading unusually long to allow for General Hill's arrival—resolved to assume the offensive on account of the losses the batteries were inflicting upon us. But this I know attributes to Banks the possession of greater skill and foresight than he is deserving of. His unaccountable silence, while betraying no fear in the midst of this deluge of iron and lead, would have been maintained for a longer period, even until the enemy's onslaught, had he not been advised by Major Perkins to advance the infantry and direct the artillery to cease firing.[19]

The orders had now been delivered to the brigade commanders, [and] the battle became general along the entire line. Generals Prince and Geary, before proceeding far, were confronted by a portion of Hill's Corps and a brigade of Early's,[20] and the preponderance of the enemy's numbers enabled them to effect a cross fire which soon caused our lines to give way and reform upon their original position. In this desperate struggle . . . Generals Augur, Geary, and Prince were wounded, the latter falling into the hands of the enemy.

General Greene, not having advanced his lines so far, held his position on the extreme left and suffered much less than the others. At this time the two brigades of Gordon and Crawford, on the right, advanced and threw the troops of Taliaferro's and Winder's Division into confusion, but Jackson, having a brigade in reserve, brought it forward and succeeded in forcing our men back to the woods from which they had emerged to make the attack.[21]

It was now apparent that this unequal contest must result in our falling back to a stronger position unless relieved by reinforcements of McDowell's Corps, [which was] known to have been promptly advanced for just such an emergency. Stragglers, wounded and demoralized, were coming back in scores. The general directed us to charge them and drive them back to the lines, but as well might one have threatened stone statues. No chagrin or mortification of defeat was observable among them, but every man spoken to pleaded a wound, and as it was physically impossible to investigate each individual case they were thus insured immunity from again resuming their place in line.

It was while endeavoring to rally this demoralized mass that one of us noticed the absence of the general's sword, as his empty scabbard was swinging loosely by his side. He was at a loss to account for the missing blade, except that in a moment of absent-mindedness he might have dropped it at the foot of the knoll while leaning over, or while giving his horse a drink at the run. Quickly riding to the foot of the hill I discovered it laying in the tall grass and returned it to him, thus preventing an additional humiliation, its engraved hilt denoting its ownership, which the enemy, [had they] discovered it, would have eagerly gloated over.

Hurried orders were now given to the aides to direct the columns that were intact, together with the batteries, to fall back slowly to a position on the other side of the woods in our rear, where Ricketts Division of

McDowell's Corps[22] was supposed to be laying in reserve. I had just returned from the hill in front of the farm where I had first established my station, [and] after conveying the general's instructions to the captain of the battery there, I observed an officer fall from his horse about twenty yards in front of the general's position. Seeing him recover himself after his horse had broken away from him, I hastily cleared the [intervening] space and recognized him as Major Louis Pelouze of General Pope's staff,[23] who was bleeding profusely from a wound in the thigh. The simultaneous movement to the rear had uncovered, to a great extent, the country in front, [and] the enemy could be seen pressing forward, so to save Pelouze from capture, I suggested his supporting himself by my saddle straps while limping back as rapidly as his situation would permit. I had assisted him to the road and within two hundred yards of the woods when he appeared about to succumb. Fortunately at this moment two mounted artillerymen emerged from the field on the right, having cut the traces of the teams from a disabled caisson, and seizing the bridle of one I ordered him to dismount and assist me to mount the major. Stolidly refusing to comply, I was driven to the necessity of forcing him down at the point of the pistol, and lifting the major up, fastened his feet in the traces and hurried him from the field to the care of a surgeon.

The cavalry charged and recharged, the Rebel lines enabling the infantry and artillery to successfully retire to the ground selected by the general, [and] but one piece was lost, a brass 12 pdr. of Best's Battery, which stuck fast in a ditch and defied the efforts of twelve stout horses to extricate it.[24]

The position taken up was about a half mile to the rear of the piece of woods referred to, and these partly afforded shelter to the Rebel columns who remained inactive, after pushing into it, until 9 p.m. At that time, thinking the opportunity favorable, they brought a battery to the edge of the timber, along our left flank, and opened briskly upon our exhausted columns. The 2nd and 5th Maine Batteries were at once put in position and opened such a rapid and destructive fire that the Rebel guns were soon silenced and driven from the field. The night was unusually lustrous, the moon clear and full, and all prominent objects as clearly discernible as in the broad light of day. Those who witnessed the artillery duel that night will not soon forget it. From twenty pieces the shells went in rapid succession, filling the air with lines of fire and sulphurous smoke that hung over the wearied troops 'till morning. The first two shots from their guns reached a group of officers composed of Generals Pope, Banks, and their staffs, who had assembled for consultation uncomfortably close to the woods. The only casualties there, however, were two horses, on one of which was seated our chief signal officer, Lieutenant Rowley. At daylight I rode to the woods and inspected the ground occupied by this daring Rebel batteryman of the night before, and counted the casualties his exploit had cost him. Within a narrow area lay twenty dead horses, ten cannoneers, and two lieutenants, one with his head taken completely off at the neck, and just back of these, two caissons so disabled that they had to be abandoned.[25] Within a few yards in front lay a cavalryman of the 1st Maine, apparently the only loss of life sustained by us from that fire.

But how dearly we had suffered the day before, the estimated figure being from two to three thousand killed and wounded, the disabilities among the field and line officers being remarkably large.[26] Among those mortally wounded with whom I had enjoyed familiar intercourse was the conspicuously gallant Colonel Donnelly of the 28th New York.[27] The survivors of that brigade will ever vividly recall his towering form as he valiantly cheered his men to greater efforts, in the thickest of the fight. Another, of whom I have before referred in the Shenandoah campaigns and who accompanied me from Warrenton, [was] Captain Williams of the 2nd Massachusetts. When after the lapse of two days the burial parties went over the field, the body of this brave soldier and estimable gentleman was found, stripped to his under-clothing, sitting against an old stump of tree, his head thrown slightly back as if in sleep. The rebel thieves had removed his uniform, taking with it some three-hundred dollars and a valuable gold watch, a present to him from Europe. Colonel Donnelly's adjutant of the 28th was discovered, at the same time, in an almost lifeless condition, with three bullet holes from which he had lain suffering, exposed and unattended, some forty-eight hours.[28] Other friends lay here and there in groups, familiar faces that had joined the corps a year before, now soon to be laid, side by side, in an earthy trench, their shroud the dusty uniform, and their coffin the blanket that had so often wrapped them in slumber.

General Pope, in his orders issued later, claimed this as a victory for the reason that although our troops were pressed back some half a mile from the lines first established, Jackson fell back, two days afterwards, across the Rapidan River, fearing to engage Pope's other troops, [and that this] clearly confirmed Pope's claim to a victory. It was a rather doubtful assumption in my opinion, and one shared in by most of our troops. Our experience in the military field, however, since that day, fully justifies the belief that had General Pope, who was but a mile or two in the rear, sent forward a portion of McDowell's or Sigel's forces, both of whom were within supporting distance, the result would have been a disastrous rout to Jackson on the evening of the fight, quite equaling his emphatic repulse at Winchester of the March before.[29]

With Sunday came a day of rest for those of the troops not detailed for after duties connected with the battle, [which was] a respite truly enjoyed from their arduous labors of the day before. Little rest, however, did the members of the Signal Corps get. Their prompt and accurate transmission of messages had taken such a firm hold upon the affections of General Pope that that gentleman's persevering appetite for news of the enemy's movements would not be appeased until he had seen us scattered to prominent points of observation, with directions to forward half-hourly reports to his headquarters.

My station on this beautiful Sabbath morning was on the right flank of the army in the yard of a shabby looking farm house whose occupants, though once well-to-do, were now literally on the verge of starvation. So reduced were they that the woman of the house came to me with two children, crying bitterly, while I was eating dinner on the grass and begged a share of our food to assuage the pangs of hunger. Although our stock of provisions was small, I could not resist her piteous appeal, and after sharing a portion of it with them was thanked again and again. . . .

This afternoon a flag of truce was sent in by General Pope to Jackson, asking permission to bury the dead which under the hot August sun were rapidly decomposing. The truce being accepted, there was a cessation of hostilities from 2 until 5 o'clock. Between the lines the soldiers of both armies mixed freely, interchanging courtesies, arguing upon the respective fighting qualities of the two sections, and [on] the ultimate results of the war.

The experience of Sergeant Gillespie,[30] of our corps, was rather an amusing one. While strolling around among the burial parties, he was approached by a Rebel soldier, who, mistaking the letters S.C. (Signal Corps) on his cap, addressed him after the following manner: "Hello South Carolina," says the Johnny, "the Yanks have got a right smart of men to bury yere?" "Yes," says Gillespie, keeping up the joke, "serves 'em right, no business to come down yere to subjugate we'un." "That's so," replied

Johnny, "wher'd you'uns get the blue trousers?" "Off'n a dead Yank," re-turned Gillespie. "Bully for you'ns, come over to our camp awhile got some good whiskey from a still, back of yere yesterday." "All right," says Gillespie, and in a few minutes they were in the camp of the 12th Virginia Infantry.[31] After several strong pulls at a canteen (for Gillespie was particularly fond of the beverage), he was taken by the Johnny to the tent of the lieutenant of the company and introduced, and another round indulged in. By this time, the effects of the ardent were beginning to tell upon Gillespie, who fearing that a wagging tongue might lead to trouble, and concluding that the truce had almost expired, made an excuse for getting back to the field, and invit-ing the Johnny along, parted from him in the most cordial manner, the Reb never supposing for a moment that he had entertained a Yankee member of the Signal Corps.

On Monday morning the 11th Jackson executed his retrograde move-ment across the Rapidan, and by night we were again in possession of the ground upon which the battle had been fought. Many bodies of the dead of both armies lay exposed, they having been too far within their lines when the burial parties were at work under the truce. Sigel's Corps was advanced to the river banks, and remained there several days, driving back and defeating frequent attempts to harass our troops.

On the 16th we were still further reinforced by Maj. Gen. Reno's di-vision of Burnside's Corps arriving at Culpeper C.H. from the vicinity of Fortress Monroe, their assignment being [to guard] the right flank of Pope's army.[32]

CHAPTER 4

SECOND MANASSAS AND THE SIEGE OF HARPERS FERRY

AUGUST 19–SEPTEMBER 6, 1862

Following the fight at Cedar Mountain, Stonewall Jackson fell back to Gordonsville, where he united with Lee and James Longstreet, who had moved there from the vicinity of Richmond. Lee had correctly surmised that McClellan would evacuate the Army of the Potomac from the Virginia Peninsula and wanted to consolidate his forces and destroy Pope before McClellan could join him. Pope, however, sensed the danger approaching and fell back behind the line of the Rappahannock before Lee could trap him between that river and the Rapidan River. Lee then determined to turn Pope's flank and accordingly, on August 25, sent Jackson, with nearly half of the Army of Northern Virginia, on a sweeping movement around Pope's right. Jackson's troops, shielded by the Bull Run Mountains, circled behind the Federals, reaching Bristoe Station, astride Pope's main supply line, the Orange and Alexandria Railroad, on the evening of August 26. Jackson's movement prompted Pope to abandon his positions along the Rappahannock and pursue the Confederates, who were ransacking his trains at Manassas Junction and burning anything they could not carry off. Lee and Longstreet, no longer faced by Pope, moved north, following the same flanking route that Jackson had utilized earlier, passed through Thoroughfare Gap and united with Stonewall near the battlefield of First Manassas. With Pope thoroughly confused about the intentions and dispositions of his opponents and the Rebels lying in wait, a battle was imminent.

As a result of the severe losses Banks's Corps had suffered at Cedar Mountain, it was assigned the inglorious task of guarding the army's supply trains during the Second Manassas Campaign. Accordingly, Fortescue served on the periphery of many important events, yet he recorded a finely detailed account of his experiences.

At 12 o'clock on the night of *Tuesday, August 19th,* orders were received to get our signal kits in readiness and saddle up, prepared to join the main column falling back to the Rappahannock River. I had been ensconced in my blankets about two hours, having turned in somewhat fatigued, and was sleeping soundly when the orderly arrived with the instructions. In a moment all were alert, and none but those who have experienced it can realize the intense anxiety that attends the receipt of an order of this character at so unseemly an hour. Where are the enemy? . . . Have they flanked us? What's their strength? Is the retreat to be conducted quietly? Who commands them? These and a dozen similar questions are asked on every side. Few are able to answer them correctly, except by vague surmise, until the columns are in motion, and then little by little, the main facts leak out, gradually spreading from lip to lip, becoming after the lapse of a couple of hours very generally known to every soldier of the command.

In fifteen minutes after receiving the order, we were in motion and found, as we proceeded, the roads filled with a heterogeneous mixture of batteries, wagons, infantry and cavalry. A confused condition of affairs naturally occasioned by the necessity of a hurried march after darkness had set in. But the veriest snarl, or tangle, if attacked by a resolute man can be straightened, and the man to fill the breach on this occasion was the much maligned General Irvin McDowell.

Upon the bank of a small stream on the outskirts of Culpeper, and facing two roads which here forked in a northerly direction, he stood directing the troops, who were all required to pass this point. To every teamster he would shout, "What corps do you belong to?" If to the First, they were ordered to take the road to the left. If to the Second or Third, the road to the right. And a few moments observation was only needed to convince one how beautifully sandwiched they had become. Here, for some three hours until daylight broke in the east; sometimes in the water and then in the road, batteries, wagons and infantry, many on the double quick, in almost inextricable confusion, were halted and started fresh, thus by a little tact, and no little exhaustion, order was restored out of chaos.

[*August 20, 1862.*] All that day, through heat and dust, footsore and thirsty (for proud Virginia boasts of but few streams in this vicinity, and these so roiled by the tread of armed hosts, that horses and mules though parched their throats, refused to drink) we toiled in the direction of the Rappahannock R.R. Bridge. Not until the rear guard had reached Brandy Station (the first south of the bridge) did the Rebel advance come in view. There they opened on our cavalry, who fell back slowly to the bridge. Thinking to easily carry that point, their infantry charged as soon as they arrived, but our men, though exhausted physically, with the aid of Matthew's Pennsylvania and Thompson's Maryland Batteries, repelled and drove them back in great disorder.[1]

Thursday, August 21, 1862. With the dawn commenced the thunder of the artillery. At least forty pieces were posted along the north bank commanding the bridge, and about an equal number of theirs were in position opposite, all being kept constantly going until noon. Our batteries were skillfully served and we saw, with our glasses, the execution wrought by several well-directed shots. The appearance of an occasional hillock along their bank indicated the hastily thrown-up rifle pit of a sharpshooter, [and] was a sign readily understood that our cannoneers would be the targets. Soon their accurate aim was seen in the number of blue uniforms and horses left upon the ground as a disabled piece was gradually withdrawn from the field.

About 9 a.m. Lieutenant Miner and I started down the river to Kelly's Ford to open communication between General Reno's column, at the latter place, and General Pope's headquarters. General Reno had fought

Longstreet very early this morning and defeated him, and his division now lay in line of battle opposite the ford.[2]

The nature of the country prevented us from carrying out our intentions, and we were thus compelled to return to general headquarters, where a camp had been established in a small piece of woods about a quarter of a mile back from the river, and just west of the road leading to the bridge. Just at noon superhuman efforts were made upon the enemy's part to storm the bridge. Strong lines of infantry were reformed and advanced as fast as they were broken, but signally failed each time to overcome our artillery, which poured an incessant and galling fire into their ranks.

Wishing to observe some of the action at this point, I started along about 1 p.m. intending to go to the river a mile above, and ride down under cover of the timber. I had proceeded a short distance only, after reaching the stream, when I came to a cleared space of about five-hundred yards between the woods, across which a full view was had from the banks on the other side. Not desiring to retrace my stops to cross this space further back out of line of a possible fire, and as no signs denoted the presence of the enemy on the opposite side, I started to ride leisurely on, at the same time scanning closely the other shore, an instinctive knowledge of the wily foe rendering me suspicious of the deathlike stillness prevailing there.

Judge of my surprise, when about a third of the distance had been traversed, to see a puff of smoke from a clump of bushes opposite, immediately followed by the shriek of a shell over my head which struck the ground and exploded some two hundred yards back. This was succeeded, as I quickened my pace, by the whiz of several rifle balls, one so close as to slightly cut the lower lip of my horse. Finding that I had innocently made myself the target for a concealed force of the enemy, I put spurs to my horse and soon reached the woods, but not before a half dozen more shots had passed uncomfortably near me.

Passing under cover of the first few trees and loose brush and thinking myself secure, I brought my horse around for the purpose of studying the situation more carefully with my marine glass, and taking off my cap gave it a flourish, indicative of the poor opinion I entertained of their skill with fire-arms. In this I made a most egregious mistake in underrating the marksmanship of a sharpshooter, for scarcely had I reached for the glasses swinging over my shoulder when my horse gave a violent lunge to the left, reared upon his hind feet and fell in a heap, partly pinning my left leg under him. A rifle ball had struck him squarely in the right eye, [and] he scarcely drew a breath after falling.

I extricated myself with little trouble, and stepping behind a tree, took a survey with my glass. The first object that met my eye was a waving cap over the parapet of a rifle-pit. [This was] a sort of responding wave to mine of a few moments before, which I could not but acknowledge with another, in token of my safety, and I then made my way on foot in back of the timber without being further molested.

Fortunately for me the horse killed was an extra one of little value, my own being somewhat indisposed with the wagon trains in camp. I soon found an idle cavalryman, who for a small consideration rode back to our quarters and brought a led horse, and in the dusk of the gathering twilight we removed the saddle and bridle from the dead animal, thus enabling me to again report before dark at headquarters.

When we stretched ourselves under a strip of canvas tonight it was with a feeling that our slumbers would not remain unbroken 'till daylight. The positive injunction to keep all horses saddled and tied as near to the rider as safety from a restless horse would permit suggested our dangerous proximity to the bridge, and [was] a fretful hardship to the suffering animals, proportionately equal, I imagine, to the efforts of a man trying to enjoy a night's sleep in a pair of tight boots. I awoke about midnight, and quietly slipping the saddle from my horse, placed it under my head, and then just before daylight as quietly slipped it on him again, giving him at least a short breathing spell, though at some risk I admit.

[*August 22, 1862.*] When their artillery opened at daylight, it brought our camp in a direct line with the fire, and in consequence, shells and solid shot dropped around us in profusion. One shell struck the edge of General Banks's table a few moments after he had risen from breakfast, and strewed the dishes and cooking utensils in many directions, causing a colossal stampede of contraband cooks, who very reluctantly returned when ordered to gather up the debris.

At 4 p.m. during the tumult at the bridge, General Sigel, under orders, attempted a crossing two miles above, but was repulsed with some loss, losing among others one of his brigade commanders, General Bohlen of Philadelphia, who was struck by a sharpshooter.[3]

About 8 p.m. a large body of our cavalry, together with the Signal Corps, were massed in the woods near the bridge awaiting the advance of the enemy, or orders to fall back, when a violent thunder storm broke upon us and drenched us to the skin. The lightning was so vivid, and played through the trees so incessantly, coupled with the terrific peals of thunder, that it was with the greatest difficulty the hundreds of frightened horses were prevented from stampeding. The trembling of a terrified horse was never so perceptible to me as was [that of] my own as I sat upon him that night during this tremendous downpour. Several trees were struck by the lightning, and a sulphurous odor filled the woods. It was a relief, indeed, when near midnight the orders came to quietly retire, the rain having continued with great violence until that time.[4]

[*August 23, 1862.*] On [Saturday] morning at daylight the rain had ceased and the atmosphere was clear and pure. From the position assigned me to watch the opposite country, [which was] a small knoll near the scene of my horse adventure of yesterday, I could see the Rebel columns moving up the river in the direction of the Sulphur Springs, with the evident intention of crossing at that point.

Before starting with our signal detachment at noon on a short cut to the Springs, I was directed to order our wagons by a designated route, and while riding across an open field to reach their location in the woods, I was surprised to find a body of our troops in line of battle facing west, an attack being threatened by a Rebel column rumored to have crossed just above during the forenoon. I was riding at a pretty stiff gait in the rear of the 14th Brooklyn (Beecher Regiment), when the boys, in a spirit of fun, set up a yell, startling my horse and causing him to shy and plunge both fore feet into a partly covered post-hole.

The suddenness of the movement unseated me and landed me on to his neck, causing him to break and frantically dash through their lines, knocking down two of their men. He ran at the top of his speed for about three-hundred yards before I succeeded in reining him in, then riding back, I had the pleasure of passing along their entire front, receiving a polite salute from the colonel, who evinced much vexation at the extremely hazardous situation I had been placed in by the idiotic playfulness of some of his men.

General Pope was successful in frustrating every design of the enemy to cross by moving up on the north bank in a parallel line with theirs. As on

Thursday and Friday, again Saturday the enemy kept working up the river for the purpose of effecting a crossing at one of the many fords above, but always found our advance occupying them upon arriving there.[5]

As on the preceding day, again Saturday the grand artillery duel was kept up, the cannonading being heavier, now at McDowell's position, now at Sigel's, now at Banks. We were successfully guarding the whole river bank and all the fords [between] Kelly's Ford [and] Warrenton, and the enemy with an army of nearly 100,000 men had been held in check by Pope with a much inferior numerical force.[6]

At twilight on Saturday evening, our party passed around the foot of hills overlooking the Sulphur Springs and the Rappahannock beyond. Outlined against the sky could be seen a line of our batteries being rapidly served to prevent a crossing by the Rebel troops. Now and then, through the dense smoke from the artillery fire that occasionally lifted, was revealed the forms of the cannoneers as they ran to and from the pieces to the ammunition boxes in their efforts to pulverize the Johnnies, and in the midst of this highly exciting spectacle could be seen the figure of a female with a gracefully fitting riding habit, leisurely guiding her horse along in the rear of the guns, seemingly wholly intent upon the work they were engaged in. I inquired of several, who like myself were admiring the coolness of this amazon, as to her affiliations or connections, but it was not until the following day that I discovered her to be a "lady of title"—the "Princess Salm Salm," wife of a colonel of one of General Dan Sickles' regiments in his "Excelsior Brigade.". . .[7]

Upon riding around to the locality of the celebrated Springs Hotel after dark what a scene of destruction was presented. Only a remnant of the walls still remained to remind us of this once luxurious summer resort. A dense smoke filled the air from the smoldering ruin whereon had stood the attractive buildings with their spacious dining halls and billiard parlors. Its elegant surroundings had vanished before the fierce and devastating violence of contending armies, and blackened debris alone marked the spot as a memory of its wooded groves and former magnificence.

As I crossed the well-kept drive that led to the river between the hotels, I met a company of our sharpshooters (Berdan's) returning from the scene of their work during the day. They had been relieved by a detachment of the same regiment, who, under cover of the darkness, were about posting themselves behind rocks, or in tree-tops, to pick off Johnnies on the other side of the river, who recklessly heeded not the rifles of their antagonists. The returning riflemen, begrimed with mud and powder, were rejoiced at an invitation from me to join in a full bottle of "commissary" that, added to the delicious spring water gushing from the iron mouth of a lion that stood in front of the principal hotel, put them in a talkative mood, and I was regaled with some rare, descriptive feats of marksmanship that day.

Said one, "A chap with a cheese-knife," meaning an officer with sword, "was looking after the picket-posts, going from tree to tree to cover himself from our shots. I watched him and winged him and he dropped. I noticed him, a little later, slowly trying to crawl out of range, and I winged him again. That settled him 'till after dark, and I could then hear the ambulance drive away with him." The hardened expression of the man in relating this so impressed me at time, that I have always remembered it as being the most cold-blooded statement I had ever heard from the lips of a soldier. Another told me, though somewhat reluctantly, that he had hit a staff officer in a group reconnoitering near the river, as well as two private soldiers about going on picket; the first being a fatal shot.[8]

We halted for the night and camped in a piece of woods near Waterloo, with orders from General Banks to proceed at day-break to Piney Mountain, a prominent cone on the Warrenton Turnpike just north of the Sulphur Springs.[9] [We were told to] take an observation of the movements of Lee's army, then supposed to be heading north along the eastern base of the Blue Ridge.

[*August 24, 1862.*] Upon reaching the top of Piney Mountain [this morning], we found the general's diction verified by a long line of dust extending far to the south, at the base of the ridge, indicating the march of a large body of troops; and immediately west of our position, we discovered, with the aid of our glasses, a clearing, through which we were enabled to distinguish the various arms of the service as they hurried along in their efforts to outflank our forces. In pursuance of our instructions, we remained here counting and estimating the strength of this column until the afternoon of the second day, [August 25] when we made preparations to return with our report to headquarters.[10]

Our abandonment of Piney Mountain was not without the usual animated incident met with in the hazardous trips of the Signal Corps when actively campaigning. . . . Upon our reaching the turnpike a short distance from the foot of the mountain, we observed a six-gun battery in position on a knoll on the opposite side of the road, the guns being trained in the direction of the river, or pike, to the south. Crossing over we entered the field with the intention of riding to the top of this knoll to pay our respects to the commanding officer, and to note the situation of the road towards the Springs. While doing this we perceived the captain of the battery hurriedly giving orders to change the direction of his pieces by reversing them, and bringing them to bear upon us. No particular attention being paid to this, our party continued to ride leisurely up until within a few feet of the muzzles of the cannon, when we were very unceremoniously halted by the captain. Lieutenant Fralich, who was riding by my side, had in the meantime taken out his handkerchief to wipe the perspiration from his face, and at the command to halt, rode forward to inquire the meaning of the captain's actions. He was summarily ordered to dismount and the batterymen directed to dismount us and take charge of our horses. They all had, as we now saw, their revolvers cocked, ready to give us a volley should we make any show of resistance.

The only demonstration we had in mind now was to try and explain to this German batteryman the absurdity of the whole situation, and this we found no easy matter in view of his excited condition, and the fact that few of us Sig's were in uniform, simply wearing a blouse without any insignia of rank. We convinced him finally, however, and then learned to our astonishment that his battery would have opened on us as soon as we had reached the foot of the hill had not the officer displayed a flag of truce. Fralich's accidental use of his handkerchief to mop his face had been taken as an indication that we were a part of the enemy's forces, and [that we] were displaying the customary signal to prevent his firing before proceeding to surrender. A startling revelation, truly; and although we had a hearty laugh afterwards over the scare we gave this "Teutonic" artilleryman, there was food for reflection in the thought that unless first carefully feeling the way, it was a trifle unhealthy, when in proximity to the enemy's lines, to risk a second adventure of this sort, which might end more seriously and prove to be a genuine scare to us. . . .

In the vicinity of the Sulphur Springs, about midway between the Rappahannock River and the bluff on which were posted our batteries during the recent shelling, stood a small insignificant looking habitation of a proud Virginian, whose family numbered some five people, the eldest child being a boy about ten years of age. When this family observed the preparations for an artillery duel, they gathered together their livestock, and deeming the cellar the safest place to secure them from the prying eyes and foraging propensities of the "invaders of their soil," as well as from the destructiveness of the cannon shots, proceeded to stow them in this repository designed for provisions, etc. The floor space of this apartment could not have been more than about 12 x 16 feet, and yet they succeeded in getting in there a cow, a horse, some fifteen sheep, several pigs and a number of geese, ducks and chickens. The boy was left in the cellar in charge, and the rest of the family skedaddled for safer quarters until the rumpus was over.

After our episode with the German battery, just related, and before leaving to report to General Banks, we concluded, as there were no indications of the enemy on our side of the river, to take another look at the surroundings of the hotel ruins, and while riding around, a couple of our men strayed off up the hill in the direction of the house referred to. We presently heard a shout, and saw them beckoning us to come up, pointing to the cellar of the establishment as an inducement to hurry.

Here an astounding spectacle met our sight. From the effects of two Rebel shells, cleanly outlined in their course on the top of the foundation wall that had burst in the cellar, every semblance of life there had been destroyed. It would be difficult to imagine a more amazing scene of disorder. Not a creature escaped the destructive power of those two shells, which must have entered at nearly the same time. The boy and cow were frightfully mangled, and blood was bespattered over almost every inch of the space. The sheep and pigs were in a mass, with the horse on top of a pile of them, and the poultry lay in every direction.

The marvelous part to us was how it was possible to have forced the horse and cow down this cellar. The entrance was by the old-fashioned flat doors, lifting up, measuring not over four feet each way, and yet here were two animals, much bulkier than the opening measured, that had actually passed through it. The stench from the putrid mass was sickening, and we had about concluded to set fire to the premises and burn up the whole disgusting business, but upon reflection decided that it would be wiser not to disturb them, lest a charge would be made that a murder had been committed and the place burned to cover up the crime, hence, we retired, leaving them in the same condition as we had found them.

This evening [*August 25*] orders were received at the various corps headquarters to move at once back towards Warrenton. From thence McDowell was to keep on in the direction of Manassas, Banks east to Fayetteville, and Sigel [was] to occupy Thoroughfare Gap to prevent the passage through of Longstreet's Corps, which was then endeavoring to form a junction with Jackson, whose corps had passed through successfully the day before.[11] It was rumored that this movement had been ordered by General Pope . . . without consulting the corps commanders, which seems to have greatly displeased General Sigel. His plan was to attack the enemy in the rear at Waterloo with [both] his and Banks's command and compel them to turn (through a fear of having their communication with Richmond menaced), thus allowing for the arrival of McClellan's column from the lower Potomac, where they had disembarked after leaving the Peninsula.

It was not to be presumed that General Pope, with his well-known disposition, would brook any interference from those whom he considered his subordinates, especially General Sigel, with whom he had some previous misunderstanding. Consequently the impetuous Sigel, like all natives of the "Fatherland," immediately penned his resignation. Whether it was forwarded to the War Department or not I have never learned; suffice it to say he continued in command. I have heard it said, upon unquestioned authority, that it was no infrequent thing for the authorities in Washington to receive letters of resignation from Sigel for alleged grievances. Needless to say, Sigel, in the contemplated operations at the Gap, failed to intercept Longstreet, who succeeded, much to Pope's disgust, in forming a junction with Jackson.[12]

On the 26th, Halstead and I were ordered to return early and remain near Waterloo upon Watery Mountain,[13] from which we were to watch the movements of the Rebel columns. Here at three or four points, looking west, we had an unobstructed view of the roads skirting the base of the Bull Run Mountains, and upon these we permanently fixed our glasses. There was little difficulty in seeing numbers of troops, wagons, artillery, and horsemen all bending their energies northward in an endeavor to flank our forces at or near Warrenton. For hours we carefully noted down the various branches passing, Halstead counting the artillery and cavalry, and I the infantry.

Our station had been partly occupied the day previous by some of Sigel's artillery, but at this time our situation was precarious in the extreme, [with] not a Union soldier between us and Anderson's Rebel division of Longstreet's Corps, which, along with some cavalry, we knew were awaiting orders to cross near this point.[14] In fact, there were none of our troops within ten miles of us, and our liability to capture increased with every hour. Although diligently noting down for the information of Pope and Banks everything of importance within the scope of our vision, we could only hope to maintain our position until noon at least, hence, three of our five men were posted where they could see the roads leading to the river, with instructions to ride to a point on the pike where they could be seen by us in the event of danger. A simple wave of a handkerchief would be the signal to leave, immediately, if we wished to avoid a trip under Rebel guard to Richmond.

Near noon the handkerchief signal came to us, and our departure was indeed a hurried one. Upon reaching the foot of the mountain, we observed in close proximity thirty Rebel cavalrymen riding along the Sperryville Pike directly towards us, but they were utterly oblivious of our presence. Considering their company anything but agreeable, we quickly crossed the road unobserved, and galloping into a piece of timber, were off across the country for Fayetteville.[15] Before proceeding very far, we were fortunate in securing the services of a contraband guide whose thorough knowledge of this region of the country enabled us to reach the troops of our command by dark. I had the pleasure of reporting the results of our observation to General Banks, receiving in return the customary flattering assurances of satisfaction and consideration.

[*August 27, 1862.*] This day found us halted, for the nonce, on the banks of the memorable Bull Run overlooking the Stone Bridge, where exultingly the issue of battle [had been] met, and subsequent dire disaster overtook our too-confident boys about one year ago. Here, over a single road, all tending towards the Manassas plains, we saw thousands toiling along covered with dust and mud, worn out with the heat and long weary marches, yet murmuring not; cheerfully, hopefully pressing forward in the expectation of foiling the pretensions of that traitor Jackson. The spirit of tolerance, ever characteristic of the American soldier, was never more [evident]. Obedient and light hearted, cajoling each over some unlucky incident of camp life, yet quick to criticize the errors of omission or commission in our too numerous boastful pretenders, or in heroically defending him whose potent influence had captured their admiration.

[*August 28, 1862.*] The following morning we moved to within three miles of Manassas Junction, and very shortly after our arrival we received a summons to report to the general's quarters. We were met by an order to prepare at once for scouting; each to penetrate as far as possible to the vicinity of the Rebel lines, gathering whatever information attainable for use in future operations.

Briggs and I selected a road leading westward in the direction of Haymarket, and rode to within two miles of that place. Here we came in sight of numerous Rebel cavalry videttes and straggling infantrymen, and concluded not to venture further. We were more than delighted, too, to discover a couple of trees loaded down with luscious peaches which we could not forbear sampling, even though the owner earnestly and viciously protested against this perfectly business-like proposition. During the afternoon we could distinctly hear volleys of musketry and salvos of artillery north in the direction of Groveton, indicating an assault of the enemy on General McDowell's Corps.[16] So after a scout around Haymarket for a couple of hours, and becoming convinced that only stragglers were in that neighborhood, we returned to headquarters near Bristoe Station and reported the results of our reconnaissance to the general, whom we found resting in an ambulance.

About 6 p.m., Spencer, Briggs, and I started out with the grim determination to find a supper composed of rarer delicacies than those to be found in the army ration, upon which we had been subsisting for many days. Our success exceeded our most sanguine expectations in finding, near Brentsville, a larder not to be despised by the most fastidious. But [in this instance] our shrewdness in going so far from headquarters to unearth a square meal nearly resulted in an unlooked for disaster. Instead of repressing our ardor in returning, which a contented mind and full stomach should have done, we elatedly rode into our pickets, who, mistaking us in the darkness for Johnnies, fired, but luckily missed us, although we were in easy range of their rifles. Our explanations proving satisfactory, we reached camp at 9 p.m. and sought shelter from a drenching rain under trees, which afforded our only shelter.

[*August 29, 1862.*] At daylight the orders to move came promptly, our destination being Manassas to support McDowell, Sigel, and a portion of McClellan's army. All signs pointed to a battle of no mean proportion within the course of the day. At 10 a.m., in a redoubt at Manassas Junction commanding a view of the plain, General Banks temporarily established his headquarters.

Leaving the general, Miner and I embraced the opportunity of inspecting the debris left by Jackson after his night raid of the 26th. It was indeed a humiliating admission that forced itself from all who witnessed the destruction the Johnnies were permitted to perpetrate by a movement in our rear, and one that might easily have been prevented. Evidences of the torch were perceptible wherever the eye rested, in twisted iron of locomotives and box-cars; the remnants of thousands of barrels of bacon, salt beef, flour, and hard tack; and of finely assorted sutler stores, forage, and uniforms. But the greater mortification to General Pope was in the capture of his private baggage, papers, etc., and the immoderate jubilation of the enemy, who made the most of a resplendent uniform, belonging to Pope, which fell into their clutches.[17]

At 1 o'clock, Sigel's Corps became engaged near the left of the line, about one mile from our position, and from this time until dark, gradually extending from division to division, the battle raged with furious impetuosity. A short time after Sigel, McDowell also became engaged, then Hooker and Kearny's [divisions] of Heintzleman's Corps, and so on until all were hotly contesting the field, with the exception of our little corps, [which was] held in reserve near the left flank with sadly decimated ranks from our previous action at Cedar Mountain.

Posted on the parapet of the redoubt with our glasses, the range of sight, extending over the greater portion of the line, was unimpeded. Acts of conspicuous bravery on the part of our men, although at times greatly outnumbered, were noticed again and again, their brilliancy exciting in us the liveliest imagination. . . . The mind reels in an attempt to describe some of the scenes of heroism witnessed. Our boys fought stubbornly against the tremendous odds hurled upon them until forced to fall back, at 6 o'clock, by a flank movement that nearly enveloped the right of our line.[18]

[*August 30, 1862.*] General Pope's evident intention had been to concentrate, and by a vigorous attack endeavor to pierce [the Rebel] center and divide them. For this purpose our cavalry were sent in on the left flank to feel and possibly divert their attention. This, [however,] had been anticipated, and they were met by a galling fire from the enemy's batteries, compelling a retrograde movement, which was followed by an overwhelming column that forced back our entire left. A terrible disaster was averted by the checking of Longstreet's Corps at the Henry House by the four brigades of Generals Tower, Meade, Seymour, and Buchanan, who sustained the brunt of the attack there, but retained their organizations intact.[19]

Near dark, our corps was ordered to return to Broad Run, at Bristoe Station, to protect the railroad trains detained by the destruction of the bridge there from raiding. These trains, consisting of several locomotives and freight cars, were filled with supplies of every description: commissary, quartermaster, ordnance, and medical stores, the estimated value being not less than two million dollars. What a prize would they have been for the Johnnies? I don't wonder [that] they looked with longing eyes on these luxuries so opportunely thrown in their way, and were arranging for their pillage when the appearance of Banks's Corps precipitately scared them off.

We accompanied General Banks that night in personally superintending the disposition of the troops against any plans of the enemy to surprise them, and saw him retire at midnight to take a few hours much-needed rest. Rowley and I then made o ur way to a little shanty attached to a tumbledown plantation which we had our eye on in the early evening. We thoroughly enjoyed a repose therein . . . securing a substantial breakfast for ourselves and our horses in the morning. It is not to be presumed that men and horses were fed by the lean and lank inhabitants of this section through a sublime admiration . . . of the soldier who wore a blue uniform. The magnetic charm that overcame their scruples to our demands was the plethoric pocket-book containing Uncle Sam's promises to pay [which] exercised the greatest influence, although I am frank to say that we knew that occupants of farms or plantations had the necessary provender we required, [and] it would have certainly been forthcoming when demanded, or trouble might have ensued.

Sunday, August 31 will ever be remembered as one of the most eventful days of my existence. Imagine our consternation, upon awaking in the morning, to find that during the night, after our army had retired within the fortifications of Centreville, the enemy had occupied the country between that point and our corps, thus almost completely cutting us off from the main body. What a world of meaning is conveyed in that little word "flanked," and what soldier has not heard it and instinctively shuddered? "The best laid plans of mice and men aft gang aglee." In endeavoring to protect the trains, somebody had neglected to insure our safety.

Every avenue of escape seemed closed, and Banks's Corps was entangled in the meshes of the enemy's net with no visible way of extrication. What anxious hours we passed that morning, soaked to the skin from the rain then falling, and how refreshing was the look of expectancy on the face of the homely matron who had furnished us breakfast after she learned of our predicament and the promised early arrival of some of her "butternut" friends.

About 8 a.m. an orderly dashed up to headquarters, his horse reeking with foam and mud, and delivered a communication from General Pope. The dispatch stated that the road to Alexandria via Brentsville was open, and that the general would at once move, with his corps, in all haste in that direction after destroying everything in the shape of transportation.

The troops were hurriedly formed, and details made to apply the torch to the railroad trains and to the wagons that would in any way encumber our retreat. The crackling flames, as they swept from car to car down the track, presented a truly grand and awful spectacle. Companies of cavalry would dash up, tear apart boxes, and array themselves in new uniforms, some with artillery jackets and infantry trousers. Infantrymen were filling their haversacks with sugar, coffee, and beans, and clothing themselves in cavalry uniforms. Teamsters, with their mules harnessed together, were building fires under the ammunition wagons, blowing them up, while others were tying pairs of shoes to the harness, strapping on bundles of blankets, or riding away with clothing piled so high on the pommels of their saddles that only their nose and eyes were visible. A squad of men, with hammers and wrenches, were engaged on the engines destroying the works. Five large and magnificent locomotives, with all the improvements that skilled mechanism had introduced, were literally smashed and heaped on each other in Broad Run, a mass of rubbish. One car, the foremost in the train, was filled with old muskets gathered from battlefields. When this had been partly consumed, the scattering of the crowd was astonishingly precipitate. Volley after volley of minie [balls], from the heated and irregularly piled muskets, flew through the air; a trial to the boys amid the confusion prevailing.

Every ammunition wagon was blown to pieces, leaving nothing to be hauled through this heavy, sticky Virginia soil but the artillery. In fine, the order to the men to destroy had been so literally carried out that it needed not the surveillance of the officers to insure a thorough compliance with it, and when the command to move was given, the line of cars, 180 in number, extending half a mile, were in a sheet of flame, the smoke of which was distinctly seen at Alexandria, a distance of twenty miles. Naught was left to the enemy but smoking ruins.[20]

The question ordinarily asked is why was the bridge [here] not rebuilt and the valuable trains with their stores saved from destruction? For three days they had stood there after the bridge, measuring about one hundred feet only, had been destroyed. [This was] certainly sufficient time to have accomplished the work, inasmuch as bridges larger than this have been built for the passage of troops in less than two days. A conclusion can naturally be partly reached, if this were all, however, by ascribing the failure to incompetence. Pope had committed errors, though his gallantry was unquestioned, and these errors, industriously fostered by the burning animosities and violence of factions among his corps and division commanders (who were to him more formidable antagonists than the enemy confronting him), lost him the respect of the troops. He could not reunite these disturbing fragments by displaying any heroic fighting attributes to which his natural disposition inclined, nor could he prevail upon them to promptly execute his orders. Neither victory in battle nor successful achievement in handling troops could be accomplished under his leadership, hence the greater the disaster and losses in men and property, the sooner the change (desired by these recalcitrants) in the commanding general.

Evidently Pope was woefully mistaken in the issue at Manassas. Being a man of more than ordinary discernment, he should have been fairly well advised of the conflicting elements, principally political, with which the destinies of war had encompassed him. He anticipated victory in the enemy's repulse and subsequent defeat through Thoroughfare Gap . . . and presumed that he would then have ample time to rebuild the bridges and save the property. [This was] a fatal blunder, realized by him too late, and his jealous subordinates contributed not only to his defeat, but to the complete discouragement of his troops, and, per consequence, to the destruction of the stores.

At 10 a.m., Banks's column took up the line of march eastward towards Brentsville, the outline of the town being clearly discerned some five miles ahead. The morale of the troops was of a very low standard, induced by the demoralizing performance required of them in the early morning. Straggling in squads, the various commands seemed to be only intent on finding ground solid enough to sustain their weight, and less tenacious to the sole of the shoe. . . . The different regiments were scattered here and there, unmindful of the fact that near them hovered large bodies of the enemy. I venture the assertion that had our march been interrupted by a corps of the enemy, Banks would have suffered a crushing defeat, if not annihilation.

We had passed through Brentsville, fording several streams greatly swollen beyond their usual depth, and were pursuing a northerly course when an orderly who, judging by his appearance, had ridden some distance, reined in his bedraggled steed in front of the general and handed him a message from General Pope. Upon reading it, he at once halted the column, held a short consultation with his staff, and dispatched two of them to a farm nearby, returning with a venerable-looking Secesh tiller of the soil, mounted on a decrepit frame of a horse. A few minutes conversation ensued between he and the general, and [then] Banks and the Virginian rode to the head of the troops, changing direction to the west, apparently pushing now for Centreville.

We entered the fortifications there about 1 p.m., and waited under orders until 5 o'clock. At this time, feeling somewhat concerned about our baggage and wishing to inform ourselves of the true situation, Rowley, Briggs, and I, in company with three flagmen, trotted off up the main road, determined to sleep under canvas that night if possible. Our teams had been in charge of Lieutenant Harvey since the battle at Rappahannock Bridge, and being reported on the Fairfax Road,[21] thither we bent our steps.

Thousands of army wagons crowded this main road, all moving northward, but without demoralization or panic. It looked like an herculean task to find ours amid this mass of similarly fashioned vehicles, which, though designated in bold letters on their canvas covers, could not be singled out a few yards away. The gathering twilight and approaching storm admonished us that we must abandon our search and seek shelter in another quarter if we would pass the night unexposed to the elements. To say that we were disgusted would but faintly express our feelings, so observing a lane to our left, which proved to be the Germantown Road, and assuming that as no troops could be seen the coast was clear for an uninterrupted bivouac, we hastened into [it]. After riding a rod or so [we] entered an apple orchard to the right, where we unsaddled and turned the horses loose to graze for the night. A fire was quickly going under a tree, and the package of bacon carried in our haversack [was] nicely sliced for broiling on a forked stick. I had arranged mine and was seated with a couple of hardtack in one hand and my improvised toasting fork in the other when a battery of three guns rapidly opened, not fifty yards from us, so close, [in fact], that we could feel the concussion and pressure of air on our faces after each discharge. Here was a dilemma indeed. We were between these guns and the troops of the [1st] New Jersey Brigade[22] who, in moving along the Fairfax Road, had come in plain view of this artillery, which had opened upon them over us.

Fancy our position when we saw the infantry halt and prepare to advance up the hill towards us. Our horses, entirely devoid of even a halter strap, were dashing around the orchard (which was fortunately fenced in), frantic from the screeching shells which went crashing through the branches of the trees and into the road among the teams. . . . Inspired by the commotion they were creating, the Rebel gunners were working their pieces with extraordinary rapidity.

Dropping my juicy slice of bacon, I ran . . . among the huddled and stamping horses, and seizing mine by the forelock, pulled him to the tree where [I had] hung my tied halter strap. [While] in the act of buckling it around his neck, a shell burst directly overhead, scattering iron about us and causing him to bolt upright, snapping the halter strap in his mad effort to get free. After much exertion, we partly quieted the horses and succeeded in holding them near the saddles, which we threw on and buckled in a moment. Mounting, we cast down one or two rails and leaped into the road.

The difficulty here presented was how to avoid the fire of the infantry line who might mistake us for Rebel cavalry, so concluding to run the gauntlet in preference to being captured, we dashed down and through them to the Fairfax Road, escaping the volleys of musketry that opened simultaneously with our passing through. Some twenty-five shots were discharged by this battery before they retired in the face of our infantry column, who followed them up closely but were not successful in preventing their escape. The only damage inflicted was the killing of two team horses and the wounding of several mules on the Fairfax Road; a remarkably slight return considering the risks taken by [the artillerymen] and the short range from their position to the road. This battery came from the little village of Germantown, not over four miles north west from Centreville, and passing around the right of our lines, it recklessly penetrated our rear to within 500 yards of the Fairfax Road. . . .[23]

Having been unceremoniously driven from the shelter of the apple trees and deprived of our salt pork, the prospect of a supperless sleep upon the wet ground appeared anything but inviting. It was too dark to institute a search for an acquaintance upon whom to thrust ourselves and test the sincerity of his hospitality, so while aimlessly wandering back in the direction of Centreville, we mechanically dismounted in front of a camp fire, around which were seated several Vermont cavalrymen. In the goodness of their hearts, they not only invited us to share their fire, but their coffee and hardtack, and at a suggestion generously permitted us to coil ourselves under their wagon, where, barring the restless mules tied to the pole, we indulged in a deep sleep. I was not unmindful of the generosity shown by the cavalrymen in tendering the shelter of their wagon body, but on awaking just before dawn I was impressed with an overwhelming desire to vacate my damp, sticky couch, which a driving mist had rendered very unpalatable. Thanking my benefactors for at least one dry side of my body . . . as I had not turned during the night, I quickly saddled and in a half hour spied our wagon train in the distance. Here a tip-top breakfast greeted me from our camp chest, which had been spared from the shells of the marauding battery of the night before. . . .

[Robert E. Lee had told his corps commanders prior to the campaign that he wanted the "miscreant" Pope "suppressed"; what the Army of Northern Virginia accomplished between late August and early September far exceeded mere suppression. "Pope," wrote one of his contemporaries, "had been kicked, cuffed, hustled about, knocked down, run over and trodden upon as rarely happens in the history of war."²⁴ The Federals, who had lost fourteen thousand soldiers during the campaign, limped back to the fortifications of Washington. The president relieved Pope from command, replacing him with McClellan, who, although he had done Pope a material disservice by delaying sorely needed reinforcements (and behind his back heaping opprobrium on him to anyone who would listen), was the commander best suited to bring order out of the disarray that Second Manassas had produced. "I must have McClellan to reorganize the army and bring it out of chaos," said Lincoln. "McClellan has the army with him."²⁵

Lee, whose Army of Northern Virginia lost approximately eighty-five hundred men, decided to take his army north, across the Potomac into western Maryland, and fight what he hoped would be another successful battle against the Federals. Taking the war to Maryland would alleviate pressure on Virginia, allow him to provision his troops from the countryside, and disrupt the Baltimore and Ohio Railroad and Chesapeake and Ohio Canal, both of which passed through western Maryland and provided supplies to Washington.[26] It would also, he hoped, provide him the opportunity to repopulate his battle-thinned ranks with Confederate-sympathizing Marylanders. A successful battle fought by the Confederate army on ground that many in the North considered Union territory might convince the Northern populace that the war was unwinnable, producing political pressure sufficient to bring an end to the conflict and guarantee independence for the South.]

[*September 1, 1862.*] Breakfast over, I started at once for the apple trees, a fine bridle and my gum coat, (left behind in the stampede), making me somewhat solicitous for their return. An inspection of the place showed that everything was there as when we left, and the opportunities that the battery had for doing murderous execution, if only operated with a trifle more deliberation, [were] satisfactorily ascertained when we stood upon the spot occupied by it the evening before.

Having surfeited our curiosity regarding the preparations made and the determined hostility of the enemy . . . we rode back to the general's quarters at Centreville for instructions as to our duties of the day. Here a most important distribution of the signal officers had been promulgated by the alert Banks in the hope of obtaining information about the enemy's designs. Lieutenants Rowley, Miner, Briggs, and myself, with flagmen, were to establish ourselves on the Catoctin range of mountains on the south side of the Potomac, and have all reports of our observations taken across the river and telegraphed to Washington, then from there to his headquarters at the front. Everything noted was to be forwarded for his consideration.

At 2 p.m., the hour fixed, we started to Fairfax Court House, passing on the road many familiar faces in the corps of Generals Sumner, Heintzelman, and Franklin, recently returned from the Peninsula Campaign.[27] From Fairfax we took the Vienna Road, but were extremely cautious, as every indication pointed strongly to its probable occupancy by the enemy between ourselves and the Catoctin range. When near Flint Hill, a few miles out from Fairfax, it was seen to be impossible to reach our destination by the south side of the river. A large force of their

cavalry was visible in the distance, precluding all thoughts of going farther, and we returned towards Alexandria, intending to try the Leesburg
Turnpike. In consequence of a heavy storm which set in late in the afternoon, it was found impracticable to pursue our investigations until
morning, so establishing ourselves under our own canvas, we lunched
and turned in for the night. Sleep, however, though courted assiduously
until near midnight, forsook our eyelids in the ceaseless thunder of the
artillery engaged at Chantilly.

Tuesday, September 2nd opened up clear and beautiful, but all of nature's
beauty could not dispel the gloom occasioned by the immeasurable loss
in the death of Major General Philip Kearney, reported killed in the engagement last night. Few lives in the annals of war had been more eventful
or conspicuously useful, more noble or brilliant. . . . A veteran of wide
experience, whose knowledge of the requirements of the common soldier,
and who unselfishly devoted himself to their welfare, gained for him their
esteem. . . . Who now can command the devotion of his brave division and
display his prodigious activity and dash in fighting and driving the forces
of the enemy wherever the issue of war led him? How many now, with the
spirit of gallantry which ruled his military life, can be found following the
precept he established of never ordering a subordinate where he would
not willingly go himself? Few indeed there are who at the first sound of
picket firing would mount and gallop away to ascertain the cause, leaving
his escort to follow after.

This desire to personally observe the situation, rather than trust the ver-
bal reports of others, led Kearney, in the darkness, within the enemy's lines.
Discovering him and seeing his attempt to escape, they poured a volley after
his retreating form. Thus he fell, his warlike and turbulent soul going out
amid the storm of elements and battle which raged about him. This morning
his body was brought through the lines under a flag of truce, the Rebel general kindly delivering it to the troops of the 57th Pennsylvania Infantry.[28]

We suffered another loss last night in the killing of General Isaac I.
Stevens, a distinguished soldier who had been identified with the 9th
Corps under Burnside at Roanoke Island, but of whom I knew personally
very little.[29]

[We] were saddled up and on the move by 9 o'clock to endeavor to
reach, by way of the Leesburg Pike, the point named in the general's order.

The troops were all astir, those encamped around being General John Sedgwick's old division, formerly on duty with us in the Shenandoah Valley campaign. The general himself, standing on the steps of a little house in which he had spent the night, was buttoned up in a much worn suit of "sou-wester" oil cloth liberally bespattered with yellow clay, and soaked from the storm of the night. His looks betokened the grim warrior that he is, and although not usually overscrupulous in the matter of dress, his well-known fighting qualities have made him the idol of his division, and fully compensate for any absence of showy apparel.

A short distance beyond the camps we abruptly came upon our cavalry videttes, who politely informed us we would have to take the back track, as the enemy's cavalry were within half a mile and the intended route therefore blockaded. Thus were we again brought to a standstill, and the prospect of carrying out the general's wishes remote indeed. We were about relinquishing the idea of going entirely and [instead] returning to headquarters when Rowley proposed crossing the Chain Bridge and trying the Maryland side of the Potomac. The proposition being acceded to, we about faced for the bridge, arriving there at noon.

When nearing a fortification adjacent to Upton's Hill on the road to the bridge, we were mistaken for a squad of Mosby's irregulars by a picket belonging to a New York regiment that had but recently entered the service. This episode might have had a serious termination had not our experience taught us that when mingling with strangers, the command to halt should at once be complied with. The officer commanding the detachment . . . had observed us, for quite a distance, riding towards him, and failing to discover any distinctive mark or color indicating our army connection, determined to capture us. Quietly posting his company at short intervals along a corn field skirting the right of the road, [he] awaited our coming. We had ridden to within fifty yards of him when the command to halt was given, all in our party instantly obeying the order, except myself. My object in riding forward was to act as the official spokesman, but in this the officer smelt danger, and I was peremptorily ordered to halt, dismount, and advance on foot. . . . Satisfactorily establishing our identity with the Signal Corps, we were allowed to pass. . . .

We found a strong force at the bridge, with the planking for several yards taken up and the approaches covered by artillery on the north bank, their position able to completely rake the inside of the structure in the event of the troops being overpowered on the Virginia side. Once in Maryland we struck the river road, and at dark reached the old stamping ground and [the] scene of our early studies in signal duty, Darnestown. . . .

[*September 3, 1862.*] In the morning, after a good night's rest and a breakfast with the Darby family, with whom we had formerly spent some pleasant hours, we were again off, arriving at Poolesville at noon.

In this little town there lived a family named Meterker, noted and respected throughout the ranks of the United States soldiers for their outspoken loyalty to the Union. Their allegiance to the old flag, surrounded as they were by traitors, had been recognized by the government in the selection of their home for the post office, and of one of their number to conduct it. It was in an upper room of their [house] that the body of the lamented Colonel Baker lay after the fiasco at Ball's Bluff, and here, during my army service, it had been my invariable custom to stop that they might have the benefit of any disbursements of money from me when away from camp. It was to this family that I now led our party and around whose welcome table we enjoyed a hearty dinner.

Our destination at the Point of Rocks was reached by way of the Monocacy Aqueduct and the tow path of the Chesapeake and Ohio Canal at 5 p.m. In view of the important events that transpired almost immediately after we had traversed this tow path it seems surprising that no obstacle was met or evidences observed of the crossing of the river by Lee's army, who were undoubtedly watching our movements from the south bank of the river. Only the narrow tow path separates the canal from the river, and between the aqueduct and Point of Rocks, some ten miles, the Potomac is not navigable except to the smallest craft and does not exceed three hundred feet in width. A sharpshooter could have picked us off this afternoon with perfect ease, and yet we were unmolested. Why [we were not], with the opportunities of short distance and concealment in their favor and no armed Union soldier within many miles of us, is to me a profound mystery. . . .

Any belief we may have entertained of re-crossing the Potomac at Point of Rocks was quickly dispelled upon reaching there by witnessing the arrival, on the Maryland shore, of thirteen hundred paroled Union prisoners, captured in the battles around Groveton, [who were] now being ferried across under a flag of truce. This effectually squelched any likelihood of complying with General Banks's orders and from this moment the project was abandoned.

This evening I renewed my acquaintance with the Bassant family of this place, of whom I have made frequent mention, and [along] with Briggs was kindly provided with accommodations. Lieutenant Rowley now decided to make a distribution of his small squad in as advantageous a manner as possible, and directed Briggs to return to Poolesville, Miner to go to Sugar Loaf Mountain, and me to occupy Maryland Heights. Between Sugar Loaf and Maryland Heights was an unusually long distance (eighteen miles "as the crow flies"), to successfully operate stations at all hours of the day, hence Miner and I arranged to communicate only between the hours of 9 and 12 a.m. and 2 and 5 p.m. [Additionally], the lack of provender for man and horse and the shortage of covering at night compelled each of us to vacate the summits of our respective mountains before darkness set in. . . . Miner, stationed to the east with dense trees for a background, would use a white flag which, in the afternoon with the sun's rays thrown upon it, could be distinctly read by me, but not so in the morning with the sun behind him reflecting brightly upon the object glass of my telescope. The background of my tower was the clear horizon, hence a black flag was necessary and was more easily read in the morning than in the afternoon with the sun's glare behind me.

[*September 4, 1862.*] I needed not a second call from Jim Bassant when at daybreak he informed me of rumors from below that Lee was crossing at or near Edward's Ferry.[30] Anxiously saddling I hurried to the tow path, a hasty cup of coffee supplying the place of a breakfast in my impatience to hear from Miner. In less than two hours I had reached Sandy Hook and prepared to ascend Maryland Heights. Several infantry soldiers passed me on my way up, indicating Union troops on the summit, [and] I soon succeeded, though considerably winded, in scaling it. Judge of my surprise when about to swing my flag in answer to Miner, whom I could see calling me, to be informed by a lieutenant of the 5th Maryland Infantry that he had orders to prevent signaling of any kind unless by permission of Colonel Miles, commanding the post.[31]

Here was an unlooked for obstacle that the most persuasive arguments failed to remove. I took the lieutenant's objections as a cool assumption of authority which, in the isolated position he had been placed, was preposterously exaggerated. . . . He persistently refused to acknowledge my

An undated Alfred Waud sketch of the signal station on Maryland Heights near Harpers Ferry. Fortescue manned this station on September 5 and 6, 1862. Note that several signal towers have been constructed and the flagman is at upper left. Courtesy Library of Congress, Prints and Photographs Division.

interpretation of his orders, and directed a file of his men to take charge of the tower, constructed by our very men over a year before, and not to allow anyone to disobey his orders. Finding him thus obdurate, I sent my man Ryan[32] down post haste to see the major commanding the batteries below with instructions to either bring him up or get an order to let us open communication, but either through the major's stubbornness or the difficulty of getting up and down the stony path Ryan did not return with the required permission until after 5 p.m., by which time Miner had ceased calling and left the mountain for the night. This was a most unfortunate and grievous disappointment, the later campaign establishing the fact that Miner was then witnessing the crossing of the Potomac River by the Rebel army.

Nothing remained now for us now but to return to Sandy Hook for the night (the lieutenant in the meantime having received instructions to permit us to signal in the morning), so crossing to Harpers Ferry I rode up into Bolivar, took supper with my old friends the Beal family, and in the evening returned to the hotel at Sandy Hook for the night.

[*September 5, 1862.*] Bright and early after breakfast I again climbed the Blue Ridge in anticipation of something important from Miner, well assured from experience that the little lieutenant was itching to let us know the condition of the country around Sugar Loaf, so unceremoniously meddled with by the Maryland sapling last evening. At 9 o'clock I observed him calling Poolesville and endeavored to read the message he flagged there, but owing to the confusing movements which were [made] away from and towards me, (Poolesville laying to the south of Sugar Loaf while I was west), instead of from side to side, I finally gave it up and began calling him for news. Before he had finished with Poolesville his flag suddenly disappeared and I saw him no more. I learned afterwards, from an old gentleman of strong Union proclivities named Howard living at the foot of Sugar Loaf, that Miner discovered, upon his arrival on the mountain, the Rebel columns preparing to cross into Maryland, and desiring to apprise the commandant at Harpers Ferry, commenced calling me at once. His information, but for the interference [of the Maryland lieutenant], would have reached Colonel Miles before their advance was on our side of the river. Briggs, at Poolesville, from some cause (probably the enemy's near approach), was not at his post in the afternoon, and the mutilated message sent the next morning did not reach Washington until Stuart's entire cavalry corps had crossed. Their advance had already reached the foot of

Sugar Loaf when Miner's flag so suddenly disappeared. He had stuck to his hazardous post in the performance of his duty until escape was well nigh impossible, relying on his familiarity with the many bridle paths of the mountain for [his] opportunity to escape. He succeeded in eluding the party intent upon his capture and reached terra firma, but was seen getting away, pursued, and taken prisoner.[33]

It was not until late this afternoon that we were aware of the enemy's designs, [which were] brought to the Ferry by a squad of convalescents who had beat a hasty retreat from Frederick one hour before Stuart's entry into that place. The day so long dreaded had arrived. The spell of ill-luck under which the Army of the Potomac had rested seemed to be still unbroken and too gloomy for positive belief. The Rebel army found itself in possession of a country where the most glowing of hopes appeared to await them. . . . Their announcement to the people of Maryland that the time was now at hand when the situation must be reversed carried with it the joyous anticipation and appreciation of the rewards now to be realized under a commander of their own famous doctrines. The sudden development of the preference of these same Marylanders for the government at Washington was a notable revelation, and disclosed, in no uncertain terms, the fact that Lee's enthusiastic army had founded their strength upon a broken reed. They would have been truly grateful for even the smallest display of recognition as victors who had earned and expected their laurel wreaths. But the distinction they enjoyed was shivering disappointment . . . and the predicted unprecedented outpouring to their ranks failed to materialize. Being a border slave state much had been expected, but their illusion was short-lived, [as] the far-seeing Marylander was not prepared to join hands with the ragged horde now overrunning his state.[34]

Lee's movement had completely cut us off from the capital, except by a circuitous route through western Pennsylvania, and rendered our position precarious in the extreme. Unless relieved, we would be encircled by Lee by way of Hagerstown, Williamsport, and Martinsburg, which was evidently a part of their plan, as seen afterwards.

The action of Colonel Miles in remaining [at Harpers Ferry], idle, and detached from any command, was unaccountable unless by direct orders of General Halleck, whose supervision over these troops . . . was supreme. Miles' indifference was manifest to everyone. His soldiers collected in groups and discussed his strange imprudence. They were positive that he intended to surrender them, called him traitor and coward in their indignation, and wondered that one of their many regimental colonels did not assume command and place him in arrest. This they were sure would be sanctioned by the War Department. But none came forward. Even General White at Martinsburg, who ranked Miles (the latter being colonel of the 2nd U.S. Infantry and detailed only to command here), instead of making an effort to extricate the beleaguered garrison, politely declined to assume command, alleging as a reason that Miles, having been commandant for some time and familiar with the topography of the country and the precise number and disposition of the troops, would be best left in control.[35] The result is now well known to all.

[*September 6, 1862.*] Saturday morning passed without anything of special note occurring, but all showed the nervous strain to which they were being subjected. At 2 o'clock I conceived the idea of attempting to reach Washington by the towpath, assuming that the entire Rebel army had by this time reached Frederick, and were [probably] moving westward leaving the river roads open. My intention at starting was to swim the canal with my horse near the Point of Rocks and use one of the roads near the river, or remain on the towpath if that proved preferable. When within a quarter mile of the Point I observed a detachment of cavalry approaching, who [proved] to be a part of Captain Cole's Maryland Battalion,[36] and I was informed that they had ridden to within rifle shot of the Rebel videttes at the Point without learning anything of importance, except that the plan devised by me was not feasible. I therefore changed my direction and returned to Sandy Hook, a Rebel parole staring me in the face.

Saturday night witnessed a despondent body of troops, hopeless as to Miles' future course, yet withal willing to encounter five times their number under any leadership that promised relief. I was invited this evening to spend the night with Colonel Maulsby of the Potomac Home Brigade,[37] and at 10 o'clock retired, fully resolved to start at daylight, by Pleasant Valley, to Hagerstown. Better to risk capture in an honest attempt at resistance than lie quiet at the Ferry and suffer this rabble to walk over one rough-shod.

CHAPTER 5

THE CAMPAIGN AND BATTLE OF ANTIETAM

SEPTEMBER 7–OCTOBER 7, 1862

H emmed in at Harpers Ferry by the approach of Confederates under Stonewall Jackson, Fortescue concluded that to avoid capture he had no choice but to strike out on his own and attempt to reach the Army of the Potomac by circumventing the northernmost elements of the invading Confederates. His departure, however, was not without consequences in that it deprived the Harpers Ferry garrison of a vital communications link to the outside world. Had Fortescue remained on Maryland Heights and persevered in his attempts to establish contact with other signal posts, the fate of the thirteen thousand troops who were to be captured there might have been different.

Fortescue's journey took him north through Pleasant Valley, Maryland, into Pennsylvania, where he headed east to Gettysburg. From there he proceeded southeast to Baltimore and finally due south to Washington, D.C. Eventually, after eight days and more than two hundred miles on horseback, he reported back for duty to the signal detachment of Army of the Potomac, then at Sugarloaf Mountain, some twenty-five miles from where he had started out a little more than a week earlier.

The lead elements of Robert E. Lee's Army of Northern Virginia had crossed the Potomac on September 4 and by the seventh had assembled near Frederick, Maryland. McClellan continued the process of reorganizing his forces to begin his pursuit of the Rebels, and on this day he left Washington to assume field command of his troops.

Sunday, September 7, 1862. With the information ringing in my ears that Lee's army was moving towards Hagerstown, and that to outstrip it I must cover twenty miles, I was off with my flagman Ryan up the valley by 7 a.m. The morning was delightfully cool and our horses were kept at a stiff gait until noon, when it grew excessively hot and dusty, and became evident that the strength of the animals should be husbanded.[1]

The distance to the pike near Boonsboro was said to be about eighteen miles, and this I reached at 11 o'clock, having met in the meantime a farmer who joined company in a desire to evade armed Rebels known to be cognizant of his pronounced Unionism. He remarked, when first accosted in the valley, that, "Perhaps we should be late in striking the pike ahead of their advance," but [that] in that case, his knowledge of the bye-roads would enable us to avoid the pike until within two miles of Funkstown, and he was positively certain that their cavalry had not yet occupied that place. We fortunately found the roads in front open, but with strong evidences of the enemy's recent occupancy, so considering our safety assured we rode leisurely to Hagerstown.

My entry into this well known place at 3 p.m. was indeed an odd one. [It was] a quiet Sabbath afternoon with not a sign of human beings to disturb its repose. As Ryan and I rode up to the curb of the Washington House[2] (kept by a Rebel named Yingling), to procure dinner . . . this deserted street suddenly became an animated one, and we [became] the center of a body of citizens upon whom it seemed to have gradually dawned that all strangers were sufficiently important to interrogate. Anxiety and impatience was

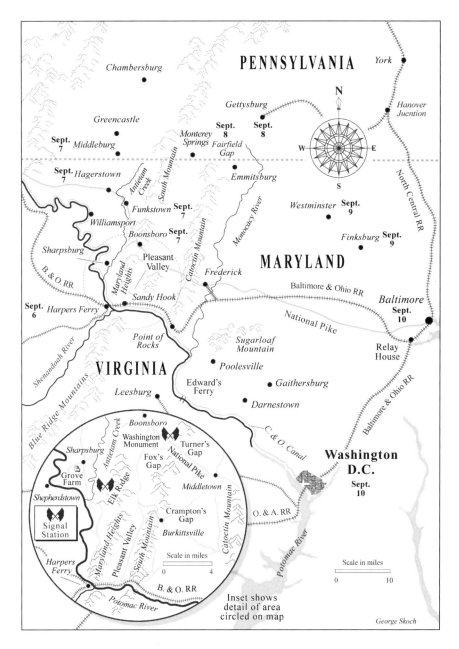

Fortescue's Antietam Campaign and the ride around Lee's army, 1862.

depicted on every face as they emerged simultaneously from their houses opposite the hotel and gathered around, regarding us as Rebels, yet loathe to commit themselves until we had spoken.

I directed Ryan to watch the crowd and the main street closely for signs of Rebel sympathy or danger while I was arranging for meals inside, and as a signal to discharge his pistol in case his suspicions were aroused. At the same time, [I told] him quietly that for the sake of expediency it would be well to keep these people in ignorance of our army connection until we should be prepared to leave. Swallowing a hastily gotten-up dinner, I relieved Ryan at the curb and directed him to soon rejoin me. In a few minutes he returned, and I then lightened the anxious minds of the burghers by informing them that we had that morning ridden from Harpers Ferry to avoid being caught in an unpleasant trap, and that my destination was out the pike in the direction of Greencastle; a revelation that met an earnest and satisfied response in their expressions as we rode away. Concluding that my safety depended upon putting several more miles between Hagerstown and myself before night, we trotted out the Chambersburg Pike, learning on the way that my Company A of the 29th Regiment had taken the same route the day before from Hagerstown, where they had been performing provost duty.

At dusk I reined in at the little village of Middleburg,[3] through which runs the state line dividing Pennsylvania and Maryland, and procuring supper for ourselves and our horses, [we] spread our blankets on a pile of hay in a stable loft and were soon asleep, a ride of thirty-five miles under a blazing sun having completely exhausted us.

Monday morning [*September 8*] found me much refreshed but puzzled as to future plans. Not a blue uniform had I met since leaving the Ferry. The choice of two roads lay open, that to Chambersburg and staying with my company until the advance of the Army of the Potomac should uncover the roads back, or eastward around Maryland, avoiding the outposts of the Rebel army. I had reason to believe that our army had engaged the Rebel rear guard, although nothing had been heard in reference to the matter.

Deciding upon the latter course I obtained the necessary information regarding my line of travel and set out early, keeping Fairfield Gap of the Blue Ridge before me. In this decision I considered it preferable to rejoin headquarters as soon as possible, even though the risks assumed might prove disastrous. At noon I gratefully tasted the waters of the celebrated

Monterey Springs Hotel on the summit, and saw before me, nestling in all its loveliness of foliage and luxuriant green, the quiet valley backed by the white dots of the village of Gettysburg. Arriving there at dusk, I found the villagers in the highest state of excitement. Scouts, farmers fleeing from the imaginary foe, and convalescent soldiers were passing through, bringing the most extravagant reports of the strength and intentions of Lee's army. A few of the more courageous citizens had formed a mounted battalion and were picketing the roads leading southward. Finding suitable quarters for man and beast at the hotel fronting the plaza, I determined to remain here for the night, the outlook for anything more comfortable at this hour being rather remote.

[*September 9, 1862.*] Obeying my instructions to call me at daylight, the rising sun's first peeps saw me trotting down the Baltimore Pike, leaving the residents in that glorious state of uncertainty [while] I, rugged and enthusiastic, was in anticipation of a successful and early [reunification] with the boys of our command. . . .

Becoming oppressed by a feeling of loneliness and anxiety in the absence of any intelligence, I sought a shady spot at noon to lunch and rest the jaded horses. When about to mount again I was surprised to see a middle-aged man, apparently a farmer, riding towards us. Ordinarily this man would have attracted no attention, but our surprise was due to the fact that not a person had been passed since leaving Gettysburg. Waiting until he checked his horse I met him with a "Good morning, sir." His timidity was noticeable at once in his reply. "Excuse me gentlemen, but as you have no regular uniforms, but [are] well armed and mounted, might I inquire whether you belong to the Confederate or Union army?" "We are Union soldiers sir," I replied, "and are endeavoring to circumvent the Rebel lines and rejoin our command with the Army of the Potomac." Glad to hear it sir," said he, "I have been obliged to leave my farm and was just thinking of going to Gettysburg, but as your destination is probably Baltimore, why I guess I'll change my mind, and with your permission, accompany you." "But you can't go through Westminster," he added, "which lies ahead of you. When I left there half an hour ago, the Rebel pickets could be plainly seen moving towards that point from Frederick. If you wish to go safely, strike off to Hanover; it is some miles out of the way, but then you run no risks."

His advice seemed reasonable, but I preferred to take the chances rather than deviate from the path I had selected, and finding him reluctant to endorse our views, I called Ryan to mount, and we withdrew from his companionship.

Under the circumstances I approached Westminster with considerable misgiving. It was a small place and lay a short distance off this main road. A lane from there intersected ours at a sharp angle, and at the junction there stood an old style country tavern with pump and horse trough near the wagon track. Some few horses could be seen beyond the group of houses in the distance, but nothing [was seen] by the tavern. Directing Ryan to unsling his carbine, and unloosening my pistol holsters, we rode boldly to the trough and gave the horses rein to drink. As we did so, about a dozen rough looking loungers came out and sauntered to the trough. Not desiring to be taken unawares, I drew my pistol, and pointing it at the crowd, said, "You men remain on that porch or I'll shoot," Ryan at the same time bringing his carbine to a ready. This was enough, they turned, and stepping on the porch, stood in line, one of them venturing the remark that "they belonged around there and wanted the news." I made no reply, but seeing that the horses had satisfied their thirst, moved slowly away, keeping my eye on them until several hundred yards had been covered, when we saw a horse and rider emerge from the yard of the tavern and gallop furiously down the intersecting road towards Westminster. This was our cue, and putting spurs to our nags, we were soon beyond danger.

That some of this gang were Rebel soldiers I had not the slightest doubt, and why they permitted us to get away is something difficult to explain. Those of the group [who were] not soldiers were evidently sympathizers, desperate enough to attempt our capture, and they very likely contemplated undertaking the attempt. . . . Our appearance this afternoon was rather sensational in the villages we struck , the natives eyeing us curiously but not deigning to offer suggestions or to question, simply contenting themselves by staring.

At 7 o'clock we reined in at a farm on the outskirts of Finksburg, some two miles from Baltimore, and I boldly sought accommodations for the night. It happened that the occupants of the place were two elderly ladies who were much perturbed at the thought of soldiers being in the house overnight, at least this was my surmise from their manner, and to quiet their apprehensions without noting their embarrassment, I assured them that I only asked consent to occupy the barn with my man and horses, as my depleted pocket-book prevented my stopping at the wayside inn on the road to their place. This was freely given, along with a nice substantial supper, and my blankets were once more spread upon a pile of hay.

At three in the morning, we were awakened by a great commotion on the main road, the rumbling of racing teams leading to the impression that possibly a Rebel column was aiming to enter the Monumental City. Quietly investigating the cause by slipping across the fields under cover of darkness, I soon discovered them to be panic-stricken farmers, making good time through fear of plundering Rebel cavalrymen.

Not daring to indulge in any more sleep after this scare, we dressed and saddled, and at dawn found the feminine farmers already astir, presumably from the same cause that had startled us. Taking a greatly relished hasty breakfast, we pushed ahead for Baltimore, entering there at 2 p.m. Without delay I made a bee-line for the quartermaster's department on Holliday Street with the intention of securing transportation for my man and I, with our horses, to Washington. The reply was a flat refusal insofar as it applied to the horses, but [it was] proffered to us on condition that we turn the horses over to his department. This offer was emphatically rejected, as was the offer to furnish passes over the turnpike, which I considered of minor importance after having ridden, as I informed him, from Harpers Ferry without paying toll or requiring a pass. Had I known the true state of affairs between these two cities, the pass would have been accepted with thanks, inasmuch as I was subjected to interminable trouble and inconvenience on the way.

From Baltimore to Washington, a distance of thirty-eight miles, there were at least 300 picket posts, and at each one a passport was required before you were allowed to proceed. At the first one I was promptly arrested by the guard and conducted to the officers quarters, where, after much scrutinizing and cross examination, the major in command adjourned the meeting and granted me a pass. This condescension on his part, I found, simply carried me beyond his post, the intimation being that I should probably meet with like interruption at the next post, 300 yards distant. Not wishing to appear officious or dictatorial to strangers in my extreme poverty, knowing that their term of service was but one week old and ended in nine months, I suggested his making it good for the trip, inasmuch as he had assured himself of my reliability and I needed to go further than 300 yards. But he was deaf to my entreaties because they likely lacked the chastened repose of manner and refined diction which his royal nibs had been accustomed to in the elegant circles he had torn himself from, for nine long months, to seek "a bubble reputation at the cannon's mouth."

The strained supervision [of this route] by a continuous line of picturesque, epauletted greatness (which secured tranquility to the suffering storekeepers of Washington), was owing to the threatening attitude of the Rebel invasion. . . . The fatigue consequent [during] this grand round of surrenders, which exasperatingly frittered away a day and part of a night, filled me with mixed gloom and profanity. At 11 o'clock p.m., when I rode perspiringly into the Signal Camp at Georgetown and dismounted, my horse, with a mournful sigh, recklessly lay down in front of the commanding officer's tent before I could remove his saddle and bridle.

Saturday, September 13, 1862. Having recuperated the exhausted energies of ourselves and horses by remaining quietly in camp all of yesterday, this morning found me again in the saddle prepared to try the identical line of travel that Rowley and our squad had gone over less than two weeks before. The fact that I was now on the home stretch, following in the wake of our troops with the expectation of coming up to the rear guard before many days should elapse, calculated to inspire me with confidence and renewed hope in being able to render my full measure of duty in the active campaigning now in progress.

General McClellan was restored by President Lincoln to the command again, and was eliciting admiration in the rapid movements of his army. The teaching this officer had undergone in being deprived of [his] command after leaving the peninsula had now induced the people to expect a faithfulness and devotion on his part commensurate with that displayed by our President in overlooking the disappointments experienced by him in McClellan's previous campaign, and by magnanimously consenting to his restoration. Generals Pope and Banks had been relegated to distant fields to endeavor to win laurels with troops less familiar with their methods as leaders.

The evening shadows were lengthening as I again approached the Darby farm beyond Darnestown and sought shelter for the night, my replenished exchequer imparting a firmness to my solicitations that only a goodly store of "shekels" can exercise.[The family] was at supper when I entered, and places were made for Ryan and I at the table to satisfy appetites enormously increased by the many miles ridden that day.

Whether the exacting fatigues we encountered since early in August had unnerved Ryan, or whether the sight of the luxuries spread before him had induced him to attempt "a perfect gorge" I was unable to discover, suffice it to say that a most distressing and embarrassing accident occurred while at the table that diffused a melancholy gloom over the family, and led me to fear they would look upon me coldly, [and] perhaps in future, pass by me on the other side. I heard [Ryan] give a sort of smothered gurgle and catch his breath, and the next moment he had jumped from his chair and emitted, all over the floor matting, a vomit which would have done credit to a full-grown mastodon.

"Great Heavens, man!" I said, "show me where you're hit and I'll call an ambulance." I tried to induce some pleasing style of conversation that would draw the attention of the host away from the dreadful exhibit, but all to no purpose. The women ran for a pail and cloths, and with Ryan's help, for of course he couldn't allow them to wallow in the entire undigested outlay, which was about six inches deep, they soon had the disgusting fragments and relics removed to the rear of the hog pen, and we resumed, half reluctantly, our instructive remarks while filled with earnest swearfulness at the nauseating turn our tete a tete had assumed. . . .

A night's repose had decisively settled Ryan's digestive apparatus, and on Sunday morning after breakfast I conveyed to Mrs. Darby a modest hint that a piece of soap would be acceptable, as I had a duty to perform which to the folks at home might seem highly ludicrous and lacking in dignity to a shoulder-strapped hero of Uncle Sam's aggregation. But a time-honored custom, dating back far in our family history, had taught me that under clothing habitually worn for three weeks needed laundering. So being supplied with a generous hunk of the brown farm-made variety . . . I hied me to a running brook back of the woods and gave my duds a good bathing. . . . In about an hour I again looked the pink of perfection, and introduced myself to Mrs. Darby arrayed in clean habiliments.

[*September 14, 1862.*] [Due to the fact] that my horse had secured a good rest in the Darby stable, I soon reached old farmer Howard's place at the foot of Sugar Loaf Mountain and arranged to stop with him overnight. The society he was enjoying, I learned, was not the most agreeable, there being two wounded Johnnies attended by two well ones on parole staying with him, but a good bed in the house of a good Union man was awaiting me, and rather than forsake that luxury on account of his un-polished guests, I remained.

Howard informed me that after Lieutenant Miner's capture, the Rebel cavalry retained possession of the mountain until the appearance of our advance at Barnsville, some five miles distant. At this time, the Rebel general Fitz Hugh Lee,[4] who had taken farmer Howard up the mountain with him, was perched on top of the tower there viewing our troops when one of our batteries of flying artillery went into position and threw a shell directly over the tower, causing a stampede of those occupying that perilous elevation, [resulting in] their hurried descent and desertion of old Sugar Loaf.

I found my old friends of the Signal Corps, Lieutenants Rowley, Spencer, Hall, and Roe, on the summit of Sugar Loaf flagging several stations, having done good service since driving Stuart's Rebel signal officers away.[5] At 12 I lunched with them and left for Point of Rocks, where I arrived in due season and called again at the Bassant homestead. Here were stationed my old partner, Harvey, with Lieutenants Homer and Jerome.[6] The events of this morning fully justified me, in my estimation, in making the exhaustive ride of the last week, when I was informed upon reaching here that the entire force at Harpers Ferry under Colonel Miles was disgracefully sur-rendered about 8 o'clock. By this dastardly piece of cowardice 11,583 men were deliberately, shamefully forced to lay down their arms to the thieving army under Jackson. The denouement was precisely as I predicted when I decided to abandon that place, and, regardless of risk, rode up Pleasant Valley on the morning of September 7. . . .

As usual, the idol of the Rebel sympathizers in the North, Little Mac, comes in for his share of the blame, and with the usual reason given—his exasperatingly slow movements. Had he promptly advanced he might have succored the imbecile Miles. But why dwell upon the disgrace? I escaped it, feeling assured, as did every soldier in that command (including the brave 1300 cavalrymen who determinedly cut their way through after my departure), that they were doomed to everlasting ignominy and humilia-tion by rank pusillanimity or superior military incapacity. Fortunately for Colonel Miles, a Rebel shell fired from a gun posted on Loudoun Heights put an end to his miserable existence while in the act of displaying the flag of truce; else his future would have been, and justly too, black indeed. . . .

[Fortescue returned to the Army of the Potomac on the heels of the Battle of South Mountain (which was actually a series of battles fought for several passes through the South Mountain range), which resulted when McClellan, who had begun to move his army northwest from the vicinity of Washington on September 6, came into possession of a lost Confederate order that revealed that Lee had divided his force and was advancing piecemeal into Maryland. McClellan attacked through the passes in the South Mountain range about fifteen miles west of Frederick, Maryland, on September 14 hoping to defeat the scattered portions of the Army of Northern Virginia, but Lee was able to hold him off and reunite the bulk of his forces behind Antietam Creek near the small village of Sharpsburg, Maryland.]

[*September 15, 1862.*] [From Point of Rocks], I hurried over towards the location of headquarters, supposed to be on the National Pike leading west from Hagerstown,[7] and after dark had the extreme pleasure of reporting myself to the Chief Signal Officer, Major A. J. Myer, whom I found in charge. Our troops had been fiercely engaged all of yesterday and well into the night at Turner's and Crampton's Gaps in what was known as the Battle of South Mountain, and on every hand were evidences of the struggle. Wounded men were strewn along in every conceivable place that afforded the slightest shelter, and on the pike were a host of slightly wounded who had been directed to foot it to the Frederick City hospitals. I witnessed some scenes of heroism among these who bore, without flinching, the agony of dreadful hurts, yet showed the enduring patience and strength to suffer in silence. Many who had scarcely reached manhood, almost worn down by exhaustion from loss of blood, trudged along with the simple courage and faith of he who has given his best arm in defense of his flag. "Suffering, patiently and enduringly borne, is one of the noblest attributes of man." How much may be learned from the life and example of even the commonest soldier!

But few there are who give more than a passing notice to the dead and dying, so common do they become in the daily life of the soldier. The indifference to the suffering is hard to believe possible. Sights that would be heartrending to a man in civil life receive but a moment's thought, so unconcerned and callous do the daily scenes render even the most delicately reared troops.

Near the Gap on the pike lay a dead Rebel soldier who had been one of the first to fall when our advance made the assault. He lay with his head on the footpath running at the side of the pike, his feet extending to the wagon track along which the army trains and artillery were moving. The stoical apathy and insensibility of man, degenerated by the baser influences of war, was never more strikingly exhibited here, as wagon after wagon loaded with supplies and ammunition had passed over his lower limbs until all that remained were the flattened stumps partly ground off by the successive wheels of disinterested teamsters. "Man's inhumanity to man makes countless thousands mourn."

General Reno, with Cox's Kanawha Division and Willcox's Division (afterwards supported by Sturgis), and Rodman's Division, led the fight at Turner's Gap.[8] Hooker's three divisions, under Generals Meade, Hatch,[9] and Ricketts, reached the ground and took part in the general attack ordered by McClellan, which successfully surmounted the obstacles on the mountainside and carried everything before them. At Crampton's Gap the principal fighting was done by General Franklin, who took Slocum's and Smith's Divisions up the slope and soon drove old fuss and feathers, Howell Cobb, from every position he sought to defend.[10] Our losses in the two engagements footed up 2100; that of the Rebels, from their own statements, over 4000. We lost the brave Reno; they General Garland.[11]

On the road across South Mountain, the signal party [was] in the advance, with instructions to look for eligible points and open communications with the columns in the rear. Is not the view of this beautiful valley a picture that will linger in the memory long after all traces of the conflict have disappeared? Before us lies in all its pastoral beauty the valley west of the range, with Middletown revealed by its dotted farms. Behind us the lines are climbing the winding paths and the pike and pouring over the slope, presenting the likeness of a huge anaconda in its undulating motion.[12] Here and there the glint of sunlight upon the polished musket barrel indicates more clearly the movement of the column.

Upon the apex of the summit we halt before a modest one story cottage, the yard encircled by a paling fence. Within its enclosure are disclosed the former traces of a housewife and industrious helpmate in its tiny gravel walks and well-arranged plots. But what a change has taken place in the situation. The vigor and industry is hushed in the stillness of death. An appalling scene greets the eye as we ride to the palings to inspect the gloomy occupants they encircle. Side by side across it are laid the forms of many men, the dingy gray uniforms denoting their possessors' former views of states-rights. No more secession in those faces now rigid and those eyes staring into vacancy. The house is deserted and its gruesome dead are the only occupants to greet the multitudes hurrying to a struggle in which many in the inquisitive groups are destined to share the lot of those lying cold before them.

While on the march tonight, in company with Major Myer, we passed a portion of the first division of Hooker's Corps, commanded by General Meade, in whom an especial interest attaches for the reason that he hails from our patriotic city. In conversing with the general, Major Myer mentioned the fact of my having been with Miles at Harpers Ferry, and of my hasty leave-taking before the disaster. General Meade evinced a desire to know the condition of the troops during my stay and their feelings while awaiting the disposition of the forces to whom they ultimately surrendered. I gave to him and Major Myer a detailed account of the conversations I had had with many of them, and of my successful efforts in evading capture.

During my interview with the general I was impressed with his strong convictions of the responsibility resting upon Miles to have saved, by any extraordinary measures, his command from the humiliation they had been subjected to. It was the opinion of Major Myer, expressed after the interview, that had it been the good fortune of those troops to have had General Meade in command no such disgrace would have been associated with his name. . . .

At noon today we reached the banks of Antietam Creek. As far as the view extends over this undulating country the troops can be seen going into position. Hooker occupies the right, Sumner the center, and Burnside the left, each having three divisions. Fitz John Porter is in reserve; all told [we have] 81,900 men.[13] Very little occurred on Tuesday to disturb the serenity of the situation except some desultory cannonading and picket firing. Major Myer had started with a party for Elk Mountain, designing to establish a station from which he could overlook the field. Before morning of the 17th, he had opened communication with McClellan's headquarters and with the Washington Monument north of the National Pike. The Elk Mountain station was some five miles southeast of Sharpsburg and was of incalculable value to McClellan during the engagement, aiding him in accomplishing much that would otherwise have been neglected.[14]

Another post-battle view of the signal station on Elk Mountain, Maryland, approximately two and a half miles behind Federal lines overlooking the Antietam battlefield. During the engagement, signal personnel stationed here relayed information about Rebel troop movements to McClellan's headquarters at the Pry House and to Ambrose Burnside's command on the Union left. Lt. Edward Pierce peers through the telescope while Lt. Aaron Jerome, seated behind him with notebook, is ready to record messages received. Pvt. Robert Morgan stands at the base of the platform; Pvt. Harrison Gardiner holds the signal flag. Courtesy Library of Congress, Prints and Photographs Division.

Wednesday, September 17, 1862. The morning opened delightfully fresh and bright, and with strong indications, in the early preparations observed, of a clash of arms before the day should be far advanced. In fact it was a little more than fairly light when [their] artillery began a fusillade, necessitating a change of position of some brigades on the left, which were found to be exposed to the fire of the enemy's guns.

Hooker, on the right [with the 1st Corps], had crossed Antietam Creek late in the afternoon of the 16th, and although opposed for a time by General D. H. Hill, maintained his position near the Dunker Church until dark caused a suspension of the firing.[15] In the early morning, however, he deployed his three divisions and charged with impetuosity the Rebel troops holding the woods around the little church. General Meade's division sustained the brunt of the action. The possession of the wood was disputed with great gallantry, but Hooker's incessant discharges of musketry and terrible fire from artillery double shotted with canister were too much for Jackson . . . and his troops fled for shelter beyond the Hagerstown Pike.

Hooker's advanced lines (now thinned by the enemy, who had obtained shelter) were beginning to break badly when General Mansfield's 12th Corps came to his relief. This vigorous officer, though much advanced in years, promptly charged through the cornfield into the woods in rear of the Dunker Church and drove the enemy back, supported later by Hartsuff and Doubleday [of the 1st Corps]. In this movement General Mansfield fell; command devolved upon General A. S. Williams, who had barely reported to General Hooker for instructions when Hooker was struck. . . .[16]

The serious fighting over the ground north of the Dunker Church ended between 9:30 and 10 in the morning. Meade succeeded Hooker, who had been borne from the field, and ordering Greene's division [up] on the left of the 12th Corps, drove the enemy some distance out of the woods towards the church. The enemy, however, concentrating upon Greene, stubbornly resisted his advance, and he was finally compelled to give way across the Hagerstown Turnpike. Here he defeated all subsequent efforts to dislodge him, being supported by the many batteries that covered his troops. . . .[17]

On the left of our lines the failure to promptly advance when ordered is attributable to the dilatory nature of Burnside. There is a diversity of opinion between Burnside's officers and those at McClellan's headquarters as to the exact time the former received his orders to attack the enemy on the heights opposite the bridge that now bears his name. General B. F. Fisher,[18] then a captain in the Signal Corps, says he carried an order [to Burnside] from McClellan not later than 7:30 a.m. Colonel D. B. Sackett of McClellan's staff says he carried an order [to him] about 9 o'clock, but it was not until near noon that Burnside commenced his movement, and not until 2 o'clock that he showed any intention of really trying to cross Antietam Creek. This is verified by General Fisher and myself.[19] While Fisher carried the order only and then returned to headquarters, I remained with Kendall of the Signal Corps and witnessed the apparent inaction of Burnside which, it is claimed by McClellan's friends, prevented that officer from driving Lee into the Potomac. Whether such a sweeping accusation can be laid at the door of Burnside of premeditatedly disobeying a positive order from his commanding officer to move, or of willfully remaining passive in the face of a . . . greatly inferior force of the enemy it is hard to believe possible. Nevertheless, the part assigned to General Burnside was of vital importance, and his delays appear inexcusable. His feeble attempts to take the bridge with a small force and his successive repulses demonstrated either timidity . . . or of obstinacy, an unaccountable charge to those familiar with his unvarying politeness and observance of military etiquette, and the warm personal friendship known to exist between he and his commander.

After successfully carrying the bridge and the heights [behind it], he waited about two hours for the remainder of his corps to cross, and then moved towards Sharpsburg. This advance met with little opposition until reinforcements arrived in the form of A. P. Hill's division, who forced Burnside back to the bridge, which he reached at dark, and the conflict passed.

From what I saw I am persuaded that Burnside imagined that additional men were needed to hold the hills south of the bridge and requested them of McClellan. This request, I am told, was referred to Fitz John Porter, whose corps, composed of 13,000 fresh troops, had not fired a shot. Porter was averse to sending any of his corps, and Burnside was notified to hold the ground at all hazards with the men he had. It is presumed that Porter desired to win the laurels his troops might achieve while commanding them himself, and his influence over McClellan carried the point.[20]

Just before dark I heard General Burnside emphatically order a captain, who was then leaving the hill north of the bridge with his battery, having exhausted his boxes of fixed ammunition and solid shot, "to return to his position and remain there, firing blank cartridge until I order you to retire." Why there should have been a lack of ammunition I am unable to imagine. An ample supply was on hand at the opening of the fight, and a resident of Hagerstown informed me that our wagons were being constantly filled at the car depot there and hurried to the field from early daylight on the 17th, and I know that an abundance was in rear of the lines at the close of the battle.

What lost opportunities are were represented upon this field? It was the universal expression that twice during the day the moment had arrived for a brilliant dash, but each time was neglected. Had Porter's Corps been thrown across the Antietam to the assistance of Burnside in the afternoon, or [to assist] French and Richardson in the morning, they would have swept the Rebel lines back like a whirlwind.[21] As the sun of that awful day went down the thunder of the artillery and rattle of musketry ceased, and one of the bloodiest battles of the war had been fought. Who is there who can faithfully picture the scenes of that terrible night in which thousands of dead and dying littered these hills and gullies?

As I returned after dark to Porter's headquarters of the 5th Corps to open communication from the roof of the house with Elk Mountain, I passed hundreds of wounded, moaning and crying piteously for medical aid, begging in the name of the Almighty for water. . . . The anguish of the maimed and bleeding, to which my nature had become partly steeled, was more heart rending than any I had ever listened to. Every fence corner, corn crib, or barn was filled to overflowing, and here and there could be seen the lanterns of the stretcher bearers and ambulance corps gathering the wounded and hurrying to points where a score of surgeons were plying the knife and saw. The troops, worn out by tiresome marching and incessant fighting, lay in groups around the flickering campfires helplessly dumb from exhaustion and deaf to the blood-curdling oaths and entreaties of those crying out in their desperation for assistance. Singular, is it not, that two armies, hotly engaged, with all the dread instruments of war thundering their noises will, on the approach of night, cease, as if by mutual consent, and in a short time become as passive as a country Sabbath day?

[*September 18, 1862.*] What a spectacle met the eye on Thursday, when at daylight I descended from my improvised couch under the roof to learn the probable intentions of the commanding general. The injured, mostly Rebel, were being unloaded from the ambulances and were laid in a row with their heads toward the house, entirely encircling it, leaving only a small space by which to enter the doorway. On the eastern side, a rude table was made of a barn door [resting] upon crotches of trees driven into the ground. Several surgeons were here probing gunshot wounds and performing amputations, a sickening exhibition and one that I was always careful to avoid from an apprehension that its ghastliness might be remembered and unnerve me when called upon to expose myself to danger.

As I stepped from the doorway between the forms, each partly covered with a blanket, and was about to take a drink of water on which floated a tin dipper, a Rebel soldier raised himself and with an arm outstretched mutely appealed to me, his lips moving but no sound being audible. It was the extreme throes and superhuman strength that comes at last to a dying man, for scarcely had I reached his feet to alleviate his distress when he dropped back, outstretched and lifeless.

Over in the cornfield where the 2nd Corps had been engaged, the windrows were dotted with prostrate forms, the blue color predominating. In the sunken road near the little church, the dead lay across each other, the gray being more conspicuous than the blue, though frequently seen in deadly embrace. Hundreds of horses were strewn around, many frightfully mangled, others badly hurt and limping about with an imploring look for feed or water, seemingly conscious that the end was near when once they succumbed and lay down. No attention whatever could be paid to them, the united efforts of the hospital staff being directed to the thousands of men scattered around needing prompt assistance.

Near the sunken road beside a disabled limber box lay a battery horse which, with his head partly raised, winnowed as I rode by. That plaintive recognition touched my most tender sympathies as I saw that both forelegs below the knees had been carried away by a cannon shot. I could not leave the poor brute to linger in such agony, so quickly dismounting, I placed my pistol to his ear and ended his suffering.

It was rumored this morning that the fight would be at once renewed, but stillness prevailed, the troops resting quietly awaiting orders. McClellan I was told was anxious to commence hostilities, but was dissuaded by some of his corps commanders, principally Sumner, who hotly opposed so rash a proceeding, as he termed it. Standing on an elevated point and viewing the Rebel lines they appeared to have been heavily reinforced and preparing for an assault. Such were the impressions of the signal officers too, on Elk Mountain, whose reports were being constantly flagged to McClellan. It proved to be a trick of Lee's, as shown subsequently, and was no doubt known by McClellan at the time, who, although "spoiling for a fight" (?) permitted his prudent adversary to slip away, crossing safely, owing to the low stage of the river at the Shepherdstown Ford. I learned afterwards from a resident near the Potomac that just before they fell back, and while the flag of truce was on the field in behalf of the wounded, every one of their available men was hurried to the front. Their cavalry were out scouring the country for stragglers, all of whom were placed in line to make it as imposing as possible . . . to deceive our officers into the belief that an attack was premeditated, when in fact it was but the prelude to a retreat. The retrograde movement must have commenced late this afternoon of the 18th and continued uninterruptedly during the night, as scarcely a vestige of their army remained north of the Potomac on Friday morning.

Although Thursday passed without a renewal of the engagement, we fully expected an encounter on Friday. Innumerable camp fires scattered over their territory on this dark and glowering night, and apparent activity in readjusting their lines gave that impression. The tantalizing discovery [in] the morning that all this uproar was simply a ruse to cover their escape dampened much of the frequent hurrahs for their idol, and McClellan's complacent countenance gave place to one of anxiety and uneasiness.[22]

The limited transportation of the enemy compelled them to abandon thousands of their wounded whom we found crowding every place of shelter; many without covering of any sort. Of course all who could pull one foot after another or could persuade comrades . . . to assist them in their efforts to escape capture got across; the helpless and stretcher patients were left to us.[23]

[*September 19, 1862.*] As early as possible this Friday morning I rode to the river opposite Shepherdstown, and could easily distinguish, with my glass, the straits the enemy and their friends were in. Confusion, ludicrous to us, was pictured in the thronged streets. Wagons, ambulances, women, and children [were] moving out household goods. A mass of negroes and whites [were] wedged and jammed together in ungovernable excitement lest the Yankees should get across and gobble the entire place. The retreat had the appearance of a stampede, and glorious would have been the results if McClellan had only awakened to the fact and pressed Lee. . . . [The Maryland Campaign] was a very dear excursion for Robert E. Lee, and was equally important to our cause. The venture showed that the assumption that Maryland only needed a chance to assert its preference for the Southern view of the question proved to be a fallacy unmistakable in its positiveness.

On our side of the river bank stood the Douglas mansion, occupied by the father of Colonel Henry Kyd Douglas of Stonewall Jackson's staff.[24] A very pretentious residence that overlooked the little town opposite with its precipitous road to the river, it was regarded by the "pore white trash" hereabouts evidently with reverential awe and wonder. Being unaware of the pronounced quality of secessionism it sheltered in its owner (though conscious that so much antiquated grandeur must be inwardly tainted with rebellious proclivities), I stepped politely inside its hallway at noon and asked to be furnished with dinner, expecting, of course, to hand over the equivalent in cash. My suspicions as to its character were confirmed at once by a bluff refusal that there was nothing to eat in the house. Noticing what appeared to be a gray uniform moving around in the principal large room or parlor, I boldly pushed the door open, and there lying on mattresses were two wounded Rebel officers, attended by another soldier with his right arm and head bandaged. They were also receiving much attention at the hands of three or four female contrabands attached to the house, one of whom, on passing through the hallway a moment later, quietly assured me that her master had a well-stocked larder, but evidently for Southern soldiers only. This put me on my mettle, and walking into the room I said to the head of the establishment, "I intend taking dinner here, sir, today, and seeing that these officers are badly hurt and need the services of a surgeon, if they desire it I shall take pleasure in bringing one who is not far away at this time." Instead of appreciating the offer, the officer lying nearest, who was writhing and groaning with pain from a gunshot wound in the bowels, turned on me with some of the choicest South Carolina profanity. [This] instantly checked the flow of sympathy welling up within me and brought out an emphatic notification that a guard would be promptly ordered there to prevent their getting away if such were their intentions.

The services of a guard, implied in my threat, were little needed, however, as I saw in the ghastliness [of their wounds] and in the vital parts in which they had been struck that death was hovering near and they [were]

The Douglas Mansion, known as Ferry Hill Place, where Fortescue encountered the wounded Confederate officers. Photograph by J. Gregory Acken, 2014.

beyond the skill of any surgeon. This surmise was shortly verified; their undressed and neglected wounds blotting out their lives before the night had half gone.

Dinner was prepared for me and I dined alone, no member of the family deigning to join me at the table; a slight that had no appreciable effect on my appetite. . . .

The hasty departure of Lee's army from the Maryland side of the river did not suffice of itself to repress the ardor and hopes of their leaders, however much it may have temporarily demoralized the rank and file.

[*September 20, 1862.*] Anticipating an early forward movement on the part of our commander . . . Captain Fisher and I started early on Saturday morning to locate suitable stations so that communication might be established nearer the river with Maryland Heights, and [with] a point known as Brian's Iron Works on the Blue Ridge, northeast of the field. Proceeding westward along the river for several miles, we observed many wounded of the enemy who had succumbed in despair after a great effort to reach succor on the south side. Others bewailed their fate at being abandoned by their friends and despondently inquired for surgical relief. We returned to the Sharpsburg Road opposite Shepherdstown just as a portion of two brigades of the 5th Corps were re-crossing, they having been ordered to cross the river very early that morning.

Some eight or nine hundred yards below we dismounted to observe the movements of our troops, a comparatively small force who were in sight on the opposite field in line behind a stone wall, evidently waiting an attack. We were surprised to find, upon inquiry, that the commandant of the brigade, one Colonel Barnes,[25] in temporary charge only, had returned with three of the regiments, leaving the fourth, the 118th Pennsylvania (Corn Exchange Regiment of Philadelphia), unsupported on the south side.

The withdrawal of a portion of the brigade seemed to be the signal for an attack by an overwhelming force of A. P. Hill's division of Jackson's Corps, who flanked the 118th from their position at the wall and forced them to the bluff overlooking a dam that crossed the river near an old mill at this point. Simultaneously with the appearance of the Rebels, our batteries, which lined the bluff on the north side and commanded the ground occupied by the contending troops, opened, but with little effect. The immense strength of the enemy compelled our men, though resisting stoutly, to vacate [their position] and rush down the precipitous bluff in an attempt to reach the bank on our side by way of the dam, the top-stones of which were then dry. Fisher and I were standing amid the pieces of a battery of 20 pdr. Parrots, and with our glasses could see these shells dropping among our men at the top of a ravine where they were concentrated, creating confusion and panic and inflicting much damage to them instead of upon the enemy. Calling the attention of the officer to this, he directed a higher elevation of his guns, but too late to retard the murderous fire and fearful slaughter that followed from the Rebel infantry, who pressed our men to the shore and picked off numbers of them while crossing, many no doubt dropping into the water and drowning.

We saw but a remnant of that large regiment ascend the bank among the batteries bearing their colonel, Prevost, whom the surgeons at once began operations on behind a stack of hay in the rear. The inexcusable blunder of leaving a regiment of infantry exposed in this manner, with a river fordable only at certain points in their rear . . . can be traced to the headquarters of the 5th Corps, General Fitz John Porter, who ordered the movement, supplemented by the unpardonable stupidity of the officer, Barnes, to whom was entrusted its execution.[26]

After the river had been cleared of our men, the Rebel sharpshooters began their amusing work upon the artillerymen who kept up a hot fire on their columns. Stepping back a few paces to a clump of trees, we fastened our glasses to one of them by screws carried for that purpose that we might watch the effects of our shells. With my eye to the telescope, Fisher was directing my attention to a sharpshooter screened behind some rocks in the ravine, when a puff of smoke rose from his rifle, and a twig about a foot above my head was clipped off and dropped upon the top of the glass. Not desiring to deliberately permit this squirrel hunter to perfect his aim . . . . we mounted and rode back to headquarters, making the discovery while ascending my perch to the roof that several of the rooms were now occupied by [wounded] officers of the 118th Regiment just brought up from the river.

During this afternoon I vacated my station at Porter's headquarters, packed up my traps, and by orders of Captain Fisher established a station near the river, having for a companion officer Lieutenant Jed C. Paine of New York.[27] This point Fisher and I had agreed upon before witnessing the lamentable disaster to the Corn Exchange Regiment, and as it was in close proximity to the Douglas mansion, we decided to make that abode our stopping place, unmindful of the obstacles to be encountered. These proved to be rather insignificant upon a second visit, it being revealed to us that in one of the wings of the residence lived an old housekeeper whose love for the Union remained unshaken, hence we were not only very welcome guests and bountifully provided for, but entrusted with secrets respecting the family that she had shrewdly obtained from a long connection with it.

She informed us that the two wounded officers met on my first visit were lieutenants, the one with the private attending him belonging to the Palmetto Sharpshooters, the other to the Louisiana Tigers.[28] It was the Palmetto boy who had assailed in such rare Billingsgate, and who had been the first to take his departure to the happy hunting grounds. It was the old man, Douglas, who had advised against bringing a surgeon of the U.S. into the house, his embittered feelings influenced by his late affiliation with the choice spirits of Rebeldom rendering him indifferent to the fatal character of the wounds of his guests. His aversion to the Northern soldier was so deep rooted and insidious that he would rather his friends should die than accept surgical aid, however dexterously administered at the hands of an enemy, or have his homestead polluted by the tread of a Yankee by invitation. Not a great while after, he was forced to accept the hospitality of the U.S. by sharing a cell in the Old Capitol Prison. . . .[29]

[*While George McClellan believed he had fought a "masterful" battle at Antietam, history has not validated his assessment. His uncoordinated attacks allowed the heavily outnumbered Lee to parry every Federal thrust and shift reinforcements around the battlefield, while his cautious nature prevented him from employing reserves that might have altered the outcome of the fight. In the balance, Lee lost almost 11,000 of the 40,000 men he brought to Sharpsburg, while McClellan lost 12,500 out of approximately 75,000 effectives. Lee, as Fortescue has noted, abandoned the field and retreated back to Virginia, allowing McClellan to claim, on September 19, that his "victory was complete." Three days later, Lincoln took advantage of the strategic victory at Antietam and issued a preliminary draft of the Emancipation Proclamation, deeming that all people held as slaves by the Confederacy would be free after January 1, 1863. The Northern war effort, from this juncture onward, was now inextricably linked with the struggle to end slavery.*]

On *September 23*, our station was withdrawn from further operations and we returned to headquarters under instructions to be in readiness for the early movement of the army. During this lull, from the continuous labor to which we had been subjected, I embraced the opportunity of visiting the boys of the 29th Regiment, who were having a nice easy time of it Boonsboro, performing Provost duty. They were under the command of Major Michael Scott[30] in the absence of Colonel John K. Murphy and Lieutenant Colonel Charles Parham, the former being still in the hands of the enemy, having been captured in the Valley near Winchester during the Spring campaign; the latter at home in compliance with an urgent demand for his resignation. He had gone to Philadelphia without permission during a fight at Front Royal, Va., creating a popularity towards his retirement unmistakable in its zeal.[31]

I found Scott the same uncouth, unkempt specimen as when this regiment was first inflicted with his presence. Unfortunately for the service there were many others like him who ought to be carrying the hod or peddling clams instead of fancying they could eke out a subsistence posing as military curiosities. Company A was in fine feather, and was anxiously awaiting orders to lay aside the monotonous routine of guard duty around private residences for those of a sterner character. Before my departure I accepted an invitation from Lieutenant Theo Coursault,[32] my former orderly sergeant now in charge, to take tea with a family living on the farm in rear of the camp ground, among the younger members of whom was a buxom daughter, who, I was informed, might become in the dim future the better half of the aforesaid lieutenant.

This morning, *September 24*, a genuine surprise reached us in the shape of a Proclamation of Emancipation by President Lincoln which declares that on or after January 1, 1863, all negro slaves of persons within the states then in rebellion shall thenceforward be free. The President further says that he will designate those slave states not in rebellion before that date and exempt them from the proclamation. That I think will be a tough question for him to decide. But the news is glorious and will be a bitter pill for the johnnies to swallow. Of course they will pooh-pooh it and call it buncombe, and pretend that it has no effect. It will be carried out though and no mistake. The President tersely says, "My paramount objective is to save the Union, and not either to save or destroy slavery. If I could save the Union without freeing any slave, if I could save it by freeing all the slaves, or if I could save it by freeing some and leaving others alone any one of these I would do." And we believe him implicitly. When I say we, I don't include Little Mac and his staff, all of whom I am sure disagree with the president in his views.[33]

Within a week after the receipt of the Proclamation, we find the President visiting us and prepared to review the troops. How inexpressibly sad his countenance always seems, and yet his enemies charge him with undue levity. It may be that he makes the occasional opportunity fit some well-timed joke, but beyond that certainly his appearance does not warrant such an insinuation.

A few days later another ride was projected by Captain Fisher, who desired to inspect the station on Fairview Mountain, a spur of the North Mountain range beyond the village of Clear Spring, Maryland. If there was one thing more than another for which our Captain Fisher was pre-eminently distinguished it was his faculty [for] withstanding the fatigues of the saddle. No potentate of feudal times was more exacting or insistent upon levying tribute upon the energies of his followers than was Fisher upon his horse-flesh. Nothing seemed to fret him more or greater disturb his equanimity than enforced idleness, which, as a subaltern, he was compelled to endure while under instruction at Georgetown, and nothing seemed to afford him more genuine pleasure than when ordered to the field in charge of a detachment, in [the] opportunities then offered for the widest scope of his peregrinated disposition. . . .

It was no uncommon thing for Fisher to break into the midst of a group of Sig's enjoying the fragrance of their pipes while intently listening to one of their number reciting the details of an adventure . . . with orders to Lieutenants Smith, Jones, or Brown to saddle up at once and accompany him on a tour of duty, the duration of which might occupy twenty hours or, perhaps, a week. These displays of enthusiasm by him, although often viewed as a hardship by those singled out . . . were calculated to win the

Center, Benjamin Franklin Fisher at the end of the war; right, Capt. Joseph Spencer; left, an unidentified officer. Courtesy Library of Congress, Prints and Photographs Division.

admiration of the chief signal officer as well as the commanding general, inasmuch as they were obviously prompted by a desire to make the Signal Corps an adjunct of the greatest value to the army.

The ride to Fairview by Fisher and I was uneventful with the exception of one nauseating experience that upset our stomachs and sorely tempted us to join in a noble resolution to discard the unfortunate habit we had contracted of seeking water as a thirst allayer when "commissary" of the rye pattern could be had for ninety cents a gallon. A roadside pump which stood temptingly in front of a farm lured us to its side, and the tin dipper had been emptied once by each of us when the matron appeared at the door, and in reply to our inquiry as to the cause of its vomit-like staleness, coolly remarked that a decayed cat had been maliciously dropped down it by disgruntled Johnnies prior to their flight beyond the Potomac. The flavor of convalescent glue, I can aver, persistently clung to my taste apparatus for quite a spell afterwards.

How grand the scene that met our gaze from the summit of Fairview. Before us to the south, looking from the broad pike that crosses the mountain, the range of country, even to Winchester, was unobstructed. To the north from another spur could be seen Chambersburg, Pennsylvania and the many smaller towns that dotted here and there the landscape. Lee's entire army was plainly visible, their camp fires and moving trains filling the atmosphere with smoke and dust many miles south of the river. Lieutenants Rowley and Roe were operating this station in front of the old "Wayside Inn," and finding them nicely quartered there we concluded to remain overnight and leisurely find our way back on the morrow.[34]

CHAPTER 6

FROM MCCLELLAN TO BURNSIDE

OCTOBER 8-DECEMBER 7, 1862

Following the slaughter at Antietam, the Federals lay idle north of the
Potomac for nearly six weeks. Lincoln's repeated entreaties to McClellan
to move his army south went unheeded, prompting General in Chief
Halleck to remark that it required "the lever of Archimedes to move this inert
mass."[1] Frustrated by McClellan's indifference to his requests and the general's excuses for his inactivity—which ranged from the overworked condition
of his horses to his need for thousands of reinforcements before he could advance—Lincoln's patience was nearly used up. "I think myself he errs on the
side of prudence and caution," one of McClellan's division commanders wrote,
"and that a little more rashness on his part would improve his generalship."[2]
Little Mac finally began his advance on October 26, but after eleven days he

had covered only thirty-five miles.³ In a war that called for hard men, re-marked historian Bruce Catton, McClellan had no hardness.⁴ Lincoln relieved McClellan on November 7 and replaced him with Ninth Corps commander Maj. Gen. Ambrose Burnside.

Wednesday, October 8, 1862. Early this morning tents were struck and everything moved to the vicinity of Sandy Hook. We are now back in Pleasant Valley again near the identical campground where the 29th Regiment spent its first night in front of the enemy over one year ago. The same crest of the Blue Ridge rises before us, stretching its wooded and rocky slope far to the north, and abruptly dipping into the Potomac to the south. Who can fail to be entranced by the loveliness of the surrounding scenery at the Ferry, which Thomas Jefferson, in the exuberance of his spir-its was wont to exclaim—being a Virginian of course—was worth a trip across the Atlantic to behold.

Today Harvey and I rode to Bolivar Heights and dropped in to see our old friends at the Beal homestead. Quite a number of officers take their meals at the table of this well-known Union family, and enjoy the society of its members. At dinner today we had Lieutenant Colonel Kane, with his wife and daughter on a temporary visit, and Major Devereaux, both of the 69th Pennsylvania. On my return late in the afternoon I called at the headquarters of one of Pennsylvania's noted batterymen, Captain Joe Knap, encamped near Sandy Hook, and at his invitation took tea and spent the night with him, his lieutenants, Atwell, Ned Geary, and Magill⁵ aiding by their presence in the pleasures of the evening.

In the morning, the old signal line of yore was again established be-tween Sugar Loaf, Poolesville, Point of Rocks, and Maryland Heights, Captain Charles S. Kendall of Boston and myself going to the familiar post at Point of Rocks. Our stay here was principally to watch the country opposite, which embraced quite a portion of Virginia, and to notice and re-port promptly any indications of movements observed. This order enjoin-ing on us a careful observance of dust or smoke was impressively imparted by Major Myer as coming from General McClellan, who must have been in possession of information relating to contemplated operations of the Rebel army, and yet no effort was made (or if made [was] in a half-hearted way only), when after a few days our signals apprised him of more than usual important data concerning the enemy's designs.

On the morning of *October 10*, General J. E. B. Stuart, with three brigades of cavalry under Wade Hampton, Fitz Hugh Lee, and [William E.] Jones,[6] about 1800 men, crossed the Potomac near the signal station on Fairview that Fisher and I had recently visited, and owing to the foggy condition of the weather nearly surprised the signal party stationed there. Lieutenants Rowley and Roe succeeded by a close shave in eluding the Rebel troopers, but lost all of their equipment [and] two flagmen, who were captured.[7] Stuart's destination was evidently Chambersburg, as that was the extreme point reached, although the immediate occupation of that place by him was of no particular moment. His purpose no doubt was to replenish their army with horse flesh, the recent campaigns having considerably reduced both armies in that direction.[8]

On the evening of *October 11*, a message came through to our station from Major Myer, at McClellan's headquarters, stating that information had been received that General Stuart, with his cavalry column, would attempt to cross the Potomac at Noland's Ferry below the Point of Rocks this evening or the following morning, and that a diligent watch must be kept and messages constantly flagged informing him every half hour of the appearance of the country from our station. We learned during the night of the 11th from a resident who had ridden hard to Point of Rocks that Stuart was not far from Frederick, heading for the river, and would probably attempt to cross near the place indicated by McClellan. This we promptly signaled to headquarters. In the early morning, Stuart's column was distinctly noted, and this information flagged to Myer. Yet notwithstanding our vigilance, [which was] spurred by McClellan's instructions, no effort was apparent to us of any intention to intercept this raiding party. [They] crossed between 9 and 10 AM, and were safely on Virginia soil with all of their plunder and hundreds of led horses from the farms of Pennsylvania by noon of that day. Our cavalry force under General Pleasonton,[9] which were little better than so many mounted monkeys, arrived just in time to see their adversaries securely landed, and received by way of a compliment half a dozen shells from a battery opposite, posted in position to protect the crossing.

Thousands of dollars' worth of clothing and supplies, blankets and horse equipments were carried off to the intense gratification of their people, who I am told look upon Stuart as the possessor of a charmed life. A division of our infantry under General Stoneman[10] were encamped at this time below Edward's Ferry, not over three miles from the point of crossing, but they seem to have made little or no attempt to harass Stuart. Why it is difficult to imagine. He appears to have had his own way completely, and could not have more successfully carried out his plans than if sanctioned by McClellan himself. McClellan's headquarters at this time were about two miles back of Knoxville, a small settlement on the Potomac some three miles east of Sandy Hook. Had Stuart known its precise location and the disposition of the troops in that vicinity, he might readily have captured the general, staff, and entire escort. But perhaps he was aware of this and didn't care to molest a friend? The order to remove the headquarters nearer the river, where the body of the army lay, was, however, soon promulgated, and the semblance of danger averted.[11]

During the rest of this bright Sabbath Day Kendall and I kept closely to our quarters, intently noting and reporting the movements of Stuart's cavalry opposite, which was reinforced by a column of infantry from Lee's army to aid in any counter demonstration by us. They lay encamped a short distance back of the river, their camp fires stretching to within a stone's throw of Leesburg. In two days the forces opposite had disappeared in the direction of Lee's headquarters at Winchester, and nothing remained confronting us but their weak line of cavalry videttes.

THE INTELLIGENT CONTRABAND

A careful research has demonstrated that only five men out of a possible two hundred and fifty know how to select a colored pilgrim who shall refrain from pilgriming and be content to reside with the family, do chores, and give the balance of his time to the care of the horses. I never knew that I was a particularly hard man to please, but in the experience I have had with help of this sort, I have lost my self-respect, to say nothing of other bric-a-brac of more substantial value.

When I returned from the general's headquarters quite late yesterday . . . I was accompanied by a highly recommended African, upon whom, I had been assured, no vague or indefinite hint of a desire for an artistic meal would be wasted, or whose training in the manipulation of plain army fare into the most delectable and palate-tickling dishes had been overlooked. Of course, after this seductive phenomenon of an oppressed race had been sprung upon me, my heart seemed lighter and I hired him, for I needed just such an addition to our aggregation of morbid appetites, and was afraid the war would close before I could secure one.

His name, he informed me, was Sancho Panza, and once or twice on my way back I checked myself in an audible chuckle over the surprise I had in store for Kendall. Sancho had a shy reluctant way about him that won me more than I can tell, and when we reached the post and I found Kendall engaged in signaling, Sancho seemed so abashed that I told him to forego the trouble of preparing any tempting viands that night, as it was after dark, but to muster his reserve powers in a breakfast that would paralyze Kendall; and with this I bade him to retire.

Twice during the night I had to answer signals, and as I passed Sancho's "A" tent, I though there grated harshly upon my ears the sonorous and deep-toned breathing of my Ethiopian prize. Perhaps it was the sighing of the wind through the timber around us, or the rippling waters of the Potomac . . . that carried past me as I hastened to the tower to respond to the impatient glimmer dimly seen on the distant mountain. I think now it must have been Sancho doing the "opossum act," and audibly calculating the hours before sunrise when his presence as a chef was to be seen and felt. The last call with the torch had been answered, and at 3:30 AM I sought my blankets, overcome with the loss of sleep and prepared to reimburse my exhausted energies until with a yearning gladness I should respond to Sancho's announcement of breakfast.

The hours sped by and I awoke to find it 8 o'clock and the expected announcement still due. At 8:30 the sound of wood chopping roused me and I ventured to speak to Kendall, whom I heard moving in and around the tent, as to the delay, and was greeted with a reply that "The d——d nigger was missing," and that with the aid of our men coffee was nearly ready. I thought too that I detected, while dressing, the sound of a strange voice intermingled with those of our men, and then in the midst of this I heard an exclamation that sounded like "Great Scott," or perhaps it was a little stronger than that, adding, "Well, that's gone too!" I concluded now that I had enough clothes on, although they were very brief, and stepping outside I met the astonished gaze of our entire detachment, reinforced by the well-known features of a farmer residing nearby.

Kendall was mad clean through. His usually unruffled calm was succeeded by a scathing treatise that was splitting the air in streaks through the blue halo that encircled his form. The contraband was non-est, and with him had disappeared one of our best saddles, a bridle, and the farmer's gray mare. Sancho had probably meant well at the start, but the recommendation that came with him was a little too ponderous for him to carry, and sooner than disappoint me, had concluded to tear himself away. That was my charitable view of it, but not the farmer's, who discovered Sancho's tracks, and the next day the "nig," with a subdued and pensive countenance, was deliberating on the uncertainties of this life in a Maryland jail. . . .

With the arrival of *Tuesday, October 28* came permission to make a flying visit to Philadelphia—an opportunity that few soldiers have been known to decline—and on the following day I was in the Quaker City, fully prepared to indulge myself in the little extravagances obtainable at home but denied us in the field. On November 1, three days later, I was speeding back again, by way of Baltimore, to my post.

On the train between the latter city and the Point of Rocks I found my old chums, Captains Joe Knap and — Fletcher, Provost Marshal of Harpers Ferry, in company with General A. S. Williams, afterwards in command of the Blue Star Division of the 12th Corps.[12] The general, as those in the army well know, was an ardent devotee of distilled rye, and whether the quality was good, bad, or indifferent, [he] was rarely known to decline an invitation to test a sample. Wishing to present some to a resident here, I had purchased two bottles in Philadelphia, and when I found the trio together on the train, I concluded to open one for their especial gratification. In consideration of his seniority in rank, the general was voted the first taste; a proposition that made his eyes sparkle. How to indulge him without being observed by those around (the car being filled with private soldiers), was a question that puzzled me somewhat. I [soon] hit upon the happy expedient of examining the texture of his military cloak (an ample one which lay upon his lap), and holding it between he and the light, I enveloped his head long enough to allow him about four inches which, despite the noise of the train, could be heard gurgling down like an overflow of water in a rain-spout.

The day following my return from home found me up early and saddled [for] a ride to headquarters, whither I had been summoned by Major Myer to decide a question relative to my rank and future status in the army. This vague message, which conveyed no other intimation of the true character of the summons, naturally quickened my desire to learn more, and ere many minutes had elapsed after our breakfast of toasted bacon and coffee,

I was galloping up the tow-path to Knoxville, eager to be acquainted with the continuation of the story, the mysterious import of which was reserved by our chief signal officer until my arrival.

Upon being seated . . . I was handed a document profusely covered with endorsements, [which] requested [me] to signify, by letter or verbally, my wishes in respect to its contents. A glance showed me that the War Department was giving me the option of remaining with the Signal Corps as a first lieutenant, or of returning to the 29th Regiment in command of Company A should the commission as captain, to which I had been recently promoted, meet with my acceptance. This paper . . . had been playing hide and seek with me for some weeks in an effort on the part of Major Myer to secure my retention with the promotion added, without the necessity of requiring a decision from me. It should also be remembered that I was now being carried on the rolls of Company A as captain on detached service. . . .

Here was a highly interesting dilemma for a young man to be confronted with. Reject promotion in a company in which I had entered the service as lieutenant, and by so doing permit the next in rank to become my senior officer? He, who had been orderly sergeant under me, [should] become my captain, and I, if fortune should so favor me as to preserve my life, [should] return home with a stigma of this kind to torture my after years? A thousand times no! On the other hand, I had been with my company but three weeks in the field prior to my detail for this duty, having left them more than a year ago. I had laid aside and placidly banished from my thoughts the duties of a company officer for those that now engrossed my whole attention, the signal service, one to which I knew scores of officers of higher grades than captain had asserted they would willingly enter as lieutenant at the sacrifice of their then-greater rank.

In my vexatious predicament, which I knew was the work of a jealous malcontent in the regiment, I appealed to Major Myer, whose advice I prized most highly, determined to accept it whatever the ultimatum. His answer was prompt and decisive, and I have ever treasured it as coming from one who truly appreciated the conscientious faithfulness of those entrusted with the success of his corps. He stated that it was his wish that I should remain with him, that he had become attached to those detailed early in the war for duty in the Signal Corps, and that it would be a grievous disappointment to him, after his selection and instruction of officers whom he found courageous, capable, and of good judgment, to find them returned to their commands at a time when their experience was so essential to him as commanding officer. I was also given to understand that my declination at this time was not by any means the final settlement of the case, but with his assistance it might be yet arranged satisfactorily and the commission retained. The major's dignified frankness added to my reluctance to sever the many attachments formed with the officers and men under him, and I at once penned my reply. . . .

Thus, principally out of regard to Major Myer, I laid aside that sweetest boon to the soldier, increased rank, that eventually would have found me at the close of the war in the uniform of a field officer. The major . . . pigeon-holed my [reply] and handed me my commission, telling me to put it safely in my trunk, and delayed action thereafter. The company muster-roll appeared monthly with my name at the head as captain until the end, although I drew pay as a first lieutenant on detached service, but with the increased pay allowed cavalry officers, because of my being mounted. At the same time the first lieutenant of the company drew pay on the company roll as an infantry officer. Hence, I claim the rank to which I was commissioned, as captain of Company A of the 29th Regiment Pennsylvania Volunteers.[13]

Sunday, November 2, 1862, again marked the crossing into Virginia of the Army of the Potomac. The engineers had promptly laid the pontoon bridge connecting Berlin, [Md.,] with the other shore, a few of the troops were sent across and thrown forward as skirmishers to protect it, and today the general movement is forward . . . with the 9th Corps in the advance. Kendall and I, agreeably to orders, packed up and with our team crossed about 8 p.m., going into camp for the night near Lovettsville.

In the morning we were off bright and early anticipating an order that would assign us to a station, but the services of the Sig's were not needed by McClellan today, hence the shadows of evening found our corps unpacking for sleep at the little town of Philomont, Va.

While at Salem, Va., where we had halted for a short rest on the afternoon of Tuesday, November 4, Kendall and I noticed two artillerymen of one of the Regular batteries robbing a house and maltreating the inmates, two females. Prior to our appearance, they had secured a pile of quilts and blankets belonging to the family, and seeing us moving towards them [they] galloped off with their plunder. The owner of the place happened to ride up at this time, at once pursued them, and by promises induced them to return.

They were very drunk and insisted upon retaining the goods until the owner had complied with their demand, which was two gallons of whiskey. Kendall and I laid low and as they rode up [we] approached them on either side, and seizing their bridles ordered them to dismount. The effects of the bad whiskey they had imbibed, [combined] with the chagrin of being cornered by, as they rightly guessed, volunteer officers, made these drunken and overrated foreigners very pugnacious, and the fellow whom Kendall was detaining whipped out his saber and prepared to make a "sweeping front cut against infantry." Kendall's pistol was out in an instant, and the bold Irish Regular immediately succumbed. My gallant Corkonian[14] was not so easily brought to terms. Instead of a sabre he drew his pistol, and was about to use it when he got a stunning blow in the back from the butt of the carbine of one of my men. It took all the wind out of him, and before he could recover he was dragged from his horse into the mud. Having restored the stolen articles to their owner, we were taking the drunken loafers with us with the intention of placing them under guard when, opportunely, a corps provost marshal hove in sight and we rid ourselves of our disagreeable company.

This Tuesday afternoon we received an order from signal headquarters to move at daylight and establish a station at Snicker's Gap, where Fitz John Porter's corps was stationed, [with] instructions to keep communication open between his corps, Maryland Heights, and McClellan's headquarters at Rectortown. This, upon arriving there after a rough ride, we found extremely difficult to do until we had traversed the ridge about a half mile south of the Gap, finding here the only point from which the station on South Mountain could be seen. It was bleak and exposed to the weather, being intensely cold and windy from all directions, making it impossible to keep a fire going although there was wood in abundance.

Duryee's Zouaves, (5th New York),[15] were picketing around us, and to protect themselves from the cold they had, with the aid of their shelter tents, built some brush huts in the hollows below the brow of the mountain. These poorly served the purpose for which they were intended, but as the boys were supplied with a couple of rations of commissary whiskey during the afternoon, they managed to ward off any ill effects from their exposure. Kendall and I were forced to leave our wagon on the road in the

Gap on account of the rocky condition of the ground, and [we] were thus deprived the benefit of our tents, a loss we keenly felt. Luckily our stay here was short, or I fear this detachment of Sig's would have been found stark and stiff at their posts.

Our first night at this place was an experience that had rarely happened during my life, but [which was] fraught with portentous significance regarding the true existence of the despised poor white among his neighbors the slave owners. As evening drew near I concluded to ride back to the Gap on a foraging errand, leaving Kendall to take charge of the station in my absence, but I promised to return with a supply of provender or information as to where it could be procured. The 5th Corps was in full possession [of the Gap], and luckily the first two persons I stumbled on were lieutenants Cal Wiggins and Fred Homer, signal officers with Porter's headquarters. This was indeed auspicious, particularly as they, with true soldierly foresight, had reconciled themselves to the barrenness of this portion of Virginia and procured a supper, to which they volunteered to conduct Kendall and I with our men.

Having ridden with some difficulty on our return to Kendall owing to darkness, we all descended a path on the east side of the mountain to a cabin wherein, they averred, a supper was awaiting us, but which, upon entering, we found to be swathed in the rankest poverty, filth, and ignorance. The family consisted of several children, all squalid and dirty, living in one little room, which was all the cabin contained. An old bedstead [which] stood in one corner [and] a rickety table centre, with a bench and two dilapidated chairs alongside, constituted the entire furniture. When we entered, the family were sullenly crouching around the fireplace endeavoring to extract some warmth from the few smoldering embers that remained of the fire that had served to cook our promised suppers. Ugh! The thought is nauseating.

Wiggins had provided the food, a fat sheep taken from a pasture by one of his men, as well as the necessary coffee. The ewe had been boiled, and the pieces were smoking on a leaden platter which looked as though it had been used by the family for such purposes for many generations, and still retained some evidences of each meal. They had steamed the coffee in an old iron tea kettle, the spout of which had long since gone to the dogs, and a wooden plug supplied in its place. The beverage was served us in four rusty tin cans and a saucer, mine being in an oblong tin canister that in the dark ages contained pepper, yet retained the spicy qualities of that condiment to the extent that once or twice I was tempted to inquire whether it was not pepper-tea. One knife, a fork almost prongless, and two spoons made up the list of eating utensils (we supplied the deficiency by using our pocket knives), and the repast was soon over. The surroundings were so uninviting and destitute of the plainest household commodities that as we sat down our appetites suddenly took wing, and we with one accord exclaimed that we did not feel a bit hungry, but would take a bite just for company sake. For my part I silently shuddered at every mouthful taken, and forgot my hunger while reflecting upon the preposterous assumption of a people, living in such abject and half-famished squalor, daring to rebel against a government that exemplified all that was good, practical, systematic, and powerful, for the spectacular promises of the fire-eating South.

I had never witnessed a scene more degrading to my senses than this, even in the lowest slums of our large cities. We returned to our hurriedly built brush protection near the summit, truly grateful that our lines had been cast in pleasanter associations, and having firmly resolved that our breakfast on the morrow should possess at least the elements of cleanliness, if lacking in variety, prepared ourselves to avert the probability of freezing to death before the welcome sunrise again appeared.

At daylight [*November 5, 1862*], I was not long in seeking the headquarters of General Sykes, commanding the 2nd Division, 5th Corps, for instructions regarding the final disposition of our wagon and occupation of the station, to which the general replied that the 5th Corps would evacuate the Gap by 9 a.m. and that our position on the mountain would be untenable after that time. Our teamster was accordingly directed to proceed with the headquarter train to a point near Bloomfield and there halt and await our coming, as we should remain on the mountain until afternoon unless driven from it by the Rebel cavalry, whose videttes were then but a mile on the other side in the direction of Winchester.

Punctually at 9 o'clock the corps commenced leaving, and we retired along the ridge to the station, keeping a close watch for the appearance of the Johnnies. At 4 p.m. we could see them riding about in the Gap, and being fearful lest they should scent our hiding place, recourse was had to the uncanny occupant of the cabin (with whose shivering and lightly clad family we had supped the night before), as to the possibility of getting away without discovery. True to his Southern instincts, he was loath to part with his knowledge of the country to Yankees until persuaded by a show of authority, and a further promise of a substantial reward. He then agreed to guide us safely away that night by a secret path known as "The trap." Having retained him in our company until dusk—the wisdom of which was quite apparent considering our precarious situation and our suspicions as to his honesty—we commenced the descent, the trap referred to by him beginning a few yards below his dingy and dreary log cabin.

The moon's dim and uneven rays . . . made it just light enough through the trees to discern a narrow, winding defile that bordered the left of precipitous rocks to the level plain below. The rocks were of a whitish shade and . . . had been so nicely distributed that they bore the semblance of a falling cascade. . . . The six horses (the guide was on foot and led the column holding the bridle of my horse), followed each other slowly in this stealthy ride, scarcely a word being exchanged by us in the half-hour it required in the descent. At last our eyes were relieved, as we emerged from the thicket, by the luminous bars of light that revealed to us the clear open country, and being now assured of our safety, we recompensed the bold Virginian and put spurs to our horses in the direction of Bloomfield.[16]

South of the town about one mile back in the woods stood our team, the teamster having hailed us in the road, and alongside the team he had pitched two small tents. Into these we pitched ourselves for the night, exceedingly glad to have found such welcome shelter from the snow then fast coming down.

Friday, November 7, 1862. This was a day well-remembered by the soldiers of the Army of the Potomac, as it was the last one in which General George B. McClellan ever had command of that army. When we awoke this morning the ground was covered with snow; a somewhat unusual thing at this period of the year for the residents of Virginia, and very likely unappreciated by the Rebel soldiers from the cotton states, who have rarely, if ever, experienced . . . a genuine old-fashioned Philadelphia snow storm. It was not very deep, however, not so much so as we would rather [have] had it in order to freeze up a lot of Johnnies, but deep and cold enough to give them a biting taste of winter.

We had scarcely prepared our early breakfast, in readiness to move, when an orderly from headquarters galloped into the woods with an order for us to report without delay. We learned that this courier was the second one sent out to find us, the first having started the night before, but not returning the second had been sent forward. Captain Cushing of the 2nd U.S. Inf., now in charge of us, had concluded (after Wiggins and Homer had reported to him our exposed condition at the Gap, and after the failure of the first orderly to return) that we had been gobbled and [were] probably on our way to Richmond as prisoners, but thanks to our Virginian guide of the night before we had escaped this harassing experience and were soon enabled to reach headquarters near Rectortown and report to him for further orders.

The morning following our arrival in camp was one indeed of excitement. Those of us attached to headquarters were early informed of the removal of McClellan, which had been conveyed to him the night before from Washington by General Buckingham,[17] who also conveyed the order assigning General Burnside as McClellan's successor. The magnitude of the change caused thousands of his admirers to boldly assert their intention of quitting the service. His strong hold upon the hearts of the men was apparent at once in the noisy ovations tendered him when it became known that he was to leave, and the enthusiasm displayed exceeded all former demonstrations in his honor. They had learned to look upon him since Pope's defeat as the saviour of this army, and his removal at this time came with such a shock that they could scarcely realize the fact that they were to lose him. There was no mistaking the genuine grief and absolute and undisputed control he exercised upon their affections in the manifestations of devotion witnessed everywhere.

So thought the young soldiers at that time when the mere mention of his name was sufficient to call forth the heartiest cheers and unbounded ecstasy. The open and avowed opposition by him to the administration soon dispelled all the greatness that clustered around his standard, and evoked instead indignation and ridicule, and we saw him later stripped, in a figurative sense, of his pretend trappings—a pigmy compared to the masterly generalship displayed by those who afterwards commanded that army.

The order relieving him, and which directed him to report to Trenton, N.J., assigned no reason for the course pursued but left all to conjecture. His failure to promptly move against the enemy when peremptorily ordered to do so; his neglect to perform a duty when directed by his superior officer, the President; his disregard of the soldier's first and most important obligation, submission and obedience to those in authority [were] without doubt the secrets of his retirement. He, the exponent of enforced discipline, the dignified example in the essential rules and duties of thousands of Union soldiers, from whom he expected immediate and absolute compliance in the enforcement of methods of subordination, is removed for dilatoriness and disobedience of orders?

This was pretty rough on the "Young Napoleon" of the Army of the Potomac, but suppressing his chagrin and mortification he at once started in, backed by a glittering staff, to take formal leave of the various corps he had commanded. And this I affirm was a sad exhibition. The salutes fired, the cheers that rent the air, the tears shed and the indignation expressed, came from many true hearts of his soldier boys, and clearly demonstrated their admiration and confidence felt in him as a leader. . . .[18]

Lee, by this time, had escaped from the Army of the Potomac, and pushing through the many gaps in the Blue Ridge was now serene in his position near Gordonsville, and between us and Richmond. He knew he could not safely assume the offensive against the strong reinforcements which [we] added when the campaign into Virginia opened, hence he remained quiet, intently watching Burnside to frustrate any plans looking towards the main object, the capture of their Capital.

The prevailing opinion was that this time an attempt would be made by our commanding general to take Richmond by way of Gordonsville, Orange Court House, and Hanover Junction, striking the city on the north side; every indication favoring such, in which case the grand battle would take place on the Rapidan near the old ground at Cedar Mountain. This it seems was McClellan's favorite plan after the Peninsula failure, but President Lincoln's ideas were different, and although no soldier, his views were certainly far in advance of McClellan's, who had the benefit of a thorough military education, both theoretical and practical. McClellan had, as seen, virtually disregarded or refused to accept the plans of the President; Burnside had assented [to them, and] it now remained to be seen how successful he would be in adopting them. . . .[19]

[*On November 12, Fortescue was appointed senior officer of "Set D" (a set consisted of two officers and four flagmen), which was one of sixteen signal detachments assigned to the Army of the Potomac, and he and his fellow signal officer, Capt. Charles Kendall, received an order to report for duty at the headquarters of Gen. Orlando Willcox, who had risen to command of the Ninth Corps when Burnside became commander of the Army of the Potomac.*]

In pursuance of this, Kendall and I, with our signal party, reported at the general's headquarters near Waterloo at 10 a.m., relieving Lieutenants Hebrew and Yates[20] who returned to camp. These two gentlemen had been wedded for some time in the same set, but being of opposite dispositions were disposed to quarrel a great deal over their respective duties. This came to the ears of Cushing, [and] he wisely concluded to relieve them from this post.

We established a station at Willcox's headquarters communicating with General Burnside at Warrenton, some twelve miles distant, an intervening station being necessary on Watery Mountain about six miles north of us. Here we were kept exceedingly busy during our two days occupation of the place; messages were constantly flagged between these two headquarters, giving us the impression, from the frequency of Willcox's visits, that that gentleman, who appeared to be somewhat of a "martinet," had embraced the opportunity, while lying quiet, to work our corps under a mistaken notion that we needed exercise. However, he could find no fault with the quality and importance of the work we performed, and later seemed really desirous of complimenting us on the rapidity with which the messages were transmitted.

Quite early on Sunday morning, the 16th, we broke camp and moved to the Sulphur Springs, where after a short rest the line of march was taken up for Fayetteville, a place noted for its intensely Rebel tendencies, which under the erroneous protection given it by many of our general officers, the female portion took little trouble to conceal. Why so much consideration should have been evinced for the security of the poultry and livestock of these Rebel Virginians I never could imagine, yet frequently after a hard days march, men who should have had a much needed rest would be detailed to stand guard over the property of some contemptible Rebel whose possessions should have been taken and distributed to the troops compelled to protect it.

Many instances have come under my notice of guards being placed over spring-houses wherein the supply of pure fresh water was ample for the needs of the troops lying near, yet all would be forced to seek a stream inconveniently far away to avoid giving offense to the gray-headed traitorous owner under a ridiculously mistaken idea that his secessionism might be mollified, or else through the maudlin sympathy or cowardice of the officer granting the protection. Rebel officers have freely admitted to me that frequently our guards have protected property, at the instance of the owner, solely that it might be enjoyed by their troops who were expected along after our departure.

There were many notable exceptions to this groveling spirit among some general officers, but none that I can recall quite equal to that displayed by Generals Pope, Kearny, or Sedgwick, whose refusals to accede to appeals from these people were remarked [upon] on numerous occasions. A declination of this sort naturally soon drifted to the ears of the Johnnies and a howl would be heard about the suffering families compelled to submit to indignities by our soldiers. No officer, however, seemed more repulsive to them, or came under their ban of displeasure to the same extent than Pope, whom they derided and threatened in their proclamations without stint, even to extending their maledictions and bombastic menaces to the officers serving under him.[21]

With the reinstatement of McClellan came a return to the sycophancy and servility towards the erring brethren of the so-called Confederacy, and the troops that had recently commended Pope for his determined interpretation of the proper treatment due Rebel sympathizers discovered that while relieved of the direful consequences threatened in the southern journals had they become prisoners of war while Pope commanded, they were to again return to the practices in vogue prior to his introduction to the eastern army, and guarding Rebel property became once more fashionable.

On the morning following our stop at Fayetteville, the plan of operations marked out by General Burnside was quietly given to the signal officers in an intimation that our destination was Falmouth, Va., and orders were at once issued to prepare to start.

But I must return to that last evening to relate an "Amusing Episode," with a slightly tragic ending, that took place at a farm a short distance from this highly tainted secession village, which Kendall and I are chuckling over, and will continue so to do for many a day.

As usual we were foraging for sweets to satisfy the inner man, and as nothing tempting could be found within the lines, [we] concluded to chance it outside to a point where snugly resting among the foliage stood an inviting farm house. What seemed to us like a reluctant assent, as we

An unfortunately blurry albumen photograph of signal officers attached to the Army of the Potomac, taken sometime late 1862 to early 1863. From left: on horseback, Capt. Charles S. Kendall, who would serve directly with Fortescue during several campaigns; Capt. Lemuel B. Norton, who would rise to be chief signal officer of the Army of the Potomac; Lt. Seymour Pierce, Fortescue (with sideburns); and Lt. William S. Stryker, who served as adjutant of the Army of the Potomac's signal detachment. Seated, left to right: Lt. Frederick Owen and Lt. Norman H. Camp. Courtesy of The Civil War Museum of Philadelphia and The Heritage Center of The Union League of Philadelphia.

entered, was the greeting from a young lady in response to our inquiry for supper. [It was] a stereotyped form of expression we were not totally unprepared for in view of the snubbing met with our boys in this locality, and from the fact that we could hear before knocking, the clear plaintive notes of a lady's voice seeking consolation in the treasonable melody of "Maryland My Maryland."[22]

A sullen silence prevailed after we sat down to await the preparation of the meal, which was not broken until we politely indicated our preference for some toothsome fried chicken. There was a decided hesitancy at first to accede to our wishes, but suddenly brightening up, the lady remarked that to gratify us a chicken would have to be killed, and if we could wait, she thought we could be accommodated. Going to the door she called a sable helper on the farm and directed him to get a chicken ready, and almost immediately after went out, presumably to give further instructions. My suspicions were aroused at the apparent change in her manner from that perceived on entering, and as soon as she had passed out by the back-way I slipped to the front door where our horses were tied to a tree, and tip-toeing along the porch to the side of the house, peeped around and saw her earnestly gesticulating to a darkey who held a horse bridled but without saddle. Quickly descending the porch I walked under the cover of the trees (it being quite dark) to the main gate, where presently came Mister Darkey, quietly leading the horse with the intention of mounting it in the road.

Waiting until he had closed the gate and was about to mount I rose up and seized the bridle, [and] under cover of my pistol demanded of the black whelp the nature of his errand. It didn't take him more than a second to slide from the back of that horse and almost down on his knees in terror at the sight of the pistol, and in answer told me that his young missus had ordered him to ride hard to a cross roads some two and a half miles away, where she knew some soldiers were stopping, and to bring them right away back to the house for a couple of Yankee officers.

The lady intended holding us there waiting for supper, and perhaps some pleasant conversation during the meal, and this accounted for the noticeable change in her behavior. . . .

Still holding his horse by the bridle I directed him to bring my horse to the gate, then mounting and taking [both] he and his horse to the cavalry vidette stationed about half a mile back on the road I cautioned the vidette to keep him covered until I returned, promising to do so in half an hour.

Upon reentering the house I found the supper nearly ready and the lady in blissful ignorance of what had occurred. Kendall was entertaining her, but appeared decidedly anxious as to what had become of me.

In order to give her a taste of her own medicine I accounted for my absence by saying that I was in charge of the cavalry pickets and had been instructed to advance them about a mile further up the road where they could ambush any inquisitive Southern soldiers venturing to inspect our lines. The solicitude of that woman to hurry up the supper and get us away in order to save those whom she fancied she had summoned to be entrapped was ludicrous indeed, and as we did not care to linger any longer than could be helped supper was soon over, and paying the accustomed stipend we departed.

But wasn't Kendall surprised when I told him what had happened, and didn't we get back at a pretty lively gait to avoid any further unlooked for developments? The vidette was relieved of Mr. Contraband, and he was taken with us to camp and placed under guard for the night.

I confiscated the animal, ridden by the boy, and in the morning the "Nig" was started back home on foot bearing our compliments to his "missus" for the excellent supper she had prepared, and our regrets for her loss of a favorite bay mare.

At noon in a driving rain we reached Bealton Station on the Orange and Alexandria R.R., and halted with the headquarters train to refresh our bedraggled steeds and to stock anew our semi-famished stomachs which had been enjoying somewhat of a holiday since the feast of fried chicken of the night before. Having satisfied our craving appetites, insofar as hard tack and salt pork would accomplish it, we wrapped the drapery of our gum ponchos around us and set out to brave the Virginia mud, now rapidly increasing in depth and stickiness from the numberless wheels and horses, aided by the deluging rain, that seemed bent on drowning us should we mire at any soft place on the line of march. . . .

It was quite dark when we halted at Deep Run, and after many unsuccessful attempts [we] succeeded in dragging our wagons out of the road and into a field of the wettest kind of grass. Tents were pitched for the night and we sought consolation around the division headquarters camp fire of General Abner Doubleday.[23] In a little while coffee was boiling, pipes were lighted, and by 9 o'clock, under the soothing influences of that downiest of all pillows, the tree of a McClellan saddle, I slept the sleep of the moist patriot, and dreamed of a perpetual "Turkish bath."

At noon of Tuesday, Falmouth was sighted, not that much was seen when the eye fell upon that antique village on the shores of the Rappahannock, with its ten or a dozen rookeries, but it having gone forth that the columns would halt here for a few days, we hailed it with some degree of satisfaction, and forthwith selected a spot to pitch tents and make ourselves "To hum."

The advance under General Sumner reached this dilapidated old settlement yesterday, the 17th, but just prior to the general's arrival, Captain Ulric Dahlgren, commanding "Jessie's Scouts," a company of good riders formerly attached to Fremont's headquarters in Missouri and named in honor of Mrs. Fremont, forded the river opposite Falmouth and made an heroic dash through the streets of Fredericksburg. Without accomplishing much they gave the Johnnies a stirring up and retired to the north side again without losing any men.[24]

Just before entering Falmouth, General Burnside's order reorganizing the army was read to us consolidating the force into four Grand Divisions. The Right Grand Division was assigned to General E. V. Sumner, and consisted of the 2nd Corps, General D. N. Couch, and the 9th Corps, General Willcox. The Centre, under General Joseph Hooker, consisted of the 5th Corps, General Dan Butterfield, and the 3rd Corps, General Stoneman. The Left, under General W. B. Franklin, consisted of the 1st Corps, General John F. Reynolds, and 6th Corps, General W. F. "Baldy" Smith, and the Reserve Division, under General Franz Sigel, was composed of the 11th Corps, General Steinwehr, and the 12th Corps, General H. W. Slocum.[25]

Kendall and I were still with Willcox's headquarters, [and we] accompanied that officer to the Lacy House,[26] a fine old deserted mansion that stood upon the bluff immediately overlooking Fredericksburg. Here we composed ourselves in anticipation of an early forward movement across the Rappahannock, the only impediment to a prompt transfer to the south side being the non-arrival of the pontoon train hourly expected from Washington.

Scarcely had we made preparations for seats at the mess table of Willcox's staff, and selected suitable quarters for locating a station to communicate

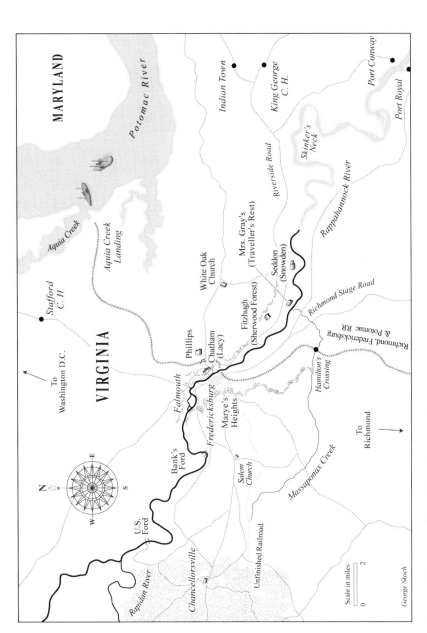

Fredericksburg and Chancellorsville, 1862–63.

with Lieut.'s Hall and Taylor[27] ([located] near the headquarters of General Sumner, at another well-known family mansion called the "Phillips"),[28] when an order came from our very changeable and extremely uneasy Captain Cushing, now in command, to report to Captain P. H. Babcock, Signal Officer commanding detachment at Hooker's headquarters.[29]

This exasperating interference with the successful workings of our corps, at times when the best results by a means of rapid communication were expected by leading generals formerly in ignorance of its obvious utility, tended to greatly discourage the subordinate officers interested in its welfare, and fomented an indifference and carelessness more observable now than when the Chief Signal Officer had held the reins at headquarters.

Having made known to General Willcox the purport of our orders, we reported to Babcock and there endeavored to extract some comfort from the contracted accommodations of a small "A" tent to which he had temporarily assigned us, that being the only piece of canvas obtainable in the Quartermaster's Department. Owing to this unpleasant beginning, I had for some time after a lively and lingering recollection of the excessively cold weather to which I was exposed. [I thus] hailed with supreme satisfaction the change to a more comfortable wall tent when, at the expiration of three days, we again saddled up and Hooker's headquarters were established on Potomac Creek below the celebrated railroad bridge.

During our stay at this camp, (and who could have then predicted its duration until the 11th day of December), I made the most of the opportunities offered and hunted up the various friends of my youth who like myself were doing service in the garb of Uncle Samuel's soldiers.

The rains were frequent, the cold weather increased, the mud grew deeper, and the want of fuel for so large a body of men caused the timber to become as scarce as home-made pies at the commissary. The well-seasoned and eagerly sought fence rails had long since disappeared, but a day or two sufficing to eradicate them completely from the face of the country. . . .

The Aquia Creek landing on the Potomac, where all the supplies were brought for the army in vessels from Washington, was a favorite spot to visit and while-away the leisure hours watching the discharge of the cargoes. On the road to the landing lay Stafford Court House, around which were camped the 11th and 12th Corps. At these headquarters were several "Sig's" with whom I often enjoyed sweet converse, that is to say, swapping army lies, a sociable game of draw, or supping a dipper of coffee with an occasional sup of something stronger.

Thanksgiving Day came and went and [there was] still no apparent change in the quietude that had prevailed since our arrival. An ominous silence was preserved at headquarters regarding our future; the rumor being that a missing pontoon train [was] left out over night, and some midnight prowler in want of a few boats took upon himself to carry home to his wood shed, [and] is responsible for our irksome detention.[30]

To fill in the time agreeably I secured yesterday, *Friday, November 28*, through the good offices of Col. Joe Dickinson, Hooker's adjutant general,[31] a pass to visit the City of Washington. [It was] ostensibly to investigate the cause of my failure to receive a new uniform ordered by express from Philadelphia, but [was] really to listen to the music and hum of civilization in that city of war memories and "Whited sepulchers." . . .

Upon arriving in Washington I received an intimation that my before mentioned clothing might have been sent to the old rendezvous at Point of Rocks, so registering at the Metropolitan for the night I composed myself, and in the morning hied me to that place.

Again was I doomed to disappointment and compelled to swallow my indignation, and though inwardly showering imprecations on the heads of all tailors, my own in particular, I prepared to devote the day with the Bassant family, and return to Washington on the morrow.

Washington! That Mecca for bediamoned female pilgrims, who, freed from the law's restraint which doth hedge their domiciles in most of the northern cities, have flown hitherward in great numbers, prepared, with the aid of their brother sharks, "the Sheenies,"[32] to fleece the unripe youth who, with his hard earned monthly pay of thirteen dollars, comes to the city to scatter it lavishly in the purchase of experience.

Washington! With its broad muddy principal Avenue, filled with army teams, lumbering artillery and recklessly riding cavalrymen, the horses and mules sinking half-way to their knees and the wheels half-way to the hubs in mire. The stranger approaches the city filled with veneration for the stately grandeur of the buildings devoted to government purposes, which his mind has pictured from the many published descriptions as equaling in gorgeousness those of the famed cities of the Orient. But once within its shadows, how changed the scene, how commonplace the edifices.

The Executive Mansion and its distinguished occupant, around which cluster the memories of a line of Presidents, is the cynosure of all eyes. Surely nothing can exceed the interest that centres here, as well as in the few old stately departments that surround it and from which emanate the daily official bulletins that tell of the heroism of battle or direct the movements of the armies and navies.

But turn your back upon these and any northern city can boast of finer structures than are here represented in the dwellings and stores. No northern city, however, enjoys the unenviable distinction of such an unprecedented outpouring of vice and crime as now throng these thoroughfares. Women with hectic complexions and blonde hair, lolling in the procession of open barouches that line the avenues, or scattering their invitations to the brilliantly lighted houses, convey to the mind of the stranger the belief that the brothels of the world have been drained of this class to prey upon the boys who are here to defend the flag.

Soon tiring of the hypocrisy of those whose sudden acquisition of wealth had raised them to a plane somewhat above the average soldier, and not desiring to mingle with the thieves and gamblers who crowded the corridors of the hotels, I decided on Tuesday December 2nd to return to the comforts of my wall tent among the troops, [away] from the horde of blacklegs[33] to the congenial companionship of the mess tent and camp fire.

Embarking on the little steamboat at the foot of Seventh St. for another delightful ride on the Potomac, I reached Aquia Creek at 2:30 p.m., and this time secured, on the train, a seat among the freight destined for Falmouth.

Among the boys returning to duty were a number of convalescents who were directed to find accommodations on the platform cars already loaded with barrels of salt-horse or sow-belly, and on these the boys seated themselves, the chines,[34] from the rough jolting, making deep inroads upon the under side of the legs resting thereon. When we arrived at "Stoneman's Switch," the boys stiff and sore helped each other down and were engaged in rubbing the creases out of their legs, when a chap who had remained on the car said, "Boys, just see how tender the heads of these casks look." Then passing his hand gently over the head of the one he had sat on, said, "Do you know I've got the top of this barrel so d——d sore, I can hardly touch it."

Upon my return to camp I found the weather extremely cold, and every article of bed-clothing in our possession [was] needed to cover us after retiring. The days were spent in the different quarters around blazing fires, the Centre Grand Division staff of Hooker vying with our signal party in the fund of anecdote. . . . Our detachment consisted of Captains Kendall, Pierce, and Babcock, and Lieuts. Fred Fuller, Clarke[35] and myself who, with an equal number of staff, including the jovial Captain Motley of the 1st Massachusetts Cavalry,[36] commanding the escort, made the time pass merrily by an animated flow of spirits that enlivened the evenings gatherings, and diffused a grateful warmth even though the lack of sufficient covering dispelled it and substituted a chill after "Taps" were sounded.

Motley was a splendid fellow and possessed the rare but happy faculty of winning, by his geniality and courtly ways, the good opinions of all those in whose society he united. His sincerity and bright honesty of character was in striking contrast to many I had served with especially a few from New York City, whose manners, smacking of the "parvenu,"[37] offensively estranged those forced by a stern military duty to serve with them. Motley never forgot that a military uniform was invariably the garb of a gentleman. . . .

CHAPTER 7

FREDERICKSBURG

DECEMBER 3-31, 1862

*eluctantly assuming command of the Army of the Potomac, Ambrose
Burnside abandoned McClellan's line of advance along the Orange and
Alexandria Railroad and instead moved southeast to Fredericksburg on the
Rappahannock. His plan was to cross the river there and advance on Richmond
along the Richmond, Fredericksburg, and Potomac Railroad before Lee and the
Army of Northern Virginia, who were west of the Army of the Potomac in and
near the Shenandoah Valley, could move to counter them.*

*Burnside's advance reached the river opposite Fredericksburg on Novem-
ber 17, but due to miscommunication, the bridging equipment he needed to
allow large portions of his army to ford the Rappahannock was not at hand.
The first boats began arriving just over a week later, but even when the full
complement of pontoons and stringers was available at the end of November,*

he waited two additional weeks to attempt his crossing. Lee, given ample time and opportunity to confront the Federals, marched east and settled in on the heights in back of Fredericksburg, awaiting Burnside's next move. Hampered by weather and indecision, Burnside finally crossed the river on the night of December 11–12 and prepared for a two-pronged attack against the entrenched Confederates.

Posted at various positions in and around the city during the fight, Fortescue's most trying experience came the day after the battle, when he was ordered to man a signal post in the cupola of the city courthouse, in full view of the Confederates posted on the heights beyond.

There could only be one answer to the innumerable questions that be-set the officers of the Signal Corps, who were mistakenly supposed to be the repositories of all the secret intelligence the commanding general possessed, and that was, "we really do not know when the contemplated movement will take place, or at what point an assault will be made."

The pontoon train, although late in arriving, and through no fault of the engineer officer in charge, had been here for some days, and the impatience to learn something official regarding the general's intentions increased with every hour. It is a characteristic of the average soldier to be impatient and complaining under a stress of imaginary disappointment, but to bear the pangs of privation and exposure with an heroic fortitude if the outlook admitted a promise of success.

To the rank and file McClellan was still a favorite, towering above his successor, or prospective successors of the Army of the Potomac, like a colossus, fostered as his claims were by political admirers at home, through the press, and by certain shoulder-strapped rank. These men, who were well-known, were desirous of playing the heroic as devotees of their idol by threats of resigning, and were not in this unmindful of the odium of voluntary retirement in the face of the enemy, and [of] the consequent humiliating penalties for so doing.[1]

We had now been confronting this secession town, with the Rappa-hannock flowing peacefully between, for some three weeks, and the time designated for crossing [was] still securely locked in the breast of the Commander in Chief. It was apparent to all that Lee's army in its en-tirety occupied the heights in the rear of the city, and were daily adding to its impregnability by redoubts and traverses. [These] obstacles could have been avoided and the smaller forces then concentrated easily overcome had General Burnside permitted General Sumner's advance, on November 17th, to cross, as advised by Sumner, the river being fordable at Falmouth at that time.

The pickets of the two armies now patrolled the opposite banks within easy rifle-shot of each other, and frequently bet—when not under the eye of an officer—for the interchange of reciprocal courtesies. This practice on the picket line had been repeatedly indulged in on former occasions, when the opportunities were more favorable by reason of no intervening river. [It was] always [undertaken] at risk, owing to its positive prohibition by the commanding general in order to prevent information of our strength or disposition of the troops leaking out, [which was] usually the true reason for the enemy's desire for a half-way interview, though professedly [for] a swapping of supplies only.

The methods adopted here were less liable to detection and precluded the possibility of secrets being conveyed because of the width of the river, and the absence of boats, hence nothing went to their side but newspapers, coffee and sugar, and nothing came back but newspapers and tobacco.

The boys would take a small keg in which vinegar had been issued to them by the commissary, and having cut a square hole in the side, would weight it directly underneath to prevent its rolling in the water. A piece of stout twine [would] previously [have] established communication by means of a large float; the string was then kept concealed beneath the surface and tied to projecting roots or reeds at the water's edge.

Each side had a signal denoting the absence of the officer in charge, and when this was seen the keg would be freighted and pulled over and back, the twine being made fast to nails driven in either end of the keg. I have seen them sitting around a picket camp-fire in the most friendly intercourse, engaged in story telling or venting their opinions of certain general officers, when at a signal that a shoulder-strap was approaching, [they would] quietly creep away to their respective posts and resume an appearance of watchfulness and firmness, highly dangerous thereafter to any of the same little circle who should venture a fraction beyond their respective lines.

Being young and susceptible to the charms of the softer sex it was a source of chagrin, accompanied by some degree of envy, to many of us accustomed to frequenting the bank of the river to see the streets of

Fredericksburg daily crowded with the profusely decorated uniforms of the rebel officers promenading with the lady residents and enjoying their hospitality. Of course we had our amusements to divert the mind, but in the entire absence of female society, a few residing within the army limits being utterly uncongenial to us, the best we "sig's" could do was to bring our long range glasses to bear upon the promenaders and thus fancy ourselves mingling with the gay throng.

The scenes presented to us this Wednesday morning, December 10, told plainly that the imperturbability under which this army had been resting was to change to that of the most exciting character and assume a gravity the like of which we had never before experienced, even under the popular and exaggerated McClellan. Orderlies with dispatches could be seen galloping in the direction of the various corps and division head quarters, premising an early forward movement upon the rebel columns now serenely and securely fortified upon the heights in full view of our troops. The place of attack was the problem that all strove to solve, and in the absence of definite knowledge every eye was centered upon the pontoon train as the significant guide to a solution of the forthcoming point of assault.

Late in the afternoon, the horses having been harnessed to the wagons containing the boats, the train commenced moving, and after reaching a point on one of the roads opposite the city but about half a mile back from the river, halted and remained there for the night, leaving all still in doubt as to its exact destination.

Captain Kendall and myself had reported to Captain Cushing in the afternoon in response to a message to that effect, and we were notified to be in readiness to move at 2 o'clock next morning. At that hour we arose and found the troops in motion heading for the plains in the rear of the Lacy House. This large open flat, which descended in a gentle incline from the river bluff, was the point of concentration, and concealed from the glasses of the enemy the vast body of men that halted in echelon awaiting the completion of the pontoon bridge. Swallowing a hasty breakfast we mounted and at 6 a.m. reported at General Burnside's headquarters at the Phillips House.

The morning was damp and chilly and a dense fog hung over the country entirely obscuring the city from our view. It lifted, however, after an hour or two and revealed to Kendall and I, who had proceeded to the river, a long line of our batteries, some two-hundred pieces, extending along the bluff as far as the eye could reach. Looking down from the Lacy House to the foot of the bluff could be seen several boats made fast in an attempt to build the bridge. After these had been anchored in position, they were abandoned owing to the deadly fire of the [Rebel] sharpshooters, the smoke from whose rifles occasionally floated from one of the many rifle-pits along the opposite shore or from the corner of a house. Several dead pontoniers lay around upon the bank and upon the uncompleted bridge, and in a thick mass of reeds to the left of the boats were hidden a number of our sharpshooters, who, as a head was shown, silenced one more of the annoying Mississippians.[2]

The engineers finding it impossible to proceed with their work, (as the hulls of the boats were being made a target as well as those handling them), the batteries were ordered to open, those immediately in front to direct their fire at the houses and rifle-pits, those on either flank to shell the works on the heights, the distance and length of fuse having been very accurately ascertained.

For five hours these guns thundered on, the cannoneers working with extraordinary rapidity. General Hunt, Chief of Artillery,[3] was constantly riding from one point to another, now directing the fire of this battery or changing the position of that, his never tiring and aggressive manner presenting to the men a bright example of alertness and endurance well calculated to achieve the best results.

About 3 p.m., during a lull in the firing by a battery of brass smoothbore Napoleons to the left of the Lacy House, Kendall and I rode over to them to interview the captain commanding, and to offer him the benefit of our long-range glasses in observing the execution he was doing. The guns had become overheated and fouled, and the men were drenching them with pails of water and swabbing them out preparatory to resuming. The cannoneers of the first gun on the right of the battery dried their piece and rammed down the sack of powder, and were about placing in a solid shot when the sergeant sighting the gun was horribly mangled by a similar shot from one of the enemy's cannon on the heights. The sergeant had been stooping with his eye on a level with the sights, and was in the act of straightening up when their solid shot struck the breech of his gun and hit him almost squarely in the face, leaving but a vestige of the head upon the body.

Simultaneously with this shock, my horse suddenly threw his head up, and upon examination I found that a sharpshooter's bullet had nearly severed my bridle rein a few inches from the mouth of the horse; the whiz of the ball and snap upon the rein causing him to momentarily rear backward. The ball that killed the sergeant passed on and frightened, but did not injure, the horses of the caisson, and they . . . suddenly wheeled and dashed across the plain towards the mass of troops waiting there with arms stacked, the bounding carriage creating an uproar and confusion, terrific for the moment, until the capture and return of the team.

It is marvelous that any portion of the buildings fronting the river, all of which were filled with sharpshooters, remained intact after the iron hail that was hurled against them. Time after time the city was on fire at several points, remote from the other, but the incessant roar of the artillery and bursting shells, joined with the sharp fire of the infantry and flying bricks, precluded any efforts to extinguish the flames.

It must have been a very hell itself to the rebel sharpshooters trying to conceal themselves, and yet a few of the inhabitants, as we afterwards discovered, were hidden throughout the bombardment in the houses. During the heaviest shelling an old colored woman appeared at a window waving a white cloth tied to a pole, but [she might] as well [have] tried to stem the river's current with an oar [than] to prevent the concentration of the firing wherever the smoke from a sharpshooter's rifle was visible.

Through all of this activity and excitement along our line of artillery, the rebel batteries replied shot for shot, and there were some tall efforts to gain cover as three or four shells would burst simultaneously overhead, indicating a concentrated fire upon that point.

Orderlies dashed by from headquarters with messages to the engineers every few minutes, but nothing could be accomplished until Barksdale's sharpshooters had been driven back, and this the batteries seemed unable to effect. This state of suspense lasted until 5 p.m. An entire day [was] wasted and still nothing around that unfinished bridge of boats barely floating from the bullet perforations but the dead engineers and horses stretched upon the damp shore. At that hour, with darkness fast approaching and all filled with anxiety and mortification at being retarded by a thin line of sharpshooters only, General Burnside appeared on the ground to the right of the Lacy House, where lay the 2nd Division of the 2nd Corps, and riding to the commander of the division, General Howard,[4] called for volunteers to cross the river.

Two regiments of Baxter's Brigade, the 19th Massachusetts and 7th Michigan,[5] at once stepped out and were double-quicked to the shore, when with a yell they sprang into the boats and with poles pushed into the stream amidst a galling fire from the riflemen. Thousands had rushed to the bank to witness this preliminary movement of a gigantic struggle, and every eye was now bent upon these boats. Shot after shot struck down those poling or at the oars, but their places were quickly refilled, and slowly, steadily they appeared on the opposite shore.

The Rappahannock being narrow, only a few more efforts are required and they have reached the south side. As they clamber from the boats and charge up into the streets their musketry fire is drowned amidst the yells of our troops now thronging the banks. Soon one prolonged shout goes up as we see them desperately fighting hand to hand, while from every window the curling smoke from a rifle indicates that their ranks are thinning. God! nerve, and spare them is the prayer that is uttered as we see them dart past and disappear beyond the street leading from the bridge. The point is now gained and the engineers are rapidly laying the bridge, while another regiment, the 20th Massachusetts, frantically poles across to reinforce those who have cleared the rifle-pits and houses.

The bridge is quickly completed and over goes the 2nd division, regiment after regiment, until all of these have rejoined the brave fellows who preceded them. The streets are cleared, the town is practically ours and naught remains of the boasted chivalry along the river front but their dead and dying, who with ours thickly cover the sidewalks.[6]

Shortly after the advance of the division entered the town, Kendall and I crossed under orders to establish ourselves near the division commander's headquarters and, if practicable, open communication with the north side of the river. Failing in the intense darkness of the night to find a suitable place for the purpose, we rode up into town on a tour of inspection, and our curiosity came near leading us into a snarl from which the direst consequences might have ensued.

After reaching the third intersecting street from the river and seeing none of our troops, we were about to proceed still further when my bridle was quickly snatched and the person in a subdued voice excitedly inquired who we were. Responding in a low tone with the information, we were told to hastily dismount and keep under cover of our horses, [because] the house on the opposite corner was filled with sharpshooters, into whose clutches we had nearly ridden. I had felt my horse stepping very carefully as we moved along and imagined it to be on account of the debris in the streets from the shattered buildings that he was trying to avoid, but upon dismounting and stooping close to the ground was surprised to find the street strewn with dead men. I was told by the officer who halted us that the hottest encounter had taken place at that corner.

Leading our horses by the bridles we got back as rapidly as possible, though we experienced much difficulty in doing so from the number of bodies laying in the streets, the sight of which kept my horse in a constant tremor, compelling me to frequently straighten up and soothe him by patting, before I could get him past them. One of those pointed out on the sidewalk was the Chaplain of the 16th Mass., the Rev. Mr. Fuller, who had shouldered a musket and fell fighting with his regiment.[7]

At the next corner, being then out of range, we breathed a trifle easier and we bid the officer a good night with a deep sense of obligation for his timely warning, and returned to the pontoons and re-crossed to the Lacy House.

This old residence was rapidly filling with wounded from the fight in the streets, and [because] Kendall was solicitous about his Boston friends in the two Massachusetts regiments, we entered, but remained but a few minutes. The operations of the frigid and passionless surgeons were of a nature ill-calculated to preserve in one the requisite amount of courage in view of the heavy battle about to take place, hence we gladly beat a hasty retreat to the cooler atmosphere of the open piazza.

[*December 12, 1862.*] At reveille next morning we again crossed to the south side, in pursuance of orders, and proceeded to an old brick grist mill opposite Falmouth, there to open communication with Colonel Hays, commanding the right of the reserve artillery on the north bank.[8]

Captain Cushing informed me, when starting, that an attack was premeditated against their works on the extreme right, and it was feared that the smoke would either prevent the artillery from firing, or so obscure our infantry as to endanger them from our shells. To obviate this we were to leave the mill and advance with the infantry line, and take a position where the signal officer with the batteries could read our flag and thus divert their fire from our own troops.

The divisions were now crossing in a continuous line and taking positions in the streets running parallel with the river preparatory to advancing. As large bodies move slowly, night came on without a conflict, although the batteries kept up a hot fire all day. Many of the enemy's guns were directed at our pontoon bridge, of which they had excellent range. It was entirely hid from them by the houses, but its location was accurately known, and as the bridge at no time was clear of men and horses but generally crowded, many were killed during the day.

Simultaneously with our crossing in front of the city, two bridges had been laid by General Franklin some two miles below, and the 1st and the 6th Corps were reported crossing to commence action on the extreme left in the morning.

Our detachment had first-rate quarters in the mill for the night, the deserted dwelling attached to it, standing in the rear on the bluff, furnishing an ample supply of excellent bed-clothing. This dwelling was raked with shot in every room. On the first floor a shell had struck a book-case, and the entire room was littered with mutilated literature. A large old-fashioned bedstead on the second floor had stood directly in the line of a round shot that went through the room exactly across the centre of the bed, its course being sharply defined on the quilts. Had any person occupied that bed when the shot entered, they must inevitably have been disemboweled.

Saturday, December 13th opened with a fresh and nipping air. A fog still enveloped us and hid the enemy's works from view, but after an hour or two it lifted, leaving the atmosphere bright and beautiful. There remained but a few troops on the north side, and these were now coming over in small detachments at long intervals. Their appearance on the bank, before descending to the bridge, was plainly visible to the rebel gunners, [and] was the signal for them to open, which only ceased when the last man would disappear.

About 10 a.m., a hitch occurred between ourselves and the signal officer with Colonel Hays's batteries, and after a fruitless effort to get a message to him, I decided to ride to his station, the better to have him clearly understand Captain Cushing's orders to us.

This tour, which proved to be an expensive one to me, would take me along the streets near the river, thence across the pontoon, and up the river road, below the bluffs, to the extreme right of the artillery. I found the streets nearest the river "en masse" with artillery and infantry; so hid, however, by the houses that the town, from the enemy's works, had a deserted appearance. Care had been taken to avoid, as much as possible, any exposure of the men on the streets running at right angles, and here, in this crowded condition on window shutters and doors wrenched from their fastenings, they had bivouacked for the night.

Halting for a short time to greet the boys of the 2nd Corps, those of the 2nd Brigade, 2nd Division being composed entirely of Philadelphians (notably Colonel Owen commanding the brigade and Ferd Pleis his adjutant general),[9] I continued to the bridge and crossed, the enemy's artillery practice, in their efforts to strike that structure, carrying away an occasional chimney or tearing up and scattering the shingles of the little white-washed houses bordering the river.

As I reached the north side of the pontoons I was met by an army newsboy with a huge pile of papers on the pommel of his saddle, and [I] stopped him to get a supply, the excitements of the hour interposing no obstacle to the pressing desire for the news of the day. Having secured a copy of the New York Herald, Baltimore American, Philadelphia Inquirer, and the Washington Chronicle, the sheets usually circulating throughout the army, I started along the river road at a fast gallop. About half-way down [I] found my way barred by a fallen tree through which I was compelled to lead my horse by separating the branches—an embarrassing obstruction to encounter as here the shells striking and ricocheting upon the water entered the bank just above the line of the road.

When about to remount I instinctively felt for my pocket-book and discovered that it had departed. Twenty-six dollars, my entire possessions, and not a cent left. Having concluded my errand I returned to the bridge in the vain hope of finding it, but alas, I was penniless. After purchasing the papers I had slipped it down between myself and the saddle, instead of in my hip-pocket—a sorry plight for a patriot with a roving commission like mine own.

On entering the streets again I found the troops preparing for an advance from the rear of the town instead of on the right as explained by Cushing, and at once drew from this an inference that Burnside had either changed his plans since yesterday or had no settled plans at starting. . . .

To reach the works our troops would have to move beyond the town and then cross an open plain [of] some five or six hundred yards, a barrier intervening in the shape of a deeply dug ditch, impassible except by the aid of ladders. This was covered by a well-constructed stone wall some two hundred yards on the other side, behind which were concealed a heavy line of infantry. Fifty yards in the rear [of this] commenced three lines of fortifications, rising tier upon tier, consisting of redoubts, traverses and earthworks of every description, so arranged as to completely sweep this plain and enfilade each other in case of the abandonment of either.

Between 11 and 12 o'clock noon General French's division of Sumner's Corps, supported by Howard's [division], advanced to the works at a double quick. As the solid columns of these divisions emerged from the streets to the plain, the batteries opened upon them from several points. After deploying (which consumed much time owing to the many small rail fences on the outskirts), the order to advance was given. The line preserved an unbroken front until within a hundred yards of the ditch, when the execution became so great that it was found impossible to proceed further.[10]

The plunging fire from the batteries was tearing great gaps, [and] for twenty minutes our men stood up boldly exchanging shot for shot, but flesh and blood could not stand such slaughter. Slowly they fall back, shattered and broken to reform, [while] other divisions arrive: Hancock, Humphreys, Getty and Sykes.[11] They form and advance and again this avalanche of flame darts from a thousand points into the faces of these brave fellows. The troops strive but in each effort they are obliged to retire. For four hours this dreadful scene is enacted, then Hooker orders forward his reserves. A lull takes place; the reserves form and advance with the lines; and again the deafening roar is heard from the batteries repelling the attack. The whole line wavers; it is too much, and they fall to the ground to escape the fire when night closes the scene. . . .

The horrors of that gloomy and dispirited night to those in line lying prone upon the field, surrounded by hundreds of dead comrades, can be but faintly imagined by those who have never underwent the trying and awful ordeal. To be compelled to hug the ground on a bleak winter's night chilled to the bone, with no covering to shield you, while on every side is a mangled corpse of a friend, and a like fate imperils your own life if to relieve your aching limbs there is the slightest exposure of any part. To be completely and utterly disheartened by the wasted lives that were so buoyant but a few hours before, to have the spirits so affected by the confusing opinions of those in whose hands are held the fate of your own and those who have thus far been spared, is an experience that few have had except the campaigners in the Army of the Potomac, and even they dare not reflect upon a probable like recurrence without a shudder.

[*December 14, 1862.*] The Sabbath morning broke upon a scene presenting the acme of suffering and anguish. Thousands of the wounded and dead dotted the plain from the rear of the houses up to the very stone wall. Our lines of battle still lay upon the ground behind a gentle rise of ground that hid them from the sharpshooter in front but not from the batteries encircling the heights. How quiet everything seemed compared to the thunder and rattle of yesterday. Now when an occasional shot broke the stillness, it drew the attention of every eye as the wreath of smoke curled from the rifle that yesterday would have passed unnoticed. The houses in the town were filled with the wounded, and scores lay around the streets exposed to the damp and piercing cold.

These scenes were presented to Kendall and I as we looked from the Court House steeple in the centre of the town where, through an unforeseen circumstance, we had been ordered at sundown of the day before.

It is deeply humiliating to refer to this "unforeseen circumstance," involving as it does disgraceful cowardice upon the part of a member of our corps, especially in the face of the many letters of commendation from generals in the field, telling of individual acts of bravery of nearly every member, and yet it remained for one of our number, Lieutenant Yates of a New York Reg't., to stultify his record by conduct so censurable that only a prompt resignation at the dictation of the chief signal officer prevented his escape from a summary dismissal.

Yates, who gloried in the fact of his former membership in Ellsworth's crack Chicago company,[12] was ordered to the Court House steeple in company with Lieutenant Fuller during this battle—a post of observation of extreme danger to the officers and men stationed there by reason of its bold and unprotected prominence from the enemy's artillery in front, as well as from the flying missiles of our own batteries in the rear, but of the greatest importance to General Burnside.[13]

Twice during the heaviest fighting of yesterday, Captain Fisher, when visiting the steeple, found Fuller alone there faithfully executing the duties required of him and endeavoring to discharge those required of Yates, whose absence he was unable to account for. Upon instituting a search for the missing Yates he was found, by Fisher, on both occasions, ensconced in the doorway of the jail in the rear of the Court House securely protected from the enemy's flying shells. Fisher was not to be deceived, and a sharp reprimand sent Yates, the first time, back to his post. When after an hour or two he was again discovered shirking, he was peremptorily ordered to hand in his resignation, or prepare for a Courts Martial, so deeming it the better part of valor to return home without the disgrace of a dismissal, we were rid of the worthless cur.[14]

We found Fuller occupying a space octagonal in form and some sixty feet above the ground. The steeple stood to the left of the structure which was built with its side to the street, the entrance to it being immediately underneath us on a level with the pavement, the whole being enclosed by an iron spiked railing. Our space was on the top or fifth floor and about four feet in diameter. To reach the first floor above the street a long ladder was required. This led to a trap door over which hung a large bell that, with its supports, filled nearly the entire space. Above the bell was a heavy upright that extended to the top of the steeple, and was apparently the main support, the outer brick-work being but a mere shell. On four sides of our apartment were round openings for clock dials, some two feet in diameter, but as the dials had never been placed there, in consequence of the poverty of the county, the spaces answered excellently for the purposes of observation, care being taken that the enemy did not observe us moving past the opening looking towards their works. The opposite one, toward our lines, was used for flagging.

For this purpose a small flag was used, two feet only, with a short pole that prevented the flag being seen when waving it on either side of the steeple, and yet [it] permitted the messages being easily read at the Phillips House by the signal officer with Burnside across the river.

Here in this coop seven of us, three officers and four flagmen, watched carefully every movement visible within their lines and reported it promptly to Burnside, the rumor having reached us that he intended again assaulting the works during the day.

Leading from the city and crossing Marye's Heights on its way to Orange Court House is a plank road, out which many of the troops advanced under cover of the few houses. On the right of this road, about midway between the city and the heights, was a small cemetery containing, among others, a monument erected over the grave of the mother of Washington. The ground here sloped towards the city and hid the troops lying in line completely from the works. About 3 o'clock in the afternoon, two companies of infantry became tired of lying in the mud, and concluded to make a break for the town, regardless of the fact that retreat was

A portion of the city of Fredericksburg, shown in this detail from an Alexander Gardner photograph. Taken from the Federal side of the Rappahannock River, the rounded cupola of the court house from which Fortescue and his fellow signalmen communicated is shown at right, to the left of the church steeple. Courtesy Library of Congress, Prints and Photographs Division.

more dangerous than to remain. At a signal they arose and started pell mell for the city. Scarcely had they risen when a line of fire opened on them from along the stone wall. The running of this gauntlet of hundreds of shots would have been ludicrous but for the mortal suffering inflicted upon many of them. One after another could be seen pitching headlong from a shot, and until night closed down upon us we could see many of them writhing in agony with no possible chance to afford them relief. It was sad to witness their terrible plight and hear their moans fade away into silence without the chance to help them.

Just after this fusillade had died away my attention was called to two men on the left of the plain, who while lying down were endeavoring to place a wounded man on a stretcher near them. After much labor they succeeded in getting the helpless man comfortably placed, and summoning courage, they each rose, grasped a handle, and started for the rear, trustfully hoping that the nature of their errand would shield them from the deadly aim of the sharpshooters. But flushed with victory, and careless of the humanitarian boldness of the two men in an effort to succor a comrade, the shots from the wall rang out and soon brought down the leading carrier. The other dropped a moment afterward and we thought him mortally hurt, but in a few minutes [we] observed him creeping slowly away until about fifty feet had been covered, when he started at full speed and reached the houses safely.

During the day vague rumors had come to us of the enemy's intention to bombard the city with cannon balls heated for the purpose, but plainly Lee would not attempt so desperate an undertaking, however brilliant to him might be its results. They did give us some excitement early in the afternoon by opening some of their artillery, the shells from which, for fifteen or twenty minutes, were distributed over the city and in the direction of the pontoon, after which they quieted down again.

[*December 15, 1862.*] On Monday the morning passed without a resumption of the firing, scarcely a shot breaking the stillness or disturbing the situation of masterly inactivity forced upon us in consequence of the proximity of their lines, and the necessity of keeping up, at any cost, a vigilant outlook. About half past three one of our officers observed a group in a small redoubt, a little to the right, intently watching us with a glass. The interest so suddenly shown for us was manifestly occasioned by the asinine conduct of an officer of our army, one Captain Long, of the Provost

Marshal's Department, who, finding himself at leisure, had clambered up to our perch for a birds-eye view of the situation. Before we were scarcely aware of his presence, [he] had obtruded half of his body out of the round opening facing their works, and with the full glare of the sun beaming upon his resplendent uniform was calmly surveying the batteries.

It was rather late now in the face of the mischief done to remonstrate with him upon his oppressive stupidity, or to suggest in any way a diversion in our favor, but we did express in rather plain terms our indignation at his conduct in revealing our presence there and in intruding himself upon us.

We were morally certain now that our post of observation, although carefully concealed from the enemy for the past three days, was untenable, and with much anxiety and impatience awaited the outcome of their sudden interest in us. And we didn't have to wait a great while either before they were seen to run a gun back and a cannoneer step into the embrasure with a shovel for the purpose of widening it, the better to bring the gun to bear upon us.

Having completed these preliminary details they commenced loading, and ere a moment had elapsed a curl of smoke arose followed by the crash of a shell that struck the further corner of the Court House, tearing up the slate shingles and throwing down a large gothic-shaped chimney into the street, where it killed two men and wounded some others of the Regular infantry temporarily quartered on the pavement. The shell continued its course into the Court House where lay a number of wounded, several of whom it injured before it lodged. While the gun was being reloaded, our intruder, who had already commenced his descent, could be seen frantically endeavoring to disentangle the chains of a huge pair of Mexican spurs that had caught on the rounds of the ladder below the bell.

We now began to be cognizant of our extremely dangerous situation, the exact range of which would be ascertained after a couple of shots, and the propriety of abandoning the steeple was proposed by Kendall. Our further remaining and attracting the fire would be hazarding the building, now converted into a hospital, along with the greater number of the houses around it, a contingency that might involve disaster to disabled men and therefore contrary to military custom, it being an axiom in warfare that no urgency should jeopardize the inmates of a hospital, either by firing into it or doing that which would draw the fire of others. But the orders of the commanding general were imperative and although we had been importuned by many surgeons, who usually exhibited a dread of being under fire, to leave, our unanimous opinion was that it was the bounden duty of all to stick to the observatory, unless the fire became too hot to continue there.

In less than two minutes the second shot came and burst with a shriek within a few feet of our round opening, sending a shock through the whole structure. Several general officers could now be seen in the street wildly gesticulating and threatening dire consequences if we did not at once vacate the steeple, so deeming their expostulations too serious to be disregarded we prepared to descend, first dispatching an orderly to General Burnside to acquaint him with the fact. . . .

As the first man was disappearing through the trap door to the top of the bell, a shell struck the latticed window of the same floor, and exploding, tore out the brick-work some two feet on either side, but fortunately did not injure him. The next shot went through the spire above the top floor and lodged in the street beyond, and the last burst before it reached the building, doing no damage.

By this time our entire party were safely on the ground floor besieged by a frantic horde of surgeons who seemed to be growing warmer upon the subject of using hospitals for signal stations. At this opportune instant Captain Fisher appeared and appeased these wrathful dispensers of calomel and quinine by rehearsing General Burnside's orders to him, an authoritative argument so obvious as to be unanswerable.

Once clear of the crowd, Fisher quietly informed us that we might leisurely take our way to the other side as the entire army would retire about 9 o'clock and abandon the town to Lee.

This information, coming as it did with such positiveness, is conclusive to my mind that Fisher obtained it from Burnside himself, who at that time, 5 p.m. of the 15th, had fully decided to fall back to the north side again. How then can we reconcile the statements of some of the leading generals, especially those allied by the closest intimacy to Franklin, when they assert, and I have heard them remark it, that they were ignorant of Burnside's intention to evacuate the south side on that evening, the 15th, but supposed he would hold the town and possibly make an assault again upon their works the next day? Certainly they are either untruthful or Burnside made a confidant of the chief signal officer for the benefit of our corps, to the exclusion of several trusted corps commanders.[15]

While the shelling was going on the rumors of firing the city with hot shot were again disseminated through the hospitals. Those of the wounded able to walk were started off, and a corps of ambulances hurriedly began the work of transporting the more desperately hurt. The streets soon became quite animated with those who lost no time in making for the north bank of the Rappahannock.

While awaiting the return of the orderly we had dispatched to the general, we betook ourselves to an old hotel-stable on the next street above. Here on the porch of the hotel lay many men who had died in the building, and [who] were now arranged in rows for burial. Among the number was one that attracted more than usual attention; a drummer boy whose sweet though sad expression, now blighted in death, drew a sigh as we remarked upon his youth and uncommon neatness. The fatal ball had entered his side just below the pit of the left arm, leaving a clear clean round hole there, without discoloration of bruise or blood outside. He had removed his shirt and raised his arm over his head to be operated upon, and had died in that position. He looked, as he lay there with lusterless eyes, as though [he was] showing us the deep ugly wound in his side, and imploring [us for] relief from the dreadful pain he was suffering. A thought of the loved ones at home, who would wearily watch for his coming, yet never see his boyish face again, impressed us distressingly as we turned from the scene to retrace our steps to the river.

The work of our party in this campaign was now at an end. With the exception of one station at the abutment to the bridge on the south side which must retire before daylight of the following morning, none of our corps would be needed, so taking our wagons to a cleared space near the railroad at Falmouth station, we pitched our tents and were soon soundly wrapped in slumber after the season of intense fatigue and excitement all had undergone.

By daylight the last of the army had re-crossed, and the bridges [were] taken up. At 10 o'clock last evening the order for the evacuation was communicated to the troops. An officer rode along the picket-line and in a whisper informed each individual of its purport. Upon the receipt of the order, each one was to slowly fall back to the reserve, which in turn was to execute a like movement to the grand reserve, and in this manner re-cross.

The scheme, with a single exception, was admirably carried out so quietly that the rebels were not aware of our retrograde action until daylight disclosed the fact to them. As soon as the discovery was made they mounted their works with a yell and shortly afterwards occupied the town and their old posts along the river. A detachment of the 91st Penna., under the command of Major Lentz, were overlooked by those entrusted with the duty of notifying the pickets, and only succeeded by the merest chance in eluding the elated Rebs and reaching our side from opposite Falmouth.[16] A delay of a few moments and even the skillful handling of the Major would not have prevented their capture.

And now, forgetful of the sacredness that should have animated the breast of the soldier for his dead antagonist, reveling only in the joyous anticipation of the indiscriminate plunder that awaited them, [there] commenced a scene of pillage and ruffianism that would have disgraced the barbarian of old. Pouncing, like so many vultures, upon the bodies of our dead that strewed the plain, they stripped them of every thing even to their shirts, and left them lying, mercilessly exposed, without the rudest burial. Said a well-known spectator within their lines, "The morning after the battle the field was blue; but the morning after the Union troops withdrew the field was white."

The night of our withdrawal was intensely cold and the dead froze to the ground, but the greed for spoils from the bodies of the Yankees, even though it were well-worn clothing, blood-stained and frozen, was a prize too rich to be overlooked, and it was only after Burnside had communicated by flag of truce and received permission to send a burial party over that our noble dead were interred in their last resting place. The detail of our men for this service were several days performing their work before the last man was laid beneath the sod. . . .[17]

Not a word is said of the jealousy towards Burnside that existed among a few of the leading generals upon the left, although the defeat, to those on that portion of the line who had the facilities for knowing the state of feeling of the corps and division commanders, deemed it clearly attributable to that cause. It has been decisively shown that while all of the forces on the right, which consisted of ten divisions, were brought into action, but two divisions were hotly engaged upon the left, notwithstanding there were eight under Franklin, and the burden of this exhibition of mismanagement, provoked solely by a spirit of envy, is attempted to be laid at the door of Burnside, whose now waning prestige under the weight of disappointment is already foreseen. Manifestly the odium should rest where it rightfully belongs, and Franklin undergo the same rebuke meted out to Fitz John Porter for his McClellanism at the Second Bull Run battle. . . .[18]

[*Fredericksburg was an unqualified disaster for the Army of the Potomac and the Union cause. The Federals lost nearly thirteen thousand men, while Lee lost less than half that number. Though he was ill served by several of his subordinates, Burnside took the blame for the reverse. "For the failure in the attack I am responsible," he wrote several days after the battle, but it was of little consolation to Lincoln, who was distraught. "If there is a worse place than Hell," he was overheard saying, "than I am in it."[19]*

Whatever faith the army had in their bewhiskered commander prior to the battle dissipated. "There is no disguising the fact that confidence in Burnside is gone," lamented a New York colonel. "There is scarcely an officer of intelligence here but that feels it. It is a most deplorable state of things."][20]

Wednesday, December 17th, 1862. Our camp at Falmouth Station having been but a temporary one, we received orders this morning to strike tents and move with Hooker's headquarters to Stoneman's Switch on the Richmond, Fredericksburg, and Potomac Railroad. Here in pursuance of instructions a detailed report of the services performed by each officer of our corps during the recent campaign was made and submitted to the chief signal officer.

On the morning of the second day following, I received a letter from father informing me of the death of Uncle Harry C. Fortescue, his name having been published with the list of those killed in the furious onslaught of Saturday morning last. I immediately sought the location of the camp of the 126th Pennsylvania Vols., in which he was a lieutenant, and there learned the particulars attending his death from eye-witnesses in his company.

The regiment had been lying in the mud in line of battle for several hours, and being ordered forward to storm the enemy's works, were in the act of rising when a volley was poured into their ranks from the stone wall. A small number dropped from the fire, among whom was Harry, a minie ball entering his head just behind the left ear causing instant death. Two or three of the company carried his body to the rear and laid it beside an old barn, where, after removing his sword and valuables, they left it and returned to their posts. This was the last they saw of it.[21]

I returned to camp and prepared an application to Lieut. Col. Taylor of General Sumner's staff,[22] who had charge of the truce boats, for permission to cross and secure it for transmission north for burial. I intended if consent was given to take with me one of the men who had carried the body to the barn, and avoid any difficulty which might be experienced in ascertaining its precise location, as well as the trouble of identification in consequence of the removal of the clothing by the enemy.

My request was refused by Col. Taylor upon the ground that all applications of this character required the approval of the War Department before parties in quest of bodies could cross. This being the extent to which I could prosecute my inquiries, I dispatched a letter home containing the particulars and suggested the prompt filing of an application to the authorities with subsequent telegrams to me of the success met with.

It was found upon further inquiry that, owing to many difficulties encountered in consequence of the multitude of applications on file at Washington for the same object, nothing could be done before decomposition set in; this, with the knowledge that he lay within the enemy's lines, forced the relinquishment of the effort to secure it, and his body was left to repose within a short distance of where he fell, a most honorable death and burial; that of a soldier upon the field of battle.

What a man wants to do about this Christmas time of year in camp is to solemnly rise in the morning, peep out between the flaps of his tent, and commune with nature. That is, the kind of nature Virginia furnishes. Dancing torrents all around the outside of your frail habitation, with moist rheumatic vapors floating around inside, to be supplemented a few hours later by the feathery snow-flakes that send chill after chill chasing merrily down your spinal column, until you have reached that degree of coldness supposed to exist only in the latitudes adjacent to the Polar regions.

If I were to trust to earlier observations, I would sincerely vow and affirm that this identical sort of weather has been dealt out to the good citizens of Philadelphia in past years, but without the concomitants that make a soldier's life so cheerful, the alluring comforts that go along with a canvas dwelling. What with the whistling and penetrating blast outside, and the green smoldering faggots within that require constant blowing to keep them from going out (thereby loading the atmosphere with smoke so dense that every one sits literally weeping) it takes a man with a Christian spirit so prodigious that if he is not a trifle careful he will find little trouble in deteriorating from the choice and elegant diction of the Sabbath school teacher to that of the toughest bar-room manipulator of morning cocktails.

He can sit around in the tent, shrouded in the fragrant haze that thickens with each minute from the entire lack of ventilation, and shiver and think of the bells— those clear Heavenly chimes of his childhood, and the holly sprigs and berries so gloriously pictured by Dickens, and then let his mind go back in deadly horror to the poor boys sleeping beyond the river there, mangled and torn as they were in the piercing, searching cold, struck down within the shadow of saintly Christmas Eve.[23]

The holidays were fast receding. A period now mournful indeed, and crowned with the ghastliness of yonder heights, that left no pleasurable memories to us of the Divine occasion, or that could be turned to veneration for the kind, forgiving and charitable time so dear to all the world.

New Year's Day was near at hand. Perhaps it might be the last for scores of us youthful defenders of the Union. It was therefore the craving of a fulfillment that persuaded me to take a few of the boys into my confidence through an elaborate gastronomic surprise. . . .

To this end I sent a letter post haste to a friend of mine in Washington, on December 29, to buy and forward me promptly a pair of fat ducks with the necessary accompaniments nicely boxed, so that a few intimates, as invited guests on the closing night of the year, might enjoy the hospitality of the Senior Officer of Set "D." In all respects, I am pleased to say, the project was an entirely satisfactory one. The ducks arrived in good season, New Year's Eve, were stuffed and roasted, and under the combined attack of four such rapacious appetites as Pierce, Fuller, Kendall and Jerome, soon disappeared. The greater part of the night was then given over to wishing the old year, with its disasters and disappointments, a hilarious farewell, with the hope indulged that the termination of the incoming one would find us enjoying good health, no missing limbs, and a Country reunited and prosperous.

CHAPTER 8

WINTER ON THE RAPPAHANNOCK

JANUARY 1–MARCH 27, 1863

*A*lthough he had no way of knowing it, the hopes Fortescue expressed for the success of the Union cause would not be realized for nearly two and a half more years. The defeat at Fredericksburg and the weeks that followed it marked a low point in the fortunes of the Army of the Potomac, and the quiet period after the battle led many in its ranks to despair as they reflected upon what they had passed through and speculated about their future. "Our large army has met with defeat after defeat, and yet we are always boasting of superiority," wrote a New Hampshire surgeon. "When will we see ourselves as we are?"[1] This introspection also led to finger pointing, and many officers in the upper ranks of the Army of the Potomac were consumed by scheming and conspiracy (indeed, as consumed as the lower echelons were *by dismay and uncertainty), as a number of McClellan's supporters, disgusted with Burnside's handling of the Battle of Fredericksburg, actively sought their commander's removal.*

Burnside, with Lincoln's half-hearted approval, attempted to move against the Confederates again by advancing up the east bank of the Rappahannock River in hopes of crossing it at Bank's Ford and turning Lee's left. The movement, which became known as the Mud March, began on January 20 (Fortescue did not join in until the early morning hours of January 21), but a rainstorm that had commenced at nightfall on the twentieth halted the Army of the Potomac far short of its objective. Burnside ordered the army back to their camps on January 22, and three days later he was relieved, replaced by the supremely self-confident Joseph Hooker.

January 1st, 1863. The opening of the year of 1863 finds us still facing the armed forces of rebellion with the same doubts and crafty enmities besetting us, but with the same firm and patient conviction that in the end the struggle to enforce obedience and the authority of the Government must inevitably be a triumph for the North, and the difficulties overcome, which now doth hedge us about.

How very few of the many thousands of mounted men attached to this large army ever had experience with horse-flesh prior to their becoming soldiers. This thought has often flashed upon me when seeing the vast columns of cavalry in motion, made up largely from the young men of our northern cities, who prior to their inception were unacquainted with the back of a horse. And the wonder has been at the admirable showing they make compared with the cavalry of the rebel army, who are credited with a life-long knowledge of that noble and docile quadruped.

The remarkable precision shown in drilling and maneuvering would belie the thought that they were inexperienced prior to their muster-in, were it not for the fact that the average man requires but a brief period to achieve that familiarity with the saddle necessary to fit him for the mounted service.

Although I confess to a partial unfamiliarity with that noble animal prior to that time, and must have exhibited a miserable nervousness when my brute was introduced to me at the close of my examination and assignment to signal duty, yet the magnitude of the work set apart for those marshaled under the banner of Major Myer enforced and quickened them in the management of that most devoted and faithful servant of man to the extent that within a very short space of time all had acquired a proficiency equal to the roughest rider trained from boyhood.

Strange is it too how a dumb animal, particularly the dog or horse can, by the wonderful instinct of the brute creation, attach itself to the human heart, and in no profession is this friendship between man and beast so obvious as with that of the soldier. On several occasions when the pitiless storms were raging this winter and the shelter of the pine boughs, rudely roofed over an improvised stable, inadequately shielded my horse from the blasts, have I taken him inside my wall tent for the night, fastening him, upon one side, by tying a rope tightly between the poles while I occupied the cot upon the other, a kindness rarely attempted on account of the erroneous idea of injury from hoofs but the true appreciation of which I fancied I could detect in the eye of my horse.

A fatality highly dangerous to my companions in the saddle seemed to cling to me whenever an outing or visitation to friends in other camps was suggested that threatened, at one time, to deprive me of the association of my brother officers through fear of accident, so common had the occurrences become.

The first of these happened one afternoon shortly after the beginning of the year to Lieutenant F. J. R. Collin, Ass't Quartermaster of our Corps,[2] when he and I accepted an invitation to visit the headquarters of General Sedgwick, for an enjoyable time with Ned Pierce and the staff.

Collin had a very fine bay mare, and wishing on our way back to impress me with some of her remarkable qualities, put spurs to her and started off ahead, reminding me that I should ride leisurely and take in her many brilliant points. A few rods ahead the mare came to a depression in the road, and in trying to clear it stumbled and pitching forward and rolled over Collin, leaving him lying there a wreck of his former beautiful self, while she bolted riderless to the camp.

This was a sorry and undignified disappointment to Collin, and seriously ruffled his confidence in the mare, for besides permanently wrecking a new uniform into shreds, it left him with a rupture of the intestines that necessitated surgical attendance with the temporary use of a pair of crutches, and very likely tended, by those cunning little twinges peculiar to a misplacement of one's interior, to harass his slumbers through the balance of his life.

I led him into camp seated upon the back of my horse, where I had succeeded in lifting him, a spectacle, with his forlorn and desolating look, fit to make the gods shake with suppressed laughter.

A week or two later, of a delightfully bright Sabbath afternoon, another ride was projected by Lieut.'s A. M. Wright[3] and Stryker, and we freshened and brushed up, with cheerful anticipations of an easy canter. . . .

About a mile from the quarters we struck a long stretch of corduroy road made necessary by the miry condition of the country, as well as to insure the prompt transit of supplies, and filled with a wild infatuation of our skill as horsemen we recklessly touched up our chargers and broke into a gallop. A movement so fraught with fractures and dislocations should have been shunned by three [such] intelligent Anglo-Saxons as ourselves, but with an exhilarating abandon we continued to urge on our now excited animals, the only thought of each being the out-distancing of his companions.

In turning a sharp corner we were confronted by two privates of a battery riding deliberately along in the same direction, wholly unconscious of the mad pace of the steeds now almost upon them. Before we could rein in to a slow trot on the slippery logs forming the roadway we collided with their horses, throwing Lieutenant Wright, who rode on the right of the party, out of his saddle and over into a field; myself, in the centre, up onto the neck of my horse where I clung, losing the control of both stirrups; while Stryker, on the left, fortunately saved himself by throwing his right leg over the back of his horse, but badly scraped the leg of the artilleryman he was passing. Stryker, seeing Wright's horse still dashing on with an empty saddle made after and captured him, while I, finally dismounting, went to Wright's assistance. Finding him insensible we carried him to the cabin of an aged colored Virginian, and with the aid of hot stones to the soles of his feet, soon restored him to consciousness. He never fully recovered from the shock to amount to much as a signal officer, and was shortly thereafter relieved from that duty and returned to his regiment.

These two interesting episodes, occurring within so short a period of each other, gave me something of a notoriety as a "Hoodoo," which clung to me with such a deep pertinacity that members of the Corps, when about to start out would tremulously inquire "If I was going too?"

It gradually wore off, however, and my shattered ambition was regaining its standing as a safe card to draw, when in an unguarded moment I was persuaded by Cal Wiggins to spend an evening again at Sedgwick's headquarters and help the staff discuss the merits of a new brand of cordial just received from Boston. At a late hour of the night, overcome by fatigue from the warmth of the discussion, we mounted to return, and had nearly covered the two miles between their quarters and our own, when encountering a ten feet wide ditch, which in the darkness I mistook for three feet only, I put spurs to my horse and urged him to jump. When about to make the leap, he saw on the opposite side a column of cavalry approaching, and instead of nobly responding to my spur he balked on the brink, landing me on my head and shoulders on the other side, my feet going into the mud and water. Seeing me safely landed and relieved of my weight, he impulsively jumped over me, and disappeared among the many horses of the cavalry moving along. It was now my turn to be assisted to the saddle of another horse, and [I was] led to the signal station occupied by Wiggins at the Fitz Hugh Mansion,[4] where I spent the balance of the night, my fall fortunately leaving no bad impressions except a temporary soreness.

This midnight adventure, affecting as it did the person of the "Hoodoo" himself, banished completely the spell hanging over the rest of the Sig's—as they affirmed—and that gulf which threatened to isolate the writer was closed over. Their freedom from accident as equestrians, at least while in my company, [was] again absolutely assured.

For the best part of three weeks after the opening of the New Year we did literally nothing except to lay around and indulge to the full our fancies in works of fiction, or moralize upon the uncertain specimens of weather produced in this region. I don't think that any one can patiently enjoy and do accurate justice to this subject—the roads—at this season of the year in Virginia, as can the patriot who does business in canvas quarters. Whether it be the shivering infantry sentinel with the lock of his rifle carefully covered from the moisture by the cape of his great-coat; the cavalry vidette, slowly riding and ever and anon retracing his steps on the extreme outpost; or the lonely signal detachment straining their eyes at the glass to decipher the waving message or variation of the enemy's designs, it is to each the same unchangeable vicissitude of season from which little consolation can be found. When the storms beat the hardest and the fogs thickened the atmosphere, precluding the transmission of messages by flag or torch, and enforced retirement to the tent, then everything was subordinated to the ravenous appetite for literature.

I had my favorite authors, and who has not? In poetry, Byron and Tom Hood; in prose, Charles Dickens, Bulwer and Eugene Sue. How often have I wrapped my blankets about me when the fire was low and fuel scarce, and under the soothing influences of a meerschaum pipe, read and re-read the works of these distinguished writers. The active life of a soldier in the field, and the limited means of transportation, combine to interfere with the purchase and accumulation of books, hence the necessity of re-reading the few at hand, although the subject may have become threadbare, the matter thoroughly digested, and the taste satiated.

On *Wednesday, January 21, 1863*, commenced that ever memorable and discouraging campaign known as the "Mud March." For a few days previous to the 20th, the weather had improved sufficiently to warrant the success of active operations if skillful handling could be assured; but on this night a cold and driving rain storm, with sleet, set in, swelled the creeks and rivulets to rivers, and rendered the roads impassable. We had been directed by Cushing to move at 3 a.m., and had made all preparations that evening intending to retire early and secure as much sleep as possible, but at ten o'clock the rain was beating with such violence, and our tent leaked so badly, that we abandoned all thoughts of sleep and resolved to brave it out huddled around our little camp-stove. At half past three our horses, which had been piteously winnowing from exposure to the fearful elements, were rubbed down with wisps of hay and saddled, our tents— what was left of them—were struck, and we mounted amid falling torrents prepared to move.

The greater portion of the army had started late in the afternoon and evening of the 20th, and were moving in parallel lines up the river roads when the storm commenced, all heading in the direction of Banks Ford,[5] a few miles above Fredericksburg. At daylight we passed along the lines of Hooker's Grand Division, strung out for miles, wallowing through mud and mire, the men wearily staggering in the furious gale that pelted in their faces and drenched them to the skin.

The many horses and teams had cut the clayey soil so deeply that wagons and artillery were stuck so tight that an additional six mules failed to budge them. The pontoon boats had been moved up the river before the rain set in and parked about half a mile back of the ford, in the rear of a dense woods, to screen them from the lynx-eyed enemy.

We arrived in the vicinity of the ford at 8 a.m., bespattered with mud and chilled to the bone, just as the order was issued to get the pontoons nearer the river bank. A few were moved with little difficulty, but the mud getting deeper as each team went over it, it soon became a veritable "Slough of despond." A light wagon upon which rested a boat could not be moved although twelve horses were harnessed to it, [even] with the addition of a full regiment manning stout ropes attached to either side.

The shouting and swearing of the men while tugging at the ropes, the lashing of the horses and spattering of the mud, combined with the fury of the storm, rendered it one of the most exciting and discouraging spectacles I had ever seen. Failure was depicted on every countenance from the chaos of confusion that met the eye.[6] The recent terrible slaughter at Fredericksburg had left its impress so forcibly upon the army that all were filled with gloomy forebodings.

The soil upon the opposite side of the river, had we succeeded in effecting a crossing, was even worse than upon ours; for with the addition of lime there it was transformed into quagmires through which it were impossible to advance, even had the way been clear of obstructions, in the shape of fortifications similar to those on the heights below.

It was 11 o'clock in the morning, while awaiting further orders in a small piece of woods near the ford, that I saw General Burnside approaching with a single member of his staff only. He was walking his horse slowly through the soft watery-like paste that extended almost to its knees, and had reached the timber where we stood when an orderly, seeking the general, came from an opposite direction galloping furiously. He came upon the general so suddenly that to avoid running him down he was obliged to quickly check the animal, throwing him back upon his haunches. The planting of the fore feet of the horse so solidly sent great splotches of mud flying, thickly bespattering the general's face and uniform. At any other time the orderly would have been severely upbraided for his recklessness, but Burnside, whose expression had a tinge of despair at the failure and hopelessness of the campaign, was too sick at heart to offer a word of reproach. Calmly wiping the mud from his eyes, he read the dispatch, returned the receipt to the orderly, and rode on.

About noon an orderly whom we had dispatched to Captain Fisher with the information that we had reached the ford and were awaiting his

The Mud March, January 21, 1863. Sketched by Alfred Waud. Courtesy Library of Congress, Prints and Photographs Division.

pleasure returned with an order for us to proceed to a place called "Ballard's Farm," some two and a half miles up the Rappahannock River.[7]

This farm stood in the centre of a piece of land around which the river formed a horse shoe, the opposite bluffs on either side being dotted with rifle-pits and manned by their pickets, completely enfilading every portion of our position. The distance across the neck of this diminutive peninsula was some three hundred yards which brought the opposite shores, owing to the narrowness of the stream, only some four hundred yards apart, so that their pickets could easily call to each other across the ground we occupied. They had also posted their artillery so as to sweep this neck rendering its occupancy, either by the rifle or large guns, extremely unpleasant and dangerous. Not a cover of any description affording protection from their fire was apparent excepting an old barn, under the shadows of which we stationed our flagman and arranged the telescope, having an excellent view of the station at Scott's Farm below,[8] and of that on the bluffs overhanging Banks Ford, to either of which we communicated by signal.

No troops of ours were within a mile of us excepting a six-gun battery of 10 Pdr. Parrots, out on the point overlooking the river, which Capt. Smith, Chief of Artillery of the 3rd Army Corps,[9] had posted to rake any flanking column of the enemy attempting a crossing, a movement considered highly probable owing to the excellent condition of the ford here; a contingency which it was a part of our duty to guard against.

The Ballard family living on the farm consisted of a very old man, his wife, and several grown-up children, two of whom, a young man and girl about 18 and 20 years, appeared to me to be marked with more than an ordinary form of dementia. As usual in this land of the F.F.V.'s,[10] everything about the place indicated destitution; the result of extreme indolence and dependence upon the black help. From this I hesitated at first to inquire for meals during our stay, as there seemed to be little for a single person to subsist upon, least of all [from] a family of this size, but upon application I found them in possession of provender, so the display of a greenback soon gained the old lady's consent.

Lieutenant Camp[11] and I (Kendall having departed a day or two before on a leave of absence) then made our horses comfortable in the barn and ensconced ourselves on the parlor floor. The parlor, as they termed it, was of the usual type met with in this uncultivated waste of unkempt dignity now over-run by hated Yankees. [It consisted of] a room about twelve feet square, a worn-out scratched and tuneless piano, a leafless table, and three Windsor chairs. [Also], a floor bare of carpet and littered with green pine wood for several feet around the fire place, upon the hearth of which lay a few expiring sticks.

The female contrabands, who failed to conceal their delight at the embarrassment of the family when in our presence, tried to add to our comfort by putting in the middle of the floor a faded ticking poorly stuffed with corn husks. This was more than we had expected and so we didn't complain when this relic of antiquity was dragged into the room, but hailed it with mingled veneration and respect on account of its hallowed associations with the earliest settlers.

Scarcely had we concluded our arrangements with our aged hostess when she launched a tirade of abuse upon the Washington authorities for arresting her old man the day before and conveying him to the guard house near Falmouth. A polite intimation to this high-toned ruin that a continuance of such language would consign her to an apartment similar to that of her husband had the effect of restraining her vituperative twaddle, and she was docility personified, at least during our enjoyable stay.

It was developed that General Burnside, anticipating some deviltry from the natives of this section, and to prevent any communication with the enemy respecting his movements, had, before issuing orders to start, quietly sent a detachment of cavalry to arrest every male resident along the river for twenty miles. A considerable squad of these aiders and abettors were therefore collected and placed under a strong guard at the head quarters of the Provost Marshal, where they were kept in ignorance, of course, of the cause of their arrest until the campaign closed.

On *Friday morning, January 23,* our friends of the battery received orders to limber up and return to the vicinity of Banks Ford, leaving us quite alone. An isolated situation truly! The enemy's pickets on almost every side and no opportunity, owing to the heavy mist and mucky weather that prevented signaling, to keep ourselves informed of the intentions of our army. At 11 a.m. I determined to ascertain the condition of affairs and endeavor to find our wagon which had thus far failed to reach us, so taking an orderly with me I rode back to the ford. Here a sight greeted me of which I am sure history furnishes but few examples. The army was literally and firmly fast in the mud. Upon the roads leading in the direction of Hartwood, entire divisions were hewing down the timber and corduroying [roads].

The wagons, pontoons, and batteries had commenced moving slowly back by being lifted with their burdens on to the portions corduroyed, and were thus keeping up with the men felling the trees. Whole pieces of woods stretching for miles thus disappeared every hour. My wagon, a light four wheeled one, had been lifted to the side of the road and was now standing sunk to the hubs, where I was forced to let it remain.

I encountered many of our general officers, upon whose faces were depicted utter dismay and heart-sickness at the fruitlessness of their labors. A conviction of bitter despondency seemed to pervade the entire command and the anticipations for the future of our Country looked blacker than ever. With a deep feeling of sadness and regret over the causes which had rendered the movement so abortive I returned to the farm and awaited the order to abandon the station.

The night had far advanced, and being now alone with my four flagmen, Lieutenant Camp having gone to headquarters, I deemed it advisable to vacate the farm house and retire from the neck of land the better to prevent surprise, while keeping up a post of observation. A wooded knoll some two-hundred yards back of the main road was selected, and to this I moved about 10 p.m., first posting a picket with instructions to keep a sharp lookout.

About 2 a.m. we were hurriedly aroused by our guard who reported hearing voices in the direction of the farm, which he was positively certain came from a detachment of Johnnies who must have crossed at the ford, as no troops of ours had come by the road. Our horses had been saddled and the signal equipments properly strapped ready for mounting. I directed one of the men to hold the five horses while I, with the three others, made a reconnaissance to the edge of the timber.

A ray of light could be seen reflecting from the farm and several voices [were] heard, but the darkness prevented us seeing what manner of persons they were. Being no longer in doubt as to the wisdom of having withdrawn from there when I did, I concluded to lay quiet and await further developments. The time became tedious after a while owing to the cold and damp ground, and one of my men asked permission to creep a little nearer to assure himself, promising to return in a few minutes. He had scarcely gotten fifty feet from us when I heard him exclaim, "Halt, or you're a dead man!" In another instant a reply came, and then a shot rang out, followed by a cry of pain, and my man came running back to us with a hurried exclamation to get away as quickly as possible. He said that he had fired at a man after commanding him to halt, who instead of obeying, had called to his squad, "to hurry; that we were in the woods."

Rushing back to our horses we hastily mounted and were soon clear of the timber, [and] on the open road. As we left the woods several shots followed us but we were too far distant in the darkness now to fear any danger. I learned later from the contrabands in that vicinity that a squad had crossed the ford to capture us, and that one of them was taken back the next morning dying from a shot he had received from a Yankee the night before.

As the early dawn peeped out we found the roads leading towards the river, near which many of the troops were met returning to their former camps, [and] our apprehensions as to the barrenness of Burnside's designs was now fully confirmed. At many places along the river road between Banks Ford and Fredericksburg our boys were jeered by the Johnnies over their dismal failure, a sign board at one point conspicuously announcing "Burnside was stuck in the mud."

It now became a matter of serious import as to whether General Burnside was to retain the command or not after his two discouraging attempts to dislodge General Lee. The experiment of conducting aggressive operations in the face of conflicting elements had proven a misfortune that few men could have withstood. It was evident to us that there had been a stormy scene between the grand division commanders and Burnside, and that news of a startling character was about to be disclosed. That he had been maligned at Washington by some of his subordinate commanders, and his generalship censured was apparent from the tone of certain prominent journals, whose correspondents were "Entre nous" at the Departments, and whose adverse comments Burnside could not bear.[12]

These rumors, which also coupled the name of a prominent officer of the Western Army to succeed Burnside, culminated in a few days after our return to camp in a sweeping general order styled "No. 8," which we saw for the first time in a copy of the New York Herald; it having been, so stated, surreptitiously obtained for that paper by someone connected with the War Department. In it General Burnside recommended for dismissal Major Generals Hooker, Brooks and Newton, and Brigadier General Cochrane. It also asked that the following officers be relieved of their commands: Major Generals Franklin and W. F. Smith, Brigadier Generals Sturgis and Ferrero, and Colonel Taylor of General Sumner's staff.

Of course the President would not consent to the approval of this wholesale order, however much he may have coincided with Burnside with respect to some of those named, notably Franklin, W. F. Smith and Sturgis, whom I am sure, from my observation, were heartily detested by the greater majority of the soldiers of this army. The President reminded Burnside, with whom there was much sympathy, that these general officers had differed with him in opinion only and were therefore not amenable to the charge of insubordination.

At his own request General Burnside was relieved and the President named General Hooker in his stead. Also [relieved was] General Sumner, [who] refused to serve under Hooker, with whom he had previously had some misunderstanding. General Franklin was relieved from the Left Grand Division, Baldy Smith from the 6th Corps, and General Cochrane then resigned. Of the last three a good riddance. [Their departure was] thoroughly appreciated by the boys, as I can truthfully aver. . . .[13]

Burnside went west taking with him his old 9th Corps, leaving under Hooker seven full corps commanded as follows: 1st, Reynolds; 2nd, Couch; 3rd, Sickles; 5th, Meade; 6th, Sedgwick; 11th, Howard; and the 12th, Slocum, thus abolishing the Grand Divisions.[14]

General Hooker assumed command of this army January 27, 1863. On the day prior to this event I was vividly reminded of the heretofore neglected necessity of preparing for the soul's salvation by an acceptance of the Divine faith, through an invitation to dinner at the table of one whom I had heard frequently referred to as the "Christian Soldier."

Lieutenant Fred Owen[15] of our corps and myself, deeming it peculiarly fitting that we should be provided with a supply of our national currency in order to maintain our credit and successfully cope with the extravagant reminders received weekly from the commissary and sutler for table supplies, paid a visit, the only thing we could pay at this time, to Major Alvin Walker, disbursing officer at Falmouth,[16] who kindly handed over, after receiving our vouchers, a very welcome two month's salary.

With this earthly blessing to improvident patriots, i.e., fat pocketbooks, we strolled over to the headquarters of Maj. Gen. O. O. Howard to pass some idle moments with Captain Owen, a brother of Teddy and ordnance officer on Howard's staff,[17] who, after permitting us to sample some of his superior "regalias," invited us to stay for dinner.

We were thereupon conducted to the large mess tent and sat down to a substantial repast in company with the general, his staff, and six clergymen. The general's reputation for pronounced religious views were widespread, and I knew he courted the society of those clothed in the robes of the Master. I had expected to witness some evidences of this before my departure, but must confess that I was simply unprepared for the extreme array of clerical enthusiasts presented, and the theory propounded by them for conducting the war.

A blessing was asked by one of the elderly ministers before we commenced the attack upon the edibles, and at its close the general's servant prepared his food by cutting his meat, etc., so that he could conveniently eat, the general having lost his right arm at the battle of Fair Oaks. The conversation was then taken up by the clergymen and the general, and the subject of Christianity in the army and the various means essential to bring about a religious fervor among the troops [was] freely discussed. In their opinion the highest satisfaction to a soldier should be in outwardly following Christ, all other perfections being otherwise forbidding and foreign to his preservation and success.

Many of their remarks, I fancied from their glances, were directed at the staff and us unconverted guests. But with all their benign and amiable dexterity in handling the subject, so convincing as they thought, I was still far from being persuaded that the boys would take them seriously. It was indeed a capital dinner, both gastronomically and spiritually considered, but to us young bloods, a very, very solemn one.

From February 3rd to the 16th, I enjoyed a leave of absence which enabled me to renew many old associations in Philadelphia, with whom I had been in correspondence, and from whom I parted with sincere regret.

Shortly after my return to duty I visited the camp of the 73rd Penna. Vols. at Stafford Court House, in pursuance of an injunction from Mother to deliver to Brother Joe, who belonged to that regiment, a package made up by her of the necessaries of life. I found him in good health and fair condition considering his foreign surroundings. It was a mystery I could not fathom how a boy, comparatively, being a trifle over sixteen then, could connect himself with a regiment composed almost exclusively of Germans and show no signs of discontent. They were attached to the 11th, a German corps, and even when away from his regiment [he] heard very little spoken but the language of that country. They had performed rather good service to this time, and he was correspondingly happy.[18]

The principal services rendered by me, for some time on, were in aiding to keep open a line of stations connecting the headquarters of Gen. Hooker with the lowest point on the Rappahannock consistent with safety. The present military administration seemed to be largely guided by a policy of inaction since the retirement of General Burnside, hoping therein to profit by the deplorable example set by that general in his unsuccessful wrestle with Virginia mud and await the more picturesque spring to again tackle the wily Lee.

My post, in company with Lieutenant Hill,[19] was at the Seddon's House, so-called from the name of the family who occupied it, who were closely related to the rebel Secretary of War. This was one of the finest residences along the river, of modern build, the third of a line (the Fitz Hugh Mansion being the second) that stood upon the bluffs commanding a view of the Rappahannock River south of Fredericksburg.[20]

These were the aristocratics, the real sure enough F.F.V.'s. No bogus "pore white trash," posing as pretenders, about them. They owned their niggers and displayed a spirit of independence quite refreshing to us "Mud Sills."[21] Their plan of government, when they made us invaders hunt our holes, was to be a revelation to all existing nations. The old car of progress was to be yanked along at a rate of speed that would have made the eyes of the outside people of ancient Greece bulge with admiration.

Come to think of it, I fancy that our mode of conducting signal operations at night made some of their eyes bulge out with trepidation. We had our glasses fastened to a pillar on the front porch, and on the lawn, within a few paces, was stationed the flagman. For many reasons we preferred the roof of this porch at night when swinging a torch, the roaring blaze of which, in close proximity to the chamber windows, was well calculated to strike terror to the dwellers therein.

These quasi-liberty loving slave holders delighted to be known as residents of the soil that held all that had been mortal of the Father of his Country, and yet rolled as a sweet morsel under their tongues the royal titles of their counties on either side of this neck of land, King George and King and Queen. There was not a Union man or woman among them, all being bitter, rabid secessionists, and each family had its representative in the rebel army.

The location of the Seddon's House rendered its occupancy as a signal station one of great peril from surprise. It was more than a mile outside the infantry pickets, but [was] covered by the cavalry videttes along the river bank, each of whom had a beat of about a quarter of a mile, where this distance presented an unobstructed view.

It was a matter of astonishment to us that no effort was made to capture us during one of the many stormy nights of this winter, when the cavalry vidette must have sought some welcome shelter as a protection for himself and horse. When the weather moderated and became mild it was not an infrequent thing to see dozens of [Rebels] in the water swimming; a few venturesome ones occasionally crossed to our side and playfully chased each other around on the grass when our vidette had ridden slowly to the end of his beat.

Our wonder at being unmolested arose mainly from the fact that [the Rebels], having a knowledge of the importance of the site as a point of observation, did not try to thus make it untenable by capturing those sent there, or by constant harassment bring about its abandonment. It was the only point from which the station below could be seen, and also afforded an excellent view of the forces and works opposite. The entire range of country from Fredericksburg to within a few miles of Port Royal, and for three miles back of the river was, by the aid of our glasses, distinctly visible.

[The house] was frequently selected by general officers, among whom were Wadsworth, Humphreys, Birney, Hancock, Sickles, Rowley and Reynolds,[22] for the purpose of observing the maneuvers of the rebel infantry encamped back of the river, and controversies often arose respecting the outlook politically and otherwise, in which their former experiences were freely discussed.

For a time General Reynolds came alone almost daily, and after dismounting and borrowing a pair of our marine glasses, would throw himself upon the slope of the lawn, appearing to be lost in reverie over the spectacular performances of the Johnnies. He was not at all communicative with us but maintained a dignified silence, scarcely ever exchanging a word except when asking for the glasses, characteristic of those graduating at West Point towards volunteer officers, and not entirely due to the fact that we were subordinate officers while he wore the "stars" of a major general.

Many of the volunteer generals calling were not only very agreeable, but anxious to glean whatever knowledge we might possess, or dared to impart. They knew the facilities the officers of our corps always enjoyed for obtaining important news not acquired by others even of the highest rank. I might also remark that we kept a gallon demijohn of "commissary rye" on tap, which on many occasions filled a long felt want and paved the way to conversations not otherwise easily brought out. On the other hand, we were glad of the opportunity this method presented of keeping ourselves posted through the medium of an occasional snifter of "liquid damnation," thereby profiting by an alliance with those who were in a position to equally dispense welcome favors to us.

There were a few officers in the Union army who had watched the gradually growing strength of the rebel position with keener interest, or who were possessed of an accurate knowledge of their numbers and dispositions, equal to the officer commanding Hooker's scouts and spies, Col. Dahlgren.[23]

It was while occupying this station at the Seddon's House that I came to know him so intimately. It was an intimacy, I am proud to say, I courted with all the fervor of a youthful ambition, desirous of attesting an appreciation and admiration of a worthy gentleman and a gallant and dashing soldier. His force consisted of between fifteen and twenty picked men who knew every path of the country, and in entering the enemy's lines in the garb of rebel soldiers took their lives in their hands, well aware that detection meant quick death with the rope.

Captain Cline[24] was the chief after Dahlgren. Then came the members of his detachment in the order in which Cline rated them: Jake Swisher, Joe Lord, Dan Plue, James R. Wood, Martin E. Hogan, Joe Elliott, George McCamick, Sanford Magee, Sid Cole, George Willard, George Ericson, G. Howard, William Dodd, and Henry Williams.[25] These men were detailed from the various commands, principally the cavalry arm of the service, and with two or three others whose names I do not recall, were credited with having sincerely carried out their arduous and precarious duties.

It was Dahlgren's custom to accompany a spy to a remote part of the lines or within a radius of a mile or two outside, and on seeing him safely off to hover in the vicinity for some days until the man's return that he might escort him to the commanding officer's quarters and hear his story. A favorite point for this purpose was on the lower Rappahannock near Port Conway,[26] where Dahlgren kept concealed a rubber boat, which when not inflated, could be compressed into quite a small bundle for carrying

Special Service Scouts, Headquarters Army of the Potomac. Fortescue has identified the individuals in this photo as follows: seated on the ground, left to right: Dan Plue (reclining holding hat), Captain Cline's son, George Willard (clean shaven in front), G. Howard, James R. Wood (holding left leg), Sanford Magee, and George Ericson; seated in chairs, left to right: Sid Cole, Captain Cline (in uniform), Joe Elliott; standing, left to right: William Dodd, George McCamick, Henry Williams (leaning on Cline's chair), Jake Swisher, and Joe Lord (hand on tree). Cline, Cole, and Plew (Fortescue misspelled the name) were members of the Third Indiana Cavalry; Wood was a former member of the Sixth U.S. Cavalry; and there is evidence that McCamick (also spelled McCamack) may have been a citizen of Virginia residing near Ely's Ford on the Rappahannock River. Courtesy Library of Congress, Prints and Photographs Division.

or concealment. With this inflated a man could readily cross, and having exhausted the air, hide it in the reeds or brush to be used on his return. . . .

Captain Cline was an Indianan whom Dahlgren usually reserved for special work. The information brought by this man in the past had proven of incalculable benefit to our cause, and [when] confirmed by subsequent reports made him invaluable, so Dahlgren compelled him to stay for days, mingling with rebel soldiers and hovering on the flanks of Lee's army.[27]

In all of these trips Dahlgren would make our signal station a stopping place and share much of the information with Kendall and myself. A greater part of Cline's success was due to his Southern appearance and homeliness, stolidity, and indifference. Among the varied types of men of the Army of the Potomac, none would have passed so readily for a Southern soldier as Cline. His complexion was sandy, and his face deeply pitted from small pox. Lean and lank, in a loosely fitting butternut uniform, he was the ideal Johnny. To these [features] should be added a perfect Southern dialect and his rebellious origin would pass unquestioned.

How often have I sat entranced over his intensely interesting conversation and hair-breadth adventures, wondering why a man should risk so recklessly an ignominious death for the paltry gold it brought him. Perhaps his daring indifference should not be attributed wholly to sordid motives but rather to inflexible patriotism, which made him insensible to fatigue or danger. Certainly he endured bodily exhaustion with a faith that argued belief in the righteousness of our cause, and not that which breasted temptation for purely mercenary reasons. . . .

During Burnside's engagement at Fredericksburg, Cline and Hogan, who were personally known to each other (although as a rule this was guarded against by Dahlgren, whose aim was to keep them in ignorance of each other's movements if possible) met inside the rebel lines in the same cavalry command of Texans, and both succeeded in getting a good horse formerly ridden by men who had lost their lives. It happened that on the night after our forces had re-crossed the Rappahannock, December 16, Cline, while in a tent, overheard two Texans conversing in an undertone in an adjoining tent expressing their suspicion of a man who had ridden with the regiment that day, and who answered Hogan's description. Cline was soon convinced that they intended investigating Hogan's case in the morning by consulting their captain, in which event it would have been difficult for Hogan to have explained his presence with their regiment, or in fact with any command, an extremely hazardous predicament to be caught in.

It now devolved upon Cline to acquaint Hogan with this information at once, it being unsafe to delay a moment, and [it was] equally important that Cline look also to his own safety. Fortunately he had noted the tent which Hogan was occupying with two or three others, but being unaware as to which one of the sleeping forms was he, Cline took the chances of his being partly awake by calling out, "Rodkins," (the name Hogan had assumed), "you're wanted for a detail." Hogan was awake, and without arousing the others, responded to the summons. Cline quickly told him of the danger; that all was up with them, and [that they should] quietly make their way to the picket rope with their saddles.

Luckily for them a scouting party had actually been ordered out that night and were getting their horses ready to move, so they avoided any difficulty or suspicion upon the part of the guard on duty with the horses. Having buckled the saddles they led the animals to a small stream on pretence of watering them, and once out of sight of the guard mounted and commenced their escape.

A detour was made of several miles before they turned their noses towards the lower Rappahannock, but in this encountered numerous picket-posts of infantry and cavalry whom it required the utmost caution to successfully evade. They succeeded by noon of the next day in reaching Port Royal, and swimming their horses over behind the rubber boat soon joined headquarters.

Cline informed me later that this was the closest call he had ever struck, that everything seemed to favor Hogan and he that night. It was only by boldly assuming that they were members of the regiment, the darkness of course aiding them, that they were enabled to so completely baffle the guard, for without their horses the chances of getting away were remote indeed.

This desperate experience . . . would, we think, have deterred a less courageous man than Cline from risking his life so soon again, particularly where his accidental identification was now so probable. And yet within a week we find him again around Lee's headquarters, questioning staff officers and the escort with all the assiduity and "Sang froid" of a regularly enlisted Confederate soldier.

Cline's unpolished heroism and sense of duty was never more strikingly displayed than in his invaluable service rendered at the opening of the second Maryland campaign, and [was] the last which I had the pleasure of listening to from his lips. This one act of his in conjunction with his chief, Dahlgren, stamps him as an inspired patriot, and is worthy of one of the brightest pages in human history.

Cline joined Lee's army just prior to that general's vacating of Fredericksburg, and moving with it around Hooker's army crossed the Potomac with their cavalry via the Shenandoah Valley. Once on Maryland soil he hurried to Dahlgren's headquarters with the information that an important mail was on the way from the rebel President Davis to Lee, in charge of a courier who would cross the Potomac at a certain hour and seek Lee's headquarters by way of the Greencastle Turnpike.

Dahlgren at once took a detail of some fifteen or twenty picked men, mostly those known to him in his scouting expeditions, and started to intercept that mail-bag. Cline's report was literally true, although how such accurate knowledge of it was obtained by him I never learned, and after they had reached the vicinity of the pike they concealed themselves, awaiting the coming of the mail carrier. They had but a short time to wait before Cline notified Dahlgren that the coveted mail-bag was approaching.

It so happened that a wagon train was on the pike moving towards Greencastle in charge of several companies of their infantry, while the mail carrier with a detachment of cavalry as an escort reached the point where Dahlgren was concealed; the two thus crowding the road fortunately enabled Dahlgren to use the train as a cover to his operations.

Dashing with his men among the wagons, he broke up the morale of the infantry guarding them and started to engage the cavalry escort, first directing Cline to capture by all means the bag, and leave the task of stampeding the escort to him. This they both successfully accomplished, and the mail was soon at General Meade's headquarters.

It proved to be of the greatest value, containing among other important documents a letter from Jeff Davis to Lee written in a despairing tone, deploring that officer's imprudence and implied want of tact in venturing so far within the enemy's country. He doubted the wisdom of such a movement, said it was ill-advised, and counseled him to return as soon as possible, averring that no reinforcements could be sent him as the troops with each command were so disposed as to make it impolitic to disturb them. It then gave the number of troops in the south and their location.[28]

The significance of this intelligence was seen at a glance, and Cline was sent in haste to Washington to convey the mail to the Secretary of War, who complimented him very highly, something that Secretary Stanton was not often guilty of doing, on the praiseworthy achievement of himself and Dahlgren. Cline received, as Dahlgren afterwards informed me, a large sum in gold for his share of the glory.

When I saw Cline the next day after his return from Washington, he was decked out in a Rebel rangers uniform with the well-known fuzzy mouse colored felt hat pinned up at the side with a single star. The disguise was perfect. His whole appearance denoted one of their cavalry even to the brown heavy felt saddle cloth so dear to the heart of the rebel troopers (a memory of successful blockade running), that Cline artfully arranged, with the aid of his crupper, to hide a deformity to the spine of his horse.

Dahlgren was leading the animal the scout was riding for a two-fold purpose, that of conveying to strangers the belief that Cline was a rebel prisoner, for until the substitution of a blue uniform his safety in our lines without Dahlgren would be limited to a few minutes only, and to prevent his occupation becoming [known], at once destroying his entire usefulness should he be spotted by any rebel spy circulating in our territory. Dahlgren, Cline, and I spent about a half-hour having the shoes of the horses made firmer at a little blacksmith shop near Emmitsburg, Md., and it was here they related the particulars of their last exploit. I must now return to our station on the Rappahannock and reserve Dahlgren's further operations for a later date.

[*Having organized the scattered detachments of cavalry serving in the Army of the Potomac into a unified corps of some eleven thousand troopers, Hooker was anxious to see how they would perform. Embarrassed by a Confederate cavalry probe across the Rappahannock on February 24 that resulted in the capture of 150 Federals, Hooker, in mid-March, ordered his troopers to cross the river and engage their Southern counterparts. Accordingly, William Woods Averell's Second Cavalry Division splashed across Kelly's Ford in the early morning hours of March 17 and battled outnumbered Confederates under Fitzhugh Lee to a draw some two miles west of the river.*]

On *Sunday, March 15, 1863*, a small detachment consisting of four signal officers and eight flagmen received orders to promptly report to General Averell, commanding cavalry division, [which was] made up of three brigades under McIntosh, Duffie and Reno, at Potomac Creek Bridge.[29]

We had had a premonition that something unusual was premeditated by the following rocket instructions, accompanied by the usual supply of parachute pyrotechnics, furnished by Captain Cushing to each officer before leaving.

Signal Department
Head Quarters, Army of the Potomac
March 15, 1863

Rocket Signals to be used on this Expedition.

None of the Signals are to be made until it positively and unmistakably decided that a certain result is obtained—

Green—All is well. Have met no enemy in force.

Green & Red—We have arrived at our destination-met the enemy in superior numbers and are now retreating, send us reinforcements.

Red & White—We have arrived at our destination-found the enemy and routed them.

Red & Green—We have arrived at our destination-found no enemy and are returning.

White & Red—We have been successful and are now returning

Answering Signal—
Green—The message is received.

The signal officers accompanying the expedition—and at intermediate stations—will throw up the necessary rocket and then wait five minutes, and if not sent forward by the next station will repeat the signal, or if a mistake is made by the next station as to color, the proper colored rocket will be again thrown up. The answering rocket will be immediately thrown up upon the message being received at the terminus station. The message will be immediately forwarded from the last station to these head quarters.

The officers will constantly keep two lookouts scanning the horizon in the direction whence the signal is expected and this watch will under no circumstances be remitted until the expedition has returned.

One of our light wagons was to be taken with small tents and supplies for three days, but our further destination was not known to us, or at least not divulged. Upon arriving [at Potomac Creek Bridge] we found the brigades making preparations for an expedition and the boys on the "qui vive" for a start that we learned was not to be made until an hour or two past midnight. Accepting the generous offer of a staff wall-tent for the night we were cozily enjoying a sound snooze when at 3 a.m., the column commenced moving, passing around the camps of the sleeping troops and heading for a point on the upper Rappahannock at one of the many fords.

The enthusiasm manifested among the men at the prospect of a season of activity and relief from the oppressive dullness of camp life appeared to extend even to the horses in the vigor and nimbleness shown, and foreshadowed trouble to the enemy wherever encountered. It was also felt that this was the initial movement towards the concentration or cooperation of . . . employing and fighting cavalry by brigade or division, the consolidation of which had been one of Hooker's pet projects since his assumption of the command of this army. A remark of his, "That he had never seen a dead cavalryman," or words to that effect, irritated the chaps who wore the yellow trimmings, and added fuel to a desire to be recognized as something better than mere followers of general officers in the guise of orderlies, as well as a growing distaste for the spectacular pomp of escort duty to which they had been subordinated by the former commanders of the Army of the Potomac.[30]

It was known that Fitzhugh Lee with his brigade of Virginia cavalry was near Culpeper Court House protecting his uncle's left flank, and we had not been on the march many miles before an intimation was given that this was probably to be our objective point. An event of which us Sig's had no previous intimation, however, occurred on the Telegraph Road just prior to reaching Hartwood Church at 1 p.m., in the accidental upsetting of our light wagon, which by the way was the only one with the column, and the tumbling out of our mess-kit, etc., much to the amusement of the boys hurrying along with their commands. . . . [This] prevented us from rejoining the head of the column again until it had reached Morrisville at 5:30 p.m.

We were now but a short distance from Kelly's Ford on the Rappahannock, and General Averell decided to remain here until early morning, so pitching our small tent and satisfying the inner man we made ourselves comfortable for the night.

My location when beneath the blankets was on the flank of the party lying down, or immediately under the slope of the canvas of our "A" tent, and two or three times during the night I was awakened by a person outside, apparently asleep, crowding me by laying against the canvas. I did not resent it very passionately because of the coolness of the night and my commiseration for the chap who was shivering there, but when in the "wee sma" hours I crawled out to be in readiness for an early start, I was not a little surprised to find the intruder upon my space to be no less a person than Averell himself.

The general, not caring to disturb the inmates of the solitary frame house that marked the village of Morrisville, had spread his blankets on the grass adjoining our tent, the only one standing in the entire division, and had unknowingly rolled over on the canvas while asleep. An apology and a regret that we did not know of his presence, [coupled] with an invitation to take coffee with us put us on a solid footing with him again, at least in our discomfiture we fancied that he appeared reconciled, his usual demeanor being one of austerity and reticence.

Our proximity to the ford was evidently not unknown to the Johnnies, and yet they had not set themselves very strenuously to work to oppose any advance we might have contemplated. The rifle-pits along the opposite bank we found occupied by a small force of dismounted cavalry only, when our advance attempted at 4 a.m. to cross the ford. The 1st Rhode Island urged their horses across and [there] then commenced a race between they and the Johnnies to reach a piece of woods some distance back where their horses were tied. In this the rebs were unsuccessful and our boys bagged the entire outfit. The reserve picket stationed beyond got away, however, and carried the news to Fitzhugh Lee, whose squadrons were soon observed forming to meet our onslaught.

The crossing of the command was effected without much delay although everyone was more or less soaked, the surface of the water on the ford extending to the tops of the saddles. When the batteries were taken over but a small portion of the breech of the guns could be seen, almost the entire carriage being submerged, necessitating the carrying of the ammunition in the arms of the mounted men. Once on the opposite shore the brigades were rapidly formed and a running fight kept up several miles to Brandy Station.

When the columns moved forward Kendall and I were directed to remain at the ford and keep communication open between them and the reserve remaining there. Not an easy task considering the many patches of intervening timber, compelling frequent changes of our position.

Fighting continued all day, commencing about 8:30 a.m., and lasted until dark, when the forces returned, re-crossed the ford, and retired to the tenting ground of the night before at Morrisville. We had a few wounded, not over forty or fifty, among the first being Major Chamberlain of Averell's staff.[31] Our men brought over and kept corralled during the engagement more than one-hundred and fifty prisoners, the ever truthful enemy reporting only thirty-five taken by us.[32]

At an early hour we were again moving back to Falmouth, stopping on our way at Hartwood Church, and again near Barnett's Ford to feed horses and men. Upon reaching the camps, where the reverberations of our artillery were distinctly audible, we were met by a hearty welcome from the boys who had been curbing a natural inclination to be further acquainted with the cause of the racket in the vicinity of Kelly's Ford. So impressed had they been with the notion that their services might be needed that the distant roar of the guns had much interfered with a Saint Patrick's Day celebration, gotten up in the 2nd Corps under the auspices of General Thomas Francis Meagher,[33] and resulted in many being ordered to camp in readiness to move at a moment's notice.

The sight of the squad of prisoners brought in added to the "eternal fitness of things," and put the cavalry, especially, in capital good humor with themselves.

The interruption to the festivities of the 2nd Corps on Saint Patrick's Day by the cavalry fight called for a renewal of that program, and ten days after, on Friday March 27, in honor of the visit of Governor Curtin of Pennsylvania and the Governor of Maine,[34] General Meagher again invited everybody to come over to his race-track and enjoy themselves.

The principal features [of the festivities] were speeding horses interspersed with leaping hurdles and ditches, [and were] attended with the usual mishaps; among the injured from the fall of his horse was the Prince Salm Salm, who was conveyed to Sickles's quarters on a stretcher. Another of the injured was a scion of royalty, a grandson of Blucher of Waterloo fame, now serving as a lieutenant of one of the siege batteries parked near Hooker's headquarters.

Foot racing and climbing greased poles were also included in the program, General Meagher being ubiquitous in a strikingly grotesque costume patterned somewhat after that of the well-known figure of Brother Jonathan. The entire day was devoted to amusements, and as a diversion from the insidious ennui prevailing, was declared a delightful success.[35]

CHAPTER 9

THE CHANCELLORSVILLE CAMPAIGN

APRIL 5-JUNE 17, 1863

The demoralized *Army of the Potomac* that *Joseph Hooker* had inherited from *Ambrose Burnside* was imbued with a sense of optimism as the spring campaign drew near, much of it drawn from its new commander. "He certainly has one good quality," recorded an observant young Massachusetts officer who dined with him that spring, "and that is self confidence and a sure feeling he will be successful."[1] Hooker had reorganized the army, consolidating the cavalry into a single unit and disbanding the Grand Divisions in favor of an organization made up of seven separate infantry corps. He granted furloughs to deserving soldiers, cleaned up the camps, improved food and rations, and bolstered the esprit de corps of the army by first assigning distinctive badges to each of his corps and then holding grand reviews so the men could *see that they were a part of something greater. "The winter of our discontent is past," wrote a New Jersey soldier. "Soldiers who wanted to go home on any terms, a few months since, are now red hot to try their luck in another great battle."*[2]

[*April 5, 1863*] After a short season of rest the army was graced with the presence of Uncle Abe and Mrs. Lincoln. I presume the President needed recreation and desired to escape from the intolerable political boring so persistently indulged in by the wise-acres who not only knew how to prosecute a war better than he, but [knew] the correct method of conducting the general Government, particularly when the theories they had to advance tended to enrich their own pockets. The President knew that among his soldier boys there was absolute freedom from petty hostility and ponderous fanatic dissent with every conscientious idea advanced, and wisely sought the rest a few days of camp-life would bring him. He also brought with him Little Tad, his son, for whom every Union boy in blue felt a devotion sincere and heartfelt. Tad's eye was soon fascinated by a boy bugler of nearly his own age, belonging to one of the headquarters batteries, and mounted on ponies the two took in everything within the range of this army. Early and late these youngsters could be seen galloping among the camps, welcome guests at every tent or picket post.

On *April 6*, the day after the President's arrival, he reviewed the cavalry and artillery of this army, commanded respectively by Generals Stoneman and Hunt. The exercises were of the most impressive character, the mounts of these two branches, in which over twenty-five thousand horses participated, eliciting unqualified admiration; first passing in review at a walk and afterwards at a gallop.

An amusing occurrence that is worth relating took place on our way to the reviewing ground in which the doughty S. B. W. Crawford, the former surgeon but now brigadier general, figured in his customary role of dignified magnificence. Lieutenant Halstead and I were riding in company and had proceeded but a short distance when we overtook Muhlenberg's Regular Battery with everything trim and shining for parade, and being quite intimate with the captain,[3] rode slowly by his side for a few minutes conversation, not noticing, nor caring particularly, that riding ahead some fifty yards were a small group of officers.

In a very brief interval we were confronted by a staff officer from this group who announced to the captain that he was the bearer of General Crawford's compliments, and was directed to say that it was unmilitary to be conversing with others when on the march in command of his battery.

The little minor details that go to make up the picture of superlative contempt that shot from the captain's eyes when he had recovered his breath we will omit in the present instance, and simply remark that the two young men at whom the general's remarks were aimed, being fully cognizant of the fact that the road was a public one, politely saluted the captain, trotted their horses in front of this group headed by the grandiloquent "pill dispenser," and brought their nags down to a walk some ten feet in advance, leading the procession to the place of review.[4]

Two days after, on the eighth, the President with General Hooker reviewed the infantry, and an inspiring sight it was indeed. Many ladies and wives of officers, including Mrs. Lincoln, graced the occasion, having embraced the opportunity of witnessing a superb military spectacle, and of viewing the enchanting scenery of the Potomac by steamboat from Washington.[5]

The promulgation of the following circular letter to the officers of our corps called for additional study upon that which we had already absorbed, to assure the further efficiency of our work in the transmission of messages:

Signal Department
Head Quarters, Army of the Potomac
Camp near Falmouth, Virginia, April 11, 1863
Circular.

The officers when upon stations forming a continuous line will, when messages must pass through intermediate stations, transmit them by "repeating." The call intimating that a message is to be repeated to a certain station will be made by adding to the call of the station, 1422.

Thus if the [number] of the station is 234, the call for repeating to said station would be 234–1422–5. The station calling will continue so, until he sees the next station has taken up the call, when the second will continue until the third receives it and so on through the line; the answering 11–11–11–5 will come from the station called upon to receive the message, and will be repeated back through the line. The message will commence with 11–11–11–5, which will be repeated through the line as if it were part of the message. If the message is not received and a "repeat" is called for, the 234 will be sent back to the first station and the "repeat" given from there.

No intermediate station will presume to meddle with the message, save to transmit it by "repeating."

By order of the Chief Signal Officer,
William S. Stryker,
1" Lieut. & Adj't Signal Corps
A of P.

This innovation was distinctly an advance in the art of talking by flag, and overcame an unavoidable detention heretofore existing when operating in a flat country interspersed with patches of woods. Instead of each station, which under the above conditions would necessarily be but a mile or two apart, receiving the message entire before calling and forwarding it to the next one, it went promptly through from start to finish with but a trifle more of hindrance than there would have been had no intermediate stations existed.

We soon found after a short season of practice that it worked admirably along the Rappahannock, the economy in time between sending a message through the four stations, a distance of twenty-five miles, in the old way being quite considerable.

The approach to the Seddon's House was by a road which skirted the river from Falmouth to the Potomac. This was a favorite route for the wagon-trains of the various quartermasters, as well as the cavalry commands in going and returning from vidette duties, it being at a safe distance from the river while affording those using it an opportunity of seeing the banks on either side.

On Monday afternoon *April 20*, a message came through to our station directing Kendall and I to be prepared to move with General Doubleday's division of the 1st Corps on the following morning, and promptly at day-break the troops of that command could be seen stretched out along the river road in plain view of the enemy.

At 8 a.m., Captain Fisher, accompanied by Wilson, Jerome, Kendall, and myself, started for the lower Rappahannock, passing on our way to the head of the column a pontoon train, indicating a crossing below. Now, thought I, the much hammered Army of the Potomac will have a chance

Capt. Charles S. Kendall of the First Massachusetts Volunteers. The thirty-year-old East Boston resident had served as a signal officer with the Army of the Potomac on the Peninsula, serving the Seven Days' battles and the Antietam Campaign. Paired with Fortescue throughout much of 1863, Kendall would be captured several days after Gettysburg and survived a succession of Southern prisons before leaving the service in 1865. Courtesy of Mollus Mass Collection, United States Army Heritage and Education Center, Military History Institute, Carlisle, Pennsylvania.

to reassert itself. Will we get across in good shape ahead of the Johnnies or will it be only another Fredericksburg fiasco?

It was soon evident, however, that something else beside a demonstration in force was intended from the little effort made at concealment, and we were quietly given the tip by Fisher that it was a feint only to draw Lee's army away from Fredericksburg. We were to proceed with the troops as far as Port Conway and use every effort to persuade the enemy that the movement to penetrate their lines was a bona-fide one, and upon reaching there other orders would be awaiting us.[6] At 5 p.m. the division arrived at Port Conway, and as darkness came on the troops were deployed in the timber and across the fields, building small fires that in the early evening dotted the country for miles, giving it the semblance of a mighty encampment. The canvas pontoon boats were driven close to the river's edge, the blazonry of war being conspicuously obvious by the unlimbering of batteries and the multiplicity of bugle calls and drum-taps by the same performers who were transferred from place to place to repeat their work.[7]

Our equipment being simply blankets, we sought a negro's shanty about midnight, Fisher enjoining upon us the importance of being in readiness to report before daylight.

Before the dawn we were off on the return trip minus breakfast, until arriving at the station at Doctor Ashton's house[8] where our brother Sig. Lieutenant Gloskoskie[9] had a meal ready, at which we fell to work, the early morning canter adding a zest to our appetites so significant as to startle our host and paralyze him beyond form of expression.

Our assignments were to points from which the roads on the other side of the river could be seen and a calculation made of the number of troops passing down to oppose our feigned threatening at Port Conway. From my position I noted almost the first that came hurrying along to Port Royal, the village opposite our halt of the night before. Here I remained the entire day counting and counting: wagons, batteries, cavalry, and infantry, until darkness prevented further observation and compelled my immediate return to headquarters with the figures of the day's operations. . . .[10]

[*Hooker planned to divide his 135,000-strong army in two, sending three of his corps (the Fifth, Eleventh, and Twelfth) up the north bank of the Rappahannock to cross it (and the Rapidan River, which flowed to the south of it) and land in an area known as the Wilderness on Lee's flank and rear. Once there, they would advance through the thick tangle of second-growth forest and underbrush to the open ground just behind Fredericksburg, taking Lee in reverse. At the same time, John Sedgwick's Sixth Corps would prepare to conduct a frontal assault on the city and the Confederates ensconced on the hills behind it. Lee, Hooker hoped, would be caught between the two Union attacks, and with his two remaining corps (the Second and Third) available to reinforce wherever necessity dictated it, Hooker would, if all went according to plan, destroy the Army of Northern Virginia.*]

General Hooker had measurably succeeded by his diversion towards Port Conway. Each member of our corps, from his post of observation, corroborated the others in estimating the strength of the enemy, which thrown forward to meet our pretended crossing, weakened their centre. But no advantage was apparently taken of the absence of this large body of men and materiel from Lee's forces. Whatever propitious results were encompassed from the march of Doubleday's division Hooker disregarded, and from our position we saw the enemy returning in large numbers, either glorying in having thwarted us, as they imagined, or temporarily disgruntled at being subjected to a fatiguing march that only provoked their temper and disgust. . . .

It may have been the inclement weather that deterred Hooker from reaping the fruits of his successful movement, as the storm blasts were in high feather again before we had fairly become settled in camp.

[*April 27, 1863.*] It had cleared off beautifully, however, when four days afterwards another batch of distinguished visitors put in an appearance in the persons of the Secretary of State, William H. Seward, and the Prussian Secretary of Legation, for whose gratification the 3rd Corps was trotted out for review and inspection.[11]

I learned this afternoon that while the review was taking place, the 5th, 11th, and 12th Corps were quietly moved to the vicinity of Kelly's Ford. It looks as though Seward's visit, and the publicity given to the review in front of the city, was a blind to cover the movement of the three corps in anticipation of a general engagement up the river.

In the evening the 1st, 3rd, and 6th Corps moved below from in front of the city for the evident purpose of holding Lee there and preventing his interruption of the operations above.

This Tuesday morning, *April 28*, Kendall and I were ordered to occupy the station at the Fitzhugh House, Lieutenant Marston[12] going to the Seddon's. Ours being the intermediate [station], we flag both Tyler's Hill, near the Phillips House on the right, and the Seddon's on the left. Hot work [is] expected, but what a splendid condition the army is in. Hooker's abilities as a re-organizer, after the series of misfortunes that have befallen us, must be conceded. The eminent gentlemen and ladies who have recently honored us with their presence were delighted with the marked excellence that characterized the commands passing before them. From a disheartened and lukewarm indifference of three months ago, we see an energetic and forcible firmness, inspiring and imposing in its effects.[13]

As evening approaches the engineers with the pontoon trains are getting them into position near the river with the evident intention of laying the bridge to-night or early in the morning.

[*April 29, 1863.*] At daylight we find it still very rainy and disagreeable. As predicted last night, the engineers are constructing the bridge at about the identical spot where Franklin had his in the last campaign.

"A heavy fire is concentrated on the boys, but no delay is noticeable and the bridge is soon completed."

"In the dash across a few of the boys were wounded before the rifle-pits were reached and those occupying them gobbled."

"Having obtained a footing on the south side the entire 6th and 1st Corps are crossing under the command of Sedgwick."

"Have about two-hundred prisoners, many of them wounded on this side of the river."

These and similar messages were flagged by us as the troops progressed in their work, keeping our flag going with very little intermission the entire day. At 3 p.m., the enemy opened a battery of Whitworth guns on the station and for a short time the peculiarly tumbling and discordant sound of these bolts made it interesting;[14] particularly to Commissary Gerker and Surgeon Nordquist of a 1st Corps division,[15] who were keeping us company, as they thought, out of range. They presently concluded, however, to stand not upon the order of going, but went. The orders to open on this battery were responded to by some of our artillery, and the Whitworth's soon silenced. One of their heavy bolts pierced the soft earth within ten feet of our flag but without exploding, and it remained there with its ugly nose sticking out during our stay.

What can be the cause of Hooker's slowness? Our men have been within speaking distance of the enemy's skirmishers for three days and no further advance made than when Sedgwick first crossed. Reynolds, with the 1st Corps, has gone to join the main body, and the 6th Corps is alone, with a fragment only of the 2nd Corps on the north side.

[Fortescue omits any mention in his memoir of his activities on the first of May but notes in his diary that "it was very quiet all the morning" and "heavy firing commenced on the right some ten miles above at 12:30 p.m.; can distinctly hear heavy volleys of musketry. . . . Our men are in the best of spirits."[16]

Over the course of the next six pages in his memoir, Fortescue describes in detail events he claims to have participated in between May 2 and 6 and specifically recounts his experiences while attached to John Sedgwick's Sixth Corps, from its May 3 assault on Marye's Heights through its retreat at Banks's Ford on the night of May 4–5. Based on the diary entries and other memoranda he recorded over the course of these five days, however, it seems unlikely that he took part in the events he relates.

In his memoir, Fortescue states that the he was ordered to cross the Potomac and attach himself to Sedgwick's headquarters on May 2; he makes no mention of it in his diary. On May 3, his diary entry, worded as if it had been written by someone who witnessed Sedgwick's assault but was not a direct participant in it, notes that Sedgwick "this morning attacked and successfully carried the Heights back of Fredericksburg." Additionally, the events he described on May 3 in his memoir relative to the activities of the Signal Corps detachment assigned to Sedgwick's command are detailed both in the Official Records *and in Brown's* History of the Signal Corps; *in neither of these instances is Fortescue reported to have been present with these signalmen.*

In his diary on May 4, he writes that Sedgwick crossed Marye's Heights to attempt to join Hooker near Chancellorsville "but came back and fought a terrible battle," which again reads as if it were written by an observer rather than an active participant. In his entry for May 5, Fortescue records that he "understood [emphasis added] that Genl. Sedgwick has recrossed the river" and that "things look rather unfavorable. . . . Slept in a shanty adjoining the

Fitz Hugh House." Had Fortescue been, as he claims forthwith, with Sedgwick
and the Sixth Corps on May 5, it seems unlikely that he would have confided
to his diary information about the corps' movements in the secondhand manner
in which he did. Finally, his handwritten record of signals transmitted and
received during the fighting leaves no doubt that he did not leave the vicinity
of the Fitz Hugh House station he had been assigned to prior to the battle.[17]

What seems probable is that Fortescue gleaned the details of the events
involving the Sixth Corps from signal officers who were stationed with it and
incorporated these into his memoir, as these occurrences were markedly more
exciting than the relatively mundane tasks which he performed during the
battle.]

This the *2nd day of May* has been a most delightful one, and excepting
the spasmodic outburst of artillery, nothing has been accomplished. This
afternoon [I] was ordered across the river and joined Sedgwick's headquarters. He had commenced moving up towards Fredericksburg after ordering the pontoon bridge removed behind him. Can see the enemy closely
following us and re-occupying their rifle-pits along the river that we had
possession of.

Sunday, May 3, 1863. Once more we are in the streets of Fredericksburg,
having moved up from our place of crossing yesterday, and everything
points to an assault on Marye's Heights again this morning. Feel somewhat used up after being for the greater part of the night in the saddle. My
horse too, looks anything but bright, although he has not suffered for feed.

The day had not far advanced before the lines began preparing for the
assault. Took a position where I could see the advancing columns, and
communicated with Hall and Taylor near the Phillips House. Near noon
the boys started up the principal roads, where the losses had been so heavy
under Burnside. With my marine glasses I could distinguish the movement of every man, so close were we to the lines.

With a yell the columns on both roads spring forward, and clambering
over the stone wall charge up the slope among the rebel batteries that are
frantically endeavoring to limber-up and escape the onslaught. But the
panic-stricken Johnnies are too late and our boys bag piece after piece of
their artillery. What a supremely radiant and brilliant picture is this compared to that of December 13 last. In a dozen different places our boys can

be seen in a desperate hand to hand conflict, and in each case the enemy [is] giving way pell-mell, and in large squads rushing to the rear.

The drivers of a gun are endeavoring to get their piece up to the summit of the ridge. In their mad efforts to escape they are leaning forward and lashing the horses furiously. The suspense is intense as a portion of our advance is seen to pour a volley into them. The pole horses stagger from the fire and drag the others back with them to the head of a ravine where the six horses, gun, and men go down in a confused and hideous mass.

Onward go the lines, the fleetest man being the color-bearer of the 6th Maine, and as he outstrips the others, he can be seen outlined against the horizon, waving his colors until his companions have joined him, and all disappear over the ridge in pursuit. Everybody is now on the run up the roads leading to the heights after the panic-stricken Johnnies who have divested themselves of blankets, knapsacks, and even their muskets in their hurry to reach cover and safety.[18]

Where are Barksdale's valiant Mississippians now? These same brave Southerners that lay concealed in rifle-pits picking off our unprotected engineers in their efforts to lay a bridge in December last. Now they are so fleet-footed that their lady friends would fail to recognize them the blood-thirsty warriors of a few weeks ago.

At last our forces hold the ridge of Marye's Heights, and all honor is due the boys of the 6th Corps, who have indeed achieved a notable victory. Everybody is exultant and with confidence we look back over that sanguinary field to the old town with, to us, its well remembered Court House spire.

And now comes the most curious part of this glorious day's work. Our troops, wearying of keeping up their pursuit of the Johnnies . . . , are returning to the ridge to reform the lines. Those retaining their formation are already moving up the river, to the right, and as fast as the others reform, they take up the line of march in the same direction.

Our light wagon stands on a nicely cleared space on the ridge near the Telegraph road, and we have received an order to establish a station there to communicate with Hall and Taylor on the north bank. In an amazingly short interval the last of the troops have passed us and our small squad of Sig's are alone, the works being cleared of all save the dead. Before we can scarcely realize it, a rebel skirmish line is swinging around to envelop us and cut us off from the Telegraph road and the troops. The demoralized Johnnies have effected a re-formation, are returning to the attack, and there is not a moment to spare to avoid capture.

A couple of valises that had been hastily thrown out to reach a signal kit lying underneath are lying on the ground. These are quickly hurled in as the driver, grasping the lines, gives the four horses the lash; his instructions being to keep to the Telegraph road and secure safety with General Gibbon's forces occupying the city,[19] as the only alternative that presents itself, while we put spurs to our horses and make for the troops that can be seen moving on about a half mile ahead.

As we gallop away we can see our team going at a break-neck speed down the Telegraph road towards the city, a line of fire from the skirmishers directed towards it; but the driver is not visible. His only salvation may lie in reaching the pontoon bridge before its removal. Fortune has certainly favored him in his flight, for the speeding white canvas body had disappeared among the houses and is assuredly safe for the desultory skirmish fire has ceased.

After a short ride we reach the rear of the troops, and mentally resolve to stick by Sedgwick come weal or woe, all heartily agreeing that in the way of a curiosity, this last experience is ahead of anything yet met with. When we later inspected that same wagon, we found that in running the gauntlet of those skirmishers it had received several bullets through the canvas cover and body, but the horses and driver were unhurt, the latter having slid down to the pole between the horses while going at their headlong pace, and probably by so doing escaped one of the bullets that struck the wagon.

Not the slightest opportunity was afforded us this evening of swinging a torch, and the only thing we could do was to remain with General Sedgwick's headquarters and await the outcome of the terrific engagement that enveloped Salem Church as the central point. Lee was evidently moving to overwhelm Sedgwick, and our only hope seemed to be, in view of the quietness prevailing at Chancellorsville, the holding of the enemy in check until a crossing could be effected at Banks Ford, around which our lines had been thrown and were protecting.

The sanguine expectations that filled the breasts of the elated boys of the 6th Corps after their work of this morning [was] that Hooker would attack and prevent the concentration of troops on our front. [This] was dispelled after dark, and we realized fully that this corps would not be able to fulfill that part of the program which provided for their joining the main body at or near Chancellorsville, nor indeed receive any assistance from the commanding general, but [would] be compelled at day-break to ingloriously fall back and save themselves as best they may.

With this understanding, careful attention was given to the details necessary to insure our safety by digging rifle-pits and preserving communication with the river, and preparations [were] made to spend the night, the boys snatching sleep as well as they could, lying on their arms with an alert enemy directly in front.

Prior to composing ourselves for the night in the sparse woods where we found ourselves located, it was decided to boil a pot of coffee, and with hard-tack and bacon appease our hungry stomachs, which at this juncture were gnawing longingly for food owing to a fast since the hasty departure of our wagon this morning. Several smoldering camp-fires were invitingly around us and the addition of a few dry sticks soon had one of them in good shape for our coffee pot.

At a distance of about twenty-five feet lay a man on his right side in front of one of these deadened fires with his face averted from us, but it being quite dark we were unable to distinguish anything about him except the mere outline of his form. There were some troops on the other side of us, fifty or sixty feet away, engaged in the same work as ourselves, the care of the inner man, but none were in the company of the individual supposedly asleep at the fire, and in fact his being there gave us no concern or thought.

Our coffee was nearly ready, and some of us, in eager anticipation of a feast, from its delicious aroma, had seated ourselves preparatory to it being dealt out, when of a sudden the discharge of a musket near the recumbent figure mentioned and the whiz of a bullet uncomfortably close startled us to our feet. Looking in the direction of the man we saw him slowly roll over on his back, and we instinctively ran towards him prepared for this sudden and unlooked for exigency. When we reached him we were amazed to find a rebel soldier, and the curious part of it was that the man was dead.

He had been shot through the head and fallen by the fire with his musket under him, the butt resting in the hot coals. The wood-work of the piece had gradually consumed, and when the lock became hot the load was discharged, the recoil causing him to roll upon his back. The expression that flitted over the countenance of each individual as he reflected upon the peculiar circumstances attending this digression from the established method of gunning for Yanks was a study, instantaneous in its transformation from that of angry determination to one of wonderment and concern.

The effect upon the feelings produced by such an event is one that surely influences the mind towards a future state in which the question of punishments and rewards become an important factor. It most certainly impressed itself forcibly upon us as evidencing one of the attributes of the Divine Spirit, which in many mysterious ways seeks to remind us of our lack of veneration and thoughtfulness to the duties of this life. Few if any of our soldier boys could boast of an escape from a bullet discharged from a piece in the possession of a dead man, however luckily they may have escaped them in the hands of experienced squirrel-hunters, and we were almost persuaded from this that it were dangerous to be safe when confronted by dead men only.

As no portion of the enemy could be seen and the scars in a few minutes subsided, we resumed our places at the fire, finished the repast and lay down, in a blanket only, marveling much at this romantic incident of our service.

I believe that everybody was aroused and alive to the importance of sharply watching the enemy long before the gray of morning had appeared. At several points along our horse-shoe line (the two ends resting on the river above and below Banks Ford), the enemy could be seen changing positions and reinforcing weak spots to successfully brush away any efforts of ours to advance, or be prepared to advance themselves should they discover our intention to re-cross without showing battle.

Towards nightfall the centre and left became hotly engaged, more for the purpose, we thought, on the part of the enemy, to keep us busy and prevent our being too hasty in withdrawing from their front. The obvious intention on Hooker's part [was] to let Sedgwick fight his own way out, [this] being no doubt as well known to Lee, by this time, as it was to Sedgwick himself.

Scarcely a shot have we heard in the direction of the other corps during this entire day, and the mystery to us is what can they be doing? We can see Professor Lowe's balloon trying to take observations, but the enemy seem to regard the balloon with utter complacency, not even deigning to attempt the professor's interruption with one of their long-range cannon.[20] About

9 o'clock, under cover of the night, we re-cross the pontoon bridge and are again on the north bank, and another dismal failure is recorded against the long-suffering Army of the Potomac. No! A thousand times no! Not the brave boys that compose this patient army, but their miserable inefficient leaders whose lack of spirit (don't mistake this for lack of "spirits"), must render the waking moments of our great hearted President a very Hell on earth.

Not having been with the other corps at Chancellorsville I cannot speak from the standpoint of an eye-witness, but if the word of thousands of truthful men who were there, and did see, are to count for anything, then two major generals were responsible for the disaster at that place—Hooker and Howard. On April 30 Hooker had possession of Chancellorsville with three large corps, the 5th, 11th and 12th. By a combination of blunders and whiskey he became so irresponsible as to permit Lee to completely out-general him, and one week after drive him back to the river, compelling him to re-cross during the night of May 5 and early morning of the 6th.

On the afternoon of May 2 Howard, in command of the 11th Corps on the extreme right, made no effort to prevent his flank from being turned by Jackson (as hundreds of eye-witnesses positively assert), but remained positively idle in the face of reliable information brought him by his own men that the enemy were executing a movement of that description. The result [was] a paralyzing stampede, the enemy attacking the 11th Corps in the rear, creating the wildest confusion for which the men were censured and not he who was alone responsible.[21]

Hooker's condition on the morning of May 3, when a cannon shot struck one of the pillars on the porch of the Chancellor House where he was standing and floored him, was such that he was either stupid from rum or dazed from the want of it, it having been asserted that he had decided not to indulge during the campaign. The need of a stimulant after weeks of liberal indulgence had rendered him incapable of self-control. He utterly failed to convince those around him that he possessed the qualities necessary to fit him for the command of the army, except when it was lying quietly in camp, and exhibited a demoralization at the supreme moment by refusing battle when he knew that an army corps only, but a mile or two away, was desperately engaged in an endeavor to free itself from an entanglement into which he had led it. He then practically ignored [it], when the slightest demonstration on his part would have brought relief and a substantial victory instead of a retreat, [and would] have fittingly marked the close of the campaign.[22]

As it was, Sedgwick brought with him the glory and splendor of a deed well performed, the stamp and the prestige of success in assaulting and gallantly carrying Marye's Heights, and safely landing, after capture, a number of pieces of artillery with seventeen hundred prisoners. Is it any wonder that the boys who wore the "Greek Cross" loved Uncle John Sedgwick![23]

The one consolation to be derived from the operations of seven army corps immediately under Hooker at Chancellorsville was the death of the rebel General Jackson. The greatest regret was that Lee did not go down with him, and the country [be] spared a continuance of the war, for with Lee absent its duration would have been short.

[*Chancellorsville was yet another in a series of gut checks for the soldiers of the Army of the Potomac. Reverses in front of Richmond, at Second Manassas, and at Fredericksburg were tempered only by the narrow triumph at Antietam. Convenient scapegoats for the Chancellorsville defeat were found in the predominately German Eleventh Corps, which had been driven from its battle line on May 2, and the army returned to its recently vacated encampments in Stafford County.*

Lee, outnumbered by more than a two-to-one margin, had fought a masterful battle, audaciously dividing his meager forces and aggressively attacking the Federals at every opportunity. His boldness, however, extracted a heavy price. 13,000 of his irreplaceable veterans were either killed or disabled, and his most trusted subordinate, Stonewall Jackson, had been mortally wounded.

Despite pre-battle counsel from Lincoln to use every man at his disposal, Hooker (reminiscent of McClellan at Antietam) had not; almost a third of his army had been either lightly engaged or had not fired a shot. The men in the ranks knew this and felt that the only thing wanting in the Army of the Potomac was a competent leader. "Do not entertain for a moment the thought that we were whipped," commented a Sixth Corps soldier four days after the battle. "We were only out-generaled."][24]

[*May 7, 1863.*] With the return of the troops to their old camps once more we again flung our flag to the breeze at the Seddon's House and resumed our line of stations temporarily abandoned during the late Hooker fizzle.

When Longstreet re-crossed the Blackwater from Suffolk, Va., and re-joined Lee at Fredericksburg on May 9, his troops were transported over the Richmond, Fredericksburg and Potomac R.R., disembarking in the rear of their line of fortifications at a point near known as Hamilton's Crossing. At the Seddon's House this point could be seen, and the trains arriving and departing, but little could be determined regarding the number of men, although we early received information that Longstreet was reinforcing Lee.

A few days afterward Captain Dahlgren came riding up the river road from the direction of Port Conway in company with Captain Cline, and reining up in front of our tent, [they] dismounted to refresh themselves with a stimulant before proceeding to headquarters. While talking with Cline about the activity noticed with their trains, I observed him rubbing his body and wincing from apparent pain which I at once inquired the cause of. Pulling up his shirt he displayed a bruised and ugly inflamed welt around his waist which he explained was caused by being tied, for three days among the thick foliage of a very high tree near Hamilton's Crossing, where he had counted the troops of Longstreet arriving.

Cline had selected a tree in a piece of woods about 500 yards from the Crossing, and after remaining there all of the first day, came down to the crossing in the evening. Mingling with the troops, he noted those disembarking after dark. Toward daylight he returned to the perch intending to do the same thing that evening, but towards dark [he] was startled to see a squad of stragglers enter the wood and proceed to make themselves comfortable for the night by building a fire and spreading their blankets within a rod of the tree he was occupying. These unlooked [for] interlopers compelled him to remain in the position all of the night as well as the next day, at the close of which he descended, sore clean through from his frightful experience. He at once made his way to our lines where Dahlgren was awaiting him, overjoyed at his success and the valuable information he brought.

An adjunct towards facilitating the prompt report of aerial observation was attempted by Hooker after his return to camp by turning over to the Signal Corps the balloon service under Professor Lowe.[25] The professor's work had been unsatisfactory, owing principally to the necessity of having to conduct his ascensions at so great a distance in the rear to avoid the artillery fire directed at him, and his reports were vague and indefinite. To overcome this it was decided to ascend to a greater height, when the course of the wind would carry the captive balloon nearer the enemy's lines, and with the aid of our strong glasses and flags [we would] obviate the former need of frequently descending by signaling the results of the observation from the car.

The absence of standing timber, felled to supply the wants of the troops, made it impossible to screen the balloon from the enemy while inflating it, and they were generally prepared to give it a warm reception if within the range of their heavy ordnance. Several times they made an effort to reach it, and on one occasion a shell passed directly under the car as the balloon was rising, giving the professor a fright that caused its removal further back.

After testing its availability thoroughly, it was found to be impracticable for our purposes in consequence of the incessant swaying motion, although an attempt was made to prevent this by ropes drawn taught from the windlass to the four corners of the basket, but these proved ineffectual.

It was impossible to use a telescope or even marine glasses in the car with any degree of satisfaction, and equally impossible on the ground to keep a telescope bearing directly to the basket. Before its abandonment as a companion to the Signal Corps, I ventured to test it, in company with Cal Wiggins, to the height of about five-hundred feet only, and here, the shock to my aesthetic taste getting the better of me, I concluded that it were infinitely sweeter to wallow all day through snow-drifts on the level than to soar above wreathed in filmy atmosphere, trying to laugh merrily while shaking your very teeth loose for fear the ding-busted thing would collapse.

It was during the few weeks that followed, while lying [opposite Fredericksburg], that an important discovery was made in connection with our signal operations that threatened to destroy our efficiency, if not dissolve the body of men that Major Myer had, at much cost of time and trouble, called together and carefully instructed.

The rebel army had also its Signal Corps, whose mode of conveying messages were precisely similar to ours, but with a different code of numerals. Their chief, Colonel Alexander, had been an officer of the U.S. Army prior to the war and was one of the few instructed by Major Myer, in New Mexico, while experimenting with his system of signals in the Indian Country, preparatory to seeking its adoption by the War Department.[26]

The enemy also had a line of stations extending from Lee's extreme left to within a short distance of Port Royal, the flags of which were in plain view of our stations on this side.

About the middle of May our officers succeeded, after much difficulty, in deciphering their code, and our time was fully occupied thereafter in reading their messages when not flagging ours, a fact of which they were ignorant.[27] To our surprise, shortly after we had obtained a knowledge of their code, we deciphered a message sent by their officers at Hamilton's Crossing to their station further down the river, asking this question: "Did you get the last Yankee message," and upon receiving a reply in the negative, observed them repeat verbatim the message that we had just before flagged over our line.

Here was an interesting dilemma for Major Myer to wrestle with, and one calculated to make him think thoughts burdensome to his inventive ingenuity. Each corps in possession of the other's code and each reading his opponents messages was an invasion of business secrets that might well be expected to ruffle the rigid dignity of our indefatigable major. But he was equal to the emergency, and had no doubt prepared himself by devising a course to be adopted in just such a contingency. A cipher code was thereupon sent to each of the officers with instructions to cover the stations from the view of the enemy wherever practicable, but in cases where this could not be done the cipher code was to be used, when flagging important messages, and the old code when they were unimportant.[28]

A short time previous to Lee's withdrawal from Fredericksburg to attempt another campaign in Maryland, Hooker, who had a very accurate knowledge of the enemy's movements, made an effort with the aid of the Signal Corps . . . to attract Lee's attention again to the lower Rappahannock.

The fact of our knowing that the rebels were in possession of our code was kept concealed from them by cunningly devised messages flagged in plain view of their stations, that they might have the opportunity of reading and reporting them to Lee. By this means another feint towards the Rappahannock was projected, and very successfully carried out, through messages arranged by Captain Fisher and [Hooker's] chief of staff, General Dan Butterfield. . . . It was undoubtedly due to [intercepted] signal dispatches that the rebel General Hill was detained on Marye's Heights after Lee's other corps had started towards Culpeper, through a fear on Lee's part that Hooker contemplated crossing at a point near Port Conway.

[At this point in his narrative, Fortescue goes on to reprint a series of signal dispatches he transmitted that were designed to lead Confederate corps commander A. P. Hill into believing that the Federals would cross the Rappahannock below Fredericksburg and force him to move down the river to counter the thrust. In the interest of space, the messages have been excised.]

Hill's curiosity presumably got the better of him and tempted him to ascertain the truth of the signal messages just flashed over our line and he sent down, on the opposite roads, a reconnaissance in force, the numbers of which were duly noted by us and reported to headquarters. He must have also soon distrusted that Hooker's activity towards the lower Rappahannock was only feigned, a suspicion that carried with it much weight when he found Hooker, within a few hours, hastily constructing another pontoon bridge at almost the identical place of Sedgwick's late crossing. Of course this brought back the rebel troops that were ordered down the river, and we were now treated to a display of batteries going into position on our immediate front. There was no unnecessary delay after the completion of the bridge, and our boys were in a short space of time throwing up entrenchments about a fourth of a mile beyond the bridge.

I witnessed this afternoon, during a vigorous shelling of an hour by our batteries commanding the crossing, some very expert feats of marksmanship that inspire the highest confidence in our artillery officers when the opportunity is presented to them of exercising their skill at long range targets. Twice in half an hour were the cannoneers, to the last man, driven from three of the enemy's guns nearly a mile distant, and each time were they compelled to limber-up and take a new position. This very accurate practice insures the largest measure of success when vigorous work is required, and belies the statement frequently overheard that the "Doughboys" (infantry), are the only ones that do any serious execution.

A quarter of a mile from our entrenchments, on the other side, was a brick house that stood at an angle partly facing to the right of our line of artillery, and which seemed to afford excellent protection to some sharp-shooters. They used one corner of it to screen themselves, and at frequent intervals a puff of smoke was observable from a rifle directed at our advance line.

A lieutenant in charge of one of our batteries directed a piece at the corner and waited for the usual puff to be sure of his man. He had waited but a minute when out stepped Mr. Sharpshooter, and simultaneously with the discharge of his rifle, the lanyard of the 20 Pdr. Parrott was pulled. On the instant, as the man stepped back to the cover of the house, the shell was seen to carry away the entire corner, completely destroying him. [It was] a remarkable shot, and in the highest degree gratifying to those around the battery as well as the boys in the rifle-pits.

Hooker has become convinced that Lee's departure from our front is an abiding one and that he must be followed in order to quiet the apprehensions of the Washington authorities. This Friday, June 12, sees the boys in motion, heading again for that city. Lee is reported nearing the Shenandoah Valley, evidently pursuing tactics that he foresees may this time land him nearer the city of "Magnificent Distances," or enable him to threaten some of our large northern cities.

From what I hear, the crisis at the War Department must be critical indeed, and calls for the exercise of patience, when forced to rely upon Hooker after the late experience, of a higher qualification than is possessed by the astute Stanton.

Our troops are withdrawn from the south bank and the pontoon bridge removed, and I am directed to remain here on the rise of ground in front of the Fitzhugh mansion and closely scrutinize the surrounding country for signs of any advance. One man is left with me, and in the event of the Johnnies crossing, we must be very alert and make a run of it to escape them.

What a sense of loneliness steals over one, with such mingled feelings of the uneasiness from capture, and a rightful intention to observe strictly the orders given. Absolute quiet prevails where but a few hours since so much activity and bustle was apparent, and not a soldier in blue excepting ourselves can be seen; naught but deserted camp-grounds and the debris from the accumulations of many months occupancy by a large army. . . . Squads of the enemy are moving about on the other side, their batteries still in position, and cavalry videttes patrolling the bank. All seem oblivious of the fact that a retrograde movement has started on this side.

Directly in our front on the river bank, some five-hundred yards away, stands a farm known as Mrs. Grey's,[29] to which a straight path leads from our position. To better observe the few houses on our side that prominently overlook the river, and detect if possible any signs of communication from them to the enemy regarding the departure of the troops, I directed my man Ryan to remain on the knoll while I rode down to the river under cover of Mrs. Grey's house. Tying my horse behind the barn I crawled along the side and dropped into one of our old rifle-pits immediately on the bank.

On the opposite side, a distance of two hundred yards only, in a rifle pit, four bobbing heads could be seen, evidently intent over a game of cards. Having arranged my telescope on the parapet of the rifle-pit I was calmly surveying them and the troops beyond when an officer came riding along the trench, parallel with the river, and reaching the group at this picket-post, remained seated on his horse while watching the game.

One of the boys suddenly looked up and espied the end of the telescope from the Sun's reflection upon the object glass, and instantly all heads went down, the officer sliding from the back of his horse and laying low with the others. Presently a head popped up and a voice called out. "None of that yer' yanks, no shootin' tween pickets yer' know," supposing my glass to be a rifle.

Divining their error and being least desirous of drawing their fire, I at once held up the telescope to reassure them, showing the straps for the shoulder, and closed the glass by pressing the sections together. This had the effect of restoring their equilibrium, and the officer again mounted and the game went on.

I remained in the pit the greater part of the afternoon, scanning the banks for any signs of their crossing, and seeing no signal from my man of danger (the size of the stakes on the little game in progress being too important to permit of further interruption by a solitary Yank), I concluded to return unobserved by them to the knoll. I prepared to leave before darkness shut us in and rendered our route a difficult one, [attempting] to reach the moving column of troops, now many miles away.

It was with much reluctance that I was forced to leave behind a most beautiful gray horse that had been painfully trying to graze near our post of observation all day. This magnificent animal, the former property of an officer of our artillery, had been abandoned in consequence of a gunshot wound in the left thigh [and] was limping badly and evidently suffered much. Foreseeing that once he laid down it would be almost impossible for him to rise again, I piled near him a portion of a bale of hay and an old camp-kettle of fresh water, which I felt might tend to prolong his days until relief came to him.

Not desiring a deeper insight into the world of rebeldom than that discovered within the scope of vision from our hillock, and fearing for my health from the miasmatic taints already rising from the tortuous river, which might grow thick enough to screen a sudden dash across by the enemy, I waved an "Adios" to the Johnnies, and putting spurs to my nag set off in the direction of the White Oak Church.[30]

The unsunned air of evening was delightfully pleasant considering the humid atmosphere of the afternoon, and naught disturbed the serenity of the scene as we threaded our way through the deserted camps of the troops until reaching the Church at midnight, where we found a small detachment of our cavalry, the first we had seen since early morning of that day. Here we had to run the gauntlet of a searching examination by the officer commanding before my man and I were pronounced of the proper standard and recognized as "real sure enough" wearers of the blue.

This early dawn of Sunday, June 14 saw us mounted and off to seek the moving infantry; traces of which were now clearly discernable in the recently abandoned fires and scraps of rations. . . . At noon we encountered the trains of the various corps. Teams innumerable blocked the roads and portions of the fields on either side for miles. The heat was oppressive in the extreme, and the dust from the grinding wheels clouded the atmosphere to suffocation. By 3 p.m. I observed my horse showing signs of weakening from the heat and excessive fatigue, and dismounting I led him by the bridle for the balance of the day, halting for the night in a grateful clump of trees on the bank of the Chopawamsic Creek.

[*June 15, 1863.*] It was scarcely daylight when we were awake and saddling. A deep far away hue, leaden in color, with here and there a fading star was giving way to the tints and shades of early sunrise. The lumbering teams loaded with camp equipage and stores of all kinds had been heard the entire night, and I was especially anxious to come up with those forming the headquarters train, of which our own was a part.

The high temperature and humidity of the atmosphere betokened another enervating day to man and beast, and it behooved me to turn my back upon the camp of the night, while yet the dews covered the field and dripped from the leaves, and seek rest and shade from the promised terrible exposure of the noonday sun. My precautions in starting early and my predictions of a scorching day were fully verified when at noon I reached the inartistic and homely village of Dumfries, and halted under a tree to test the qualities of some bacon and hard tack, with a box of sardines as a side-dish, procured from a passing sutler.

The distressed condition of the troops from the blazing rays showed that it was telling upon them with dreadful effect, and that many would fall victims if it continued long. At 3 p.m. it was still severely oppressive but fearing to delay longer I started, and during the night arrived at the Occoquan River. Crossing the ford at Wolf Run Shoals at 2 a.m., I immediately went to sleep on a log near that stream, fatigued beyond continuing a step further. . . . The following midnight I had the pleasure of reining in at Fairfax Station, where I fortunately found my wagon with the head-quarter train.

An unusual spectacle was witnessed on this march and one that the soldiers of the Army of the Potomac, although accustomed to all forms of death, have heretofore been entire strangers to—an execution by hanging.

A soldier of the 5th Corps had been detected in robbing a farm and committing an outrage upon an aged woman. There seemed to be very little sympathy felt for the man by the members of the corps, who were formed in solid columns to witness the execution. An improvised scaffold had been arranged and a grave dug close at hand, and after a few preliminary remarks, including the reading of the order for the hanging, he was swung off, not exactly, however, as a soldier would prefer to die. But discipline must be maintained even though such dreadful exhibitions require it. The hardest lesson of all, and an unsavory one to a vast majority, is that little word obedience.[31]

It will hardly be believed that this large army, with the exception of the cavalry who were compelled to closely watch Stuart's marauders . . . lay absolutely passive from Thursday, June 18th until the 24th, and all of this time Lee was moving his columns in the direction of Pennsylvania, having wisely concluded that the route to the promised land of fresh stock and a replenished commissary lay by the way of the Shenandoah Valley and Winchester.[32]

CHAPTER 10

THE GETTYSBURG CAMPAIGN AND CAPTURE

JUNE 18 – JULY 18, 1863

F ollowing his departure from the deserted Federal positions near Fredericksburg, Fortescue moved north, trailing in the wake of Hooker's pursuit of the Army of Northern Virginia.

After his one-sided victory at Chancellorsville, Lee, with his government's blessing, had decided that another invasion of the North was his best course of action. Taking the war away from Virginia would help alleviate the toll that two years of active campaigning had wrought upon the state and would allow him to gather supplies and horses in Maryland and Pennsylvania. Fighting a battle north of the Mason-Dixon line might force the Union to pull forces from the West, where relief was needed, with Ulysses Grant besieging Vicksburg and William Rosecrans readying an advance in Tennessee against Braxton Bragg.

Additionally, should the battle prove to be yet another victory for the Rebels, they might gain the elusive diplomatic recognition from France and England they had long sought.

As Lee moved northeast down the Shenandoah Valley, Hooker sidled along to the east, keeping his army between the Rebels and Washington, D.C., but the War Department, having lost confidence in him after Chancellorsville, seized an opportunity that presented itself when Hooker offered his resignation over a dispute about the disposition of a garrison manning Harpers Ferry and relieved him, replacing him with Fifth Corps commander George Gordon Meade.

Fortescue was back with the main body of the army on June 18, and after resting near Fairfax, Virginia, for a week, he moved out with the other signal attachments toward western Maryland, crossing the Potomac at Edward's Ferry on June 26. Two days later, with the Army of Northern Virginia ranging throughout the countryside to the north and west, Fortescue and his companion signal officer, Capt. Charles Kendall, who were then at Taneytown, Maryland, were ordered to locate an observation post on a mountain range near Emmitsburg, Maryland, and from there communicate any intelligence of note back to Meade's headquarters at Taneytown. On the morning of June 29, Fortescue and Kendall, with their complement of enlisted signalmen, established their station on Jack's Mountain, a commanding height in the South Mountain range that provided views south six miles to Taneytown and northeast ten miles to the crossroads market town of Gettysburg. Over the next two days, the Northern and Southern armies converged on Gettysburg, and Fortescue, following orders, remained on Jack's Mountain. From there, he and his detachment had the opportunity to experience what was arguably one of the most panoramic views of the largest battle of the Civil War. Fortescue and Kendall were essentially behind Confederate lines, attempting to communicate their observations of Rebel movements over the heads of their enemies to signal stations in and around Gettysburg.

About 4 p.m. of [June] 18th I reached Fairfax Court House during a downpour of rain that deluged everything exposed to the elements, and learned, to my regret, that Captain Fisher, our chief, was captured last evening in company with a member of General Meade's Staff near Aldie. Fisher, I am informed, was captured while awaiting the preparation of a supper at a farm-house, the place being surrounded by the reb cavalry before he was aware of their presence.[1]

This places the command of the Signal Corps in the hands of Lemuel B. Norton, a rather inconsequential captain of one of the Pennsylvania Reserve details; who, although possessing the confidence of our chief, Myer, to no inconsiderable extent, by no means possesses the love of the rank and file, and is infinitely inferior in all respects to Fisher as a commandant at headquarters. The transfer of the command was made by Captain Sam Cushing, who visited us this Sunday, the 21st . . . accompanied by Adjutant W. S. Stryker.

Prior to our removal from Fairfax Court House, I obtained a leave of absence to visit Washington and while there purchased some fine trappings for my horse and a very fashionable straw hat for myself, the oppressive heat necessitating lighter head-gear than the regulation cloth cap.[2] Thus equipped, I mounted to return at about 3 p.m. of the 24th, via

Signal Officers of the Army of the Potomac, taken during the Peninsula Campaign of 1862. Left to right: Lt. Lemuel Norton, Maj. Albert J. Myer, and Lt. William S. Stryker. Courtesy Library of Congress, Prints and Photographs Division.

the Long Bridge, and had a most exciting experience with my spotted horse "Pete," who never seemed to admire the appearance of a locomotive, and on such occasions was pretty apt to attract attention in the cunning way he had of showing his dislike.

The greater part of the Long Bridge on either end is built of brick, and is simply filled in with earth, along the centre of which runs a six foot fence, dividing the track of the steam road from the wagon path. The centre of the bridge stands upon piers, and has a draw to allow for navigation, but [has] no fence here to screen the trains, hence, an ambitious horse can make a most mirth-provoking exhibition of its rider should a train be encountered where no fence obstructs his view.

Being conversant with the disposition and vagaries of my beast, and wishing to avoid a scene, I dismounted and led him on the bridge, reaching the centre just in time to see the draw open in front of me to permit a tug-boat to pass through, which emitted a volume of smoke in the draw that greatly unnerved my animal. About the time the draw closed I observed a train approaching from the Virginia side, and turning Pete around walked him back to the cover of the fence to hide the train from his view while passing. Just as the engine came opposite, it let out a huge puff of smoke above the fence, and my brute, with much earnestness, leaped partly over the wall of the bridge, his fore-legs hanging on the outer side.

This exhilarating conduct, with me clinging to his bridle and halter-strap, was witnessed by several of Uncle Sam's minions, who, although tickled at the reckless abandon of the beast, ran to my aid and assisted me to lift him back to terra-firma, suggesting meanwhile, with some profanity, that I should shoot the life out of him. Desiring to get back to Fairfax that evening, I was compelled to decline their proposition, so turning his head towards Virginia, and seeing no trains, I again mounted, and driving my spurs into him, crossed that structure at a mad gallop, disregarding the shouts of the bridge-tenders and the customary sign displayed cautioning drivers to walk their horses.

I gave him no rest until reaching Fairfax again, making the fourteen miles in about one hour, and I rather imagine that if horses are possessed of any reasoning powers, his reflections, after being unsaddled for the night, were that it was better to preserve a happy medium between utter listlessness and promiscuous shying, and retain thereby the affectionate regard of the man bestriding the saddle and avoid as well the sore effects produced by a pair of exasperating spurs.

This early morning of the 25th all is in commotion and we are to strike for Maryland again, to try and intercept Lee. Why did not Hooker make the discovery a week ago that this was necessary? The query remains unanswered, and we are led to surmise that the meaning might be traced to Washington, probably to the headquarters of Major General Halleck.

The signal officers who accompanied General Pleasanton in his fight at Brandy Station on the 9th are with us and, while awaiting the orders to move, regale us with some exciting incidents of that battle.[3] The spirit displayed by our boys rather astonished the Johnnies and surely proclaimed the fact that the Yankee cavalry are the equals, if not the superiors, of the boasted riders of the South. It developed another feature of this war, that the Southern cavalry do not take kindly to the sabre as a weapon, but prefer the revolver; the remark of a rebel officer, while flourishing his pistol to the Yankee opponent, "To put up his sabre and fight like a gentleman," being now liberally quoted.

We lost some brilliant young officers in this engagement who can ill be spared, among the number Colonel "Grimes" Davis of the 8th N.Y. Cavalry, whom I saw at Harpers Ferry with Miles, and who got away from there with his command just after my escape; and Colonel Janeway of the 1st N.J. Cavalry, the latter dying from the twelfth wound received by him since entering the service.[4]

Captain Harry Sawyer of the 1st N.J. Cavalry, whom I also knew, is a prisoner and badly wounded. His encounter was a desperate one. The captain commanding a South Carolina squadron singled Harry out conspicuously as the two commands charged each other, and their horses, while at the utmost speed, collided squarely on their chests. At the moment of striking, Sawyer leaned forward, driving his sabre cleanly through his opponents side, while [the Southerner] discharged his pistol point blank in Harry's face, the ball striking him in front of the left ear and coming out just behind it, filling the cheek with powder. The impact was so terrific and the wounds [were] so serious that both horses and men were completely shocked, and being unable to disengage themselves (Sawyer's sabre-knot held him firmly by the wrist to the rebel officer whose side was penetrated by the blade to the hilt) [they] all went down insensible in a heap. In the rally Sawyer was missed, and is no doubt now in the hands of the enemy.[5]

Contrary to expectations we remained here until the following morning, the 26th, before starting for the Potomac, arriving at 4 p.m. opposite Edward's Ferry as Hancock's 2nd Corps was crossing on the pontoon bridge. With this corps we proceeded to Poolesville and encamped for the night.

Just at daylight of the next morning we were moving towards Frederick City with instructions to remain there until headquarters left. Not receiving orders for a forward movement we spent the greater portion of this day in Frederick, the association with the Union citizens of this loyal Maryland town compensating us in some measure for the depressing news hourly received of the occupation of Carlisle, York, and other parts of Pennsylvania by Lee's ragged hordes who seem to be cutting up "high jinks" in our old Commonwealth.

Sunday, June 28th, 1863. This was an exciting day for us chaps around headquarters, the news early reaching us of a change in commanders of the Army of the Potomac, from Joe Hooker to George G. Meade, and the further unpalatable information that Lee was about entering Harrisburg.

During part of the 28th and all of the 29th, our lines were slowly moving westward, the pace being somewhat slackened no doubt to enable General Meade to grasp more fully the importance of the weighty responsibilities resting upon him as Commander in Chief. . . .

At Taneytown, which we entered shortly after the noon hour, a station was established in the steeple of a church. Norton directed Kendall and I to proceed to the mountain range to the rear and north of Emmitsburg[6] and open communication with this steeple, that General Meade, who would make this town his headquarters for the present, might be kept informed of any movements observed by us from that elevation.

Before nightfall, after a brisk ride, we reached Emmitsburg, finding it in the possession of the 11th Corps, the 1st Corps having just left going northward in the direction of Gettysburg. Without waiting we proceeded through the town and [out] along the Millerstown pike[7] at the base of the mountain, reaching a favorable road leading to the summit some three miles north of Emmitsburg. Along this road in the rear of a dense wood we came upon the farm of a Mr. Jacob Weitzel, and as darkness had now set in we concluded to buy his hospitality for the balance of the night.

June 29. Had a remarkably fine bed last night and was up at daylight much refreshed. Haven't enjoyed such a luxury for months; the neat

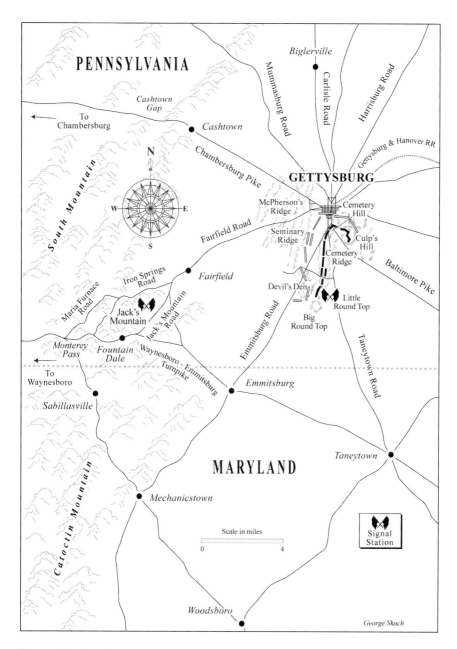

Fortescue's Gettysburg, 1863.

appearance of this Teutonic farmer's wife and her cozy surroundings made Kendall and I quite home-sick.

Located ourselves early on a spur of the mountain from which can be seen the Taneytown church steeple, and the beautiful valley north and east to Gettysburg. The mist and cloudy atmosphere, however, obscured the view greatly and prevented our seeing clearly the movements of Reynolds' corps, now midway between Emmitsburg and Gettysburg. The 11th Corps still remains near the former place and another large body of troops is moving up to join it, presumably Sickles's [3rd] corps from the headquarters flags seen.

Had a visit to-day from Lieutenants Wiggins and Camp, who have been ordered, like ourselves, to employ the time principally as a corps of observation.

Got a message through by flag to Taneytown in the afternoon, although it is still rainy, reporting the results of our observations, and received a reply that General Meade's headquarters were yet occupying that place. In the evening Kendall, Wiggins, Camp and myself found an excellent roosting

Jack's Mountain as seen from the southern outskirts of Fairfield, Pennsylvania, looking south. The Iron Springs Road (which turned into the Maria Furnace Road) is at lower right. Fortescue and Kendall would likely have manned a position near the summit shown in this view. Photograph by J. Gregory Acken, 2014.

place in an old barn near the top of the mountain that presented advantages far superior to a bivouac in the woods in this wet weather.

Wednesday, July 1, 1863. Still rainy and misty and of course impracticable for our mode of conveying information. We can see the outlines of the Taneytown steeple, but the heavy atmosphere precludes the possibility of our reading a message from them, or of their being able to decipher one from us at present.

About noon, Wiggins, Camp, and I persuaded a Mr. Wagman, who had strolled up to our station, to guide us on a reconnaissance to Sabillasville,[8] from which point a view of the country west of the range could be obtained, but as no troops were visible in that direction, we returned in time to see indications of a heavy fight in progress a short distance west of Gettysburg. The 1st Corps and the cavalry, with probably part of the 11th Corps, had struck the enemy on Seminary Ridge. At nightfall, can see firing just south of the town of Gettysburg, denoting a retrograde movement by our troops from the position where the firing was first observed.

After swinging our torch for some time in the evening, [we] succeeded in getting the Taneytown steeple and communicated the result of our observations to General Meade; the delay in attracting their notice being on account of the thick atmosphere. An answer came back from Norton, directing us to hold our position and report again promptly at daylight.[9]

Thursday, July 2, 1863. Early this morning we found the haziness of the last day or two greatly dispelled and a good view obtainable of the country in and around Gettysburg. A large force of rebel infantry and artillery are actually in our immediate front, or between us and our own troops, who are evidently maneuvering for position, as all seem to be in motion.

The station in the Taneytown steeple has probably been abandoned as no flag can be seen there, notwithstanding we have called the station, which is distinctly visible, for an hour. At nine o'clock we succeeded in locating a flag flying on the Taneytown Road, and opening communication with it were informed that the 1st and 11th Corps engaged the enemy heavily yesterday between Gettysburg and Cashtown, and all have fallen back to the ridge near the former place. . . .

The rebel troops must have been moving in towards their present position all of last night as their lines appear to extend, without a break, from in front of Gettysburg down to a point opposite, or below, Big Round Top Mountain.

About 11 a.m. we were informed by the station on the Taneytown Road that they had been ordered up to headquarters (General Meade now being near the Cemetery [in Gettysburg]) and we are therefore again in the air without communication.

At 4 p.m. the fighting commenced again heavily. Our glasses reveal a vivid picture of a desperate hand to hand encounter almost in front of the two small Round Tops. Can also see evidences of an engagement beyond and back of these two prominences, indicating a counter movement on the right flank of our position.

At 4:30 p.m. I wrote a message to Captain Norton for General Meade, giving him a detailed description of the rebel troops and their probable numbers, as viewed from our station. At exactly 5 p.m. I started my man Ryan off with directions to circumvent the right flank of the rebel lines, the position of which could be distinctly seen, and not to spare his horse but deliver his message at the earliest possible moment to Captain Norton. This he accomplished and returned during the night with orders from Norton to remain in our position and report again any movement of importance.

The firing continued 'till darkness set in, in fact heavy volleys of musketry could be seen until at least 9 o'clock, and then came that ominous lull, and gradually complete silence, so difficult to realize when succeeding the ghastly impatience and venomous impetuosity of the contest of an hour before.

Ryan reported the wounding and killing of several general officers in today's battle, the principal casualties being in the 3rd Corps, on whose front the brunt of the fighting occurred.[10]

It is now midnight, and all seems hushed in sleep excepting my flagman at the glass and myself. An inky blackness covers all the earth, with here and there in the distance a tiny spark, the remnants of lingering coals that indicate the post of the picket guard, or where the pot of coffee has been hastily prepared on the lines. . . . Not a sound but those [of the] incessant nightly insects breaks the stillness. Somewhere lying below us the enemy's lines are being strengthened, or they are moving to our extreme left flank to turn the position General Meade now occupies. If the latter, then indeed is our situation on the mountain a precarious one, and our only salvation a precipitous ride westward when dawn shall reveal clearly the route open to us.

[*July 3, 1863.*] At 2 o'clock I lay down, intending to be up the moment the breaking day dispelled the dark shadows and gave opportunity to study the situation on the plain below. The stars had first commenced to peep out, and then the moon beamed splendidly; the air, however, seemed close, indicative of a withering heat when the rising sun should fulfill these indications.

As morning broke I was up and soon enjoying a dipper of coffee. Evidently something of moment is intended as we can see several batteries of the enemy maneuvering and changing position near our extreme left flank.

At 7 a.m., I determined to ascertain what news there might be in Emmitsburg, and in half an hour had galloped into that village to find many farmers with their teams harnessed up and the wagons loaded with furniture and supplies, prepared to follow others of their neighbors who had preceded them eastward, fearful of rebel depredations. Riding a mile or two east of the town, I secured the services of a blacksmith to tighten the shoes of my horse, and while awaiting the completion of the operation, was accosted by my old friend Colonel Dahlgren and his favorite scout Cline, just returning from the successful capture of the mail-carrier, before mentioned.[11]

Returning to Emmitsburg, I encountered a detachment of the 6th Regular Cavalry, who in a movement ordered by General Merritt, their brigade commander,[12] had been ambuscaded on the Millerstown pike and compelled to cut their way back accompanied by several empty saddles of their officers and men. . . .[13]

By 10.30 a.m., I was back at our station and could now clearly observe lines of troops marching and forming in the rear of the timber lining a ridge about a mile west of the position of our troops at the Cemetery. Well on towards noon a sharp firing was observed on a portion of our line above the Round Top Mountain, and a burning building could be seen, but after a brief time all firing ceased and quiet again was restored.[14]

During the entire morning efforts were made, at intervals by us, to communicate by flag with stations that could be seen inside our lines, notably that on Round Top Mountain, but each time, after repeatedly calling, the effort was abandoned.[15]

At 12.30 p.m., I took one of my men to a farm house just below us on the side of the mountain to procure forage for our horses, and after obtaining a good supply of corn, led the horses to the gate preparatory to mounting for the return ride. As I placed my foot in the stirrup I heard the discharge of a single piece of artillery, and turning to the farmer who had followed us to the gate, I remarked that if he desired to witness an unusual spectacle to get his horse and ride quickly to the station, noting at the same time that it was exactly one o'clock.

Before I had reached the station more than a hundred guns of the enemy were hurling their fire at the elevated plateau around which our troops had formed their lines, and the air was filled with the blaze of cannon and bursting projectiles, but not a soldier of ours was visible excepting the outlines of the batteries in position, which were not yet replying to this terrific cannonade of the enemy.

In a brief interval of time our artillery responded, and now more than 200 cannon awake the echoes of this valley with the thunders of their discharges. What a scene for an artist is unfolded to us as we, in mid-air, look across the enemy's lines, and, facing our own, note the repeated whistling of projectiles and their explosions before reaching the frail improvised shelter of our men. From a point almost at the foot of our mountain extending north some two miles, a continuous line of batteries are belching shot after shot so rapidly that it is one incessant roar without intermission.

Surely the enemy are doing much execution to our artillery for we can see an occasional slack in the response from the guns. It is clear to us that the fire from our batteries is not in vain as the bursting shells temporarily scatter here and there the rebel infantry lying in rear of the woods along which their artillery is ranged.

If we could only flag to headquarters the position of the rebel lines as they appear to us from this eminence; but no signal flag is in sight, everybody must be surely under cover, awaiting a lull in this rain of shot. Fortunately our position on the mountain is such that when using our flag it is not visible, except from a distance across the valley, else we might not remain in undisturbed possession of a lookout so menacing to the comfort of the rebels movements. At all events, we have not been discovered, although it is somewhat singular that the rebel signal officers have not been prospecting over the territory we now occupy.[16]

Half an hour has elapsed and the heavy fire from the enemy's batteries has begun to slacken. Ours has ceased entirely for quite a while, and we wonder whether our boys have all been laid out. We can see their infantry in commotion back of the woods, but do not realize, fully, the next step in the program. It is soon apparent and a long line emerges from the woods, uncovered to the view of our troops. They seem to be halting for some purpose, presumably to dress their lines and impress upon the men some closing instructions. Evidently they are concentrating the greater part of their forces for one grand assault as none are now visible in the rear of the timber, where they were before massed.[17]

With my telescope I can scan this immense column, from right to left, as they now move forward to the attack. Is it possible that our boys can resist an onslaught so formidable? They have scarcely started when our entire line of batteries are again ablaze, and hundreds of shells are bursting within their ranks; the fire being concentrated on this charging column. Scores of them can be seen going down under the cannonading, and they don't appear to be moving forward as confidently, or compactly, as when they first emerged from the woods. Some of them are double-quicking forward, and the fire of our infantry is now opening. What a chance our boys have got to keep under cover and give them the full benefit of the medicine we've had to take in Virginia.

The fire from the whole of our infantry line is now open as their column sweeps across the road near the plateau, and our artillery is fairly mowing them down. We can hardly resist the temptation to get up and relieve our pent-up feelings, with one hilarious shout, so glorious is the scene compared with what we endured at Manassas and Fredericksburg.

Scarcely a breeze stirs the atmosphere and the dense volumes of sulphurous smoke slowly ascend and linger at a height of about five hundred feet, hanging there, apparently motionless, so slowly does it move, like a great flat cloud pointed up the valley, as far as the eye can reach.

The intermingling ranks of desperate combatants can hardly be discerned, but the lurid flashes of the artillery and volleys of musketry tell the fearful tale of destruction that is decimating the enemy's lines. Squads of them have broken away and are rushing back across the plain, unable to withstand the terrific scorching fire of our boys. The enveloping smoke prevents our seeing the immediate conflict where the impact takes place, but certainly their lines are wavering, and no reinforcements are going to their relief, excepting a few pieces of their artillery that are run forward to a point equidistant between the two ridges, but are useless in consequence of the hand to hand conflict now waging and the fear of killing their own men.

Scarcely twenty minutes has elapsed since their long assaulting line crossed the Emmitsburg Road, which runs almost parallel with our lines, before we see them madly rushing to the rear. There does not seem to be one-tenth of the number that advanced to the charge, and yet the few that race back are all that we see returning; our boys must surely have annihilated the command.[18]

A wagon train has driven to the rear of the timber and is hurriedly loading in their wounded, and as fast as they are filled they take the road leading to the main drive across Monterey Gap. This looks like a retreat as the firing has almost entirely ceased.

The plain is now swept clear of men excepting the dead and wounded, which litter the ground covering the front of our lines. Not a shot is heard although it is yet an hour before dark. The repulse has been overwhelmingly complete, and the greatest excitement is apparent inside their lines. Regiments and brigades are being double-quicked to fill in gaps in anticipation of more work. Can it be possible that another assault is contemplated, or are they preparing to resist a counter movement by General Meade?

The activity continues until night comes on, and our suspense on the mountain correspondingly increases as we contemplate the nearness of the enemy and their problematic future designs. Will they retire across the range by division or corps, taking to the many bye-paths to insure a speedy rearrangement of their lines on the west side, or will they all fall back in order through the Monterey Gap? The coming morn can only enlighten us, which we must patiently await, in the absence of other sources of information, and yet to tarry here may land us, before that time, prisoners in the enemy's hands.[19]

The positive instructions from Norton prevent our choosing any other alternative except to remain unless absolutely driven away, so at 6 p.m., I sent Ryan again with a message to Captain Norton containing a hastily written description of the movements of the rebels as seen from our station, [also] regretting our inability to communicate by flag earlier in the day when witnessing their preparations for the assault.

The hours seemed unusually long during the night, and our horses were kept saddled. Very little sleep was indulged in, our time being mostly occupied in watching their camp fires and listening for strange noises on the mountain paths, down which were picketed three of our men with orders to gallop to the station if they perceived any movement of troops in that direction. [*July 4, 1863.*] But daylight at last came, and with it Ryan returned and reported that he had with difficulty found Norton, who simply replied, after reading our message, that we should remain in our position until further orders.

Ryan had scarcely reached the station and delivered his message before we were apprised by a farmer, who was excitedly urging his horse up to our point of observation, that a squad of the enemy's cavalry were on the Millerstown Pike and had no doubt started up one of the many paths for the purpose of capturing us. He asserted that a detachment had fed and stabled their horses in his barn during the night, that they had been picketing and scouting on the pike as a protection to the flanks of General Lee on either side of Cashtown and Fairfield, or the Monterey Gap, and having observed the signal flag flying on Jack's Mountain, intended to surprise it at daylight.

His excited appearance left small room for doubt that whatever we did . . . should be done quickly, and gathering together our signal equipments, [we] were in a few moments on a mountain road that led to Harbaugh's Gap;[20] our informant at once consenting to play the role of guide.

Taking a southerly direction, a half hour's ride brought us to the level within a few miles of Emmitsburg, and bidding our loyal farmer a thankful adieu [we] soon reached the college buildings in the rear of the town, and passing around them, galloped with all speed towards Taneytown.

Placing a couple of miles between us and the mountain, we reined in at a farm house. The pressing necessity of the inner-man—after the desperately anxious departure of the early morning—had begun to have its effect, particularly as the excitement of a threatened pursuit was by this time wearing off. An intimation thrown out to the farmer's wife that we were ravenously hungry and prepared to reimburse her brought forth an appetizing breakfast that Kendall and I did full justice to.

Having convinced the methodical helpmeet of this Maryland border farmer that, like the majority of Uncle Sam's blue coats, we had a pleasing and ambitious capacity for bacon and eggs, we mounted again, intending to ride to Gettysburg and report to Captain Norton the untenable [nature] of the Jack's Mountain station. We had not ridden more than three miles when we met the advance of General Kilpatrick's division of cavalry, who had been ordered to make a detour around the extreme left flank of our army, by way of Emmitsburg, for the purpose of harassing Lee's rear.[21]

The coming of this body of troopers persuaded us to change our plans and like true soldiers return and occupy our station until regularly relieved. [This was] a most unfortunate decision, as will be presently seen, and one that changed the whole current of our prospectively dazzling military careers, although [it was] the most eminently proper course for us to have pursued at that time.

With this determination, we faced about, and at 9 p.m. again reached Emmitsburg. Riding out the Pike to the path leading to our station, we halted in the woods until the last of Kilpatrick's division had passed.

Having in the meantime allowed Ryan to visit a blacksmith in the village, and fearing for his safety unless we waited for his return, we discovered when he had reported that it was past midnight. [As] it was drizzling rain and smoky (a night wholly impracticable for signal operations), we decided not to ascend to the summit before morning. Stationing a man on guard duty at the road with instructions to keep us informed of anything important, we sought the friendly shelter of an old barn on the side of the mountain, and being much used-up from the day's jolting in the saddle, lay down for the balance of the night, not at all in a satisfactory frame of mind with this day's mode of celebrating our great National Holiday.

The dripping rain from the trees falling upon the roof of the little barn was the last sound I remembered before tired nature asserted itself and refreshing slumber carried me into the land of nod.

[*July 5, 1863.*] We were all enjoying a blissful repose when a half-terrified outcry of alarm brought every man to his feet, and looking in the direction of the door [we] saw our guard carefully closing it. Inquiring the cause of his anxiety, we were met by a hurried expression that for a moment almost paralyzed us. Lowering his voice he excitedly said, "My God! the Johnnies are all around us."

It was just the peep of day, and the cavalry that he had indistinctly seen passing him down the Pike for at least an hour before, and whom he had supposed to be Kilpatrick's men returning from their ride up at midnight, were really General Jeb Stuart's rebel column, seeking a gap further down the mountain to avoid that very body of our troops that had forced their way in the Monterey Gap ahead of Stuart, and prevented his rejoining Lee.

There was literally no outlet for us, for when our man had hurried to the barn, they were then, as he had declared, all around it. Not five minutes elapsed after his entering before a squad of them, far outnumbering us, were trying the door to effect an entrance, expecting, of course, to find some livestock, but little imagining that two Yankee officers and four enlisted men, trapped like rats in a cage through the insufferable stupidity of a guard, were to be their prey.

But it needed no second glance to convince them of their prize, and we were soon marched out to the roadside, minus horses and equipments, to reflect upon the well-worn proverb that "Obedience is better than many obligations," especially with the soldier, although had we followed our own inclinations we would have rejoined the headquarters of General Meade, instead of carrying out that fool-order of the bumptious Norton in returning to the station.[22]

[*As was the case with a portion of his recounting of his experiences during the Chancellorsville Campaign, doubt as to the veracity of his account has crept in to Fortescue's narrative at this point due to a significant discrepancy between what is recorded above and his contemporary diary. As he relates it here, Fortescue and his signal detachment initially rode to Taneytown on the morning of July 4 and eventually left there, passed through Emmitsburg at 9:00 p.m., and retired in a barn near the base of Jack's Mountain, where they were captured early on the morning of July 5. In his diary entry for July 4, however, Fortescue states that he accompanied Federal cavalry into the town of Emmitsburg (this he duly noted in his postwar account) but "stopped for the night at Doctor Anna[n]'s—Very fine family. Retired at 10 p.m." In his diary entry for July 5 he writes, "Was awoke at 7 a.m. by the Dr. who informed us that the Rebel Cavalry were in the town. Saw them take our men's horses. Knowing that we were in the House they threatened to burn it unless we came out. Surrendered at 8 a.m."*

Which one of the two versions of his capture is correct is difficult to determine, as there is not a surfeit of additional circumstantial evidence (as there was at Chancellorsville) that would validate either claim. Surely Fortescue and his compatriot, Capt. Charles Kendall, who was taken with him, would prefer to have it believed that they were captured near their signal station rather than sleeping in relative comfort in a house some miles away. Were it to become known that they were not near their post when captured, they would have faced the very distinct possibility of serious disciplinary action, likely combined with an attendant loss of dignity. Indeed, in every other mention of

Fortescue's capture that has come to light (either recorded directly by Fortescue in his military and pension records or in secondary accounts, such as in the History of the Signal Corps*), the capture of he, Kendall, and their enlisted signalmen is related as having occurred on Jack's Mountain. So though it cannot be stated with complete certainty what the true sequence of events surrounding his capture was, it appears likely that Fortescue was indeed captured, somewhat ignominiously, while at the Annan House in Emmitsburg.*]

It was now too late to moralize on what might have been or give vent to our feelings over the remissness of the flagman on guard who should have notified us when the advance of this column was first seen by him, so following the directions of a rebel officer of this regiment, which proved to be from North Carolina, we joined the column and started for Emmitsburg.

We soon learned from these drowsy cavaliers, who had been steadily in the saddle for some days and nights, that Lee had been, since early morning of the previous day, July 4, retreating through the Monterey Gap, and the squad of cavalry sent to raid us at daylight, of which we were apprised by the farmer, was to prevent our reporting by signal flag to General Meade this retrograde movement; our location having been discovered in some manner.

Stuart, after a hard and unsuccessful fight with our cavalry under General D. McM. Gregg[23] near the Hanover Road east of Gettysburg, at what was known as the Rummel farm, had started to find General Lee, from whom he had been separated during the three day's battle, but upon reaching Monterey Gap discovered Kilpatrick's division ahead of him. Kilpatrick, about this time, was playing havoc with the rebel general Ransom's division train, which he had captured together with over 1300 wounded prisoners, and being in possession of the Gap, Stuart was compelled to retreat southward on the roads, on the east side at the base of the ridge. He was looking for an outlet among the bye-paths of the mountain in order to get through when his lines enveloped us, and this change in the military situation, so momentous to us, had taken place in the misty darkness of the early morning without our knowledge, although enacted at so short a distance from where we lay.[24]

At 7 a.m., we entered Emmitsburg and moved down towards the center of the village that General Jeb Stuart might interrogate us. As we passed along the sidewalk, I noticed, ahead, a group of young girls ranged in line behind a white paling, one of whom was holding her white apron up by the corners, and motioning to Kendall, each of us dropped in the apron, unobserved by the cavalrymen, our handkerchiefs tied tightly, his containing his watch only, while mine, in addition to my watch, had two tightly rolled topographical maps, a small compass and a pair of spurs. It were infinitely preferable, thought we, that these young ladies, who might be of Union proclivities, should have our valuables than the "Tar-heel" cavalrymen, who were waiting an opportunity to rob us.[25]

Arriving at the intersection of the first street, we were confronted by the cavalry leader of the Army of [Northern] Virginia, whose headquarters were temporarily established there.

To those who have never had the misfortune of an introduction under such unfavorable conditions, his appearance might have awakened

An 1890s view of the Annan house in Emmitsburg, Maryland, where Fortescue and his signal party were, in all probability, taken prisoner on the morning of July 5, 1863. The house, which occupied a lot on the western edge of the town, no longer stands.

adulatory criticism, particularly by believers in his theory of southern rights. But to us his self-assumption and bombastic exaggeration of dress simply invited contempt. In stature he was six feet, and weighed about one-hundred and ninety pounds. A complexion somewhat ruddy from exposure, with light brown hair, worn rather long, and full flowing beard. His regulation gray uniform was profusely decorated with gold braid, and was topped with a broad-brimmed black felt hat, pinned up at the side with a star from which drooped an extravagantly large ostrich feather. On the left breast was a shield, about two inches in width, which held a chain attached to the handle of a small stiletto, the blade being passed through the button holes of his coat. What a gentleman's object was in adopting this spectacular ornament of decoration, it was difficult to imagine, unless to use as a handy tooth-pick? He may have meant that it should lend an air of ferocity to his appearance; a sort of brigandish style of bearing; if so it was a moderately successful achievement, the "Bombastis Furioso" standard being courted, as we were afterwards observed, by most of the prominent rebel officers.

His deportment, at the moment of our arrival, was surely an index to his imperious and haughty disposition, and a glance sufficed to convince us that he entertained a feeling of disdain and hatred towards soldiers of the Union army.

His headquarters were in the open air, and he and his staff were surrounded by their horses. [Accompanied by our] escort, we were conducted within the circle for examination, and the following conversation ensued:

> Stuart: "What command do you belong to?"
> "Signal Corps."
> Stuart: "Were you with the cavalry that passed up that pike last night?"
> "We were with the troops that moved up there last night."
> Stuart: "Who commanded them?"
> "A general of the United States Army."
> Stuart: "What infantry regiments were with them?"
> "We did not observe, nor count them."
> Stuart: "You did not count the cavalry either I suppose?"
> "No sir."

Stuart: "Nor the artillery?"

"No sir."

Stuart: "Were my men fighting General Kilpatrick
during the night?"

"Not having been there, Sir, we are unable to say."

It was our opinion, after the interview, that Stuart was misled into believing that an infantry force was with Kilpatrick, and that, in consequence, his chances of getting through safely were somewhat remote. Turning to a staff officer, presumably the provost marshal, he directed him to take charge of us, his tone and gesture indicating that while with his column we might look for no favors. In less than a half-hour his cavalry were again in motion, traversing the same road that we had used in escaping from them the previous morning.

Stuart seemed much perplexed while ascending the mountain just south of Emmitsburg, knowing as he did that the impetuous Kilpatrick was laying low to intercept him, and during this Sunday morning he made two attempts to reach the other side, but each time the head of the column was abruptly halted by advance couriers dashing up and informing Stuart of Kil's presence with his artillery unlimbered. On both occasions Stuart placed a battery in position and threw a few shells, and while doing so, compelled our squad, which had grown to about twenty, to march down and stand in line in the rear of the pieces, hoping thus to deceive Kilpatrick into the belief that an infantry force was with him.[26]

It was during one of these halts that I was introduced to the thieving methods employed by the southern chivalry towards unarmed prisoners. Partisan zeal was usually advanced by the admirers of the Confederacy as the incentive that characterized their cruel and unsoldierlike treatment of Union soldiers who fell into their hands. But such a specious plea would not avail with us when witnessing the downright robbery perpetrated upon our men by commissioned officers of every grade.

Kendall and I were seated on a rock, a few yards from the staff, awaiting the result of a reconnaissance that Stuart had ordered, and to allay the depression which we were striving to endure, I filled my meerschaum pipe, covering it meanwhile with my hand to prevent their seeing its value. After lighting it an orderly came riding up and informed me that he had been directed by Adjutant Washington to bring my pipe to him. I politely declined to surrender it, but on second thought, knowing their determination and my inability, therefore, to retain it, remarked that being an inveterate smoker I needed some such consolatory companion now, and if the adjutant had a pipe to replace mine to send it over and I would comply with is demands. This he did, the orderly returning with a cheap wooden affair, and mine became the property of the adjutant. [It was] a polite style of stealing, under the guise of bartering, by these pretended gentlemen, that ere long we grew accustomed to.

At last late in the day Stuart struck a road and successfully evaded our cavalry, reaching the level country beyond after dark. During all of these fatiguing maneuvers, although numerous led horses were in the column fresh from the farms of Pennsylvania, and every man [was] mounted excepting ourselves, he forbid the prisoners from riding, twice sending a member of his staff back to have me dismounted after I had been accorded the privilege by the cavalryman in charge. But the masculine creature has an instinctive aversion to being nagged, especially by such lordly dignity, and this oppressive display of churlishness toward those whose line of duty had been wholly in the mounted service excited ridicule even from his own command who, as they freely asserted, could see no possible avenue of escape open to us, but rather the contrary, especially while securely leading the horses we bestrode by a halter-strap.

> "The tide revertive, unattracted leaves
> A yellow waste of idle sands behind."[7]

How often in my weary imprisonment my mind reverted to this dispiriting march which only ceased when morning broke, and to the lost opportunity of escaping, that for the instant only presented itself, and then faded into an inexpressible lamentation that the eye did not comprehend its full significance and grasp its availability.

At midnight in the shadows of a wood a small stream crossing the road was encountered, made deeper, no doubt, from the recent heavy rains, but not then reaching above the knees of the animals. On the right, skirting the timber and along the outside of a worm fence, the body of an oak tree had been laid on which pedestrians might cross instead of fording.

My feet were still dry, though sore from the long tramp and the quickened step made necessary by the occasional spurring of the horses. I had been between two cavalrymen, and holding to their saddle-straps [I] was aided greatly thereby in relieving the severity of my tight riding boots. My two guardians were dozing in their saddles, and as we came to the branch I dropped behind them and sought the tree, then dimly seen, to cross dry shod. They waited but a moment only, and then slowly ascended the other side. When I had reached the centre of the log their horses had proceeded to the cover of some undergrowth, shutting out my view of them, and for the moment, and only a moment, I stood alone. Had I then dropped to the water, waist deep, I could in an instant have leaped the fence into the woods and disappeared. But to save the drenching this involved I hurried to the other side, [only] to find on looking back that another cavalryman had drowsily moved up, and seeing me, waited until I had rejoined the column, my two former companions being then several yards in advance and apparently indifferent to my whereabouts. Oh! the golden opportunities of our lives that we cast aside at the moment of success, how often do they return to plague us with their remembrance? The "hope deferred which maketh the heart sick," found me at daylight still plodding along, without the chance again of profiting by the experience so tardily recognized at the midnight stream.

[*July 6, 1863.*] At noon we joined General Ewell's corps, on the outskirts of Hagerstown, whose advance was retarded by the operations of our cavalry. Kilpatrick's division had ridden hard to outstrip Stuart, and passing around to the south of that town, had moved up and engaged the cavalry with Ewell. After Stuart's arrival he reinforced the latter and we were witnesses of some hard fighting on the main, or Chambersburg Street, resulting finally in the dispersion of our troops who were largely outnumbered by the rebel cavalry.

During our stay with Ewell's staff, who occupied a smooth grassy knoll to the right of the Chambersburg Pike, our view of the cavalry operations was unobstructed and we could readily see the futility of Kilpatrick's movements in his efforts to harass Lee's advance. The rebel infantry had taken possession of the houses and from the windows poured a steady fire into the ranks of our charging cavalry that emptied many saddles, and our little squad was soon increased by the addition of several Yankee prisoners, two of whom, Captain James A. Penfield, 5th N.Y. Cavalry, and Lieutenant Harry C. Potter, 18th Pennsylvania. Cavalry, I later became quite intimate with.[28]

An exhibition of marksmanship took place after our cavalry had been dispersed that proclaimed the superiority of the squirrel rifle, as an accurate and long range weapon, when backed by the man in whose hands it had been a familiar toy since early boyhood. One of our cavalrymen, having lost his horse, had sought the shelter of a front stoop, and by laying close behind it was enabled to use his repeating carbine to good advantage when an occasional shot offered of a protruding head from a window, towards us.

He was probably a thousand yards away, and at intervals of three or four minutes, we could see the smoke rise from his carbine and the dust fly as his bullets struck a brick wall or the pike in front. A rebel sharpshooter was watching him from an old log house on the opposite side of the street, not five-hundred yards from us, and several times we observed him bring his rifle to his shoulder and again lower it as though waiting for a better opportunity to fire. At length he fired, and we saw our cavalryman roll out beyond the step apparently in the most excruciating agony.

He had been completely disabled, and so far as we could observe, was the only man who had been keeping up the fire; a most conspicuous act of heroism, considering the tremendous odds against him. After a couple of hours this man was brought in on the horse of a rebel cavalryman, and we then saw the nature of his wound. [It was] a painful one in the extreme, a bullet having gone squarely through the heel, fracturing the ankle bone which our Reb squirrel hunter had noticed projecting beyond the lower step whenever our cavalryman assumed a stooping posture in aiming his carbine. And this amazing accuracy was obtained at a distance of at least five-hundred yards, insuring unqualified respect, on our part, for the man with a squirrel rifle.

It was while lying here that Kendall and I caught a passing glimpse, and for the last time, of the two mute companions of our army life, now gaily prancing along with North Carolinians in their saddles. This regiment had been ordered to the front to charge the street, and as they swept by the two horses were easily distinguished by the trappings we had purchased for them. Kendall's animal was a very amiable and clean-limbed bay called "Billy," mine a brown with white spots, to both of which we had rendered the full tribute of affection and admiration.

This hasty recognition of our faithful partners, from whom we had never been separated, awakened us to a mournful realization of the fact that we should never again caress them, and in the new experience we were now to undergo the lineaments of our lost friends often arose, recalling sweet memories and suppressed feeling that invariably ended with tear-dimmed eyes.

What a scene of suffering mingled with horrid oaths and execrations now presented itself on every side. Long lines of army wagons, by the hundreds, were struggling to reach the Potomac and every wagon [was] filled with their wounded. In the paroxysms of anguish and torment from the rough jolting of the springless wagons, curses loud and blood-curdling were hurled by the occupants at the Yankee army, and as we were the few representatives present, it was mainly intended for our ears. The moaning and groaning from every wagon and the shouts and imprecations from the wounded who were able to walk were hurled at us until it seemed as though we might fare badly at their hands before reaching our destination.[29]

A youthful lieutenant of the 2nd N.Y. Cavalry named Arthur Richardson[30] was marching by my side just prior to entering Hagerstown, and at one of the violent outbursts from a wounded rebel, Richardson turned to me with a smile and made a jesting remark. At this moment a soldier marching with the wagons brought his piece to his shoulder and in another instant Richardson, and probably myself, would have received the contents of his rifle had not an officer of his command riding behind shouted to him to put up his piece and move on with the column. I had to caution this young man that however much we secretly enjoyed the discomfiture of the Johnnies we had better restrain our exuberant spirits until safely out of sight and hearing of this display of blood and these frightful shrieks, else our obituaries would mingle with many others of the Gettysburg campaign.

Before starting our column for the river we were given the opportunity of seeing the principal rebel himself, General Robert E. Lee, who came down the Chambersburg Pike with a few staff officers and halted near us to confer with General Ewell. It was midnight when the order to move was given and we passed through the streets of Hagerstown and out the old familiar road to Williamsport.

A horse lay bleeding and dying in front of the Franklin House in Hagerstown which Captain Penfield, before mentioned, remarked as we marched by, was his. The captain was then a man of 45 or 50 years, and in the cavalry charge up the street his horse was struck by a bullet and fell so quickly that the captain's body was pinned beneath. While lying in this painful position, a rebel cavalryman charged over him and at the same moment gave him a swinging sabre cut across the top of the head, stunning him and severing an artery, the discharge soon thickly matted his flowing beard and saturated the front of his jacket. This splendid specimen of a Union soldier disdained the offer of a seat in a wagon, preferring to boldly march with us to the river, his head swathed in bloody rags and in stockinged feet only, his boots being lost when he was dragged from beneath the fallen horse.

[*July 7, 1863.*] At 9 a.m. we entered Williamsport and halted half a mile from the river awaiting, as we surmised, some means of transportation across. We had now been in their hands two full days and the only provender seen was a very limited quantity, grudgingly obtained from persons on the line of march, who were, as a matter of course, drained nearly dry by the rapacious Johnnies. The farmers encountered by us were as a rule close to the border line separating Maryland from Pennsylvania, and reputed to have a strong leaning towards secessionism, hence, their indifference towards a Yankee, especially when they saw him a helpless prisoner. They were thus enabled to make themselves solid with the Grayback by refusing to give to us, [and to also] exercise their latent spite on the wearer of a blue uniform, for whom they should have entertained the greatest regard.

The rebel commissary pretended to issue some rations, a pint of flour being given to each of us, but a sorry mess we made of it in the absence of cooking utensils. Having emptied six cups full on a rubber poncho, we mixed it with water, shaped it into a ball on the end of a stick, and then held it over a fire until the ball was brown. These, when taken inwardly, dropped with a hollow plunk into our stomachs strongly suggestive of the thud of a dipsey when cast overboard; an admirable foundation for a dyspeptic nightmare in its most hideous form.[31]

[*July 8, 1863.*] The scenes of disorder and confusion were heightened tenfold at the river's edge. Horses and mules [were there] in droves, [with] no apparent means of getting them across except by a frail looking flatboat, some twenty feet long and ten feet wide, worked by an overhead rope stretched to the opposite bank. The Potomac was swollen far above its usual high water mark by the recent heavy rains, and was now madly rushing by, carrying logs and trees at a terrific rate, and was the color of yellow mud. What a dilemma for Lee's retreating hordes was here presented, and what a golden opportunity for General Meade, thought we?

It was at last determined that our squad of ten or twelve should be ferried across, the reason for the haste not being then apparent to us. No Yankees were visible or firing audible, and yet there seemed to be great anxiety on our account, so we were marched on board the scow and started on the perilous trip. One piece of artillery with its limber box was on the scow, together with ourselves, and when in midstream the force of the rushing water carried us down, stretching the two upright ropes to their fullest tension and causing the overhead rope, upon which the pulley ran, to describe a semi-circle, slanting and submerging the boat inward, over half of which the water swashed. A prayer sincere and fervent went up from our squad that the on-dashing flood would snap those ropes and carry us down the stream beyond the reach of the enemy, who lined the banks watching our transit. Indeed I would have taken my chances in the waters without a boat could the snapping of the lines been accomplished by any secret means. It was not to be, however, and soon we touched the opposite bank and were ordered to spring ashore; then was the extraordinary haste to get us over manifest. A body of our officers, numbering one hundred and fifty, representing various commands captured in the first day's fighting at Gettysburg, were, under a guard of infantry, awaiting our crossing before moving on to Martinsburg, Va.

This guard of two hundred and fifty men was the skeleton of one of Pickett's Brigades that formed the assaulting column on Friday last, and was now commanded by the only field officer left, a one-armed major.[32] The chances of escaping to our lines was now becoming more remote than ever. The seething torrent was between us and the "boys," and we were again on Virginia soil with a vigilant guard watching closely our never-ceasing anxiety to enjoy once more the delights of freedom.

[*July 9, 1863.*] At Martinsburg we were greeted by many downcast looks that indicated sympathy and friendship. Some even elicited our admiration in their manner of upbraiding the Johnnies for not giving us more rations than had been doled out, and they freely distributed to our hungry boys, while passing, great slices of bread that must have been as "gall and wormwood" to the guard in charge of us.[33]

[*July 10, 11, 1863.*] Winchester was reached in the evening and the column halted near the famous Washington Spring of that town. What Heavenly purity its cool and clear waters possessed, and with what eagerness we accepted of its refreshing excellencies. Our first night here was passed supperless, a feature of life within the rebel lines to which I believe many are not strangers, and a condition, I am told, to which the stomach can be made accustomed to should the experiment in the meantime not terminate in death.

A correspondent of the New York Herald named Young, who had accompanied our column to Winchester, had been captured near Gettysburg, and made his escape the first night of our arrival, taking with him several of our names, and it was through his published accounts afterwards that our friends learned of our fate, many supposing from the silence respecting us after the battle that we were numbered among the killed.[34]

[*July 12, 1863.*] It was while lying here that we received the daily papers from Richmond containing the news of the fall of Vicksburg; a pill that seemed especially nauseating and unpalatable to the Johnnies, but glad thrilling music to the ears of the jaded Yanks, who greeted this welcome intelligence with three rousing cheers.[35]

A few hours delay only and the line of march was headed down the Valley of the Shenandoah. Before moving the brigade of infantry were relieved by General Imboden's brigade of irregular cavalry, and a motley command he had. Imagine five-hundred men mounted on mules and what may have been once a well-conditioned horse. With saddles of every description, ranging all the way down through the list of Mexican, McClellan and Citizen, to a piece of blanket, or no saddle at all, but simply a rope stirrup dangling from either side. Those with the longest legs seemed to have gotten the shortest mules, and three-fifths of the entire force carried no arm except a shot-gun.

At the head, swelling with Falstaffian pomposity, rode the general commanding, as in halcyon days other brave chieftains have marshaled their hosts. He was bedecked in new clothes, with many scrolls of gold lace encircling his arms, and looked as pretty as a red wagon. Alas! that his army of swash-buckling bushwhackers should have presented so ludicrous a spectacle to ordinary, every-day Yankees.[36]

The incessant rains that succeeded the battle of Gettysburg had made the Valley Pike almost impassable where the small streams crossed in the hollows, and our enlisted men, some thirty-five hundred who joined us shortly after leaving Winchester, were, in many places, forced to ford [in water] waist deep.

[*July 14, 1863.*] At the town of Strasburg tired nature succumbed, and I lay down completely petered-out. My tight cavalry boots, which came to the knees, were filled with water from fording, and I was compelled to cut them off my feet by slitting from the top of the toe to above the ankle. To tramp the pike in the sensitive condition of my feet was impossible, so Imboden reluctantly paroled me until his wagon train should come along.[37]

While thus waiting in front of a house in company with another prisoner we were approached by a Reb soldier, whose face was entirely bandaged excepting the mouth, with an inquiry as to whether we belonged to the 6th U.S. Cavalry. He could scarcely articulate from the nature of his ghastly wounds, but we finally comprehended, and told him we were not. He appeared disappointed and walked away, at the same time nervously handling a carbine. Another Johnnie with no wish to discourage us in the least, frankly remarked that the first, "was looking for 6th Regulars to kill."

[He said] that in a charge, the man's horse was disabled and fell on him, and while in this position one of the 6th Cavalry, in riding by, had struck him a sweeping blow with the butt of his carbine across the face, breaking his nose and dislodging several teeth. Of course, this was annoying and fatiguing after having announced in no uncertain tones his desire to surrender. So having an idea that he had been misunderstood, he was seeking, with a reckless fire-arm, that individual, or in fact any member of the same command, to convince him that he earnestly meant what he said when he lay with a ton of dead horse resting on his stomach and legs.

My fellow prisoner vouchsafed the remark, as soon as we were alone, that usually he strove to tell the truth, and only lied when some high grade of entertainment was to be introduced marking him for the sacrifice; that he belonged to the 6th Cavalry when drawing his pay, but for the nonce preferred to be simply rated as cook to the teamsters of any quartermaster until eternal stillness gathered the man with the pulverized countenance and frenzied longing.

Just before halting yesterday for the night, our boys gave Imboden a genuine scare that I think must have disturbed his slumbers greatly. The announcement to go into camp for the night came just as they were passing a newly made fence, and instinctively every man's thoughts turned to fire wood. A rush was made before Imboden could interpose, and the line of fencing immediately vanished. On looking back after we had entered the field with the advance, we observed our column of enlisted men, each with a fence rail at "right shoulder shift." The effect of over 3000 men marching in this manner was startling and I don't wonder that Imboden was on the tenter-hooks until he had the column safely encamped. Had a break been made with those rails, they could have swept his scabs from the face of the earth.

When the wagon train came up at Strasburg I accepted a seat on a pile of rags, and in company with a Reb officer, jolted on through Woodstock to Mount Jackson, recognizing many familiar points of our former campaign.

Standing behind the paling gate of a farm, shut in by foliage adjacent to the south side of Edenburg (the scene of a former signal exploit narrated in an earlier chapter) stood a southern damsel, who, ever and anon, bestowed one of her sweetest smiles upon Imboden's guerrillas, being, to all appearances, on very good terms with this exquisite concentration of blatant freebooters.

At this time I had surrendered my parole, rejoined the column, and was marching between two of the cavaliers, who seeing the young lady holding a large pitcher of fresh spring water and a glass, turned their mules towards the gate and reined in for a drink. Following their example I patiently awaited my turn after they had satisfied their thirst. The damsel, however, indignantly refused to pour out a glassful for me, and snappishly replied that she had no water for Yankees. One of the Johnnies coming up asked for a drink and then smilingly passed it to me. Whereupon I related to them how I had been present when our army was advancing down the Valley under Banks, and how this family had not only willingly taken the oath of allegiance, but volunteered the assertion that they were for the Union and always had been, and pled for a guard to protect their property, which the general had freely granted. She denied the truth of my statement until reminded of the night I took supper with the family. Then suddenly recollecting me, she laughingly remarked that everybody in the Valley, at times, were forced "to play the Yankees for suckers," in which our cavalrymen approvingly coincided, and we moved on. I stored away, however, a mental resolve to be conveniently brought forth again for future use in squaring accounts, should my line of duty ever bring me in contact with this family again.

On the evening of July 17 our jaded column halted within four miles of Staunton for the night. The prisoners were sick at heart and weary from exposure and fatigue, having tramped nearly two-hundred miles, subsisting chiefly on flour paste and water, and [we] were only too willing to welcome any change from the drenching rains to which we had been daily subjected. Whatever beauties the Shenandoah Valley may have possessed had lost their charms to us, and there was indelibly stamped on every countenance those significant words, rest and food. One night yet remained in which we were to feel the full force of the elements, combined with a vague feeling of uncertainty as to how much of our clothing would be left to us before severing the social ties that bound us to Imboden's thieves.

I lay down on the side of a hill on which sharp rocks projected, and finding that my body fit somewhat snugly between two of them was soon asleep. About midnight I awoke soaked from a pouring rain, the outlet of the descending waters being by way of the gully in which I was snuggling. How I had slept so soundly was a mystery unless from excessive fatigue, and my arousing when I did saved me from being drowned, which would assuredly have been my lot in a brief time. Above this storm could be heard the curses and maledictions showered upon the heads of the guard by our men, who were being robbed by them of their hats, boots, and clothing.

[*July 18, 1863.*] When morning at last broke in the east, and the order [came] to move forward to Staunton where the trains to convey us to Richmond were awaiting, many a Union soldier strode that pike in stockings only, or coatless and hatless, [and] swore to square accounts later with those Southern thieves.

The run to Richmond over the Virginia Central, 137 miles, required just nine hours, which included many stops, the most important one being at Gordonsville. As the train neared the station, we saw another taking in water before resuming its trip towards the front. The station platform was crowded with jubilant rebs, officers and privates, returning from furlough, etc., and the cause of their rejoicing we soon learned was not our magnificent victories at Gettysburg or Vicksburg, but the ponderous pyramidial headlines with which the Richmond dailies had that morning shrieked their delight over the draft riots in New York.[38] These same papers not only belittled Grant's important successes in opening up the Mississippi River, but ladled out to their bigoted readers fulsome hallelujahs over Lee's alleged triumph at Gettysburg. The arrival of our trains with over 4000 prisoners at this juncture tended to strengthen this absurd pretension, and the joy of the Johnnies, thereat, was unbounded. It proportionately had a depressing effect upon us. We were, in a great measure, ignorant of the results attained by those two campaigns, and the thought that our Government might have lost its grip at home, and that our armies would be compelled to retrace their steps northward to contend against an element at our very doors, filled us with forebodings we could scarcely conceal.

The approach of so large a body of Yankee prisoners to the rebel capital had, no doubt, been telegraphed in advance (40,000 said the report, the operators having added a harmless cipher with a view of booming the flagging spirits of their people) and as our train stopped on Broad Street of that city, we found a multitude gathered awaiting us. Many were noticed in the throng whose sympathies, I am sure, were with us, but the countenances of thousands betrayed their exultation at our forlorn appearance.

It required a large force of military to press the crowd back from our train before we were permitted to disembark preparatory to marching to the prison, and in the crowd I recognized two familiar Philadelphians. One, well known as Sans Long, a brother of Wm. Long, the keeper of a noted drinking saloon and museum on Third Street below German, Philadelphia, informed me that he had lived in Richmond for some time, and was now desirous of reaching the North but was unable to do so owing to the stringency of the blockade.

Half an hour later we had passed down Ninth Street in full view of the Rebel Capital building and celebrated Washington Statue, and traversing the Main Street were marshaled in front of the Libby Prison, each in turn to undergo the searching process. This species of robbery [we had become] quite intimate [with] within the few days we had spent in their hands, and there was little about us to compensate the heroes of Libby Prison for the trouble they were taking, but as there might still remain a trifle that the next fellow wanted, the Johnny to whose tender mercies you were confided always considered it incumbent upon him to go through your clothes, no matter how often this interesting ceremony had taken place before you were entrusted to his precious charge.

Fortescue entered Libby Prison on July 18, 1863, and while up to this point in the war prisoner exchanges were not uncommon, he was destined—like the majority of Union officers captured during the Gettysburg Campaign—to remain a prisoner until March 1865. The hardships he endured during his time as a captive, while not as severe as those experienced by enlisted men in the prisons at Belle Isle, Andersonville, or Florence, left an indelible mark on him and forever colored his recollection of his wartime experiences. He remained in Libby Prison until early May 1864, when the bulk of the officers held there were sent to Camp Oglethorpe at Macon, Georgia. Transferred to Charleston, South Carolina, in late July 1864, Fortescue and his fellow officers remained there until October 5, when they were shipped to Camp Sorghum, located on the outskirts of Columbia, South Carolina. While at Sorghum, Fortescue and three comrades escaped and successfully eluded their pursuers for sixteen days but were captured near Augusta, Georgia, and brought back to Columbia. There they found that the prison—due to numerous escape attempts—had been moved to the enclosed grounds of the state insane asylum. There he would remain until February 4, 1865, when the camp was vacated and the prisoners began to move north with the promise of liberation. Fortescue signed his parole on February 20, 1865, near Charlotte, North Carolina, and was finally formally exchanged near Wilmington, North Carolina, on the cold, rainy day of March 1, 1865. Partaking soon after of his first meal as a free man in twenty months, Fortescue wrote that he and his comrades offered "a fervent prayer . . . to the Supreme Being whose tender mercies and loving kindness we have much to be grateful for."]

NOTES

INTRODUCTION

1. John D. Billings, *Hardtack and Coffee; or, The Unwritten Story of Army Life* (Boston: George M. Smith, 1888), 404.

2. Paul J. Scheips, "Albert James Meyer, Founder of the Army Signal Corps: A Biographical Study" (Ph.D. diss., American Univ., 1966), 74–77.

3. Many of the details of Myer's early training and struggle to establish the signal service were culled from Rebecca Robbins Raines, *Getting the Message Through: A Branch History of the U.S. Army Signal Corps* (Washington, D.C.: Center of Military History, 1996), 4–7, and from Scheips, "Albert James Myer."

4. Scheips, "Albert James Myer," 336.

5. J. Willard Brown, *The Signal Corps, U.S.A., in the War of the Rebellion* (1896; reprint, Baltimore: Butternut and Blue, 1996), 50–51. Another officer detailed for instruction in the signal code at this time wrote that the order assigning him to this duty stipulated that the men chosen be "of temperate habits that could be relied upon." Joseph Spencer to "My Dear Sister," Sept. 1, 1861, Spencer Papers, Wisconsin Historical Society, Madison (cited hereafter as Spencer Papers).

6. Louis R. Fortescue, "Diary of Army Service," typescript, vol. 1, pp. 1–18, Civil War Museum of Philadelphia, Philadelphia (cited hereafter as CWMP). All of Fortescue's quotes utilized in the introduction are taken from his memoir and will not be cited hereafter.

7. See Fortescue's early December 1862 comments prior to the Battle of Fredericksburg and Brown, *Signal Corps,* 189–90, as examples.

8. William W. Rowley, "The Signal Corps of the Army During the Rebellion," in *War Papers: Being Papers Read Before the Commandery of the State of Wisconsin, Military Order of the Loyal Legion of the United States,* vol. 2 (1896; reprint, Wilmington, N.C.: Broadfoot, 1993), 228. The other officer detailed from the Twenty-ninth Pennsylvania for instruction in the signal code with Fortescue wrote that the assignment was "a little safer position than in the Regiment and a more pleasant one." Lt. Edward Burr to Grandmother, Oct. 6, 1861, private collection.

9. "When a lieutenant entered the signal arm, he was compelled by circumstances, over which he had no control, to resign all hope of promotion. He was absolutely condemned to stand still, although performing hazardous acts with brilliant courage, while the more fortunate, who remained in the line, carried off the honors of military preferment." Brown, *Signal Corps,* 45–46.

10. Ibid., 93. In one notable instance, a signal officer posted at Seneca Mills, Maryland, reported reading a flag signal sent from Maryland Heights opposite Harpers Ferry, a distance, he reported, of thirty-five to forty miles. Spencer to "Dear Sister," Nov. 23, 1861, Spencer Papers.

11. Brown, *Signal Corps,* 120.

12. "It is well known that the enemy can read our signals when the regular code is used," wrote a signal officer from the Army of the Potomac after Chancellorsville, "and it is equally evident . . . that our cipher is unsafe and cannot be trusted." Scheips, "Albert James Myer", 552.

13. Brown, *Signal Corps,* 125.

14. Samuel T. Cushing, "The Acting Signal Corps," in *War Talks in Kansas: A Series of Papers Read Before the Kansas Commandery of the Military Order of the Loyal Legion of the United States* (Kansas City, Mo.: Press of the Franklin Hudson Publishing, 1906), 1:108.

15. George B. McClellan, *McClellan's Own Story* (New York: Charles L. Webster, 1887), 135.

16. Myer's General Orders Number Nine, reprinted in Brown, *Signal Corps,* 132–33.

17. Ibid., 7. Higher ranking volunteer officers who lacked preconceived notions about the usefulness of the Signal Corps accepted it more readily than their Regular Army counterparts. Having benefited from the efforts of the signalmen during the Battle of Kernstown, the general who commanded there wrote, "Take it all in all, I consider this signal system in the hands of skillful and resolute men like those of this corps as one of the most extraordinary devices for obtaining intelligence of the enemy's movements—and for combining our own movements simultaneously—that has appeared in our age & country." Brig. Gen. James Shields to Maj. R. Morris Copeland, Apr. 23, 1862, copy in Spencer Papers.

18. Rowley, "Signal Corps of the Army," 227.

19. Brown, *Signal Corps,* 198, 201. The three instances cited are taken from a number of testimonials that Brown included in his history. For more examples, see 195–203.

20. Brown, *Signal Corps,* 161. A total of 146 officers were commissioned in the permanent Signal Corps as organized in August 1863 (with their commissions backdated to March 1863), while an additional 297, including Fortescue, served as acting signal officers. Many of the acting signal officers served for no more than several months with the Corps, however, and returned to their regiments, so the number is somewhat misleading. Because he was being held as a prisoner of war when the Corps was formally organized, Fortescue was unable to appear before the examining board necessary to secure a commission in the permanent organization, thus (surely to his chagrin) he always carried the designation of acting signal officer.

21. The editor is indebted to Walt Mathers of the United States Signal Corps Association for providing a typewritten copy of these entries.

22. Military Order of the Loyal Legion of the United States, file of Louis R. Fortescue, CWMP.

23. *Annual Report of the Adjutant General of Pennsylvania . . . for the Year 1879* (Harrisburg, Pa.: Lane S. Hart, 1880), 108.

24. See John P. Nicholson, *Pennsylvania at Gettysburg* vol. 1 (Harrisburg, Pa.: Wm. Stanley Ray, 1904), 217–23, for the brief summary of the regiment's war service.

CHAPTER 1

1. Brown, *Signal Corps,* 228–29.

2. Thirty-six-year-old William H. Letford of Philadelphia, originally the first lieutenant of Company B of the Twenty-ninth, resigned his commission

as adjutant on November 12, 1863. Muster Rolls, 29th Pennsylvania Infantry, RG 19, Pennsylvania State Archives, Harrisburg. (cited hereafter as MR 29 PV, Harrisburg; future references will cite the appropriate regimental designation of the individual mentioned).

3. Nathaniel Prentiss Banks (1816–1894) was the epitome of the so-called Northern political general. A former Democratic congressman, Banks was serving as the Republican governor of his native Massachusetts when war broke out. Appointed major general of volunteers by Lincoln in May 1861, he went on to serve in a variety of subordinate and independent commands throughout the Civil War, usually with less-than-desired results.

4. Edward C. Burr, a twenty-one-year-old Philadelphian, was the first lieutenant of Company D of the Twenty-ninth. He served in the Signal Corps until March 2, 1862, when he returned to the Twenty-ninth and mustered out of the service less than one week later on March 8, 1862. MR 29 PV, Harrisburg; Brown, *Signal Corps,* 737.

5. 1st Lt. Leonard F. Hepburn of Company E of the Fourth New York was detailed to the Signal Corps in June 1861 and served in the field until September 1862, when he was placed in charge of the Signal Office at Washington, D.C. He remained there until he mustered out with his regiment, as captain, in June 1863. Brown, *Signal Corps,* 791; Frederick Phisterer, *New York in the War of the Rebellion 1861–1865,* 3rd ed., 5 vols. (Albany, N.Y.: J. B. Lyon, 1912), 2:1745.

6. William S. Stryker, twenty-five, of the Ninth New York State Militia (NYSM, the Eighty-third New York Infantry), had been promoted from sergeant to second lieutenant of Company D of his regiment before he joined the Signal Corps in August 1861. He served in the field through many of the campaigns in the East and was eventually made adjutant of the signal detachment assigned to the Army of the Potomac. In early 1865 he was made chief signal officer of the Department of the Susquehanna and mustered out of the service in August of that year. First Lt. Charles R. Braine, twenty-two, of Company F of the Ninth NYSM, served only briefly in the Signal Corps and was discharged from the service on October 16, 1861. Frederick R. Shattuck, twenty-eight, the first lieutenant of Company B of the Twelfth Massachusetts, served with the Signal Corps detachments in Maryland until early 1862, when he was promoted to the position of chief signal officer of the Department of Kentucky. He resigned from the service in July 1862. 2nd Lt. Lysander F. Cushing, also of the Twelfth Massachusetts, was a twenty-five-year-old farmer from East Abington, Massachusetts. He returned to his regiment and was promoted to first lieutenant of Company G on June 25, 1862, but was killed

at Antietam on September 17, 1862. 1st Lt. R. Horace London of Company A, Second Pennsylvania Reserves, served only briefly in the war, resigning his commission in early December 1861. Isaac J. Harvey, first lieutenant of Company K of the Second Pennsylvania Reserves, served in the Shenandoah under Banks, with Pope's Army of Virginia at Cedar Mountain and Second Manassas, and with the Army of the Potomac until early 1863, when he was transferred to the Department of Tennessee. Appointed captain in the permanent Signal Corps in March 1863, he served in the West until his retirement in February 1864. Brown, *Signal Corps,* 372, 672, 732, 788, 867, 879; Phisterer, *New York in the War* 2:2918, 2928; *Massachusetts Soldiers, Sailors and Marines in the Civil War,* 8 vols. (Norwood, Mass.: Norwood Press, 1931) (cited hereafter as *Mass. in the War*), 2:16, 43; *Annual Report of the Adjutant General of Pennsylvania . . . for the Year 1866* (Harrisburg, Pa.: Singerly & Myers, 1867), 133.

7. Fortescue's comment notwithstanding, on occasion enlisted flagmen of the signal detachments became proficient in the signal code, usually through the aid of a sympathetic signal officer. See Brown, *Signal Corps,* 188–89.

8. 1st Lt. Evan Thomas of the Fourth U.S. Artillery, son of adjutant general of the army Lorenzo Thomas, served in the Signal Corps until October 1861, when he rejoined his battery. Brevetted to captain and major for his services at Fredericksburg and Gettysburg respectively, he was killed in action fighting the Modoc Indians in California in 1873. Brown, *Signal Corps,* 48, 65, 883; Francis B. Heitman, *Historical Register and Dictionary of the United States Army,* 2 vols. (Washington, D.C.: GPO, 1903), 1:953.

9. Twenty-two-year-old William W. Rowley was detailed from Company E of the Twenty-eighth New York to the Signal Corps in August 1861. He would command the signal detachment under Banks during the Valley Campaign of 1862 and subsequently served as a signal officer with the Army of the Potomac until October 1862. Assigned as chief signal officer of the Department of the Gulf on December 17, 1862, he mustered out of the service upon the expiration of the term of his regiment in June 1863. 1st Lt. Frank N. Wicker of Company A, Twenty-eighth New York, joined the Signal Corps in August 1861. The twenty-three-year-old Lockport, New York, native also served with Banks in the Shenandoah Valley in 1862 and with the Army of the Potomac through the Chancellorsville Campaign. He later served with the U.S. Military Telegraph Corps at New Orleans and instructed officers of the Mississippi Squadron in signaling. Wicker received a permanent commission in the Signal Corps in 1863. Brinkerhoff N. Miner, twenty-six, second lieutenant of Company D of the 34th New York, served in upper Maryland

and under Banks in the valley in 1862. Captured during the early stages of the Antietam Campaign, he spent a month in prison at Richmond before his parole. Returning to signal service during the Chancellorsville Campaign, he mustered out with his regiment in June 1863. John H. Fralich, twenty-six, a first lieutenant of Company B of the Thirty-fourth New York, served on the upper Potomac and in the Shenandoah through mid-1862. Assigned to the signal detachment of the Army of the Potomac, he participated in the Antietam Campaign before his discharge for disability on December 3, 1862. 2nd Lt. Joseph H. Spencer, twenty-nine, originally a member of Company A of the First Minnesota Volunteers, was detailed to the Signal Corps in August 1861 and served on the upper Potomac until the commencement of Banks's Valley Campaign. Serving with distinction at Thoroughfare Mountain in the days leading up to the Battle of Cedar Mountain in August, he also distinguished himself during the Antietam Campaign. Spencer was subsequently assigned to duty at the signal office at Washington, where he was posted from early 1863 until April 1865. Appointed captain in the permanent Signal Corps to date from March 3, 1863, he was promoted to major on October 2, 1865, and mustered out of the service five days later. William C. Larned, also of the First Minnesota Volunteers, had been wounded at First Manassas earlier in the war. During his brief time in the Signal Corps, the forty-four-year-old second lieutenant of Company C was assigned to the upper Potomac during the winter of 1861–62 and later served in the Shenandoah Valley until May 1862. Originally the first lieutenant of Company K of the Thirteenth Pennsylvania Reserves (also known as the "Bucktails"), William Ross Hartshorne, a twenty-two-year-old Curwensville, Pennsylvania, native, also spent a short time in the Signal Corps, serving as an aide attached to Nathaniel Banks's headquarters until February 1862. Returning to his regiment, he was promoted to adjutant and major, and he commanded the Thirteenth at Antietam and Gettysburg. Appointed after mustering out to the colonelcy of the 190th Pennsylvania, he was captured in August 1864 and remained in prison for most of the remainder of the war. He was brevetted to the rank of brigadier general at the close of the conflict. Silas D. Byram, a second lieutenant of the Sixteenth (not Twenty-seventh, as Fortescue records) Indiana Volunteers, served on various stations along the upper Potomac from September 1861 to early 1862. He served with the signal detachment under Banks at Kernstown in March 1862 and at Winchester in May before returning to his regiment. Brown, *Signal Corps*, 234, 241–42, 738, 787, 814, 834, 861, 874, 895; Phisterer, *New York in the War* 2:2060, 2062, 2132, 2134; John Q. Imholte, *The First Volunteers: History of the First Minnesota Volunteer Regiment, 1861–1865* (Minneapolis: Ross & Haines, 1963),

137, 144; O. R. Howard Thomson and William H. Rauch, *History of the "Bucktails," Kane Rifle Regiment of the Pennsylvania Reserve Corps* . . . (Philadelphia: Electric Light Printing, 1906), 85–86.

10. Brig. Gen. Charles P. Stone of Massachusetts (1824–1887), an 1845 West Point graduate, at this time commanded a three-brigade division of the Army of the Potomac.

11. Col. Dudley Donnelly, thirty-seven, led the Twenty-eighth New York, which was raised in and around Albany for two years' service in May 1861. He was mortally wounded at Cedar Mountain on August 9, 1862. The Ninth New York State Militia, which was later designated as the Eighty-third New York, was, with the exception of one New Jersey–raised company, recruited in New York City in May 1861. During its term of service, the Eighty-third suffered nearly 700 casualties, and when it marched home to New York in June 1864, only 107 men remained. Capt. Clermont L. Best of New York, an 1847 West Point graduate, commanded Battery F of the Fourth U.S. Artillery. He would eventually rise to command the artillery of both the Second Corps of the Army of Virginia and the Twelfth Corps of the Army of the Potomac. Phisterer, *New York in the War* 2:2052, 2058; Phisterer, *New York in the War* 3:2913; William F. Fox, *Regimental Losses in the American Civil War, 1861–1865* (Albany, N.Y.: Albany Publishing, 1889), 214.

12. Col. Edward D. Baker (1811–1861), an English-born Illinoisan, was a long-time political ally of Abraham Lincoln. Offered a brigadier general's commission at the outbreak of war (which he declined because it would preclude him from retaining his newly acquired senate seat representing Oregon), Baker instead organized the First California Regiment (so-named because of Baker's political ties with the West Coast but primarily recruited in Philadelphia and New York City), which he led until he assumed command of the Third Brigade of Gen. Charles P. Stone's division in early October 1861. The Third Brigade was comprised of the First, Second, Third, and Fifth California Regiments (which were, in late 1861, officially designated as the Seventy-first, Seventy-second, Sixty-ninth, and 106th Pennsylvania Regiments respectively), and Baker led it until his death at Ball's Bluff.

13. Pvt. Oliver Tack, a twenty-three year old Philadelphian, belonged to Company C of the Seventy-first Pennsylvania. MR 71 PV, Harrisburg.

14. Rising almost thirteen hundred feet above sea level, Sugar Loaf Mountain—in addition to providing the bountiful view that Fortescue describes—was considered of inestimable importance during the Antietam and Gettysburg Campaigns due to the strategic locations that could be observed from its summit. "The range

of vision from this point," wrote signal chief Myer in the early fall of 1862, "is un-equaled by that from any other in Maryland. It includes several prominent fords of the Potomac, the approaches to them in Virginia, and much of the country into which an army passing those fords would move." U.S. War Department, *The War of the Rebellion: A Compilation of the Official Records of the Union and Confederate Armies,* 127 vols., index and atlas (Washington, D.C.: GPO, 1880–1901), ser. 1, vol. 19, pt. 1:118 (cited hereafter as *OR;* all citations are to series 1 unless otherwise noted).

15. From Oliver Goldsmith, "The Deserted Village," 1770.

16. McClellan had instructed Colonel Baker's division commander, Brig. Gen. Charles P. Stone, to make a demonstration across the Potomac to support a Federal movement up the Virginia side of the river against Confederates stationed near Leesburg. Stone, in turn, gave Baker the option of either withdrawing a small portion of his brigade, which was already across the river, or, if he felt he could gain an advantage, reinforcing it and pushing toward Leesburg. (In the meantime, McClellan had cancelled the Federal thrust up the Virginia side of the Potomac, but he failed to notify Stone of his change of plans.) Baker, unaware that he was outnumbered, chose to reinforce the detachment and suffered a crushing defeat. Union forces lost 49 killed, 158 wounded, and 714 captured; the Southerners lost a total of 36 killed, 107 wounded, and 2 captured. Stephen W. Sears, "The Ordeal of General Stone," in *Controversies and Commanders: Dispatches from the Army of the Potomac,* by Stephen W. Sears (Boston: Houghton Mifflin, 1999), 33–34; *OR* 5:303, 308.

17. 1st Lt. Samuel T. Cushing of the Second U.S. Infantry, an 1860 graduate of West Point, was one of the first officers of the army instructed in the signal code, having been assigned to duty under Major Myer in New Mexico in early 1861. Detailed to the signal detachment of the Army of the Potomac in mid-August 1861, he became chief instructor at the Signal Camp of Instruction near Washington, D.C., in February 1862 and soon after took charge of the Signal Office in Washington. In September 1862, he was appointed chief signal officer of the Army of the Potomac, serving in that capacity until May 1863. Cushing was appointed to a majority in the permanent Signal Corps in May 1863, but he de-clined the commission and became signal instructor at West Point until February 1864. He then left the signal service and served for the balance of the war in the Subsistence Department. Brown, *Signal Corps,* 35, 753.

18. Likely referring to a group of manufacturing mills situated along Seneca Creek near the Potomac River and not far from Darnestown, Maryland.

19. Col. John White Geary of Pennsylvania (1819–1873), a Mexican War veteran and prewar mayor of San Francisco, had raised the Twenty-eighth Pennsylvania Regiment at the inception of the conflict and commanded it until his promotion to brigadier general in April 1862. Wounded at Cedar Mountain in August 1862, he recovered and in October was promoted to command of the Second Division of the Twelfth Corps, which he led until the end of the war. William Allan Blair, ed., *A Politician Goes to War: The Civil War Letters of John White Geary* (University Park: Pennsylvania State Univ. Press, 1995).

20. New York–born Capt. Joseph Knap of Pittsburgh was the commander of the battery that bore his name. Knap, a twenty-four-year-old Pittsburgh resident, was employed before the war in his family's iron works, the Fort Pitt Foundry, and was originally a lieutenant in Company L of the Twenty-eighth Pennsylvania Volunteers. In August 1861, Knap received authority to recruit a battery to serve with the Twenty-eighth Pennsylvania, and a portion of a company that had recently been recruited in Pittsburgh was combined with volunteers from the Twenty-eighth to complete its formation. Knap's battery, which was officially known as Independent Battery E Pennsylvania Light Artillery, served in the Twelfth and Twentieth Corps throughout the war. Captain Knap served with the battery until mid-May 1863, when he resigned to oversee the foundry. James P. Brady, *Hurrah for the Artillery: Knap's Independent Battery "E," Pennsylvania Light Artillery* (Gettysburg, Pa.: Thomas Publications, 1992), 4, 24–31.

21. A contemporary map of Point of Rocks shows the Bassant house (spelled "Beasunt" on the map) situated along the road leading from the Potomac River into the town on the towpath between the Chesapeake and Ohio Canal and the Potomac.

22. John Page Nicholson had been promoted from private in Company K to commissary sergeant of the Twenty-eighth Pennsylvania shortly after his enlistment. In October 1862 he was advanced to first lieutenant and regimental quartermaster, in which capacity he served until he mustered out in July 1865. Lansford L. Chapman, twenty-six, of Carbon County, Pennsylvania, was at this time the captain of Company E of the Twenty-eighth. Wounded at Antietam, he was promoted to major in January 1863. Fortescue tells more of his fate shortly. Chapman's brother, Charles, twenty-eight, served under him in Company E. He was mustered out in July 1864 at the expiration of his term of service. MR 28 PV, Harrisburg.

23. The prospect of civilians peddling alcohol to his troops drove Geary to distraction. "Our Colonel is a temperance man," a member of the Twenty-eighth Pennsylvania had written in early August, "and he does not allow whiskey within

smelling distance of the camp. He got wind that a person was selling Union Whiskey to the boys, down went a Corp Guard and brought him to the Colonels tent. the Col passed Sentance and he is now serving it out by walking around a sentinel with a heavey canon Ball [*sic*] resting on his shoulder which he is to do for an hour. there is 4 more just been brought in for the same offence who are now in the Guard House waiting for the Colonel to come." Timothy J. Orr, ed., *Last to Leave the Field: The Life and Letters of First Sergeant Ambrose Henry Hayward, 28th Pennsylvania Volunteer Infantry* (Knoxville: Univ. of Tennessee Press, 2010), 31.

24. A plaque was placed outside of St. Mark's Episcopal Church in Mauch Chunk (present-day Jim Thorpe, Pennsylvania) in memory of Chapman and his wife. According to local lore, Mrs. Chapman fainted while worshipping in the church at the same moment her husband was killed at Chancellorsville. Undated newspaper clipping in Lansford Chapman File, Pennsylvania Save the Flags Collection, Twenty-eighth Pennsylvania Infantry, United States Army Military History Institute, Carlisle Barracks, Pa. (cited hereafter as USAMHI).

25. QM Sgt. David B. Hilt of the Twenty-eighth Pennsylvania was discharged for disability on August 17, 1862. MR 28 PV, Harrisburg.

26. Samuel Logan of Westmoreland County, Pennsylvania, was one of the assistant surgeons of the Twenty-eighth. He resigned his commission due to disability on October 3, 1862. Ibid.

27. Pvt. Thomas Armer, a twenty-three-year-old Pittsburgh native, was discharged from the Twenty-eighth in December 1862 to accept promotion in the U.S. Military Telegraph Corps. Ibid.

28. Forty-year-old Hector Tyndale of Pennsylvania was promoted to lieutenant colonel of the Twenty-eighth on April 25, 1862, and during the fighting at Antietam, he commanded the First Brigade of the Second Division of the Twelfth Army Corps. Promoted to brigadier general in April 1863, he led brigades in the Eleventh and Twentieth Corps before retiring from active service in August 1864. He was brevetted to the rank of major general for his services at the close of the war. Stewart Sifakis, *Who Was Who in the Civil War* (New York: Facts on File, 1998), 667. Unless noted, all future brief biographical summaries of prominent players of the Civil War in the endnotes are taken from this excellent biographical reference and are not cited.

29. Due in large part to the fact that it was a staging area for the Baltimore and Ohio Railroad and was home to many mechanics and engineers from the North, Martinsburg, in present-day West Virginia, was one of the more Union-leaning towns in this section of the state. While retreating through it in the face

of Stonewall Jackson's advance in the late spring of 1862, a Pennsylvania officer wrote, "Never since entering the service have we received such a cordial greeting as was extended to us by the ladies of this town. Our march through the place was amidst one continued ovation, the waving of handkerchiefs and the cheers of ladies." George A. Brooks Journal, Southern Historical Collection, Wilson Library, University of North Carolina, Chapel Hill (cited hereafter as Brooks Journal). More on the Unionism prevalent in Martinsburg can be found in Edward H. Phillips, *The Lower Shenandoah Valley in the Civil War: The Impact of War upon the Civilian Population and upon Civil Institutions* (Lynchburg, Va.: H. E. Howard, 1993), 14, 17, 38–40, 42, 46.

30. Fortescue's sentiments regarding Charlestown were echoed by another member of his regiment who, when passing through it in early March 1862, "found the women very bitter towards the 'Yanks,' some of them even going so far as to spit in the faces of our troops." A Massachusetts officer who was stationed there with his regiment in February 1862 also commented on the women of the town, noting that they "took a malicious pleasure in expressing to our officers their sentiments of hatred to '*your*' president and to '*your*' government; and no amount of swearing induced them to believe in our recent victories at Henry, Mill Springs, and Donelson." David Monat, "Three Years in the 29th Pennsylvania Volunteers," Historical Society of Pennsylvania, Philadelphia (cited hereafter as HSP); George H. Gordon, *Brook Farm to Cedar Mountain in the War of the Great Rebellion, 1861–62* (Boston: James R. Osgood, 1883), 107.

31. A gunner attached to Knap's Battery wrote that after the first few Rebel shells fell into their camp, "it did not take long to get our guns in position and we returned their fire briskly. After our second shot the enemy ceased firing. . . . We still kept firing and advancing until we reached Point of Rocks. . . . The enemy only fired 13 shots in all, nine of which were found. . . . Their shots were well directed, but as it happened, there was none of us hurt." Brady, *Hurrah for the Artillery*, 61.

32. Lt. Col. Gabriel DeKorponay of Philadelphia seems to have been a somewhat controversial figure in the Twenty-eighth Pennsylvania. In a letter to his wife soon after this incident, Colonel Geary reported, "Col. DeKorponay has gone home, I think he will resign *cause* he drinks too much whiskey. I would not be surprised if he does not return." Contrary to Geary's prediction (and Fortescue's version of later events), DeKorponay remained in the service and was promoted to colonel of the Twenty-eighth in late April 1862, but he retired from active service in September of the same year. He was discharged due to disability in March 1863. Blair, *Politician Goes to War*, 29; MR 28 PV, Harrisburg.

33. 1st Lt. Thomas H. Elliott, twenty-seven, of Carbon County, Pennsylvania, was promoted from Company H of the Twenty-eighth Pennsylvania to the rank of captain and assistant adjutant general on the staff of Gen. John Geary in July 1862. He was killed at Peach Tree Creek, Georgia, on July 20, 1864. 1st Lt. Gilbert L. Parker of Company D, a thirty-year-old Philadelphian, was promoted to captain and assistant quartermaster of volunteers in March 1863 and brevetted at the end of the war to the ranks of major and lieutenant colonel, respectively, for his services in the Atlanta and Carolinas campaigns. MR 28 PV, Harrisburg; Samuel P. Bates, *History of Pennsylvania Volunteers; Prepared in Compliance with Acts of the Legislature, 1861–5*, 5 vols. (Harrisburg, Pa.: State Printer, 1869–71), 2:449; Heitman, *Historical Register* 1:402, 769.

CHAPTER 2

1. A tenet central to Maj. Albert J. Myer's thesis of his signalmen as communicators was that their responsibility not only encompass traditional (flag and torch) communications but also include field telegraphic operations. As Fortescue discloses, this position put him at odds with Secretary of War Edwin M. Stanton's belief that the Signal Corps would have no influence over military telegraphy. Additionally, as Fortescue relates, Myer shared the more conservative political leanings of George B. McClellan and was, in fact, intimate with him, a point that did not bode well for any officer hoping to remain in Secretary Stanton's good graces. Writing to a fellow signal officer after he was relieved of command in 1864, Myer explained, "I have found Mr. Stanton does not have any tangible ground against me and strikes me solely because the Telegraph Interest was jealous of our field lines, and wished to control them." Myer to Fisher, Nov. 8, 1864, Benjamin Franklin Fisher Papers, USAMHI (cited hereafter as Fisher Papers); Brown, *Signal Corps*, 180–81; Raines, *Getting the Message Through*, 16–17, 21.

2. A slightly differing version of this occurrence was recorded by a member of the Twenty-eighth Pennsylvania, who wrote that a flag of truce was at first displayed near an angular flight of stairs leading to the river from under the destroyed railroad bridge. The flagman, who appeared to be an African American, hailed the Federals on the Maryland side of the river. Two of Geary's civilian scouts, named Rohr and Rice, set out in a boat to investigate, and when nearing the opposite shore, Rohr remarked that the man hailing them appeared to be a white man painted to look black. Continuing on despite their suspicions, the men soon saw that the steps leading to the river were crowded with men who fired upon

them, killing Rohr. As a result of this, Geary ordered several railroad hotels, the Baltimore and Ohio and Winchester railroad depots, a store, and five houses at the foot of Harpers Ferry burned so they could not be used by Confederate snipers. John O. Foering Diary, HSP. A contemporary account of the incident, which essentially mirrors Fortescue's recounting, can be found in Frank Moore, ed., *The Rebellion Record: A Diary of American Events . . .* (New York: G. P. Putnam, 1862), 4:79–80. Rice would identify the leader of the group that killed Rohr as Capt. Robert W. Baylor of the Twelfth Virginia Cavalry. Baylor was later captured and brought up on charges of murder and violating a flag of truce, but the trial, which was convened at Harpers Ferry in June 1862, was never completed due to the approach of Confederate forces. Baylor (who testified that he was in Charlestown, Virginia, on the day of the shooting) remained a prisoner at Fort McHenry for nearly two years and was finally exchanged in June 1864. *OR,* ser. 2(6):127, 358–59, 426–27, 528–29; ser. 2(7):211.

3. This woman was Bridget Divers, who had accompanied her husband (a private, not a major) into the First Michigan Cavalry as a nurse. Serving throughout the war, she attracted attention not only because of her gender but also because of her bravery under fire succoring the wounded and, reportedly, rallying demoralized troops.

4. Capt. Ashton S. Tourison commanded Company P of the Twenty-eighth Pennsylvania. Five of the drowned men were privates of the Twenty-eighth Pennsylvania (George Artlip, Jacob Arnold, Alexander Helverson, Abraham Spicer, and James Wood); the other casualty was a civilian scout named James Steadman. Interestingly, the pilot of the skiff, who alone survived the disaster, was the scout Rice, who was involved in the incident mentioned in note 2 above. MR 28 PV, Harrisburg; Bates, *History of Pennsylvania Volunteers* 1:481–83; Chester A. Hearn, *Six Years of Hell: Harpers Ferry During the Civil War* (Baton Rouge: Louisiana State Univ. Press, 1996), 92.

5. Charles S. Hamilton (1822–1891), an 1843 graduate of West Point, had led the Third Wisconsin before his promotion to brigadier general and command of the Third Brigade of Banks's division.

6. Brig. Gen. John Sedgwick of Connecticut (1813–1864), an 1837 West Point graduate, would later gain fame as the leader of the Sixth Corps of the Army of the Potomac. His division was soon detached from Banks's force, designated as the Second Division of the Second Corps, and ordered back to Washington to join in McClellan's advance on Richmond. *OR* 5:18, 750.

7. Col. Dennis Kane, commander of the Philadelphia-raised Sixty-ninth Pennsylvania, was killed at Gettysburg on July 3, 1863; Maj. John Devereux Jr.

was promoted to lieutenant colonel of the Sixty-ninth on December 1, 1862. Wounded near Richmond in July 1862 and again at Antietam two months later, he resigned his commission in March 1863. MR 69 PV, Harrisburg; Bates, *History of Pennsylvania Volunteers* 2:707.

8. Union engineers had constructed a light pontoon bridge across the Potomac on February 26 to allow Banks's division to cross and gain a foothold in Virginia. According to the plan, a permanent bridge was to then be constructed across canal boats fastened in the river, on which heavier reinforcements and supplies would move to support the Federal thrust into the lower Shenandoah Valley. Upon their arrival opposite Harpers Ferry, however, it was discovered that the canal boats were too wide to fit into the lock that would transfer them to the river, and the effort was abandoned. Lincoln was uncharacteristically exasperated at the aborted attempt. "Why in the nation," he asked McClellan's chief of staff, "couldn't the general have known whether a boat would go through that lock before spending a million dollars getting them there?" Stephen W. Sears, *George B. McClellan: The Young Napoleon* (New York, Ticknor & Fields, 1988), 156–57.

9. Fortescue was mistaken. Irish-born James Shields (1810–1879), another of the North's political generals, at this time commanded Gen. Frederick Lander's old division of the Department of West Virginia. His force was combined with Banks's division to form the Fifth Army Corps, commanded by Banks.

10. Edward L. Halstead, a twenty-one-year-old native of New York City, had begun his war service as second lieutenant of Company K of the Fortieth New York Infantry. Posted to duty with the signal detachment serving with Banks's army in early March 1862, he would later be commissioned in the permanent Signal Corps and act as chief signal officer for the Middle Military Division. During the Valley Campaign of 1864, he commanded the signalmen attached to Gen. Phil Sheridan's headquarters and, later, the detachment serving with Gen. A. T. A. Torbert's cavalry. Phisterer, *New York in the War* 3:2227; Brown, *Signal Corps,* 632–36, 784.

11. Edward Corbin Pierce, twenty-four, of Augusta, Maine, originally the second lieutenant of Company B of the Third Maine Volunteers, was detailed to the signal service in December 1861. He served in the Department of Shenandoah at Culpeper, Virginia, in August 1862 and was posted to the Army of the Potomac in November. Appointed chief signal officer of the Left Grand Division of the Army of the Potomac just prior to Fredericksburg, he went on to serve at Chancellorsville and Gettysburg. Pierce was offered a first lieutenancy in the permanent Signal Corps but declined the commission. He mustered out of the service as the captain of Company B of the Third Maine in June 1864. *Annual Report of the Adjutant*

General of the State of Maine for the Year Ending December 31, 1862 (Augusta, Maine: Stevens & Sayward, 1863), 43; *Annual Report of the Adjutant General of the State of Maine, for the Year 1864 and 1865*, vol. 1 (Augusta, Maine: Stevens & Sayward, 1866), 1075; Brown, *Signal Corps*, 850.

12. Ephraim A. Briggs, twenty-four, of the Forty-third New York Infantry served as a first lieutenant during the early stages of the 1862 Valley Campaign with the signal detachment under Banks and saw active service during the Antietam Campaign and at Chancellorsville as well as in the pursuit of Lee following Gettysburg. Appointed second lieutenant in the permanent Signal Corps to date from March 3, 1863, he served for the balance of the war in the Department of the Ohio and, later, in the Department of Virginia and North Carolina. Brown, *Signal Corps*, 231, 241, 324, 351, 733; Phisterer, *New York in the War* 3:2276.

13. Their experiences in Winchester, the principal city in the lower valley, elicited a variety of uncomplimentary remarks from Northern soldiers who spent time there. A Massachusetts chaplain who, like Fortescue, rarely had anything positive to say about his experiences in the South, found the city "dirty and shiftless. . . . There are exceptional houses of good appearance, but the bulk of the town is mean." A Maine infantryman who entered the city several weeks after Fortescue was taken aback by the behavior of the residents: "I think I have seen more secession today than all the rest of my time. The citizens need a practical lesson in good manners more than any people I ever saw. . . . One old hag actually washed her steps twice where two lots of our boys sat down on them. They make any remark they choose and play dixie on their pianos as much as they can. . . . Such rank, bitter, intensified hatred I never saw evinced by anything claiming to be human." Writing in much the same vein, a Connecticut soldier recalled that the female inhabitants "were as loyal to the Confederacy and hostile to the Union and all Unionists as any with whom the regiment came in contact during its service. There was no trifling nor compromise about them, and they never for the least moment looked upon the Union soldiery in any otherwise than with unmitigated hate and loathing." Alonzo H. Quint, *The Potomac and the Rapidan: Army Notes from the Failure at Winchester to the Reenforcement of Rosecrans, 1861–3* (Boston: Crosby and Nichols, 1864), 108; William B. Jordan Jr., ed., *The Civil War Journals of John Mead Gould, 1861–1866* (Baltimore: Butternut and Blue, 1997), 122–23; William E. Marvin, *The Fifth Regiment Connecticut Volunteers: A History . . .* (Hartford, Conn.: Press of Wiley, Waterman & Eaton, 1889), 71.

14. Brig. Gen. Alpheus Williams of Detroit (1810–1878) was one of the myriad of reliable but undistinguished commanders who populated the upper ranks of the

Union armies during the Civil War. At this time he had recently been promoted to command of the First Division of Banks's Fifth Corps (which would soon become part of the Department of the Shenandoah), and he went on to serve faithfully throughout the balance of the war in various divisional and corps-level assignments with the Twelfth Corps and Twentieth Corps. Williams's star shone most brightly at Gettysburg, where on the evening of July 2 he was instrumental in defending and securing Culp's Hill for the Union. The first of his brigades moved off on March 21, with the other two following on the twenty-second. Like his counterpart Williams, the aforementioned Brig. Gen. Charles S. Hamilton had recently been promoted to divisional command, leading the Third Division of the Third Corps of Banks's army. Sixty-four-year-old John J. Abercrombie of Baltimore, an 1822 West Point graduate, commanded the Second Brigade, First Division of the Fifth Corps of Banks's force.

15. Brig. Gen. James Shields's division, officially designated as the Second Division of the Fifth Corps of Banks's army, consisted of the First Brigade, led by Col. Nathan Kimball of Indiana; the Second Brigade, commanded by Col. Jeremiah C. Sullivan of the Thirteenth Indiana; and the Third Brigade, led by Col. Erastus B. Tyler of the Seventh Ohio.

16. Col. William Gray Murray of Blair County, Pennsylvania, led the Eighty-fourth Pennsylvania, which lost twenty-one killed and seventy-one wounded at Kernstown. The Fifth Ohio lost eighteen killed and thirty-one wounded, while the Eighth Ohio lost eleven killed, forty-one wounded, and one captured. Fortescue's comment regarding the Federal Third Virginia was made in error. The First West Virginia Volunteers was the only Union infantry unit from that state involved in the battle; they lost six killed and twenty-three wounded. Total losses by the Federals at Kernstown amounted to 590; the Confederates lost 718. *OR* 12(1):346–47, 384.

17. I have been unable to locate any of the general orders Fortescue refers to; however, General Banks, in his official report submitted at the close of the Valley Campaign some months later, mentioned the "most valuable assistance" rendered by the Signal Corps. "There should be some provision," he wrote, "for the prompt promotion of officers and men so brave and useful as those composing this corps." Col. Nathan Kimball, the field commander of the Union forces at Kernstown, in an addendum to his official report, noted that the soldiers of the Signal Corps "deserve the greatest praise, and by their vigilance and efficiency have made the Signal Corps an indispensable arm of the service." Prior to the foregoing adulatory comment by Kimball, frustration had been manifested by the commander of the signal detachment at Kernstown, Lt. William W. Rowley, at the lack of

recognition received by the signalmen for their services during the battle. Writing to signal chief Myer soon after the fighting, he complained, "I would like to be returned to my regiment as this service is very expensive and hard. I believe I have labored more than any man in the division, and as yet get no credit. All of us have endeavored to do our duty, but the service is such that no one knows it or seems to appreciate it. As yet I have seen no mention of us made at the battle of [Kernstown]. I know we were of great service. The general commanding told me we were of great service, and that we should be honorably mentioned. . . . I would like to be returned to my regiment where I can stand some show for promotion." *OR* 12(1):353, 366, 552. Examples of attempts by Meyer to prod high-ranking Union officers into acknowledging the efforts of his signalmen are in Scheips, "Albert James Myer," 417, and Brown, *Signal Corps*, 195–203. Myer's politicking, while undertaken to advance the interests of the Corps, irritated more than a few general officers and officials. Gen. Phil Sheridan considered Myer a schemer who had "wire-pulled himself from an assistant surgeon to a colonel in the regular army." Brown, *Signal Corps*, 168.

18. The Rebel officer whom Fortescue encountered wounded on the field at Kernstown was Capt. James Yancey Jones, commander of Company E of the five-company-strong First Virginia Battalion, also known as the Irish Battalion. Jones was removed from the battlefield and brought to the nearby courthouse in Winchester, where he was ministered to by a surgeon and several female citizens of the town. His face had been horribly disfigured by his wound (both eyes were indeed shot out and the bridge of his nose was gone), and the captain, realizing how unnerving his appearance was, pointed to his temple as one of the nurses tried to work on him and said, "Ah, if they had only struck *there* I should have troubled no one." Jones lingered for several more days following his removal to Winchester, alternating between lucidity and delirium, and died on March 28. Gary L. Ecelbarger, *We Are in for It: The First Battle of Kernstown*, March 23, 1862, Shippensburg, Pa.: White Mane, 1997.

19. Sears, *George B. McClellan*, 176.

20. A native of New York, Col. Jonas P. Holliday was an 1850 graduate of West Point. He served in various positions in the dragoons and cavalry of the Regular Army until he was appointed to lead the First Vermont Cavalry on February 14, 1862. Heitman, *Historical Register* 1:537.

21. Fortescue is wrong concerning the date of this incident, which occurred on April 5. A court of inquiry was convened soon after Colonel Holliday's suicide to determine the events surrounding his death. The surgeon of the regiment testified,

"All the business of conducting a regiment agitated the colonel. I persuaded him to rest at a house in Harpers Ferry, and he insisted that I stay with him. He was afraid to be alone. He told me, 'If I can't get some sleep, I will go insane.' His sighs and groans convinced me that the suffering and privation of the men, both now and in the future, distressed him. He had had not more than two hours of sleep a night in the past month, but I saw no reason to fear suicide." Thomas P. Lowry, *Tarnished Eagles: The Courts-Martial of Fifty Union Colonels and Lieutenant Colonels* (Mechanicsburg, Pa.: Stackpole Books, 1997), 194–96.

22. Pvt. James Martin of Company B of the Twenty-ninth Pennsylvania was one of the soldiers mentioned by Fortescue: "When near a place called Edenburg," wrote a comrade of the dead soldier, "a shell from the Rebel Battery exploded over our company killing James Martin, one of my tentmates; the whole top of his head was tore off. . . . It was a terrible sight for us as he was a fine young fellow well liked by all the company." Later the same day, Pvt. Gottlieb Spear of Company I of the Twenty-ninth was killed during an attempt to cross the Shenandoah opposite Edenburg. Bates, *History of Pennsylvania Volunteers* 1:484–85, 525; Monat, "Three Years in the 29th Pennsylvania; Brooks Journal.

23. Capt. William B. Williams, a thirty-year-old prewar engineer from Jamaica Plain, Massachusetts, began his war service as the first lieutenant of Company E of the Second Massachusetts. Promoted to the captaincy of Company G on November 1, 1861, he was killed in action ten months later at the Battle of Cedar Mountain. *Mass. in the War* 1:106.

24. Forty-eight-year-old Samuel App of Philadelphia resigned his commission on July 11, 1862. MR 29 PV, Harrisburg.

25. 2nd Lt. George W. Wiggins Jr., a twenty-six-year-old Philadelphia native, resigned from the Twenty-ninth on May 11, 1862. Ibid.

26. The soldiers who perished in this mishap were Sgt. James Evans, a twenty-one-year-old laborer from Limerick, Maine, and Pvt. George Freeman, a twenty-four-year-old English-born Boston resident. Alonzo H. Quint, *The Record of the Second Massachusetts Infantry, 1861–1865* (Boston: James P. Walker, 1867), 316.

27. Dr. William S. King, a Pennsylvania native, was a Regular Army surgeon and medical director of Banks's corps.

28. It is difficult, based on the cursory allusions Fortescue makes toward him, to positively identify Dick Powell. The roster of the Signal Corps in Brown's *History of the Signal Corps* does list a Richard Powell (without designating a regimental affiliation), but his name is followed by the notation that he was rejected from the service. Brown, *Signal Corps*, 851.

29. In this instance, Fortescue's hindsight appears to have been clouded by events that occurred later in the war. John Singleton Mosby was certainly the most effective (and feared) guerrilla leader who operated in the Eastern theater during the war, but he did not assume his role as an independent partisan ranger until early 1863. Moreover, his raids in the section of the Shenandoah Valley Fortescue was traveling through took place during the Valley Campaign of 1864. Unlike Mosby, however, Fortescue would have had reason to dread a brush with partisans from the command of Lt. Col. Elijah V. White. White, a twenty-nine-year-old gentleman farmer from Loudoun County, Virginia, had raised an independent company for "border warfare" in late 1861 and later saw it expanded into a larger unit officially designated as the Thirty-fifth Battalion Virginia Cavalry. Nicknamed the Comanches, White's men were active in attacking Federal picket posts in Loudoun County and the lower Shenandoah Valley during the first half of 1862. John E. Divine, *35th Battalion Virginia Cavalry* (Lynchburg, Va.: H. E. Howard, 1985), 1–6.

30. Fortescue's aversion to anything Southern is apparent here. The Taylor Hotel, far from being antiquated, had been constructed in the late 1840s. Though no longer functioning as a hotel, the altered façade of the building can be seen in present-day Winchester. A contemporary illustration of the hotel is in James E. Taylor, *With Sheridan Up the Shenandoah Valley in 1864: Leaves from a Special Artist's Sketchbook and Diary* (Dayton, Ohio: Morningside House, 1989), 159–60.

CHAPTER 3

1. Col. Joseph F. Knipe of the Forty-sixth Pennsylvania (1823–1901) was promoted to brigadier general in November 1862 and led various brigades and divisions in the Army of Virginia and the Army of the Potomac before transferring west with the Twelfth Corps in September 1863. Maj. George W. Gile of Philadelphia, a thirty-two-year-old prewar actor, was promoted to lieutenant colonel of the Eighty-eighth Pennsylvania on September 1, 1862. Severely wounded at Antietam, he was promoted to colonel in December 1862 but was discharged as a result of his wounds in March 1863. Serving subsequently as colonel of the Ninth Veteran Reserve Corps, he was brevetted to the rank of brigadier general at the close of the war. QM Sgt. John T. Reilly, a thirty-eight-year-old Philadelphian, was eventually advanced to the first lieutenancy of Company K of the Ninetieth Pennsylvania and was captured in September 1864. He was discharged in March 1865. 1st Lt. William I. Augustine, thirty, of Company K of the Twenty-ninth

Pennsylvania, ascended to the captaincy of his company on November 11, 1864. The Philadelphia native was brevetted to the rank of major in the omnibus promotions of March 1865. MR 88 PV, 90 PV, 29 PV, Harrisburg; Bates, *History of Pennsylvania Volunteers* 3:75, 172, 182.

2. John Pope assumed command of the Army of Virginia, which was formed by the combination of the Mountain Department, the Department of the Shenandoah, and the Department of the Rappahannock on June 26, 1862, but did not take the field with his army until late July.

3. German émigré Franz Sigel (1824–1902) had taken command of the Army of Virginia's First Corps when Gen. John C. Fremont refused to serve under Pope, whom he outranked. The First Corps had been formed from troops formerly comprising the Mountain Department. Nathaniel Banks's forces from the Department of the Shenandoah became the Second Corps under Pope. Maj. Gen. Irvin McDowell of Ohio (1818–1885), an 1838 West Point graduate and the loser at First Manassas, commanded the Third Corps, comprised of most of the troops that had previously served under him in the Department of the Rappahannock. Determining the exact strength of the army is difficult. Fortescue's tally of 48,000 is probably close to the mark, but the 18,500 men he attributes to Banks's corps—which had closer to 10,000 effectives—is far too high. He did not, however, include cavalry in his estimate, which numbered between 5,000 and 6,500. Robert K. Krick, in his study of the Cedar Mountain battle, places the total number of Federals at 45,000, including cavalry, while John Hennessy in his Second Manassas study estimated a total Union force of 51,000. Pope's most recent biographer, Peter Cozzens, puts the number of troops at between 48,000 and 52,000, and Pope himself, who would have had an interest in understating the number, estimated his strength at 43,000, including 5,000 cavalry. Robert K. Krick, *Stonewall Jackson at Cedar Mountain* (Chapel Hill: Univ. of North Carolina Press, 1990), 5; John J. Hennessy, *Return to Bull Run: The Campaign and Battle of Second Manassas* (cited hereafter as Hennessy, *Second Manassas*) (New York: Simon & Schuster, 1993), 6; Peter Cozzens, *General John Pope: A Life for the Nation* (Urbana: Univ. of Illinois Press, 2000), 90; *OR* 12(2):20.

4. As Fortescue notes, soldier's comments to Pope's widely publicized address were numerous and pointed. The pronouncement was, in fact, written with the full approval of Secretary of War Edwin M. Stanton, who was responsible for some of its more strongly worded passages. Many in the Army of the Potomac understandably viewed it as an affront, while reactions from soldiers who would

serve under Pope were mixed: "These invidious comparisons and other offensive matters in [Pope's] orders," wrote a New York infantryman, "disgusted the Army of Virginia, who were keenly sensitive to any implied censure, and upon whose good will the fortunes of General Pope himself were peculiarly dependent." In contrast, a Maine cavalryman remarked that Pope's address "had put new life into the officers and men of his command. . . . They believed in Gen. Pope, and they welcomed him to their command with a feeling that he was the man for the place." Wallace J. Schultz and Walter N. Trenerry, *Abandoned by Lincoln: A Military Biography of General John Pope* (Urbana: Univ. of Illinois Press, 1990), 102–3, 108; Isaac Hall, *History of the Ninety-Seventh Regiment New York Volunteers (Conkling Rifles) . . .* (Utica, N.Y.: L. C. Childs and Son, 1890), 43–44; Edward P. Tobie, *History of the First Maine Cavalry, 1861–1865* (Boston: Press of Emery & Hughes, 1887), 75–76. Comments supportive of Pope (which are far less abundant than those critical of him, and almost wholly recorded prior to the Second Manassas Campaign) can be found in Mary Warner Thomas and Richard E. Sauers, eds., *The Civil War Letters of First Lieutenant James B. Thomas* (Baltimore: Butternut and Blue, 1995), 58; Jane B. Steiner, ed., *George Washington Irwin: The Civil War Diary of a Pennsylvania Volunteer* (Lafayette, Calif.: Hunsaker, 1991), 138. Statements by those expressing dissatisfaction with Pope's perceived verbosity are in Charles E. Davis Jr., *Three Years in the Army: The Story of the Thirteenth Massachusetts Volunteers . . .* (Boston: Estes and Lauriat, 1894), 90–91; Milo M. Quaife, ed., *From the Cannon's Mouth: The Civil War Letters of General Alpheus S. Williams* (Detroit: Wayne State Univ. Press, 1959), 104, 110–11; Russell Duncan, ed., *Blue-Eyed Child of Fortune: The Civil War Letters of Robert Gould Shaw* (Athens: Univ. of Georgia Press, 1992), 224–25.

5. It was not, as Fortescue relates, Pope's second general order but the aforementioned July 14 order to the Army of Virginia that was reported as having been issued from his "Headquarters in the Saddle." That it had not originated from there mattered little to Pope's opponents, who seized on it to belittle him. Fitz John Porter, whose attitude typified that of the anti-Pope, pro-McClellan faction, wrote that "Pope has not improved since his youth and has now written himself down as what the military world has long known, an ass. His address to his troops will make him ridiculous in the eyes of military men abroad as well as at home." Hennessy, *Second Manassas*, 13.

6. The reception Banks received from Pope was not an isolated incident. An officer who served under him in the Army of Virginia recalled that Pope's

"deportment towards the subordinate officers of his command, who had occasion to call on him in person, was not such as to inspire respect, but seemed rather unconciliatory, if not uncivil; as if [he was] conscious of his offence but disdained to use a little suavity to regain their good will. This unpopularity. . . . among his own officers, arising mainly from his lack of culture and tact, was enough to have demoralized any army susceptible of deep impressions, except, perhaps, the army he was called to command." Hall, *History of the Ninety-Seventh Regiment,* 44.

7. Possibly Capt. William R. Murphy of Fortescue's original regiment, the Twenty-ninth Pennsylvania. Murphy had been promoted from a first lieutenancy in Company F of the Twenty-ninth to captain and commissary of subsistence of volunteers to date from July 17, 1862. Bates, *History of Pennsylvania Volunteers* 1:520.

8. Pope acknowledged the "very valuable services rendered by the signal officers of this army" in his official report of the Cedar Mountain action. See *OR* 12(2):135–36. Butler Mountain lies south of present-day Virginia Route 522 approximately thirteen miles northwest of Culpeper; Red Oak Mountain rises north of the same road near Woodville, sixteen miles northwest of Culpeper.

9. District of Columbia–born and Virginia-raised Maj. Gen. Richard S. Ewell (1817–1872), an 1840 West Point graduate, and Ambrose Powell Hill of Virginia (1825–1865), an 1847 West Pointer, both commanded divisions that bore their names under Stonewall Jackson at this time.

10. Lieutenant Spencer had been posted on Thoroughfare Mountain—located three miles west of the Cedar Mountain battlefield near James City (present-day Leon)—since July 28 and had relayed substantive information to Pope concerning the movements and estimated strength of the Rebels. He remained there until August 18. A slightly different version of the circumstances surrounding his temporary abandonment of this signal station can be found in Marvin, *Fifth Regiment Connecticut Volunteers,* 221–27.

11. Recounting his experiences of the prior two months in a letter written after Antietam, Spencer remarked, "I have been reported [a] prisoner four times and killed once, but so far I have come out all right and am called a pretty '*tough case.*'" Spencer to Dear Sister, Sept. 29, 1862, Spencer Papers.

12. For examples of the messages Spencer relayed to Pope concerning the movement of Jackson's forces, see Fortescue, Record of Signals Sent and Received, RG 111, National Archives, Washington, D.C.

13. Brig. Gen. Samuel Wylie Crawford of Pennsylvania (1829–1892), a prewar army surgeon who gained notoriety early in the war as a result of his presence at the fall of Fort Sumter, commanded the First Brigade, First Division of Banks's

Second Corps of the Army of Virginia at this time. As Fortescue will subsequently reveal, he was not favorably impressed by Crawford.

14. New York–born and Iowa-raised Brig. Gen. George D. Bayard (1835–1862), an 1856 West Point graduate, commanded the cavalry brigade attached to Irvin McDowell's Third Corps of the Army of Virginia. He was mortally wounded at the Battle of Fredericksburg.

15. Col. George H. Gordon of Massachusetts (1823–1886), an 1846 West Point graduate, commanded the Third Brigade, First Division of Banks's Second Corps of the Army of Virginia.

16. Brig. Gen. Christopher C. Augur of New York (1821–1898), an 1843 West Point graduate, commanded the Second Division of the Second Corps at Cedar Mountain and was seriously wounded during the battle. His brigades were led by Brig. Gen. Henry Prince of Maine (1811–1892), an 1835 West Point graduate who was captured after he had assumed command of the division upon Augur's wounding, and Brig. Gen. George Sears Greene of Rhode Island (1801–1899), a West Pointer from the class of 1823.

17. In his official report of the action at Cedar Mountain, the commander of the signal detachment, Lt. William W. Rowley of the Twenty-eighth New York, made mention of Fortescue and Lt. Brinkerhoff Miner for their "great coolness upon the battle-field, carrying messages from the general commanding in the thickest of the fight." *OR* 12(2):145.

18. Maj. Delevan D. Perkins of New York, an 1849 West Point graduate, was Banks's chief of staff. Heitman, *Historical Register* 1:784.

19. What specifically prompted Banks to attack at Cedar Mountain has been the source of much controversy, especially considering that Pope had ordered him to await reinforcements before assuming any offensive. Fortescue's recounting aside, other accounts suggest that Banks may have been coaxed into his assault by a condescending member of Pope's staff, who told him, "There must be no backing out today." Cozzens, *General John Pope,* 94.

20. Brig. Gen. Jubal Early of Virginia (1816–1894), an 1837 graduate of West Point, at this time commanded Arnold Elzey's brigade of Richard Ewell's division of Stonewall Jackson's Second Corps.

21. Fortescue is slightly confused. William B. Taliaferro of Virginia (1822–1898), who commanded the Stonewall Brigade at Cedar Mountain, ascended to the command of Stonewall Jackson's division when Brig. Gen. Charles S. Winder of Maryland, an 1850 West Point graduate, was mortally wounded during the battle.

22. Brig. Gen. James B. Ricketts of New York (1817–1887), an 1839 West Point graduate, commanded the Second Division of Maj. Gen. Irvin McDowell's Third Army Corps.

23. An 1849 graduate of West Point, Louis H. Pelouze had served in the artillery and infantry of the prewar army and in a variety of staff positions throughout the conflict. He recovered from this wound and in September 1864 was brevetted to the rank of lieutenant colonel in recognition of his services at Cedar Mountain. He was also awarded the brevet rank of brigadier general for his services during the war. Heitman, *Historical Register* 1:781; Roger D. Hunt and Jack R. Brown, *Brevet Brigadier Generals in Blue* (Gaithersburg, Md.: Olde Soldier Books, 1990), 476.

24. Official Federal reports of the battle do not mention the loss of this gun; however, Confederate reports confirm the recovery of a spiked twelve-pounder Napoleon.

25. The artillery duel Fortescue describes (which was remarked upon by soldiers of both armies) was brought on when Stonewall Jackson tried to push northward to Culpeper in pursuit of the retreating Federals. In an attempt to ascertain their location in the gathering dusk, Jackson ordered his accomplished battery commander, Willie Pegram, to shell what appeared to be a Union force straddling the Culpeper Road several hundred yards in their front. Pegram initially sent the Federals reeling (one soldier in the Eighty-third New York claimed that a band in Samuel Sprigg Carroll's brigade began to play, enabling the Confederates to pinpoint where Union reinforcements were positioned), but his guns, along with their infantry supports, soon came under a withering crossfire from Capt. George Leppien's Fifth Maine Battery, Capt. James Hall's Second Maine Battery, and Capt. James Thompson's Battery C, Pennsylvania Light Artillery, and suffered heavy casualties. One of the dead officers Fortescue mentions seeing was Lt. Mercer Featherstone of Pegram's battery, who was beheaded by an artillery round. Jackson soon abandoned his plans to advance further that evening. A good overview of this aspect of the fight (and a thorough treatment of the battle with an emphasis on Southern participation) can be found in Krick, *Stonewall Jackson at Cedar Mountain*, 299–314. Accounts of the artillery duel from the Federal perspective can be found in Hall, *History of the Ninety-Seventh Regiment*, 53–54; John W. Jacques, *Three Years' Campaign of the Ninth N.Y.S.M. During the Southern Rebellion* (New York: Hilton, 1865), 91–92; Charles S. McClenthen, *A Sketch of the Campaign in Virginia and Maryland . . . by a Soldier of the 26th N.Y.V.* (Syracuse: Masters & Lee, 1862), 3–4.

26. Union losses at Cedar Mountain were 320 killed, 1,466 wounded, and 617 missing or captured, totaling 2,381 out of roughly 9,000 engaged. Of that number, 165 were officers. The Confederates lost 314 killed, 1,062 wounded, and 42 missing or captured, totaling 1,418 out of a battlefield strength of about 15,000. Krick, *Stonewall Jackson at Cedar Mountain*, 45, 368–76.

27. Dudley Donnelly, the thirty-seven-year-old colonel of the Twenty-eighth New York, died from his wounds on August 15, 1862. His regiment was decimated in the fight at Cedar Mountain, losing 213 men. All of its field officers were wounded, and of the fourteen company-grade officers carried into the fight, all were either killed, wounded, or taken prisoner. Phisterer, *New York in the War* 3:2058; *OR* 12(2):152.

28. Adjutant Charles P. Sprout of the Twenty-eighth New York was reported as having been killed outright at Cedar Mountain, not mortally wounded as Fortescue thought. *OR* 12(2):152.

29. Pope had not expected that Banks would bring on a general engagement south of Culpeper and had instructed him to wait until Franz Sigel's First Corps came to within supporting distance before assuming any offensive. Upon hearing the sounds of the engagement from his headquarters in Culpeper, a surprised Pope ordered Sigel and James B. Ricketts's division of McDowell's Third Corps forward to the battlefield. Although they arrived too late to assist in the fighting, they helped shore up the unsteady Union retreat.

30. Possibly Sgt. William B. Gillespie of Company H, Twenty-eighth New York Infantry, although the roster in the history of the Signal Corps in the Civil War states that he was discharged from the signal service in March 1862. Brown, *Signal Corps*, 777.

31. Possibly the Twelfth Virginia Cavalry, as the Twelfth Virginia Infantry was not present at Cedar Mountain, either during or immediately after the fight.

32. Maj. Gen. Jesse L. Reno (1823–1862), an 1846 West Point graduate, commanded the Second Division of Maj. Gen. Ambrose Burnside's Ninth Corps. His troops were actually positioned on the left (not right) of Pope's force, guarding the crossings of the Rappahannock south of Stevensburg, Virginia. Reno was promoted to command of the corps in early September 1862 but was killed by friendly fire less than two weeks later at South Mountain on September 14. Hennessy, *Second Manassas*, 39. As subsequent footnotes reveal, I have relied heavily on Hennessy's masterful study to validate Fortescue's account of his experiences during the Second Manassas Campaign.

CHAPTER 4

1. It was not infantry but Confederate cavalry that the Yankee artillerists skirmished with between Brandy Station and Rappahannock Station on August 20. *OR* 12(2):726–27.

2. Fortescue exaggerates the outcome of this action, and is in error regarding its timing (it occurred during the afternoon of the twenty-first). Longstreet's corps had begun to march up the west side of the Rappahannock in support of Stonewall Jackson's move around Pope's flank, but near Kelly's Ford his rear guard collided with Federals from the Ninth Corps conducting a reconnaissance toward Stevensburg. Two brigades from Cadmus Wilcox's division held the Yankees at bay until late afternoon, when they broke off the action and continued north. Hennessy, *Second Manassas*, 64, 486.

3. Brig. Gen. Henry Bohlen (1810–1862), a German-born resident of Philadelphia, commanded the First Brigade of the Third Division of Franz Sigel's First Corps. He had been sent across the Rappahannock at Freeman's Ford on August 22 to intercept a section of Stonewall Jackson's wagon train as it moved up the riverbank, but his four regiments were ambushed by Isaac Trimble's brigade, supported by John Bell Hood's division, and driven back over the river. In the midst of the retreat, Bohlen was shot through the heart and instantly killed. See ibid., 68–70.

4. The intensity of this rainstorm on the night of August 22–23 raised the level of the Rappahannock by nearly six feet. Ibid., 72.

5. Although Fortescue was evidently ignorant of it, Brig. Gen. Jubal Early's brigade, along with a regiment and two batteries of Brig. Gen. Alexander Lawton's brigade (both of Jackson's corps), had established footholds on the Federal side of the river during the evening of August 22. Separated from the bulk of their corps by the rainstorm that Fortescue has just mentioned, the Confederates assumed a defensive position covering Sulphur Springs and beat back a half-hearted Union probe before recrossing to safety on the evening of August 23–24. Ibid., 70–73, 82–88; Joseph L. Harsh, *Confederate Tide Rising: Robert E. Lee and the Making of Southern Strategy* (Kent, Ohio: Kent State Univ. Press, 1998), 131.

6. Fortescue has significantly overstated the strength of Lee's army; at this time it numbered approximately fifty-five thousand effectives. Hennessy, *Second Manassas*, 456.

7. Princess Agnes Elisabeth Winona Leclerq Joy Salm Salm was the wife of Prussian-born Prince Felix Salm Salm. Prince Salm Salm had served earlier in the war on the staff of Brig. Gen. Louis Blenker, but at this time was apparently unassigned, as he did not assume command of the Eighth New York Infantry

(which was engaged during the Second Manassas Campaign as part of the Army of Virginia's First Corps) until October 1862.

8. The men Fortescue encountered were members of the Second U.S. Sharpshooters attached to Brig. Gen. John Hatch's brigade of Rufus King's division of the Third Corps, Army of Virginia. Commonly known as Berdan's Sharpshooters, they were named after their self-promoting commanding officer, Col. Hiram Berdan, who had suggested the formation of regiments of sharpshooters to the War Department in the months following the onset of war. Two regiments, the First and Second Sharpshooters, were eventually raised (Berdan led the First Sharpshooters, which were attached to the Army of the Potomac, until he was promoted to brigade command), and their ranks were filled by men from all states of the Union who could meet the rigorous standards of accuracy that qualified them to be sharpshooters. A brief recounting of the experiences of the sharpshooters near White Sulphur Springs can be found in C. A. Stevens, *Berdan's United States Sharpshooters in the Army of the Potomac, 1861–1865* (St. Paul: Price-McGill, 1892), 170–71.

9. Piney Mountain, rising immediately northeast of Waterloo and five miles due west of Warrenton, Virginia.

10. Fortescue and his comrade were witnessing the first day of Stonewall Jackson's flanking march around Pope's right on August 25. The move (which Lee had directed in hopes of severing Pope's main supply line, the Orange and Alexandria Railroad) covered twenty-five exhausting miles and took his corps from Jeffersonton, southwest of Warrenton, to the vicinity of Salem, some eight miles west of Thoroughfare Gap. Hennessy, *Second Manassas*, 97–101; Harsh, *Confederate Tide Rising*, 134, 137.

11. Fortescue has confused the orders given by Pope to his corps commanders on August 25. Sigel was instructed to march from Sulphur Springs to Fayetteville, McDowell was to remain at Warrenton, Banks was posted to Bealeton Station on the Orange and Alexandria Railroad with instructions to extend his line southeast toward Kelly's Ford, and Jesse Reno and the Ninth Corps were moved to a position on Banks's left at Kelly's Ford. Unknowingly, Pope was shifting his troops away from Stonewall Jackson's thrust around his right rather than toward it. Hennessy, *Second Manassas*, 103–4.

12. Franz Sigel had been the unlucky recipient of a series of confusing and contradictory orders from Pope on August 25 (in one instance Pope actually ordered Sigel to move his men across the Rappahannock utilizing a bridge that Pope had earlier ordered him to burn). When Sigel sought a personal interview with Pope

to air his grievances, he was greeted with an onslaught of profanity so severe that it reportedly prompted him to offer his resignation. Fortescue is wrong regarding Sigel's inability to prevent the movement of Longstreet through Thoroughfare Gap. Irvin McDowell had issued an order directing Sigel to move his corps toward Thoroughfare on August 27 but countermanded it soon after, sending instead James B. Ricketts's division to contest Longstreet's passage. Heavily outnumbered when he approached the Gap on August 28, Ricketts broke off his engagement after sharp skirmishing and retreated toward Gainesville. See ibid., 103–5, 141–42, 153–61.

13. The ridge of Watery Mountain runs in a north-south direction just west of present-day Virginia Route 17, six miles north of Warrenton. "Watery Mountain is a fine point of observation," wrote a Federal signalman in the fall of 1863, "and it is enough to ascend the top of it to find the desired place; there is a tree known to everyone, called the 'view tree,' and the place where it stands affords view almost in all directions." *OR* 19(1):139.

14. Maj. Gen. Richard H. Anderson of South Carolina (1821–1879), an 1842 West Point graduate, was, as Fortescue details, stationed along the heights on the south bank of the Rappahannock overlooking Sulphur Springs and Waterloo Bridge and was the rearmost element of the Army of Northern Virginia at this time. Anderson would leave this position on August 28, reaching the battlefield at Manassas in the early morning hours of August 30 after a grueling seventeen hour march. Hennessy, *Second Manassas*, 117, 309.

15. Fayetteville, a small hamlet near present-day Opal, Virginia, two and a half miles northwest of Bealeton Station on the O&A Railroad.

16. Fortescue was likely hearing reverberations from skirmishing between Gen. John Reynolds' division of Irvin McDowell's corps, which was moving east along the Warrenton Turnpike toward Manassas Junction and Confederates under the command of Gen. William B. Taliaferro's division of Stonewall Jackson's corps. His comment that the sounds of battle were emanating from the north (Groveton) is curious, because if he indeed was scouting in the vicinity of Haymarket, the cannonading and small-arms fire he heard would have originated due east of his position. The heaviest fighting on August 28 took place at Brawner's Farm, also near Groveton, but this contest between the Iron Brigade, supported by other elements of Rufus King's division, and portions of William B. Talliaferro's and Richard S. Ewell's divisions took place in the early evening. Hennessy, *Second Manassas*, 147–50.

17. When he reached Bristoe Station on the Orange and Alexandria Railroad on the evening of August 26, Stonewall Jackson learned that the large Federal

supply depot at Manassas Junction several miles north was lightly defended. Two regiments of Isaac Trimble's brigade advanced up the line of the track, surprised and scattered the guard at the rail junction, captured over three hundred Yankees and, more important, tons of supplies stockpiled in boxcars, wagons, and warehouses. Most of the balance of Jackson's corps came up the following day and ransacked the depot, feasting on delicacies many had never seen and carrying off as much of the provender as they could shoulder. At midnight of the twenty-seventh, Jackson ordered the remaining stores burned, and the ensuing fire blazed so intensely it could be seen ten miles away. Pope's personal baggage was not captured at Manassas Junction but had been taken several days earlier at Catlett's Station by cavalry under Jeb Stuart raiding along the Orange and Alexandria Railroad. Theodore F. Dwight, ed., *Papers of the Military Historical Society of Massachusetts* (1895; reprint, Wilmington, N.C.: Broadfoot, 1989), 2:106–7; Hennessy, *Second Manassas*, 74–79, 113–15, 122, 129–30, 138.

18. It was not the right but the left flank of the Union army that was nearly overwhelmed by the Confederate assault on August 30.

19. Army of Virginia Third Corps commander Irvin McDowell had sent John Reynolds's Pennsylvania Reserve Division from the left of the Union line to the north side of the Warrenton Pike to reinforce Fitz John Porter's failed attack against Stonewall Jackson on the afternoon of August 30. This movement left the Federals severely outnumbered in the sector south of the Warrenton Pike (2,200 Yankees faced over ten times their number), and James Longstreet, though ignorant of the depleted condition of the forces facing him, attacked the weakened Federal flank and for a time swept everything before him, threatening to cut off the Union line of retreat. Several Union brigades (including Zealous B. Tower's of the Army of Virginia's Second Corps) impeded Longstreet's advance west of the Henry House on Chinn Ridge long enough to allow Pope to rush reinforcements back to his beleaguered left. The Pennsylvania Reserve brigades of Brig. Gen. Truman Seymour and Brig. Gen. George Meade were ordered into position just north of the Henry House and were later supported by the U.S. Regular Brigades of Lt. Col. William Chapman and Lt. Col. Robert C. Buchanan, along with brigades under A. Sanders Piatt and Robert Milroy. As darkness descended over the battlefield, these troops successfully stalled Longstreet's attack, ensuring that the road to Centreville, over which the Federals would withdraw, remained open. Hennessy, *Second Manassas*, 360–63, 393–95, 408–24.

20. Another soldier from Banks's division who was nearby wrote, "I went up and down the burning trains. Hundreds of stragglers were overloading themselves with

pants, blouses and shoes. Bridles, saddles, guns and medical stores were fast going into smoke. A hundred cars is no mean line and a hundred cars afire is no mean smoke. Smoke black, brown, green, grey and red poured from the cars according to their contents. I looked upon the grand ruin and I could not help feeling this immense loss was the result of a want of brains. Panic and fear at nothing, it is the cause of half of our reverses and misfortunes." Jordan, ed., *Civil War Journals*, 183.

21. The Fairfax Road, also known as the Warrenton Pike.

22. The First New Jersey Brigade was made up of the First, Second, Third, and Fourth New Jersey Volunteers. They formed the First Brigade of the First Division of the Sixth Army Corps and were the only troops from the Sixth Corps who were engaged during the Second Manassas Campaign. *OR* 12(2):260.

23. As he has described it, Fortescue's location at this time was very close to Germantown, likely somewhere in the angle formed by the juncture of the Little River Turnpike and the Warrenton Pike. Jeb Stuart's cavalry had been moving north around the Federal right on this day, and when they struck the Little River Turnpike turned east, advancing almost parallel with a retreating Union supply train to their south who were heading east along the Warrenton Pike toward Alexandria. Deciding after a reconnaissance that the infantry force guarding the train was too strong to attack, Stuart sent two guns from his Washington Artillery from Ox Hill (not Germantown, as Fortescue wrote) to shell the Yankees. Col. A. T. A. Torbert, commander of the New Jersey Brigade at this time, reported that Rebel artillery had unlimbered three hundred yards from the Centreville pike and fired six shots into Federal supply trains moving along it: "Drivers deserted their wagons and the greatest confusion prevailed. My guards, stationed on the road to arrest stragglers, by great exertions stopped the train and restored order, forcing men to take charge of the wagons and drive them to Alexandria and towards Centreville." David A. Welker, *Tempest at Ox Hill: The Battle of Chantilly* (Cambridge, Mass.: Da Capo Press, 2002), 98–102; *OR* 12(2):538.

24. Francis Amasa Walker, *History of the Second Army Corps in the Army of the Potomac* (New York: Charles Scribner's Sons, 1886), 91.

25. Jeffry D. Wert, *The Sword of Lincoln: The Army of the Potomac* (New York: Simon & Shuster, 2005), 139.

26. Joseph L. Harsh, *Taken at the Flood: Robert E. Lee and Confederate Strategy in the Maryland Campaign of 1862* (Kent, Ohio: Kent State Univ. Press, 1999), 47.

27. Edwin Vose Sumner of Massachusetts (1797–1863) commanded the Army of the Potomac's Second Corps on the Peninsula; Pennsylvanian Samuel P. Heintzleman (1805–1880), an 1826 West Pointer, commanded its Third Corps; and

William B. Franklin (1823–1903), also from Pennsylvania and an 1843 West Point graduate, commanded its Sixth Corps.

28. Forty-seven-year-old Maj. Gen. Philip Kearney of New Jersey commanded the First Division of the Army of the Potomac's Third Corps.

29. Brig. Gen. Isaac Stevens of Massachusetts (1818–1862), an 1839 West Point graduate, commanded the First Division of the Ninth Corps.

30. D. H. Hill's division crossed the Potomac on the afternoon of September 4; in addition to pushing brigades across the river at Berlin, Maryland, at Noland's Ferry (four miles below Point of Rocks, Maryland), and at Cheek's Ford (several miles south of Noland's Ferry), Roswell Ripley's brigade crossed directly at Point of Rocks. Fortescue was fortunate to have left the town early in the morning. Joseph L. Harsh, *Sounding the Shallows: A Confederate Companion for the Maryland Campaign of 1862* (Kent, Ohio: Kent State Univ. Press, 2000), 71.

31. Col. Dixon S. Miles of the Second U.S. Infantry (1804–1862), an 1824 West Point graduate, commanded the twelve-thousand-man garrison at Harpers Ferry. A court of inquiry convened following the Union rout at First Manassas in 1861 had determined that Miles had been drunk during the battle, but the case was never brought before a formal court-martial and Miles was sent to Harpers Ferry, where, it was thought, he could do little harm. Overmatched by Stonewall Jackson when that Confederate leader commenced siege operations against his command, Miles decided to capitulate on the morning of September 15 but was mortally wounded as the surrender details were being settled on.

32. Likely Pvt. John Ryan of the Second New York State Militia (Eighty-second New York Volunteers). Ryan was a native of New York City who had served in the Department of Washington before his transfer to the Army of the Potomac as a flagman serving under Fortescue. Brown, *Signal Corps,* 370, 862.

33. Lieutenant Miner had retired from his station on Sugar Loaf Mountain on the evening of September 5; returning to the station on the morning of the sixth, he and his flagman, Pvt. Albert Cook, captured two Confederate cavalrymen who were carrying messages from General Lee to Confederate president Jefferson Davis. Immediately thereafter, however, a brigade of Rebel cavalry arrived, capturing Miner and Cook and assuring the safety of the dispatches. The two Federals remained with their captors until just after the Battle of Antietam, when they were sent to Libby Prison in Richmond, from which they were exchanged on October 5, 1862. Brown, *Signal Corps,* 241–42.

34. As Fortescue somewhat sarcastically notes, Lee had expected to partially fill his depleted ranks with Southern-sympathizing Marylanders during his first

invasion of the North, but the anticipated groundswell of support never materialized. A good discussion of this aspect of the Maryland Campaign and the factors that led to the seeming indifference of the natives of the state is in William A. Blair, "'Maryland Our Maryland': Or How Lincoln and His Army Helped to Define the Confederacy," in *The Antietam Campaign*, ed. Gary W. Gallagher (Chapel Hill: Univ. of North Carolina Press, 1999), 74–100.

35. Brig. Gen. Julius White of Illinois (1816–1890) had commanded a three-thousand-man force posted in Winchester, Virginia, in early September. Upon Jackson's approach, he was ordered to abandon the town and link up with Colonel Miles at Harpers Ferry, which he did on September 3. Posted to command troops guarding the Baltimore and Ohio Railroad at Martinsburg two days after his arrival at the Ferry, White was again driven out by advancing Confederates and retreated back to Harpers Ferry. Although he outranked Miles, White declined to take charge of the defense of Harpers Ferry because the commander of the Middle Military Department, Maj. Gen. John E. Wool, had personally placed Miles in command of the garrison. White found himself under arrest following the surrender but eventually succeeded in clearing his name. Hearn, *Six Years of Hell*, 126–29, 154–55, 162–63, 166, 190.

36. This was the First Maryland Potomac Home Brigade Cavalry, commanded by Maj. Henry A. Cole of Frederick, Maryland. C. Armour Newcomer, *Cole's Cavalry; or, Three Years in the Saddle in the Shenandoah Valley* (Baltimore: Cushing, 1895), 41–43.

37. Col. William P. Maulsby was the commander of the First Regiment, Potomac Home Brigade Infantry. Captured, along with the entire brigade, at Harpers Ferry on September 15, Maulsby was paroled soon after and served until his resignation in August 1864.

CHAPTER 5

1. Although it is difficult to completely determine how serious a breach of duty it was considered, Fortescue's decision to abandon his station on Maryland Heights did not go unnoticed. In his official report of the Antietam Campaign, signal chief Myer remarked that officers stationed at Point of Rocks and on Sugar Loaf Mountain attempted to contact Fortescue by signal flags and rockets without success on September 12, five days after he had departed. "It was afterwards ascertained," Myer wrote, "that Captain Fortescue had in so far misapprehended the position in which he could be of most service as to leave the Heights prior

to their investment." In spite of this faintly damning statement, Myer added the caveat that Fortescue had not been given positive orders to remain on the Heights at all hazards. Even so, when the time came to single out officers for special mention for their services during the campaign, Fortescue was one of only several not specifically cited in Myer's report. *OR* 19(1):119, 124–25.

2. A popular hotel on West Washington Street in Hagerstown, Maryland. It is believed that John Brown and two of his sons stayed there under aliases en route to Harpers Ferry in 1859. See Taylor, *With Sheridan Up the Shenandoah*, 300, for a contemporary drawing of the hotel.

3. Middleburg, Pennsylvania, in southern Franklin County in close proximity to the Maryland border.

4. Brig. Gen. Fitzhugh Lee of Virginia (1835–1905), an 1856 West Point graduate, was the nephew of Army of Northern Virginia commander Robert E. Lee. At this time he commanded a brigade of the cavalry division of the army.

5. Nathaniel Banks deserves credit for having recognized, in the days immediately after the defeat at Second Manassas, the need to dispatch the signal officers attached to his corps—including Fortescue—to locales along the Catoctin Mountain range in order to observe the anticipated advance of the Army of Northern Virginia. Foiled in their attempts to scale the Catoctins, they reached strategic positions along the Maryland side of the Potomac and provided timely reports of Rebel movements. 1st Lt. William B. Roe of the Sixteenth Michigan served in many of the important campaigns of the Army of the Potomac through October 1863. In December of that year, he was sent west and served in the Department of the Gulf (as chief signal officer) and in the Department of Louisiana. In May 1864 he was appointed chief signal officer of the Department of Washington and in the waning months of the war commanded the Signal Camp at Georgetown. He resigned on May 13, 1865. John Robertson, *Michigan in the War* (Lansing, Mich.: W. S. George, 1880), 918; Brown, *Signal Corps*, 784, 859.

6. 2nd Lt. Frederick Homer of Company E of the Sixth New Jersey Volunteers was posted to the signal detachment of the Army of the Potomac in March 1862 and participated in a variety of signal assignments throughout McClellan's Peninsula Campaign. Present during the Antietam Campaign at Point of Rocks and later at Fredericksburg, he returned to his regiment and was dismissed from the service in July 1864. Aaron B. Jerome had begun his war service as a sergeant of Company B of the First New Jersey Volunteers and was soon promoted to the second lieutenancy of Company H. Detailed to the signal detachment of the Army of the Potomac in March 1862, he served on a naval gunship opposite Yorktown early in

the Peninsula Campaign. Actively engaged during the Antietam, Fredericksburg, Chancellorsville, and Gettysburg campaigns, he was appointed to a first lieutenancy in the permanent Signal Corps to date from March 1863. Assigned to act as chief signal officer of the Department of the Gulf in April 1864, he served there until he resigned his commission on September 20, 1864. Brown, *Signal Corps*, 795, 804; William S. Stryker, *Record of Officers and Men of New Jersey in the Civil War, 1861–1865* (cited hereafter as Stryker, *New Jersey Record*) (Trenton, N.J.: John L. Murphy, 1876), 1:280.

7. Fortescue is mistaken; the advance of the Army of the Potomac was still well short of Hagerstown. He is likely referring to traveling west on the National Pike from Frederick, Maryland.

8. Brig. Gen. Jacob D. Cox of Ohio (1828–1900) commanded the Kanawha Division of Jesse Reno's Ninth Corps; Brig. Gen. Orlando B. Willcox (1823–1907), an 1847 West Point graduate, led its First Division; Brig. Gen. Samuel D. Sturgis of Pennsylvania (1822–1889), a West Pointer from the class of 1846, led the Second Division; while forty-year-old Isaac Rodman of Rhode Island (who would be mortally wounded at Antietam) commanded the Third Division. These divisions were instrumental in forcing back (but not completely clearing) Confederates under the immediate command of D. H. Hill from Fox's Gap, located a mile south of Turner's Gap. See Stephen W. Sears, *Landscape Turned Red: The Battle of Antietam* (New Haven, Conn.: Ticknor and Fields, 1983), 129–35, 139–40.

9. John P. Hatch (1822–1901), a New York native and 1845 West Point graduate, had commanded the cavalry brigade under Banks during the Valley Campaign of 1862. At this time he led the First Division of the First Corps under Joseph Hooker and was severely wounded during the assault on Turner's Gap on September 14, 1862.

10. Maj. Gen. William B. Franklin commanded the Army of the Potomac's Sixth Corps. Despite Fortescue's positive spin, Franklin's attack at Crampton's Gap, six miles south of Turner's Gap, was inexplicably slow in getting under way, and though ultimately successful in clearing the passage of Rebel resistance, Franklin failed to exploit his advantage. His First Division was commanded by Brig. Gen. Henry Warner Slocum of New York (1827–1894), an 1852 West Pointer, and his Second Division was led by Brig. Gen. William F. Smith of Vermont (1824–1903), an 1845 West Point graduate. They were initially opposed at Crampton's Gap by a mix of five understrength cavalry and infantry regiments and were later reinforced by a brigade of Georgians under former Georgia governor and U.S. Speaker of the House Howell Cobb. Sears, *Landscape Turned Red*, 146–49.

11. Actual Union losses in the combined actions at South Mountain amounted to 1,813; the Southerners lost 2,685. Maj. Gen. Jesse L. Reno, commander of the Federal Ninth Corps, was killed in the action at Fox's Gap, as was Brig. Gen. Samuel Garland of Virginia (1830–1862), Confederate commander of Early's brigade of Daniel Harvey Hill's division. Thomas L. Livermore, *Numbers and Losses in the Civil War in America, 1861–65* (reprint, Dayton, Ohio: Press of Morningside House, 1986), 90–91.

12. From a vantage point on South Mountain, Middletown would have lay to the rear, while Boonsboro would have been to the front.

13. The strength of McClellan's army at Antietam was approximately 71,500; the Confederates mustered some 39,000.

14. McClellan's headquarters were located at the home of Philip Pry, two miles northeast of Sharpsburg on a bluff overlooking the battlefield. The signal station on Elk Ridge (also known as Red Hill or Elk Mountain), a commanding height approximately eleven hundred feet above sea level two and a half miles east of Sharpsburg (behind Federal lines), provided timely, accurate information on Confederate troop movements during the battle (though McClellan seems to have profited little by it), as did the station at Washington Monument, located on South Hill in the South Mountain Range. A signalman posted on Elk Mountain wrote, "Our station was in very little danger & we could see the whole battlefield & it was the prettiest sight I ever beheld—shells flying in all directions, houses burning, musketry cracking & altogether the grandest sight imaginable." Sept. 17, 1862, Luther C. Furst Diary, Harrisburg Civil War Round Table Collection, USAMHI (cited hereafter as Furst Diary). See *OR Atlas,* plate 28, maps 1 and 2, for the location of this station and of the other Federal signal stations manned during the battle.

15. Hooker's movement on the evening of the sixteenth was not opposed by D. H. Hill but by John Bell Hood, commanding a division in Jackson's corps. Hooker's stopping point that night was almost a mile north of the Dunker church. *OR* 19(1):922–23.

16. Fifty-nine-year-old Brig. Gen. Joseph K. F. Mansfield of Connecticut had been posted to command of the Federal Twelfth Corps two days prior to the Battle of Antietam and died from his wounds the day after the fight. Fortescue is mistaken regarding the sequence of the attacks he describes. Brig. Gen. George Hartsuff of New York led a brigade in James Ricketts' Second Division of the First Corps, while Brig. Gen. Abner Doubleday, also of New York, commanded the First Division of the corps. Hartsuff had been wounded during the early morning

assault through the East Woods, and his brigade suffered heavy losses before it withdrew. Doubleday's division, advancing west of the Hagerstown Pike, had gained a foothold on the north end of the West Woods and was supported (not reinforced) by the advance of the Twelfth Corps. Hooker was wounded in the foot and forced to leave the field.

17. Greene's division had gained more ground than any other Union force on the north end of the battlefield on this day, and they stubbornly held onto the terrain near the Dunker church, fending off a number of attempts to dislodge them until midday, when they were forced back in disarray by elements of John Walker's division of Longstreet's corps. Sears, *Landscape Turned Red,* 231–32, 248–49.

18. Benjamin Franklin Fisher, a twenty-eight-year-old prewar attorney from Centre County, Pennsylvania, began his Civil War service as a lieutenant of Company H of the Third Pennsylvania Reserves. Detailed to the Signal Corps in August 1861, he was appointed an instructor at the Signal Camp at Georgetown and served in the field in increasing roles of responsibility from the Peninsula Campaign through Antietam, when he was named chief signal officer of the Army of the Potomac. Promoted to a captaincy in the permanent Signal Corps to date from March 1863, Fisher served at Chancellorsville and in the early stages of the Gettysburg Campaign. Captured near Aldie, Virginia, on June 17, 1863, he spent the next eight months in Richmond's Libby Prison, successfully escaping through the infamous tunnel on February 9, 1864. Resuming his position as chief signal officer of the Army of the Potomac, Fisher served at Meade's headquarters until December 1864, during which time he was promoted to major and colonel. On December 26, 1864, soon after Myer was relieved by Secretary Stanton, he was promoted to chief signal officer of the army (i.e., the head of the Signal Corps) and served until November 1866, when, due to the expiration of his commission as colonel in the Corps, he resigned. Fisher was brevetted to the rank of brigadier general for gallant and meritorious service during the war. Brown, *Signal Corps,* 86–88, 163–65, 169, 769–70.

19. Burnside had not been ordered to begin his attack by McClellan in the seven o'clock hour; rather, McClellan alerted Burnside at that time to *expect the order to attack,* and it was possibly this directive that Captain Fisher carried to Burnside. Col. Delos B. Sackett, the Army of the Potomac's inspector general, wrote erroneously, in a postwar letter that was published in McClellan's posthumous memoir, that he reached Burnside with the attack order at 9:00 a.m., when in fact it was closer to noon. Fortescue is wrong regarding the timing of the commencement of

the assault on the bridge by the Ninth Corps; it began just prior to 10:00 a.m., not at 2:00 p.m., as he states. Sears, *Landscape Turned Red,* 235, 262, 355–56.

20. Space constraints prohibit a complete recounting of the happenings at the lower, or Burnside's, bridge on the morning of September 17. As Stephen Sears has pointed out, shoddy reconnaissance work by McClellan's staff officers (who selected an impassable ford farther down Antietam Creek as a crossing point for a flanking element of the Ninth Corps) and a confused command structure (which resulted in an unconscionable lack of familiarity with the features of the terrain over which the assault was to take place) nearly doomed the undertaking and, in fact, severely delayed it. McClellan's initial message ordering Burnside to commence his attack was received, as noted earlier, at approximately 10:00 a.m., and soon after Burnside initiated the first of three abortive attempts to carry the bridge. At 12:00 p.m., with the bridge still not taken, McClellan sent Colonel Sackett to instruct Burnside to take the span at all costs. An assault led by the Fifty-first New York and the Fifty-first Pennsylvania of Brig. Gen. Edward Ferrero's brigade secured the bridge at 1:00 p.m., but it took Burnside an additional two hours to bring up ammunition and position the reinforcements necessary to continue the attack. After ninety minutes of furious fighting, which saw the Federals reach the outskirts of Sharpsburg, the Ninth Corps troops were pushed back to their starting point by the attack of Confederate general A. P. Hill's Light Division, which had just arrived from their capture of Harpers Ferry. Ibid., 262–67, 276–91

21. McClellan's most trusted lieutenant, Maj. Gen. Fitz John Porter, commanded the Fifth Army Corps, which on paper contained just over twelve thousand men, though only half as many were on hand on September 17. With the exception of several of its Regular brigades, it was held in reserve at Antietam and experienced minimal casualties. Had the bulk of the available Fifth Corps troops been thrown across Antietam Creek to reinforce Union attacks on either the northern or southern end of the battlefield (or used to mount an independent action directly across the Middle Bridge), the Battle of Antietam may well not have ended in the tactical draw that it did.

22. Lee had designated that Longstreet's divisions in the center of the Confederate line were to commence the retreat on the night of the eighteenth, and would be followed by Stonewall Jackson's divisions on the left, with the rear of the force being covered by A. P. Hill's division and several brigades of cavalry. Longstreet left his position around 9:00 p.m., and, as Fortescue confirms,

purposely left his campfires intact to mislead the Northerners. Harsh, *Taken at the Flood*, 446–47; Harsh, *Sounding the Shallows*, 217.

23. The subject of wounded Confederates left around Sharpsburg in the wake of Lee's retreat is touched upon in Harsh, *Sounding the Shallows*, 216–17.

24. The Douglas mansion, also known Ferry Hill Place, was owned by the Rev. Robert Douglas and overlooked the Potomac River and Shepherdstown from a commanding eminence on the Maryland side. His son, Lt. Henry Kyd Douglas, served as assistant inspector general on Gen. Stonewall Jackson's staff at this time. The structure still stands, and from 1979 to 2001 it was used as the headquarters of the C&O Canal National Historical Park.

25. Col. James Barnes of the Eighteenth Massachusetts (1801–1869), an 1829 West Point graduate, commanded the First Brigade, First Division of the Fifth Corps at Shepherdstown, in place of Brig. Gen. John H. Martindale. While only in temporary command of the First Brigade at this time, he was soon appointed brigadier general and permanently replaced Martindale. He would lead the brigade at Fredericksburg and Chancellorsville, and during the Battle of Gettysburg, he commanded the First Division.

26. The action that took place at Shepherdstown on September 20, 1862, is generally overlooked due to the carnage that preceded it at Antietam three days earlier. It was, in fact, the single costliest battle fought on West Virginia soil during the Civil War, resulting in 624 combined casualties, with the majority of the Federal losses occurring in the ill-fated 118th Pennsylvania, which had been in the service for just over a month. Despite Fortescue's comment condemning Colonel Barnes for the debacle, much of the blame can be assigned to Col. Charles Prevost, the forty-four-year-old commander of the 118th who, despite having received an order to retreat before his regiment was overwhelmed, refused to obey it because it was delivered to him in what he thought was an improper manner. Prevost was severely wounded in the shoulder during the action at Shepherdstown, and the consequences of his injury plagued him throughout his life until he died from their effects, partially paralyzed and blind, in 1887. Mark A. Snell, "Baptism of Fire: The 118th ('Corn Exchange') Pennsylvania Infantry at the Battle of Shepherdstown," *Civil War Regiments* 6, no. 2 (2000): 119–42; Survivors' Association, *History of the 118th Pennsylvania Volunteers Corn Exchange Regiment, from Their First Engagement at Antietam to Appomattox*. . . (Philadelphia: J. L. Smith, 1905), 681. Good descriptions of the fighting by an officer of the 118th can be found in J. Gregory Acken, ed., *Inside the Army of the Potomac: The Civil War Experience of Captain Francis*

Adams Donaldson (Mechanicsburg, Pa.: Stackpole Books, 1998), 126–38, and in Survivors' Association, *History of the 118th Pennsylvania,* 54–94.

27. Twenty-two-year-old Jed C. Paine, a native of Brooklyn, New York, had begun his war service as first lieutenant of Company I of the Fifty-seventh New York Volunteers and was later promoted to the captaincy of Company B. He began active field service in the Signal Corps with the Army of the Potomac during the Antietam Campaign. Appointed to a captaincy in the permanent organization of the corps to date from March 1863, he served with the Ninth Corps from late August 1864 through March 1865 and commanded the signal detachment in the Department of Virginia and North Carolina in the months after the end of the war. Brown, *Signal Corps,* 846; Phisterer, *New York in the War* 3:2499–2500.

28. A positive identification of the wounded Rebel officers is difficult. The Palmetto Sharpshooters formed a portion of Brig. Gen. Micah Jenkins's brigade of Brig. Gen. David R. Jones's division of Longstreet's corps and reported losses at Antietam of eight killed and fifty-seven wounded. Two officers listed as seriously wounded were Lt. W. N. Major and Lt. H. H. Thompson, so there is a possibility that Fortescue encountered one of these men at the Douglas house. The identity of the wounded Louisiana Tiger is harder to ascertain, as that nickname was applied to an entire brigade of Louisiana regiments serving under Brig. Gen. Harry T. Hays in Lawton's division of Longstreet's corps. *OR* 19(1):906, 908; Sears, *Landscape Turned Red,* 188.

29. According to Rev. Douglas's son, Henry Kyd Douglas, on a stormy night in October the wind threw open the shutter of an upstairs window of Ferry Hill Place as Mrs. Douglas was passing by with a candle. The Federals mistook the candle for a signal light and hauled Reverend Douglas off to Fort McHenry in Baltimore (not Old Capitol Prison), where he remained for six weeks. Henry Kyd Douglas, *I Rode with Stonewall* (Chapel Hill: Univ. of North Carolina Press, 1940), 181–82.

30. Thirty-two-year-old Michael Scott of Philadelphia served as major of the Twenty-ninth Pennsylvania from July 1, 1861, until his resignation in February 1863. MR 29 PV, Harrisburg.

31. Col. John K. Murphy of the Twenty-ninth, a sixty-five-year-old Philadelphian, had been captured in the streets of Winchester, Virginia, on May 25, 1862. Early in the action that day his horse was shot from under him, and he was unable to keep up with the retreating Union forces. Returning to his regiment following captivity in October 1862, he resigned his commission six months later on April 23, 1863. Lt. Col. Charles Parham, thirty-five, also of Philadelphia, at

this time had apparently already submitted his resignation, as it was accepted to date from July 19, 1862. Incapacitated by an undetermined illness that left him lame in the days leading up to the action at Front Royal, Virginia, on May 23, 1862, Parham, who was then in command of a detachment of five companies from various regiments of Banks's division, was caught up in the rout of the Federals by Stonewall Jackson's forces and joined in the retreat. When he reached Martinsburg, Virginia, the next day, he reported that he required "medical attention and quiet nursing, also a change of linen and clothes," and proceeded, incredibly, to hop a train bound for Philadelphia via Baltimore. Ibid.; OR 12(1):560–63,624; Frank H. Taylor, *Philadelphia in the Civil War, 1861–1865* (Philadelphia: Published by the City, 1913), 61.

32. Theodore Coursault was originally the first sergeant of Fortescue's Company A of the Twenty-ninth. The twenty-two-year-old Philadelphia native was promoted to first lieutenant in July 1862 and served as such until his resignation on April 9, 1864. MR 29 PV, Harrisburg; Bates, *History of Pennsylvania Volunteers* 1:505.

33. McClellan was aghast at the pronouncement and drafted a letter to Lincoln opposing the proclamation. He was dissuaded from sending it by military and civilian confidants, who told him that coming out against it would be a "fatal error." Sears, *George B. McClellan*, 326.

34. "It is indeed a 'Fair View,'" wrote Lt. Joseph Spencer while stationed at this post in October 1862, and noted that from it he could see north to Chambersburg, Pennsylvania, Hancock, Maryland, to the northwest, Harpers Ferry and Martinsburg, and as far as Berryville and Bunker Hill, Virginia, in the Shenandoah Valley. Spencer to "Dear Sister," Oct. 22, 1862, Spencer Papers. The location of this station, which was positioned just north of the National Road several miles west of Clear Spring, Maryland, is shown on *OR Atlas,* plate 27, map 2. The Wayside Inn Fortescue refers to, though now a private residence, still stands along the old National Pike at the base of Fairview Mountain.

CHAPTER 6

1. Halleck quoted in Sears, *George B. McClellan*, 332.

2. George Meade, *The Life and Letters of George Gordon Meade, Major General United States Army* (New York: Charles Scribner's Sons, 1913), 1:319.

3. Sears, *George B. McClellan*, 337.

4. Bruce Catton, *This Hallowed Ground: A History of the Civil War* (New York: Doubleday, 1956), 171–72.

5. 1st Lt. Charles A. Atwell of Knap's Independent Battery E, Pennsylvania Light Artillery, was a twenty-two-year-old Pittsburgh native. Promoted to captain of the battery in July 1863, he was mortally wounded at the Battle of Wauhatchie, Tennessee, on October 29, 1863. Edward R. Geary, seventeen, of Salem, Pennsylvania, a second lieutenant, was the oldest son of Brig. Gen. John Geary, commander of the Second Division of the Twelfth Corps. He was killed in action at Wauhatchie, Tennessee, on October 29, 1863. Thirty-seven-year-old James D. McGill of Pittsburgh, a prewar merchant, served as a lieutenant in Knap's Battery until promoted to captain in March 1864. He resigned his commission in July 1864. Brady, *Hurrah for the Artillery*, 6–8, 12–15.

6. Fortescue is slightly confused about the men who led this expedition. The eighteen hundred troopers who took part in it were commanded personally by the leader of the cavalry of the Army of Northern Virginia, J. E. B. Stuart, and were handpicked from the brigades of Brig. Gen. Wade Hampton, Brig. Gen. Fitzhugh Lee, and Brig. Gen. Beverly Robertson. Divided into groups of six hundred, the detachments were commanded by Hampton, change to Brig. Gen. W. H. F. "Rooney" Lee (eldest son of Robert E. Lee), and Col. William E. "Grumble" Jones. H. B. McClellan, *The Life and Campaigns of Major General J. E. B. Stuart* . . . (Boston: Houghton Mifflin, 1885), 136–37.

7. Lieutenant Rowley later wrote that owing to the fog, Stuart's troopers were not spotted until they were three hundred feet away from his signal station, and that in addition to Pvt. Robert Vincent and Pvt. Peter Emge captured, they lost all of their extra clothing, three McClellan saddles and bridles, two horses, two full sets of flags, one saber, three pistols, two telescopes, two marine glasses, and two kites. *OR* 19(2):33.

8. Stuart's goals for the raid included the seizure of horses, the garnering of information on McClellan's troop dispositions and intentions, the arrest of public officials to be held as hostages for citizens of the Confederacy who had been similarly taken prisoner, and the destruction of a railroad bridge near Chambersburg, Pennsylvania, which connected McClellan with his supply base at Hagerstown. Edward G. Longacre, *Lincoln's Cavalrymen: A History of the Mounted Forces of the Army of the Potomac* (Mechanicsburg, Pa.: Stackpole Books, 2000), 109; McClellan, *Life and Campaigns*, 137.

9. Brig. Gen. Alfred Pleasonton (1824–1897), a native of the District of Columbia and 1844 West Point graduate, at this time commanded the cavalry division of the Army of the Potomac. Despite being outclassed by his Confederate counterpart, Stuart, he eventually ascended to the command of the Cavalry Corps of the army,

which he led, with mediocre results, until Grant was appointed commander in chief in March 1864.

10. New York native George Stoneman (1822–1894), an 1846 West Point graduate, commanded the First Division of the Third Army Corps at the time of Stuart's raid. Promoted to major general in late November 1862, he commanded the Third Corps at Fredericksburg but is probably best remembered for his command of the Federal cavalry at Chancellorsville.

11. When McClellan notified Washington that part of the reason for his cavalrymen's inability to intercept Stuart's raiders was the worn out condition of their horses, Lincoln would have no part of it. "The President has read your telegram," General in Chief Halleck wired back, "and directs me to suggest that, if the enemy had more occupation south of the river, his cavalry would not be so likely to make raids north of it." Sears, *George B. McClellan,* 333–34.

12. Provost Marshal Fletcher is unidentified; Fortescue's reference to the Blue Star Division of the Twelfth Corps is to its Third Division.

13. The lure of increased rank was, as Fortescue describes, a powerful incentive to induce a young subaltern to return to his regiment and was undoubtedly a situation Myer had to confront on a number of occasions prior to the establishment of the permanent Signal Corps. Writing to a highly regarded lieutenant who was similarly tempted by the promise of promotion in his original regiment, Myer commented that he "could not advise him to decline captaincies," but that if the officer chose to remain in the signal service, he would "have a chance at more prominence and distinction . . . than falls to the lot of most captains." "If this Corps be established," he continued, "those who have so faithfully done their duty will not be overlooked." Myer to William S. Tafft, Feb. 17, 1862, quoted in Scheips, "Albert James Myer," 417.

14. That is, a native of County Cork, Ireland.

15. The Fifth New York Infantry, also known as Duryee's Zouaves, were named for the wealthy New York businessman who had raised and led them, Abram Duryee, and were one of the more famous infantry commands in the Army of the Potomac. Assigned to the Second Division of the Fifth Army Corps, the Zouaves were one of the few volunteer regiments considered disciplined enough to be brigaded with Regular Army troops. During the fighting at Second Manassas, the New Yorkers had suffered the unfortunate distinction of losing 297 men out of 490 carried into battle, most of them in a space of ten minutes. Fox, *Regimental Losses,* 191; Hennessy, *Second Manassas,* 373.

16. In a letter written soon after this incident, Fortescue related that upon see-ing "the Rebel videttes not over 400 yards [away], our things were packed in 5 minutes and then there was some of the tallest *skedaddling* down that Mountain through the bushes and over the rocks that has been seen in these parts for some time—there were 5 in the party, all however got away except one of our men who was captured at 6 p.m." Fortescue to "Friend Sam," Nov. 13, 1862, photocopy in bound volume 153, Fredericksburg and Spotsylvania National Military Park, Fredericksburg, Virginia (cited hereafter as FSNMP).

17. Brig. Gen. Catharinus P. Buckingham of Ohio (1808–1888), an 1829 West Point graduate, was at this time on special assignment to the War Department.

18. Commenting on the scenes produced by McClellan's leave taking several days later, Fortescue wrote that "he emerged from his Head Quarters and pro-ceeded to a large field opposite where the Signal Camp was pitched and behind which the Infantry and Cavalry composing his body guard had been drawn in line awaiting him. His appearance was a signal for a general outburst from all on the ground, the men cheered, threw up their hats, waved their swords and gave vent to their feelings in every conceivable way—he was thus received by each Corps. At the tent of Gen. Fitz John Porter the scene was very affecting, the officers comprising this Corps crowded around him sobbing and crying like children. The General stood in the centre bidding farewell with tears in his eyes and sobs chok-ing his utterance—the scene will never be forgotten by those who witnessed it—the men were loud in their denunciations of the administration and resignations are said to be quite numerous." Fortescue to "Friend Sam," Nov. 13, 1862, FSNMP. For more soldiers reactions to the change of commanders, see John J. Hennessy, ed., *Fighting with the Eighteenth Massachusetts: The Civil War Memoir of Thomas Mann* (Baton Rouge: Louisiana State Univ. Press, 2000), 113; Acken, *Inside the Army of the Potomac,* 161–62, 164–65; J. Harrison Mills, *Chronicles of the Twenty-First Regiment New York State Volunteers.* (Buffalo: Gies, 1887), 316–17, 19. Prior to his removal, McClellan had been slowly advancing south toward Culpeper Court House, utilizing the Orange and Alexandria Railroad as his main supply line. His plans once he reached Culpeper were unclear, but when Burnside assumed command, he chose to shift the army east to Fredericksburg and operate against Richmond from that point, utilizing Union control of the waterways that led in the direction of the Confederate capital to supply him. Sears, *George B. McClellan,* 337; William Marvel, *Burnside* (Chapel Hill: Univ. of North Carolina Press, 1991), 163–64.

20. Originally of Company C of the Ninety-ninth Pennsylvania, 1st Lt. John A. Hebrew of Philadelphia served in various assignments with the signal detachment of the Army of the Potomac between March 1862 and March 1863. Returning to his regiment, he was promoted to captain of Company G and was honorably discharged on September 19, 1864. A member of Company D of the Seventy-third New York, 1st Lt. Frank Yates had served with the signal detachment attached to the Second Corps of the Army of the Potomac during the Peninsula Campaign and during the Antietam Campaign was posted in the environs of Washington, D.C. As Fortescue relates in the next chapter, Yates was returned to his regiment and discharged to date from the Battle of Fredericksburg under less than agreeable circumstances. Brown, *Signal Corps*, 342–44, 790, 901; Phisterer, *New York in the War* 4:2767; *Annual Report of the Adjutant General of Pennsylvania . . . 1866*, 540.

21. John Pope had, by virtue of a series of general orders issued soon after he assumed command of the Army of Virginia, made himself singularly repugnant to many Southerners. In them, he enjoined his soldiers to forage from the countryside over which they traversed (paying citizens for their larder with vouchers redeemable at the end of the war), stated that he would hold local citizens responsible for guerrilla-led depredations against isolated detachments of soldiers and the army's supply line, and ordered any disloyal male Southerners within the lines of his army to be arrested and compelled to take the oath of allegiance. Those declining to take the oath were to be driven from their homes and, if found again within the confines of Federal territory, were to be executed. The orders are reprinted in *OR* 12(2):50–51.

22. "Maryland, My Maryland" was a popular Southern war song written by James Ryder Randall that encouraged the people of Maryland to join with the Confederacy against the North. Their setback at Antietam, coupled with a generally cold reception by the citizens of the western part of the state during their campaign there, soured many of the soldiers of the Army of Northern Virginia on ever hearing it again. See James V. Murfin, *The Gleam of Bayonets: The Battle of Antietam and the Maryland Campaign of 1862* (New York: Thomas Yoseloff, 1965), 303–4.

23. Brig. Gen. Abner Doubleday of New York (1819–1893), an 1842 West Point graduate, was in command of the First Division of the First Corps.

24. Ulric Dahlgren, a twenty-year-old prewar Philadelphia lawyer, was the son of Adm. John A. Dahlgren. Serving at this time as an aide-de-camp to Eleventh Corps chief Franz Sigel, he had reconnoitered through Fredericksburg on November 9, eight days before Sumner arrived opposite the city. Dahlgren was

killed in March 1864 while leading a detachment of cavalrymen on a raid against Richmond. His report of the Fredericksburg foray is in *OR* 19(2):162–63.

25. Reference has previously been made to a number of the generals Fortescue mentions. Maj. Gen. Edwin Vose Sumner was appointed to lead the Right Grand Division, comprised of the Second Corps, under Maj. Gen. Darius N. Couch (1822–1897), an 1846 West Point graduate and New York native, and the Ninth Corps, under Brig. Gen. Orlando B. Willcox. The Centre Grand Division was commanded by Maj. Gen. Joseph Hooker of Massachusetts (1814–1879), an 1837 West Pointer, and consisted of the Fifth Corps under Maj. Gen. Dan Butterfield (1831–1901), a politically connected New Yorker, and the Third Corps, led by Maj. Gen. George Stoneman. The Left Grand Division, under Maj. Gen. William B. Franklin, consisted of the First Corps, commanded by Pennsylvanian Maj. Gen. John F. Reynolds (1820–1863), an 1841 West Pointer, and the Sixth Corps under Maj. Gen. William F. "Baldy" Smith. The Eleventh Corps, under Maj. Gen. Franz Sigel, was announced in the new organization as simply a reserve force, but on January 10, 1863, the Twelfth Corps, under Maj. Gen. Henry Warner Slocum, was added to it and the combined organizations were called the Grand Reserve Division. *OR* 19(2):583; *OR* 21:962.

26. The Lacy House, known as Chatham, was the home of the family of James Lacy. Standing on the east bank of the Rappahannock directly opposite Fredericksburg, Chatham was a prominent landmark during the December 1862 battle and served as a hospital both then and during the fighting around Chancellorsville in May 1863. Noel G. Harrison, *Fredericksburg Civil War Sites, April 1861–November 1862* (Lynchburg, Va.: H. E. Howard, 1995), 102–13.

27. Capt. James S. Hall of Company D of the Fifty-third Pennsylvania Volunteers was initially assigned to the signal detachment of the Army of the Potomac in March 1862 and served on a navy ship in the early stages of the Peninsula Campaign. Posted on Sugar Loaf Mountain, Maryland, during the Antietam Campaign, he served at Fredericksburg, Chancellorsville, and Gettysburg, being stationed on Little Round Top during the latter battle. Appointed captain in the permanent Signal Corps to date from March 1863, he retired from active service in March 1865. Peter A. Taylor, twenty-five, originally the first lieutenant of Company D of the Forty-ninth New York, was posted to the signal service from his regiment in March 1862. He served throughout many of the major campaigns of the Army of the Potomac through the fall of 1863 and later was attached to Winfield Scott Hancock's Second Corps during the Overland Campaign of 1864. Appointed to a captaincy in the permanent Signal Corps effective March 1863,

he became the chief signal officer of the Department of Tennessee in early 1865. Brown, *Signal Corps*, 784, 882. Phisterer, *New York in the War* 3:2392.

28. The Phillips house was the uncompleted residence of Alexander Phillips of Fredericksburg. The two-story, Gothic Revival brick house, located on the east side of the Rappahannock on a bluff one mile northeast of Fredericksburg, served as the headquarters of General Burnside during the battle of Fredericksburg and was utilized as a signal station during both the Fredericksburg and Chancellorsville campaigns. The house was accidentally burned by occupying Union troops in February 1863. Noel G. Harrison, *Fredericksburg Civil War Sites, December 1862–April 1865, Volume Two* (Lynchburg, Va.: H. E. Howard, 1995), 167–72.

29. Capt. Paul Babcock Jr. of Company D of the Seventh New Jersey Volunteers served on several naval warships during McClellan's Peninsula Campaign following his posting to the Signal Corps in March 1862. Returning to field duty in the fall of 1862, he participated in the operations of the corps at Fredericksburg, Chancellorsville, and Gettysburg. Appointed captain in the permanent Signal Corps to date from March 1863, he was promoted in early 1864 to the position of chief signal officer of the Department of Cumberland but resigned his commission four months later on April 30, 1864. Brown, *Signal Corps*, 720; Stryker, *New Jersey Record* 1:322.

30. The order directing the movement of the pontoons necessary to bridge the Rappahannock was issued on November 6 but didn't reach the engineers in charge of them until the twelfth (it was sent via mail rather than telegraph). Additionally, neither the engineers in charge of the pontoon train nor their immediate superiors in Washington were notified that the pontoons were urgently needed. Moving from a point near Harpers Ferry, the engineers arrived in Washington with their equipment on November 14–15 and were ordered to divide the pontoons into two sections. One section was to proceed by water for Belle Plain Landing, while the other section was to move overland south to Fredericksburg. The section traveling by land became mired in the rain-soaked back roads of Virginia near Chopawamsic Creek and was ultimately floated down to Belle Plain, where it linked up with the original seaborne section on November 24 and moved to Fredericksburg. A good account of this movement can be found in Bruce Catton, *Glory Road: The Bloody Route from Fredericksburg to Gettysburg* (Garden City, N.Y.: Doubleday, 1952), 34–39. Descriptions of the obstacles surmounted on the overland route by one of the engineers in charge are in Ed Malles, ed., *Bridge Building in Wartime: Colonel Wesley Brainerd's Memoir of the 50th New York Volunteer Engineers* (Knoxville: Univ. of Tennessee Press, 1997), 93–98.

31. Lt. Col. Joseph Dickinson, a thirty-two-year-old Philadelphian, was originally a member of the Twenty-sixth Pennsylvania. He was serving as Hooker's assistant adjutant general at this time.

32. A disparaging term for people of Jewish heritage.

33. That is, a gambler or con man.

34. "Chines" meaning the end section of the wooden vertical staves that extend over the ends of a barrel, forming a circle.

35. Frederick Fuller, a first lieutenant of Company I of the Fifty-second Pennsylvania Volunteers was detailed to the Signal Corps in March 1862 and served during the fall of that year at Snickers Gap and, later, at Fredericksburg. Posted to duty at Washington, D.C., in mid-1863, he later was assigned to recruiting duty for the corps at Scranton, Pennsylvania. Fortescue is likely referring to George J. Clarke, a twenty-three-year-old New York City native who had transferred to the Signal Corps from his position as first lieutenant of Company H of the Sixty-second New York Volunteers. He served continuously with the detachment assigned to the Army of the Potomac from March 1862 until August 1865 and was appointed to a first lieutenancy in the permanent Signal Corps in March 1863. 1st Lt. Thomas Clarke of the Sixth Vermont Volunteers was also assigned to the signal detachment of the Army of the Potomac at this time, but based on the fact that Lt. George Clarke was paired with Captain Babcock at this time, it appears that Fortescue is referring to him. Brown, *Signal Corps,* 337–38, 744, 774; Phisterer, *New York in the War* 3:2580.

36. Thomas L. Motley, a twenty-seven-year-old merchant from Roxbury, Massachusetts, had begun his war service as a lieutenant in the Second Massachusetts Infantry. Transferring to the First Massachusetts Cavalry in late 1861, he was at this time on detached service at Hooker's headquarters. Wounded and taken prisoner during the Wilderness Campaign, he was eventually exchanged and promoted to major and assistant adjutant general in November 1864. Benjamin W. Crowninshield, *A History of the First Regiment of Massachusetts Cavalry Volunteers* (Boston: Houghton Mifflin, 1891), 319; *Mass. in the War* 4:173.

37. A parvenu is someone who has suddenly risen to a higher class but has not been accepted socially by the class into which they have risen.

CHAPTER 7

1. McClellan had only recently departed from the Army of the Potomac, and the sway in which he held many of the subordinates he left behind was a force that

every subsequent commander of the Army of the Potomac had to contend with. McClellan's most ardent partisans at the corps and division levels of the army at this time included a number of general-grade officers in the Sixth Corps (which even late in the war was a bastion of pro-McClellan sentiment), notably its leader, Maj. Gen. William F. Smith, and two of its three division commanders, Brig. Gen. William T. H. Brooks and Maj. Gen. John Newton, as well as Maj. Gen. William B. Franklin, who commanded the Grand Division containing the corps. Maj. Gen. Darius Couch, former commander of a Sixth Corps division and now commander of the Second Corps, was a stalwart McClellan ally, as were two of Couch's division commanders, Brig. Gen. Winfield S. Hancock (who had served in the Sixth Corps until the Battle of Antietam) and Brig. Gen. John Gibbon. A Fifth Corps divisional commander, Brig. Gen. Andrew A. Humphreys, had, in a fit of emotion upon McClellan's removal, publicly expressed a wish that Little Mac would turn the army north and march on Washington rather than fight the enemy. John J. Hennessy, "We Shall Make Richmond Howl: The Army of the Potomac on the Eve of Chancellorsville," in *Chancellorsville: The Battle and Its Aftermath*, ed. Gary W. Gallagher (Chapel Hill: Univ. of North Carolina Press, 1996), 16, 20–21; Stephen W. Sears, "The Revolt of the Generals," in *Controversies and Commanders: Dispatches from the Army of the Potomac* (Boston: Houghton Mifflin, 1999), 133–167; Acken, *Inside the Army of the Potomac,* 164.

2. Though Fortescue could not have known at the time what state they were from, the Confederate sharpshooters who compromised Federal bridge-building efforts across the Rappahannock on this day were detailed from Brig. Gen. William Barksdale's all-Mississippi brigade, supported by several companies of the Eighth Florida. Reports of their attempt to slow the river crossing are in *OR* 21:600–607.

3. Brig. Gen. Henry J. Hunt (1819–1899), a Michigan-born and Ohio-raised member of the class of 1839 at West Point, was the capable chief of artillery of the Army of the Potomac.

4. Maj. Gen. Oliver Otis Howard of Maine (1830–1909) was an 1854 graduate of West Point. Nicknamed the "Christian General" because of his pious tendencies, he had lost an arm earlier in the war at the Battle of Fair Oaks. Fortescue comments in a later chapter on his personal impression of Howard.

5. Fortescue is slightly confused. Lt. Col. Henry Baxter was the commander of the Seventh Michigan, which was one of the regiments of the Third Brigade, Second Division, Second Corps that conducted the amphibious assault; the brigade was led by Col. Norman J. Hall of the Seventh Michigan.

6. A good treatment of the crossing can be found in Richard F. Miller and Robert F. Mooney, "Across the River and into the Streets: The Twentieth Massachusetts Infantry and the Street Fight for Fredericksburg," *Civil War Regiments* 4, no. 4 (1995): 101–26.

7. Chaplain Arthur B. Fuller of the Sixteenth Massachusetts, a thirty-year-old Watertown, Massachusetts native, had resigned as chaplain of his regiment and was discharged from the service to date from December 10, 1862. He was preparing to return home when he found that the Sixteenth was to be sent into action, and determined to accompany the regiment across the river. In the vicinity of a grocery store at the intersection of Hawk and Caroline Streets, he was fatally wounded by a shot passing through his hip and died soon after. Richard F. Fuller, *Chaplain Fuller: Being a Life Sketch of a New England Clergyman and Army Chaplain* (Boston: Walker, Wise, 1864), 299, 301, 303; *Mass. in the War* 2:214–15.

8. William Hays of Virginia (1819–1875), an 1840 graduate of West Point, at this time commanded the artillery reserve of the Army of the Potomac, with the rank of brigadier general.

9. Welsh-born Col. Joshua T. Owen of Philadelphia (1821–1887), originally the colonel of the Sixty-ninth Pennsylvania, commanded the Second Brigade of the Second Division of the Second Corps, known as the Philadelphia Brigade. Twenty-seven-year-old Ferdinand Pleis of the Seventy-second Pennsylvania Volunteers was the acting assistant adjutant general of Owen's brigade at this time. He was mortally wounded at the Battle of Gettysburg, dying on August 2, 1863. MR 72 PV, HB.

10. French's Division led the vanguard of Darius Couch's Second Corps attack on Marye's Heights; Hancock's (not Howard's) Division followed. Just outside of the limits of the town a fifteen foot-wide millrace obstructed the advance of the Federals.

11. Winfield Scott Hancock of Pennsylvania (1824–1886), an 1844 West Point graduate, commanded the First Division of the Second Corps at Fredericksburg; his fellow Pennsylvanian Andrew Atkinson Humphreys (1810–1883), an 1831 West Pointer, commanded the Third Division of the Fifth Corps. Washington, D.C., native George Getty (1819–1901), an 1840 West Point graduate, commanded the Third Division of the Ninth Corps, while George Sykes of Delaware (1822–1880), an 1842 West Point graduate, commanded the Second, or Regular Division of the Fifth Corps.

12. Mention has been made of Lt. Frank E. Yates in the previous chapter. He had served briefly in the early months of the war as a lieutenant in Company G of

the Eleventh New York Infantry, a regiment commonly known as Ellsworth's Fire Zouaves. The Zouaves were led by Col. Elmer Ellsworth, a Chicago attorney and intimate of Abraham Lincoln who became a martyr to the Union cause when he was assassinated by a Southern sympathizer in Alexandria, Virginia, on May 24, 1861. Prior to the war, Ellsworth had led a drill company in Chicago, famed for its skill and discipline, which had conducted a popular tour of many cities throughout the North in 1860. It is uncertain whether Yates was a member of this group. Phisterer, *New York in the War* 2:1872.

13. Pvt. George White of the Sixth Wisconsin of the Iron Brigade had been assigned to the Signal Corps in early 1862 and was posted in the cupola of the courthouse in Fredericksburg (though he mistakenly recalled that he was positioned in a church steeple) during the battle on December 13: "Hundreds of solid shot roared past me, each one seeming to call for a winding up of my career. Think of it! I was over 200 feet from the ground, charged with a sacred duty that demanded ceaseless attention and any second a shot or shell might hurl me to the street. The church was struck in a dozen places, each time giving me a jar I can never forget. A shell hit the top of the steeple and exploded a piece of iron half as large as your hand dropping within an inch of one of my feet. A solid shot went through my perch three or four feet below my platform. How did I feel? Can't tell. Thought the hour to go had come, but at that moment a message from Burnside's headquarters at the Phillips House was signaled and I repeated it. Never did a poor fellow pray for night as I did." Lance J. Herdegen and William J. K. Beaudot, *In the Bloody Railroad Cut at Gettysburg* (Dayton, Ohio: Morningside House, 1990), 81–82.

14. Lt. Frederick Fuller was the other signal officer stationed in the courthouse steeple with Lieutenant Yates on the day of the battle. After opening signal communication from the steeple, Fuller later wrote, "I . . . expected Lieutenant Yates to take charge . . . but, upon inquiring, no one could tell me where he was. I was obliged to make observations and send all messages unaided, and with only one flagman, the other being obliged to guard my horses." Burnside then sent a message to Yates directing him to keep up the station at all hazards. "Upon receiving the order directed to Lieutenant Yates from General Burnside," continued Fuller, "I again tried to find him, but could not. He came up once, when, by the greatest urging, I succeeded in getting him to send one message, after which he ignominiously fled, and openly declared, in presence of the men, that he would not stay there." This discreditable event notwithstanding, Yates would reenlist as a private in the Eighteenth New York Cavalry in January 1864 and work his way up to captain of his company by the time he was discharged. *OR* 21:160–61; Phisterer, *New York in the War* 1:1039.

15. General in Chief Henry Halleck had counseled Burnside to stay on the west side of the Rappahannock and occupy Fredericksburg following his defeat (as did Sumner and Couch); Burnside seems to have thought that the city was indefensible and was finally swayed by Hooker to cross to the east side of the Rappahannock, which he did on the night of December 15–16. Marvel, *Burnside,* 200.

16. John D. Lentz of Philadelphia was at this time the captain of Company E of the Ninety-first Pennsylvania of the Fifth Corps. He and his company had crossed to the west side of the Rappahannock on picket duty in the early morning hours of December 16 and were overlooked when the word to recross the river was given. Posted in a blockhouse guarding the Richmond, Fredericksburg, and Potomac Railroad crossing near Hazel Run south of the city, Lentz ordered his men to fire on advancing Confederate pickets and retreated to the pontoon bridges that, to his mortification, were not where they had left them. One of his men volunteered to swim the river and secure a pontoon boat, and Lentz soon ferried his entire company, less eleven men who were lost in the retreat, to the east bank of the Rappahannock. He was promoted to major four days later. See *OR* 21:403. Details on the structure Lentz occupied are in Harrison, *Fredericksburg Civil War Sites, April 1861,* 124–25.

17. Fortescue conveniently omits any mention of the wanton plunder of Fredericksburg by Union troops prior to the fight while chastising Confederates for stripping Union dead after the battle. The Rebels, for the most part, were driven by need, while the Federals who sacked the town seem to have been actuated by little more than vindictiveness.

18. Burnside had expected that Franklin would, at the very least, hold the troops on the Confederate right in place to prevent them from reinforcing against the attack of Edwin Vose Sumner on their left, and that in the course of this action he would attempt to turn the Rebel right flank by seizing the high ground near Hamilton's Crossing. Franklin instead launched what amounted to little more than a reconnaissance in force that, despite early success, was brushed back when he failed to properly support it. Marvel, *Burnside,* 175, 181–88, 191–92.

19. *OR* 21:67; Carl Sandburg, *Abraham Lincoln: The Prairie Years and the War Years,* One Volume ed. (New York: Harcourt, Brace, 1954), 328–29.

20. Wert, *Sword of Lincoln,* 209.

21. Fortescue's uncle, Harry C. Fortescue, a Philadelphia-born resident of Chambersburg, Pennsylvania, was the second lieutenant of Company G of the 126th Pennsylvania. MR, 126 PV, HB.

22. Lt. Col. Joseph H. Taylor was chief of staff to Gen. Edwin V. Sumner, commander of the Right Grand Division. The 126th Pennsylvania was a part of the of the First Brigade, Third Division, Fifth Army Corps, and in addition to Lt. Harry Fortescue, it lost eleven killed, sixty-six wounded, and fourteen missing in the battle. *OR* 21:137.

23. In spite of the somber tone of this comment (and, ironically, likely as a result of it), Fortescue and many other soldiers of the Army of the Potomac saw fit to drown their sorrows during the holiday. "Christmas was a dull day at our camp," Fortescue wrote in an early January letter, "but the army all through as a general thing enjoyed itself *hugely*. On the 24th the different commissaries issued Whiskey to all who applied for it . . . so you can probably form some idea of the crowd there was after it. The result was the Army of the Potomac on the 25th was as drunk as an *owl*. We had a Gallon on Christmas Eve and I tell you Whiskey punches flowed like rain—we turned in at 3 a.m. considerably deluged with the above article. I paid a visit to the Head Qrtrs. of Genl. Dan Sickles . . . in the evening of the 25th and found everybody, including the General, considerably inebriated—they actually had to *Buck and Gag* a Captain who got so furiously drunk that he drew his *sabre* and came very near finishing two or three Genls. who were standing near. I also stopped at Hooker's 'Fighting Joe' Hd. Qrtrs. and found things in the same elegant condition." A fellow Pennsylvanian was amazed by the tippling he witnessed around this time. "It is astonishing the extent to which drinking is carried on in camp," he wrote the day after Christmas, "and were I so inclined there is no restriction or limit to the amount of whiskey I could drink. It appears to be a qualification in certain quarters to be able to carry an enormous amount of the beverage with the least possible exhibition of its side effects." Fortescue to "Friend Sam," Jan. 9, 1863, copy in FSNMP; Acken, *Inside the Army of the Potomac*, 196.

CHAPTER 8

1. Mike Pride and Mark Travis, *My Brave Boys: To War with Colonel Cross and the Fighting Fifth* (Hanover, N.H.: Univ. Press of New England, 2001), 192.

2. Fred J. R. Collin, a first lieutenant of the Eighth Pennsylvania Cavalry, had been assigned to the Signal Corps detachment of the Army of the Potomac in March 1862. At this time he was the acting assistant quartermaster for the corps. He was discharged in September 1864. Brown, *Signal Corps*, 747; Bates, *History of Pennsylvania Volunteers* 3:119.

3. Second Lt. Alexander M. Wright of Company K of the Third Pennsylvania Cavalry was posted to the Army of the Potomac's signal detachment in March 1862. He served with the Third Army Corps at Yorktown and, later, with the field telegraph at Fredericksburg. Returned to his regiment in the spring of 1863, he was dismissed for unknown reasons on May 2, 1863. Brown, *Signal Corps*, 900.

4. There were several contemporary dwellings in Stafford County occupied by families named Fitzhugh; the Fitzhugh Mansion Fortescue refers to, known as Sherwood Forest, was located on the north side of the Rappahannock approximately four miles below Fredericksburg and a mile due east of the river. Built in 1837 on land originally owned by George Washington's mother, it served as a hospital following the battles of Fredericksburg and Chancellorsville. Though it has fallen into disrepair, the main house and several outbuildings are still standing. *OR Atlas*, plate 39, map 3; *OR* 21:377.

5. Banks Ford, three miles upriver from Fredericksburg, was the first crossing point on the Rappahannock above the city. During the Civil War there were two crossings here, the upper, which was a ford, and the more frequently used lower, which was a ferry crossing. The upper and lower crossings stood a half mile apart. Noel G. Harrison, *Chancellorsville Battlefield Sites* (Lynchburg, Va.: H. E. Howard, 1990), 199; *OR Atlas*, plate 39, map 3.

6. Commenting on the Mud March in a letter composed after the army had returned to its camps, Fortescue wrote, "It was awful, I never saw anything to equal it—about four o'clock in the afternoon I passed to the extreme right of the line and saw some scenes that really astonished me. The baggage wagons—Artillery—Pontoon boats on wagons, everything was sunk in the mud up to their hubs. I actually saw Pieces of Artillery with twelve horses attached stuck fast also boats on wagons with the same number of horses and ropes on each side manned by an entire Regt. that could not be moved." Undated fragment of LRF letter (likely written on Jan. 26, 1863), FSNMP.

7. Ballard's farm was, as Fortescue notes, located on a small peninsula formed by a bend in the Rappahannock some two and a half miles above Fredericksburg, almost midway between U.S. Ford above and Banks Ford below. Map of Stafford County, 1863. Jeremy Francis Gilmer Collection, Virginia Historical Society, Richmond (cited hereafter as Gilmer Collection).

8. Scotts Farm, also known as Scott's Mill, which is not shown on contemporary maps in the *Official Atlas*, was located on the northern bank of the Rappahannock

at Banks Ford, approximately midway between the upper and lower crossings. Map of Stafford County, 1863, Gilmer Collection.

9. Capt. James E. Smith of the Fourth New York Battery commanded the artillery attached to the Second Division of the Third Corps.

10. "F.F.V.'s," meaning First Families of Virginia.

11. Norman H. Camp, a first lieutenant of Company K of the Fourth New Jersey Volunteers, served with the signal detachment of the Army of the Potomac throughout the Peninsula and Antietam campaigns and on Little Round Top during the Battle of Gettysburg. Appointed first lieutenant in the permanent Signal Corps to date from March 3, 1863, he served later in the war in the Military Division of Western Mississippi and the Department of the Gulf. Brown, *Signal Corps*, 739; Stryker, *New Jersey Record* 1:222.

12. Two weeks after the defeat at Fredericksburg, with Burnside about to begin a new offensive against Lee, Brig. Gen. John Newton, commanding the Third Division of the Sixth Corps, and Brig. Gen. John Cochrane, one of Newton's brigade commanders, were dispatched to Washington by their respective corps and grand division commanders, Maj. Gen. William F. Smith and Maj. Gen. William B. Franklin, to attempt to convince Lincoln to suspend the move and at the same time displace Burnside with McClellan. Burnside learned of the intent of the visit (though not the identities of the messengers) from Lincoln himself during a trip to Washington on December 31 and a day later offered his resignation, which was declined. Sears, "Revolt of the Generals," 142–48.

13. Burnside's General Orders Number 8, drafted on January 23, called for the dismissal of Maj. Gen. Joe Hooker, commander of the Center Grand Division (who had been hinting to anyone who would listen of his fitness to command the army); Sixth Corps generals W. T. H. Brooks, John Newton, and John Cochrane; and Lt. Col. John H. Taylor, chief of staff to Maj. Gen. Edwin Sumner of the Second Corps. General Franklin and General Smith, the chief conspirators in the drama, were ordered to Washington to be reassigned, as were generals Samuel Sturgis and Edward Ferrero, though Burnside stated later that the portion of the order pertaining to these two Ninth Corps officers was made in error. Burnside personally presented his order to Lincoln a day later along with his own resignation and told the president to choose between him and the dissident officers. Lincoln relieved Burnside from command of the army with the promise of reassignment, placing Hooker in his stead. Franklin was relieved from command of the Left Grand Division when Hooker assumed command (he was later sent to the West), while Baldy Smith was posted to command of the Ninth Corps when

it was sent to Tennessee in early 1863. Cochrane, as Fortescue correctly states, resigned, and Brooks was shelved until the spring of 1864, when he commanded a division in the Army of the Potomac for a three month stint. Ibid., 153–57.

14. Fortescue witnessed Burnside's departure from the army, and he recorded in a letter written in late January that as he left, "he remarked, 'Farewell Gentlemen, there are no pleasant reminiscences for me connected with the Army of the Potomac.'" Undated fragment of LRF letter (likely written on Jan. 26, 1863), FSNMP.

15. Lt. Frederick W. Owen, originally of the Thirty-eighth New York, was assigned to the Signal Corps in December 1861 and served as acting signal officer through many of the major campaigns of the Army of the Potomac through Fredericksburg. In March 1863 he returned to his regiment, where he mustered out of the service with the brevet rank of lieutenant colonel three months later. Brown, *Signal Corps*, 845.

16. Alvin Walker of New York served uninterruptedly as additional paymaster of volunteers from September 1861 until May 1865. Heitman, *Historical Register* 1:995.

17. Probably William Henry Owen of Brooklyn, New York, who had begun his war service in the Third Maine Infantry, which was initially commanded by Oliver Otis Howard. William Henry Owen was promoted to captain and assistant quartermaster of volunteers in October 1861. He was later advanced to the rank of colonel and brigade quartermaster and mustered out in June 1865. Heitman, *Historical Register* 1:763; *Maine Adjutant General, 1864 and 1865*, 1076.

18. This is one of only two references Fortescue makes throughout his account of his war service to his brother, Joseph, who was a private in Company I of the Seventy-third Pennsylvania (the other, which is not included in this work, was in reference to a visit he had with him while they were both being held prisoner). Joe, whose muster-in roll lists his age as eighteen, had originally enlisted in the Philadelphia-raised Sixty-sixth Pennsylvania, but this regiment failed to meet its required quota, was disbanded, and had its enlisted men distributed among the Ninety-ninth and Seventy-third Regiments. Joe was captured, along with most of his regiment, at Missionary Ridge, Tennessee, on November 25, 1863, and was sent to the Confederate prison camp on Belle Isle, located in the James River opposite Richmond, almost within sight of his brother's place of incarceration, Libby Prison. He mustered out of the service in January 1865.

19. George H. Hill, originally the first lieutenant of Company E of the Fifty-fifth Pennsylvania Volunteers, had received his signal training in the Department

of the South during the winter of 1861–62 and served with distinction at the capture of Fort Pulaski, Georgia, in April 1862. Transferred north, he began active field service with the Army of the Potomac during the Antietam Campaign and served later at Fredericksburg and Chancellorsville. Promoted to major of his regiment in May 1865, he mustered out of the service three months later. Brown, *Signal Corps,* 253, 256, 793; Bates, *History of Pennsylvania Volunteers* 2:181, 195.

20. The Seddon House, known as Snowden, was home to the family of Maj. John Seddon of the First Virginia Battalion, brother of Confederate secretary of war James A. Seddon. Located on the east side of the Rappahannock approximately six miles south of Fredericksburg, Snowden was one of the most valuable properties in the area, with an assessed worth of ten thousand dollars. The Southern sympathies of the Seddon family would lead to a heightened degree of caution on the part of Federal soldiers stationed near the house. In the spring of 1863, Lt. James Brooks of the Signal Corps, concerned about attempts by the residents of the house to communicate information to Confederates across the river, "made arrangements that the . . . House shall undergo no change in its outward appearance from day to day—by opening or closing windows or blinds or by anything being exhibited upon the lawn in front of the house, that the inmates may not use these means for transmitting information to the enemy." Despite the precautions, there is evidence to suggest that in the days leading up to Chancellorsville the Seddon women successfully used hand signals to warn Confederates across the river of the impending Federal move. In May 1864, Union gunboats razed Snowden in response to Jubal Early's destruction of Maryland governor Augustus Bradford's home. Jerrilyn Eby, *They Called Stafford Home: The Development of Stafford County, Virginia from 1600 until 1865* (Bowie, Md.: Southern Heritage Books, 1997), 250, 252–57; Edwin C. Fishel, *Secret War for the Union: The Untold Story of Military Intelligence in the Civil War* (Boston: Houghton Mifflin, 1996), 324, 655; William A. Blair, "Barbarians at Fredericksburg's Gate: The Impact of the Union Army on Civilians," in *The Fredericksburg Campaign: Decision on the Rappahannock,* ed. Gary W. Gallagher (Chapel Hill: Univ. of North Carolina Press, 1995), 160. The editor is indebted to Al Conner of Stafford, Virginia, for supplying him with details about Snowden and its location.

21. Mud Sills was a derogatory name coined by Southerners to describe Northerners.

22. Brig. Gen. James Wadsworth of New York (1807–1864) commanded the First Division of the First Corps; Alabama-born and Philadelphia-raised David Bell Birney (1825–1864) commanded the First Division of the Third Corps; Thomas A.

Rowley of Pennsylvania (1808–1892) commanded the First Brigade of the Third Division of the First Corps; while John Fulton Reynolds of Pennsylvania (1820–1863), an 1841 West Pointer, commanded the First Corps.

23. Dahlgren was serving at this time as an aide-de-camp to Gen. Hooker with the rank of captain; he was not promoted to colonel until July 1863.

24. Milton W. Cline of the Third Indiana Cavalry, a thirty-seven-year-old prewar sailor and native of New York. Fishel, *Secret War for the Union*, 306.

25. Dan Plew was a private of the Third Indiana Cavalry; Martin E. Hogan was a twenty-five-year-old member of the First Indiana Cavalry; Sid Cole was possibly Sgt. Daniel Cole of the Third Indiana Cavalry; and G. Howard was possibly George Howard Jr. of Maryland, who had spied for Nathaniel Banks during the first half of 1862. Sanford McGee is believed to have been a member of a Unionist family residing west of Fredericksburg, Virginia, as was George McCamack; William Dodd had been a member the First Ohio Light Artillery.

26. Port Conway, Virginia, located some seventeen miles southeast Fredericksburg on the east bank of the Rappahannock River opposite Port Royal.

27. A good description of another one of Cline's extended reconnaissances through enemy lines near Port Royal in late February can be found in Fishel, *Secret War for the Union*, 306–10.

28. The dispatches captured by Dahlgren at Greencastle on July 2 were actually recovered folded inside of a shirt packed in the valise of one of the twenty-two Confederate captives. The correspondence, which was comprised of letters between Lee, Davis, and Gen. Samuel Cooper, revealed important details about the operational status of Confederate armies in the field. For a recounting of Dahlgren's Greencastle expedition and the intelligence procured from his captures, see ibid., 530–32.

29. William Woods Averell of New York (1832–1900) was an 1855 West Point graduate who at this time commanded the Second Division of the Army of the Potomac's Cavalry Corps. His brigades were led by Col. Alfred Duffie of the First Rhode Island Cavalry, Col. John B. McIntosh of the Sixteenth Pennsylvania Cavalry, and Capt. Marcus A. Reno of the First U.S. Cavalry. *OR* 25(1):48, 53.

30. One of the more significant reforms Hooker had instituted upon assuming command of the Army of the Potomac was the consolidation of his cavalry regiments (which up to this point in the war had been assigned piecemeal to various brigades and divisions) into a single nine-thousand-man-strong Cavalry Corps, commanded by Brig. Gen. George Stoneman. The army's cavalry had been consistently bested by their Confederate counterparts (due in part to the improper

way in which they were deployed) and had led Hooker to remark—in approving the offensive by Averell that resulted in the Battle of Kelly's Ford—that there had not been many dead cavalrymen lying around lately, and that should the move be undertaken, there would be. The oft-repeated quote attributed to Hooker ("Who ever saw a dead cavalryman?") appears to have been a paraphrase of that statement, though some credit Confederate general Daniel Harvey Hill with originating it. Longacre, *Lincoln's Cavalrymen*, 127; John Bigelow, *The Campaign of Chancellorsville: A Strategic and Tactical Study* (New Haven, Conn.: Yale Univ. Press, 1910), 74.

31. Thirty-two-year-old Maj. Samuel E. Chamberlain of the First Massachusetts Cavalry, division inspector of cavalry and chief of staff to Brig. Gen. Averell, was shot through the nose and left cheek while leading a charge across the Rappahannock at Kelly's Ford. The prewar policeman and Cambridgeport, Massachusetts, native recovered from his wounds and returned to the army on June 3, 1863. He was brevetted to the rank of brigadier general at the close of the conflict. OR 25(1):48; Crowninshield, *History of the First Regiment*, 115–16; *Mass in the War* 6:142; Hunt and Brown, *Brevet Brigadier Generals*, 106.

32. Fortescue has exaggerated the numbers lost by the Rebels at Kelly's Ford. Fitzhugh Lee reported a loss of eleven killed, eighty-eight wounded, and thirty-four captured (Union accounts list in excess of sixty Confederate captives), while Averell reported six killed, fifty wounded, and twenty-two captured, with nearly half of these losses concentrated in the First Rhode Island Cavalry. OR 25(1):53, 63; Longacre, *Lincoln's Cavalrymen*, 135.

33. Brig. Gen. Thomas Francis Meagher (1823–1867), an Irish-born New Yorker, had raised the Irish Brigade in late 1861, and he led it until just after the Battle of Chancellorsville.

34. Andrew Gregg Curtin (1817–1894), a strong Lincoln ally, served as governor of Pennsylvania from 1861 to 1867; Israel Washburn of Maine (1813–1883) had recently declined to serve a third term as governor of his state, resigning on January 7, 1863.

35. The festivities on March 27 were not a continuation of the St. Patrick's Day festivities that took place in the Second Corps on March 17 but a celebration thrown by Pennsylvanian David Bell Birney, commander of the First Division of the Third Corps, in honor of the visit of Governor Curtin. As on St. Patrick's Day, horse racing was the featured activity, and both young Lieutenant Blucher of the Regular Artillery and Prince Salm Salm were seriously injured falling from their horses. Thomas L. Livermore, *Days and Events, 1860–66* (Boston: Houghton

Mifflin, 1920), 188; Regis De Trobriand, *Four Years with the Army of the Potomac* (Boston: Ticknor, 1889), 427–28.

CHAPTER 9

1. Stephen Minot Weld, *War Diary and Letters of Stephen Minot Weld, 1861–1865*, 2nd ed. (Boston: Massachusetts Historical Society, 1979), 158.

2. William B. Styple, ed., *Writing and Fighting the Civil War: Soldier Correspondence to the New York Sunday Mercury* (Kearny, N.J.: Belle Grove, 2000), 178.

3. 1st Lt. (later Capt.) Edward D. Muhlenberg of Pennsylvania commanded Battery F of the Fourth U.S. Artillery and during the Battle of Chancellorsville was cited for bravery while commanding the artillery of the Second Division of the Twelfth Corps. *OR* 25(1):723, 725–27.

4. In a previous chapter, Fortescue has made clear his dislike for Brig. Gen. Samuel B. Wylie Crawford, and some insight into the general's character can be gleaned from a story related by Theodore Lyman, an officer serving on the staff of Army of the Potomac commander George Gordon Meade in 1865. During the operations around Petersburg in 1864, a sculptor was sent to the army by a wealthy citizen for the purpose of making models of Meade, each of his corps commanders, and of Gen. Alexander Webb, Meade's chief of staff. The models were to be used in the manufacture of medallions, which this unnamed citizen planned to sell for profit. Crawford, who at that time commanded the Third Division of the Fifth Army Corps, was apparently miffed at being left out of the undertaking. "Isn't General Crawford rather an odd man?" the artist asked Webb as he sat for his model one day. "What makes you ask?" answered Webb. "Why, he waked me up in the middle of the night," the artist replied, "and asked what I could make a *statuette of him for!* I told him $400 and he said he thought he would have it done!" On his next encounter with Crawford, Webb asked him if he had seen the sculptor. "Seen him!" Crawford answered. "My dear fellow, he has done nothing but follow me round, boring me to sit for a statuette!" George R. Agassiz, ed., *Meade's Headquarters, 1863–1865: Letters of Colonel Theodore Lyman from the Wilderness to Appomattox* (Boston: Atlantic Monthly Press, 1922), 312–13.

5. "Beautiful day," Fortescue jotted in his diary of the review on April 8. "Quite a crowd attended—many ladies—numerous *stars* & shoulder straps. . . . Uncle Abe delighted, ditto Mrs. Lincoln." Louis R. Fortescue Diary, 1863–1865, Southern

Historical Collection, Wilson Library, University of North Carolina, Chapel Hill (cited hereafter as Fortescue Diary, UNC).

6. Hooker's goal in ordering elements of the First Corps to march down the Rappahannock to Port Conway on April 21 was to draw a portion of Lee's forces away from Fredericksburg and, if practicable, attempt the capture of what was reported to be a small enemy force occupying Port Royal on the west bank of the river. See *OR* 25(2):234.

7. A good recounting of the hardships the Union infantrymen encountered on this march and their efforts to deceive the Confederates across the river can be found in Thomas Chamberlin, *History of the One Hundred and Fiftieth Pennsylvania Volunteers, Second Regiment, Bucktail Brigade* (Philadelphia: F. McManus, 1905), 79–83.

8. Ashton's home was located just south of the Ridge Road in northern King George County, equidistant between the small hamlets of Indian Town and Hampstead, some twenty miles east of Fredericksburg. Map of Spotsylvania and Surrounding Counties, 1864, Gilmer Collection.

9. Joseph Gloskoski, originally the first lieutenant of Company K of the Twenty-ninth New York Volunteers, was posted to the signal detachment of the Army of the Potomac in March 1862 and served throughout the Peninsula Campaign, where he was mentioned for bravery at Gaines' Mills, as well as at Antietam and Fredericksburg. Commissioned a first lieutenant in the permanent Signal Corps to date from March 1863, he participated in the Chancellorsville and Gettysburg Campaigns and accompanied Gen. Judson Kilpatrick on his unsuccessful raid against Richmond in February 1864. Ultimately declining the proffered commission in the Signal Corps, he resigned on April 26, 1864. Brown, *Signal Corps*, 778; Phisterer, *New York in the War* 3:2070.

10. Because he lacked ropes necessary to join his pontoons together to effect a crossing, Doubleday was unable to attempt to capture the small Confederate garrison at Port Royal during this movement. The maneuver was not without results, however, as the Federal's thrust quickly drew a strong Confederate countermove to Port Royal, revealing that an assault on Lee's right—which was under consideration in the weeks leading up to Chancellorsville—would be stiffly resisted. Additionally, Union signal officers were able to intercept Confederate signals relaying incorrectly that a fleet of Federal transports was moving down the Potomac. Two days after Doubleday's feint, James Wadsworth's division, also of the First Corps, successfully crossed the river and captured a small amount of supplies and several prisoners in Port Royal. Fishel, *Secret War for the Union*, 366.

11. The review of the Third Corps by Secretary of State William H. Seward took place on April 27. "I don't know who was with him," wrote an officer who was present, "but there were two four-horse carriage loads of ladies. The review came off very well." James I. Robertson Jr., ed., *The Civil War Letters of General Robert McAllister* (New Brunswick, N.J.: Rutgers Univ. Press, 1965), 291.

12. 1st Lt. Frank W. Marston of Company A of the Seventy-fifth Pennsylvania Volunteers was detailed to the signal service in late December 1861 and took the field with the Army of the Potomac during the Peninsula Campaign. Present at several different postings during the Chancellorsville Campaign, he was promoted to the rank of captain in the permanent Signal Corps and served as chief signal officer of the Department of the Gulf from February 1864 to January 1865. During this period, in July 1864, he was promoted to the rank of major in the Signal Corps (only three other officers in the corps outranked him) and he resigned his commission on February 10, 1865. Brown, *Signal Corps,* 822.

13. An enlightening treatment of the impact Hooker's reforms had on the Army of the Potomac in the months leading up to the spring 1863 campaign can be found in Hennessy, "We Shall Make Richmond Howl," 1–35.

14. The English-made Whitworth rifle fired a hexagonal-shaped bolt, which accounted for the distinctive sound the projectile produced in flight.

15. Frederick Gerker, originally the regimental quartermaster of the Ninetieth Pennsylvania Volunteers, had been promoted to his present position as captain and commissary of subsistence in August 1862. Charles J. Nordquist, forty, of the Eighty-third New York Infantry, was the surgeon in chief of the Second Division of the First Corps. Heitman, *Historical Register* 1:452; Phisterer, *New York in the War* 4:2926.

16. Fortescue Diary, UNC.

17. Messages sent by Fortescue regarding Confederate troop movements on the south side of the Rappahannock opposite his station at the Fitzhugh House between April 29 and May 6 are in his handwritten diary/record of signals sent in RG 111, National Archives, Washington, D.C.

18. The Sixth Maine, supported by the Fifth Wisconsin, led the assault of elements of Col. Hiram Burnham's Light Division of the Sixth Corps against Marye's Heights on May 3. As Fortescue correctly relates, color sergeant John Gray of the Sixth Maine is credited with being the first man over the stone wall at the base of the Heights, which sheltered its Confederate defenders. A recounting of the assault as experienced by the Sixth Maine can be found in James H. Mundy, *No Rich Men's Sons: The Sixth Maine Volunteer Infantry* (Cape Elizabeth, Maine: Harp Publications, 1994), 114–26.

19. Brig. Gen. John Gibbon commanded the Second Division of the Second Army Corps. His troops remained in Fredericksburg and were only lightly engaged during the Battle of Chancellorsville.

20. Balloon Service leader Thaddeus S. C. Lowe (who somewhat fancifully styled himself "Chief of Aeronauts" in his dispatches) had two balloons in service between April 28 and May 4; Lowe manned the balloon "Washington," which was posted on the north side of the Rappahannock River south of Fredericksburg, while the other balloon, known as "Eagle," was upriver from the city at Banks Ford. Reports from Lowe and his subordinate E. S. Allen describing their observations during the battle are in *OR* 25(2):277, 288–89, 324, 336–41, 353–56, 361, 390, 409.

21. Howard and the commander of his First Division, Charles Devens, bear equal amounts blame for the disaster that befell the Eleventh Corps on May 2. Howard, despite imprecations from Hooker to be alive to a threat from his right, failed to take any precautions to prepare for an assault from that quarter, while Devens ignored repeated warnings from subordinates that the enemy were massing on their flank. See Sears, *Chancellorsville*, 237–38, 266–71.

22. Fortescue is resurrecting a rumor that, though it started immediately after the battle, gained credence in the 1880s when Second Corps commander Darius Couch (an avowed foe of the commanding general) wrote that Hooker's courage was typically derived from a bottle, and that had he kept up his usual habits rather than trying to remain sober during the Chancellorsville Campaign, the outcome of the battle may have been different. See ibid., 505–6, for an exploration of the rumors of drunkenness that plagued Hooker in the months and years after the fight.

23. Though lauded by Fortescue, John Sedgwick's performance in command of the Sixth Corps at Chancellorsville was middling. Given discretionary orders to attack Rebel forces holding the town of Fredericksburg on May 2, Sedgwick decided not to attempt an assault despite a preponderance of evidence that showed that the enemy were continually drawing off troops from his front and moving them toward Chancellorsville. When he finally attacked and successfully carried Marye's Heights on May 3, he moved slowly in the face of what was initially a single brigade, ultimately allowing a full division to assemble in front of him at Salem Church and halt his advance. On the night of May 4, when his lines had constricted to form a protective arc around Banks Ford, he chose to retreat to the north side of the Rappahannock rather than hold his position, as Hooker had desired. Sears, *Chancellorsville*, 248–49, 384–85; 417–20.

24. Styple, *Writing and Fighting the Civil War*, 191.

25. Fortescue is in error. Although the Balloon Service under Professor Thaddeus Lowe worked in concert with the Signal Corps, Lowe reported directly to the chief engineer of the Army of the Potomac, Capt. Cyrus Comstock. After Chancellorsville, Lowe tried on several occasions to have his service brought under the command of the Signal Corps, but Maj. Myer was opposed to it, possibly as a result of his experiences earlier in the conflict. At the First Battle of Manassas, Myer had commanded the balloon detachment assigned to McDowell's army, but in his haste to reach the battlefield, the balloon was damaged and never put into use. Fishel, *Secret War for the Union,* 443; Paul J. Scheips, "Union Signal Communications: Innovation and Conflict," *Civil War History* 9, no. 4 (Dec. 1963): 401.

26. Col. Edward Porter Alexander of Georgia (1835–1910) was serving at this time as commander of an artillery battalion in the Reserve Artillery of the First Corps of Lee's Army of Northern Virginia. Graduating from West Point in 1857, Alexander had assisted future Signal Corps chief Albert Myer in testing his wig-wag method of flag signals while stationed at various locations around New York Harbor in the fall of 1859. Appointed a captain of engineers in the Confederate army soon after the outbreak of war, Alexander put his knowledge of Myer's system to good use during the Confederate victory at First Manassas, where he commanded Gen. P. G. T. Beauregard's signal detachment. Brown, *Signal Corps,* 21, 22, 43–45, 205–6; Gary W. Gallagher, ed., *Fighting for the Confederacy: The Personal Recollections of General Edward Porter Alexander* (Chapel Hill: Univ. of North Carolina Press, 1989), 13–14.

27. Federal signal officers had actually deciphered the Confederate flag alphabet in late November 1862, though Fortescue was evidently ignorant of it. Fishel, *Secret War for the Union,* 265–66.

28. Union signal officers became aware of the Confederate's familiarity with their flag alphabet in early April through a captured Confederate signal officer, yet as Fortescue tells, they unthinkingly bragged of their knowledge in subsequent transmissions. The cipher code Myer developed as a result of this information substituted letters for each other, and the pairings were changed on a daily basis and repeated weekly, thus giving the Federals seven separate alphabets to use in their work. To further confuse their foes, Myer directed his signalmen that messages which would lead the enemy believe the Federals were unaware of their possession of the signal code, as well as communications that purposely misled the Rebels about proposed Union movements, were to be sent unenciphered. Ibid., 347–48.

29. Situated on the east bank of the Rappahannock opposite the mouth of Massaponax Creek, Mrs. Gray's house was locally known as Traveller's Rest and appears as such on contemporary maps. It was located just off the River Road approximately five miles below Fredericksburg. *OR Atlas,* plate 39, maps 2 and 3; Map of Stafford County, Virginia, 1863, Gilmer Collection.

30. White Oak Church is located in Falmouth on the east side of the Rappahannock, approximately six miles from Fredericksburg at the intersection of White Oak Road (Virginia Route 218) and Caisson Road (Virginia Route 603).

31. A relatively thorough search of printed source material on the Fifth Corps has yielded no additional information relative to this execution, however, at least one case of capital punishment was recorded during the march to Gettysburg. Pvt. John P. Wood of the First Corps' Nineteenth Indiana, convicted of desertion at the Battle of Fredericksburg, was executed by a firing squad on June 12.

32. While the bulk of the Army of the Potomac, as Fortescue notes, was not active at this time, the Cavalry Corps and elements of the Fifth Corps fought a series of series of skirmishes near the eastern passes of the Blue Ridge Mountains in Virginia as they tried to break through Jeb Stuart's cavalry screen to divine Lee's movements in the Shenandoah.

CHAPTER 10

1. Fisher was captured on a farm near Aldie by a squad of Mosby's Rangers. "The man who took me," he later recalled, "came from nowhere in particular, so far as I could see, but suddenly I was confronted by a fellow 16 feet high, who almost put his revolver down my throat. I know he was not 16 feet high, but he looked like a giant to me. I instinctively put my hand to my hip to draw my own weapon, but my hand fell by my side before I completed the movement. . . . The fellow who captured me said that his finger was already on his trigger as my hand went back, and I escaped death by a hair's breadth." Flagman Luther Furst wrote that Fisher and another officer were "captured near Aldie while out at breakfast & visiting some ladies." *Philadelphia Public Ledger,* Nov. 22, 1914, clipping in Fisher Papers; June 21, 1863, Furst Diary.

2. Fortescue noted in his diary that he boarded in Washington at the Kirkwood House, "a one horse hotel awful for accommodations," visited friends, and attended the theater during his two-day stay. June 22–24, 1863, Fortescue Diary, UNC.

3. The fight at Brandy Station, Virginia, on June 9 was the largest cavalry battle of the war, involving some seventeen thousand troopers and was brought on when Joe Hooker ordered a preemptive attack on a concentration of Rebel cavalry near Culpeper, Virginia, which he feared was planning a raid on his supply lines. Cavalry Corps commander Alfred Pleasonton's two-pronged attack initially took Jeb Stuart's troopers by surprise, but after a day-long fight, the Federals disengaged and left the battlefield. Although Union losses of 866 were greater than the Confederates (575), Brandy Station proved that the Union cavalry in the East, two years into the conflict, was finally on an equal footing with their Southern counterparts.

4. Thirty-year-old Col. Benjamin S. "Grimes" Davis, a Mississippi native and 1854 graduate of West Point, had led his Eighth New York Cavalry on a daring escape from besieged Harpers Ferry on the night of September 14, 1862, and while en route to Union lines captured a forty-wagon ordnance train belonging to Confederate general James Longstreet's corps. At the time of his death at Brandy Station on June 9, 1863, he commanded the First Division of the Cavalry Corps. Hugh Janeway of the First New Jersey Cavalry (who at the time of the battle retained the rank of major) was not killed at Brandy Station but survived until killed at Amelia Springs, Virginia, on April 5, 1865.

5. Capt. Henry B. Sawyer, a thirty-four-year-old carpenter from Cape May, New Jersey, commanded Company K of the First New Jersey Cavalry. Following his capture he was brought to Richmond's Libby Prison, and it is there that Fortescue likely learned the particulars of his capture. Sawyer would gain notoriety when he was chosen at random from the captives in Libby to be executed in retaliation for two Confederate spies who had been put to death. Federal authorities countered that if Sawyer and his fellow hostage, Capt. John Flinn of the Fifty-first Indiana, were executed, they would execute two of their captives, Brig. Gen. W. H. F. "Rooney" Lee, son of Robert E. Lee, and Capt. Robert Tyler of the Eighth Virginia Infantry. Reason soon prevailed over emotion, and Sawyer and Flinn were eventually exchanged for Lee and Tyler. *OR,* ser. 2(6):87, 362, 488, 706, 991, 1127.

6. Fortescue and Kendall, as noted, were posted to Jack's Mountain, a fifteen-hundred-foot elevation on the South Mountain range six miles northwest of Emmitsburg (and ten miles southwest of Gettysburg) situated immediately north-northwest of both the Fairfield Road (present-day Pennsylvania Route 116) and the Waynesboro Pike (Pennsylvania Route 16). Their station would have faced

toward Gettysburg and was likely located on the far eastern portion of the Jack's Mountain spur. *OR Atlas*, plate 66, map 2.

7. Referring to the present-day Waynesboro Pike (Maryland Route 140 and Pennsylvania Route 16) connecting Emmitsburg, Maryland, and Waynesboro, Pennsylvania.

8. Sabillasville, Maryland, some four miles south of Jack's Mountain, seven miles west of Emmitsburg.

9. Though successful in communicating with General Meade at Taneytown (Meade left Taneytown for Gettysburg at 10:00 PM on the first), Fortescue and Kendall were unable to contact the signal station on Little Round Top, the station nearest them on the Gettysburg battlefield. This post was particularly troublesome to the Confederates throughout the battle due to its proximity to Southern lines and the view it provided of Rebel movements. "That wretched little signal station upon Round Top," recalled a Southern officer when writing about the actions of July 2, "that day caused one of our divisions to lose over two hours, and probably delayed our assault nearly that long." It was from this point that Brig. Gen. Gouverneur Kemble Warren of Meade's staff was able to rush Union reinforcements into position when he noticed Southern assault columns forming on the exposed Federal left. See *OR* 27(1):202; and Brown, *Signal Corps,* 360–69.

10. Third Corps commander Maj. Gen Dan Sickles lost a leg in the fighting on July 2; the commander of the First Brigade of the First Division of that corps, Brig. Gen. Charles Graham, was wounded and captured. Other notable casualties among general-grade officers on July 2 included Brig. Gen. Samuel Zook of the Second Corps, who was killed, and Brig. Gen. James Barnes of the Fifth Corps, who was wounded.

11. See chapter 8, note 28.

12. Wesley Merritt of Illinois (1834–1910), an 1860 West Point graduate, had been promoted to brigadier general commanding the Reserve Brigade of the First Division of the Cavalry Corps four days prior to this incident.

13. Advancing from Emmitsburg, Maryland, toward Gettysburg on July 3, Merritt was informed of the presence of a Rebel wagon train loaded with plunder moving along the Millerstown Pike near Fairfield, Pennsylvania, and sent a four-squadron section of the Sixth U.S. Cavalry to intercept it. After some early success when they surprised the column on the outskirts of Fairfield, the Regulars found themselves confronted by a full brigade of Virginians under Brig. Gen. William E. "Grumble" Jones and suffered heavily in the ensuing fight, losing 242 out of roughly 400 men engaged. See Edward G. Longacre, *The Cavalry at*

Gettysburg: A Tactical Study of Mounted Operations during the Civil War's Pivotal Campaign, 9 June–14 July 1863 (Cranbury, NJ: Associated University Presses, 1986), 235–36.

14. Fortescue's reference to Round Top Mountain is to Little Round Top. Heavy timber prevented active signaling from the adjacent (and higher) elevation of Big Round Top during the battle. The structure that Fortescue observed burning was the William Bliss farm, located west of the Emmitsburg Road almost midway between Confederate forces on Seminary Ridge and Union troops on Cemetery Ridge. A haven for sharpshooters of both sides, it was deliberately burned by soldiers detailed from the nearby Federal Second Corps on the morning of July 3.

15. Confederate sharpshooters controlled the low ground around the area of Devil's Den on July 2 and 3, frustrating the efforts of Union signalmen on Little Round Top to send and receive signals. See July 3, 1863, Furst Diary.

16. Fortescue raises an interesting point. The activities of the signal detachments of the Army of Northern Virginia at Gettysburg (and, for that matter, throughout the conflict) are considerably less well-documented than their Northern counterparts, and it would appear, based both on the dearth of reports from Confederate signal officers during the campaign and the lack of mention by field commanders who would have reason to note the services of their signalmen had commendation been merited, that the Confederate signalmen were underutilized at Gettysburg. Historian David Gaddy has noted that Robert E. Lee, while cognizant of the usefulness of the flag and torch signal system (he served as chairman of the War Department board that approved Myer's system in 1859), seems to have simply accepted its existence rather than embraced it as a groundbreaking communications system. Without an advocate in the South (like Myer in the North) constantly applying pressure on both political and military authorities for official recognition of the corps, it is understandable that the services of these men were either taken for granted or completely overlooked. For a discussion of the role of Confederate signalmen during the battle, see David Winfred Gaddy, "The Confederate Signal Corps at Gettysburg," *Gettysburg Magazine* 1, no. 4 (Jan. 1991): 110–12.

17. Fortescue is, of course, witnessing the Pickett-Pettigrew-Trimble charge.

18. Of the approximately 12,500 Confederates who participated in the Pickett-Pettigrew-Trimble attack, more than half, or approximately 6,500, were killed, wounded, or captured.

19. Fortescue's apprehension was not misplaced. Lee began his retreat from Gettysburg on July 4 using two main routes, the Chambersburg Pike, which led

west from Seminary Ridge to Cashtown Pass (Lee utilized this route to send his ambulance, ammunition, and supply trains), and the Fairfield Road, which the Rebel infantry moved south on. J. E. B Stuart's cavalry would screen the movements on both routes. Just south of Fairfield, the Fairfield road splits into two; the Iron Springs-Maria Furnace Road skirted the western side of Jack's Mountain, while the Jack's Mountain Road runs along the eastern base of the mountain and feeds into the Waynesboro Pike. Rebel forces traveling on either side of Jack's Mountain would have obviously posed a threat to Fortescue, Kendall, and their men. Kent Masterson Brown, *Retreat from Gettysburg: Lee, Logistics and the Pennsylvania Campaign* (Chapel Hill: Univ. of North Carolina Press, 2005), 69; Allen C. Guelzo, *Gettysburg: The Last Invasion* (New York: Alfred A. Knopf, 2013), 431.

20. Likely referring to the passageway through Harbaugh Valley, which lies south of Jack's Mountain immediately east of Sabillasville, Maryland.

21. Brig. Gen. Judson Kilpatrick of New Jersey (1836–1881), an 1861 West Point graduate, led the Third Division of the Army of the Potomac's Cavalry Corps. He had been ordered to proceed from Gettysburg to Emmitsburg early on July 4 with the intention of locating Confederate supply trains known to be moving in the direction of Monterey Pass, which lay directly behind (west) of Fortescue's station on Jack's Mountain.

22. The enlisted flagmen captured along with Fortescue and Kendall were Pvt. Benjamin D. Alexander, originally detailed from the First Massachusetts; Pvt. Michael T. Burke, originally from the Ninth New York State Militia; Pvt. John Ryan of the Second New York State Militia; and Pvt. Michael Sheehan, originally assigned from the Twelfth Massachusetts. Brown, *Signal Corps*, 371, 717, 736, 862, 867.

23. David McMurtrie Gregg of Pennsylvania (1833–1916), an 1855 West Pointer, at this time commanded the Second Division of the Cavalry Corps.

24. J. E. B. Stuart had not been separated from Lee during the three-day battle; rather, he had reported to him, after an eight-day circuitous ride around the Army of the Potomac, on the afternoon of July 2. Following the fight at the Rummel Farm (three miles east of Gettysburg) on July 3, Stuart had left the battlefield on the afternoon of July 4 and arrived in Emmitsburg early in the morning of July 5, reporting the capture of sixty prisoners, one of whom, presumably, was Fortescue. The action at Monterey Gap described by Fortescue took place on the night of July 4–5 and was brought on when the ambulance and supply trains of Maj. Gen Richard S. Ewell's (not Ransom's) Corps (escorted by two brigades of Rebel

cavalry) were attacked by several brigades of Brig. Gen. Judson Kilpatrick's cavalry division. As Fortescue correctly reports, the Federals captured over thirteen hundred prisoners and destroyed roughly one hundred wagons. Stuart was not involved in this action. Longacre, *Cavalry at Gettysburg*, 248–50; Eric Wittenberg, "This Was a Night Never to Be Forgotten: The Midnight Fight in the Monterey Pass, July 4–5, 1863," *North & South* 2, no. 6 (Aug. 1999): 44–53.

25. Upon his exchange from Confederate prison in March 1865, Fortescue was sent to Camp Parole, at Annapolis, Maryland, for processing. When released from there, instead of going home to Philadelphia, he wrote that he instead journeyed to Emmitsburg, to the Annan home, to retrieve the valuables he has just mentioned entrusting to the doctor's family. I leave it up to the reader to decide, based on the conflicting accounts I have noted, whether Fortescue actually deposited his valuables with the family as he passed through town a prisoner or whether he secreted them away in their house before his capture there.

26. Stuart left Emmitsburg on the morning of July 5 with the intention of striking west to Hagerstown to link up with another Confederate infantry column that was moving on that city from the north. As he pushed through the passes of South Mountain near Smithsburg, Maryland, his advance was unexpectedly contested by Kilpatrick, who had encamped there following his triumph at Monterey Gap the night before. Mistaking a retrograde movement by a Confederate brigade for a retreat (and believing he was outnumbered), Kilpatrick broke off the action after sharp skirmishing and advanced south to Boonsboro. Longacre, *Cavalry at Gettysburg*, 252–53.

27. From "A Poem Sacred to the Memory of Sir Isaac Newton," by James Thomson (1727).

28. A good description of the action that took place in Hagerstown on July 6, which developed when Judson Kilpatrick advanced north from Boonsboro, Maryland, to attack retreating Confederate supply columns, is in Brown, *Retreat from Gettysburg*, 220–33. Capt. James A. Penfield, a thirty-five-year-old Vermont-born New Yorker, commanded Company H of the Fifth New York Cavalry. Like Fortescue, he would remain a prisoner until March 1865 but was promoted to major of his regiment during his captivity. Following his release, he was brevetted to the rank of lieutenant colonel and resigned his commission on May 2, 1865. 1st Lt. Henry C. Potter of Company M of the Eighteenth Pennsylvania Cavalry escaped from confinement in May 1864 while en route from Danville, Virginia, to Macon, Georgia, but was recaptured. Transferred to Charleston and from there to Columbia, South Carolina, he escaped from prison there, but after thirty days

was again recaptured. Potter was later paroled, rejoined his regiment, and was promoted to captain to date from April 14, 1865. He mustered out of the service in October 1865. Phisterer, *New York in the War* 1:842–43; Kama Lee Ingleston and Wendy Ingleston, eds., *The 1863–1864 Civil War Diary of Captain James Penfield, Fifth New York Volunteer Cavalry Company H* (Ticonderoga, N.Y.: Press of America, 1999), 11; Regimental Association, *History of the Eighteenth Regiment of Cavalry Pennsylvania Volunteers . . .* (New York: Wynkoop Hallenbeck Crawford, 1909), 275.

29. The Confederate officer who had charge of the wagon train of wounded later wrote of the men he was transporting: "Some were praying, others were uttering the most fearful excretions that fear could bring from agony. Occasionally a wagon would be passed from which only low, deep moans could be heard." See Steve French, "Hurry Was the Order of the Day: Imboden and the Wagon Train of the Wounded," *North & South* 2, no. 6 (Aug. 1999): 35–42.

30. John Arthur Richardson of the Second New York Cavalry, a native of Troy, New York, had been promoted to the second lieutenancy of Company D less than two weeks before his capture on July 5, 1863. Like most of the officers taken prisoner at Gettysburg, he suffered a long confinement and was paroled on March 1, 1865. Phisterer, *New York in the War* 1:775.

31. "Oh, such bread," bemoaned one of Fortescue's fellow prisoners of this concoction, "you might use it in cannon for solid shot with fearful execution." Richard N. Beaudry, ed., *War Journal of Louis N. Beaudry, Fifth New York Cavalry: The Diary of a Union Chaplain Commencing February 16, 1863* (Jefferson, N.C.: McFarland, 1996), 53.

32. These men were from Richard B. Garnett's brigade of Gen. George Pickett's division, which had lost 948 out of the 1,459 men it had carried into action on July 3. Maj. Charles S. Peyton of the Nineteenth Virginia, who succeeded to command of the brigade, had lost an arm at Second Manassas in August 1862 and was wounded in the leg during the assault on the Third. Tattnall Paulding, "The Libby Prison Correspondence of Tattnall Paulding," ed. James W. Milgram, *American Philatelist* 89, no. 12 (Dec. 1975): 1118–19; Krick, *Lee's Colonels*, 305.

33. Another prisoner on this march recalled that while passing through Martinsburg, the citizens of the town learned from the guards that that they had not provided their charges with food: "There was a sudden rush for the houses, and in a few seconds the street was lined with women with dishes of cake, bread and everything they could lay their hands on with so short a notice." A near riot broke out in the streets of the town when women tried to break through the guard

line to pass food to the Federals and were pushed back by the Confederate pickets, and it was only averted when the Rebels agreed to assemble the prisoners in an open space outside of town and distribute the food from the citizens to them. See John L. Collins, "A Prisoner's March from Gettysburg to Staunton," in *Battles and Leaders of the Civil War*, ed. Robert Underwood Johnson and Clarence Clough Buel (Secaucas, N.J.: Castle, n.d.), 3:432.

34. Correspondent William Young of the *New York Herald* had been captured during the campaign by Confederate cavalry.

35. On July 16, while passing through Harrisonburg, Virginia, Fortescue jotted in his diary: "Town full of wounded. Strong secesh sentiment prevailing—everybody highly delighted at a site of live Yankees. They simmered at the mention of *Vicksburg.*" Fortescue Diary, UNC.

36. Brig. Gen. John D. Imboden of Virginia (1823–1895) and his command made a similar impression on another Federal officer. "The fierce General Imboden," he recalled sarcastically, "with a feather in his hat, fire in his eye, and profanity in his mouth, with an irregular mounted force, dressed like brigands, formed a vigilant guard on the long march up the valley of the Shenandoah to Stanton." George H. Starr, "In and Out of Confederate Prisons," in *Personal Recollections of the War of the Rebellion: Addresses Delivered Before the Commandery of the State of New York, Military Order of the Loyal Legion of the United States,* 2nd ser., ed. A. Noel Blakeman (New York: Knickerbocker Press, 1897), 72.

37. Fortescue was not alone in his plight, as a number of prisoners (including many from the cavalry who were unaccustomed to long marches on foot) were permitted to fall out in Strasburg to await wagon transportation. Officers who gave their parole not to escape were permitted to move freely within the limits of the town. Paulding, "Libby Prison Correspondence," 1119.

38. In response to the Conscription Act, which held all physically able men between twenty and forty-five liable for military service, riots had broken out in New York City on July 11. The disorder lasted for several days and was only quelled when troops from nearby barracks and several regiments of the Army of the Potomac arrived to reinforce beleaguered police and other civil authorities.

BIBLIOGRAPHY

MANUSCRIPTS

Civil War Museum of Philadelphia, Philadelphia, Pennsylvania:
  Fortescue, Louis R. "Diary of Army Service." Typescript manuscript. 5 vols.
    (Vols. 1–3 cover U.S. Signal Corps service.)
  Military Order of the Loyal Legion of the United States. Membership
    records.
Fredericksburg and Spotsylvania National Military Park, Fredericksburg,
    Virginia (FSNMP):
  Fortescue, Louis R. Letters (copies). Bound Volume 153.
  Map of Spotsylvania and Surrounding Counties, 1864. Jeremy Francis
    Gilmer Collection, Virginia Historical Society, Richmond. Copy at
    FSNMP.
  Map of Stafford County, 1863. Jeremy Francis Gilmer Collection, Virginia
    Historical Society, Richmond. Copy at FSNMP.
Historical Society of Pennsylvania, Philadelphia:
  Foering, John O. Diary. (Twenty-eighth Pennsylvania.)
  Monat, David. "Three Years in the 29th Pennsylvania Volunteers."
National Archives, Washington, D.C.:
  Fortescue, Louis R. Handwritten partial Record of Signal Communications,
    November 1861–May 1863. Record Group 111. (Typescript copy in pos-
    session of Walt Mathers, Glen Burnie, Maryland.)
Pennsylvania State Archives, Harrisburg:
  Muster Rolls. Various Infantry Regiments. Record Group 19.

Private Collection:
  Burr, Lt. Edwin C. Letter, October 11, 1861. (U.S. Signal Corps.)
United States Army Military History Institute, Carlisle Barracks, Pennsylvania:
  Chapman, Lansford. File. Pennsylvania Save the Flags Collection. (Twenty-
  eighth Pennsylvania Infantry.)
  Fisher, Benjamin Franklin. Papers. (U.S. Signal Corps.)
  Furst, Luther C. Diary. Harrisburg Civil War Round Table Collection. (U.S.
  Signal Corps.)
Southern Historical Collection, Wilson Library, University of North Carolina,
  Chapel Hill:
  Brooks, George A. Journal, 1861–2. (Forty-sixth Pennsylvania Infantry.)
  Fortescue, Louis R. Diary, 1863–1865.
  Wisconsin Historical Society, Madison:
  Spencer, Joseph H. Papers (U.S. Signal Corps.)

DISSERTATIONS

Scheips, Paul J. "Albert J. Meyer, Founder of the Signal Corps: A Biographical
  Study." PhD diss., American Univ., 1966.

BOOKS AND ARTICLES

Acken, J. Gregory, ed. *Inside the Army of the Potomac: The Civil War Experience
  of Captain Francis Adams Donaldson.* Mechanicsburg, Pa.: Stackpole
  Books, 1998.
Agassiz, George R., ed. *Meade's Headquarters, 1863–1865: Letters of Colonel Theodore
  Lyman from the Wilderness to Appomattox.* Boston: Atlantic Monthly
  Press, 1922.
*Annual Report of the Adjutant General of the State of Maine for the Year Ending
  December 31, 1862.* Augusta, Maine: Stevens & Sayward, 1863.
Annual Report of the Adjutant General of Pennsylvania . . . for the Year 1866.
  Harrisburg, Pa.: Singerly & Myers, 1867.
Bates, Samuel P. *History of Pennsylvania Volunteers, 1861–5; Prepared in Compliance
  with Acts of the Legislature.* 5 vols. Harrisburg, Pa.: State Printer, 1869–71.

Beaudry, Richard, ed. *War Journal of Louis N. Beaudry, Fifth New York Cavalry: The Diary of a Union Chaplain Commencing February 16, 1863.* Jefferson, N.C.: McFarland, 1996.

Bigelow, John. *The Campaign of Chancellorsville: A Strategic and Tactical Study.* New Haven, Conn.: Yale Univ. Press, 1910.

Billings, John D. *Hardtack and Coffee; or, The Unwritten Story of Army Life.* Boston: George M. Smith, 1888.

Blair, William A. "'Maryland Our Maryland': Or How Lincoln and His Army Helped to Define the Confederacy." In Gallagher, *Antietam Campaign,* 74–100.

Blair, William Allan, ed. *A Politician Goes to War: The Civil War Letters of John White Geary.* University Park: Pennsylvania State Univ. Press, 1995.

Brady, James P. *Hurrah for the Artillery: Knap's Independent Battery "E," Pennsylvania Light Artillery.* Gettysburg, Pa.: Thomas Publications, 1992.

Brown, J. Willard. *The Signal Corps, U.S.A., in the War of the Rebellion.* 1896. Reprint, Baltimore: Butternut and Blue, 1996.

Brown, Kent Masterson. *Retreat from Gettysburg: Lee, Logistics and the Pennsylvania Campaign.* Chapel Hill: Univ. of North Carolina Press, 2005.

Cameron, Col. Bill. "The Signal Corps at Gettysburg." *Gettysburg: Historical Articles of Lasting Interest* 1, no. 3 (July 1990): 9–15.

Catton, Bruce. *Glory Road: The Bloody Route from Fredericksburg to Gettysburg.* Garden City, N.Y.: Doubleday, 1952.

Chamberlin, Thomas. *History of the One Hundred and Fiftieth Pennsylvania Volunteers, Second Regiment, Bucktail Brigade.* Philadelphia: F. McManus, 1905.

Collins, John L. "A Prisoner's March from Gettysburg to Staunton." In Johnson and Buel, *Battles and Leaders of the Civil War* 3:429–33.

Cozzens, Peter. *General John Pope: A Life for the Nation.* Urbana: Univ. of Illinois Press, 2000.

Crowninshield, Benjamin W. *A History of the First Regiment of Massachusetts Cavalry Volunteers.* Boston: Houghton Mifflin, 1891.

Cushing, Samuel T. "The Acting Signal Corps." In *War Talks in Kansas: A Series of Papers Read Before the Kansas Commandery of the Military Order of the Loyal Legion of the United States.* Paper no. 5. Kansas City, Mo.: Franklin Hudson Publishing, 1906.

Davis, Charles E., Jr. *Three Years in the Army: The Story of the Thirteenth Massachusetts Volunteers from July 16, 1861, to August 1, 1864.* Boston: Estes and Lauriat, 1894.

Davis, William C. *Lincoln's Men: How President Lincoln Became Father to an Army and a Nation.* New York: Free Press, 1999.

De Trobriand, Regis. *Four Years with the Army of the Potomac.* Boston: Ticknor, 1889.

Divine, John E. *35th Battalion Virginia Cavalry.* Lynchburg, Va.: H. E. Howard, 1985.

Douglas, Henry Kyd. *I Rode with Stonewall.* Chapel Hill: Univ. of North Carolina Press, 1940.

Duncan, Russell, ed. *Blue-Eyed Child of Fortune: The Civil War Letters of Robert Gould Shaw.* Edited by Russell Duncan. Athens: Univ. of Georgia Press, 1992.

Dwight, Theodore F., ed. *Papers of the Military Historical Society of Massachusetts.* Vol. 2, *The Virginia Campaign of 1862 under General Pope.* Reprint, Wilmington, N.C.: Broadfoot, 1989.

Eby, Jerrilyn. *They Called Stafford Home: The Development of Stafford County, Virginia from 1600 until 1865.* Bowie, Md.: Southern Heritage Books, 1997.

Ecelbarger, Gary L. *We Are in for It: The First Battle of Kernstown, March 23, 1862.* Shippensburg, Pa.: White Mane, 1997.

Fishel, Edwin C. *The Secret War for the Union: The Untold Story of Military Intelligence in the Civil War.* Boston: Houghton Mifflin, 1996.

Fox, William F. *Regimental Losses in the American Civil War, 1861–1865.* Albany, N.Y.: Albany Publishing, 1889.

Frassanito, William A. *America's Bloodiest Day: The Battle of Antietam 1862.* London: Mills and Boon, 1978.

French, Steve. "Hurry Was the Order of the Day: Imboden and the Wagon Train of the Wounded." *North & South* 2, no. 6 (Aug. 1999): 35–42.

Fuller, Richard F. *Chaplain Fuller: Being a Life Sketch of a New England Clergyman and Army Chaplain.* Boston: Walker, Wise, 1864.

Gaddy, David L. "The Confederate Signal Corps at Gettysburg." *Gettysburg Magazine* 1, no. 4 (Jan. 1991): 110–12.

Gallagher, Gary W., ed. *The Antietam Campaign.* Chapel Hill: Univ. of North Carolina Press, 1999.

———. *Antietam: Essays on the 1862 Maryland Campaign.* Kent, Ohio: Kent State Univ. Press, 1989.

———. *Chancellorsville: The Battle and Its Aftermath*. Chapel Hill: Univ. of North Carolina Press, 1996.

———. *Fighting for the Confederacy: The Personal Recollections of General Edward Porter Alexander*. Chapel Hill: Univ. of North Carolina Press, 1989.

———. *The Fredericksburg Campaign: Decision on the Rappahannock*. Chapel Hill: Univ. of North Carolina Press, 1995.

Gordon, George H. *Brook Farm to Cedar Mountain in the War of the Great Rebellion, 1861–62*. Boston: James R. Osgood, 1883.

Gould, John Mead. *History of the First—Tenth—Twenty-Ninth Maine*. Portland, Maine: Stephen Berry, 1871.

Guelzo, Allen C. *Gettysburg: The Last Invasion*. New York: Alfred A. Knopf, 2013.

Hall, Isaac. *History of the Ninety-Seventh Regiment New York Volunteers (Conkling Rifles) in the War for the Union*. Utica, N.Y.: L. C. Childs and Son, 1890.

Harrison, Noel G. *Chancellorsville Battlefield Sites*. Lynchburg, Va.: H. E. Howard, 1990.

———. *Fredericksburg Civil War Sites, April 1861–November 1862*. Lynchburg, Va.: H. E. Howard, 1995.

———. *Fredericksburg Civil War Sites, December 1862–April 1865, Volume Two*. Lynchburg, Va.: H. E. Howard, 1995.

Harsh, Joseph L. *Confederate Tide Rising: Robert E. Lee and the Making of Southern Strategy*. Kent, Ohio: Kent State Univ. Press, 1998.

———. *Sounding the Shallows: A Confederate Companion for the Maryland Campaign of 1862*. Kent, Ohio: Kent State Univ. Press, 2000.

———. *Taken at the Flood: Robert E. Lee and Confederate Strategy in the Maryland Campaign of 1862*. Kent, Ohio: Kent State Univ. Press, 1999.

Hartwig, D. Scott. *To Antietam Creek: The Maryland Campaign of 1862*. Baltimore: Johns Hopkins Univ. Press, 2012.

Hearn, Chester A. *Six Years of Hell: Harpers Ferry During the Civil War*. Baton Rouge: Louisiana State Univ. Press, 1996.

Heitman, Francis B. *Historical Register and Dictionary of the United States Army*. 2 vols. Washington, D.C.: GPO, 1903.

Hennessy, John J., ed. *Fighting with the Eighteenth Massachusetts: The Civil War Memoir of Thomas Mann*. Baton Rouge: Louisiana State Univ. Press, 2000.

———. *Return to Bull Run: The Campaign and Battle of Second Manassas*. New York: Simon & Schuster, 1993.

————. "We Shall Make Richmond Howl: The Army of the Potomac on the Eve of Chancellorsville." In Gallagher, *Chancellorsville: The Battle and Its Aftermath*, 1–35.

Herdegen, Lance J., and William J. K. Beaudot. *In the Bloody Railroad Cut at Gettysburg*. Dayton, Ohio: Morningside House, 1990.

Hunt, Roger D., and Jack R. Brown. *Brevet Brigadier Generals in Blue*. Gaithersburg, Md.: Olde Soldier Books, 1990.

Imholte, John Q. *The First Volunteers: History of the First Minnesota Volunteer Regiment, 1861–1865*. Minneapolis: Ross & Haines, 1963.

Ingleston, Kama Lee, and Wendy Ingleston, eds. *The 1863–1864 Civil War Diary of Captain James Penfield, Fifth New York Volunteer Cavalry Company H*. Ticonderoga, N.Y.: Press of America, 1999.

Jacques, John W. *Three Years' Campaign of the Ninth N.Y.S.M. During the Southern Rebellion*. New York: Hilton, 1865.

Johnson, Robert Underwood, and Clarence Clough Buel, eds., *Battles and Leaders of the Civil War*. 4 vols. New York: Century, 1887.

Jordan, William B., Jr., ed. *The Civil War Journals of John Mead Gould, 1861–1866*. Baltimore: Butternut and Blue, 1997.

Krick, Robert K. *Lee's Colonels: A Biographical Register of the Field Officers of the Army of Northern Virginia*, 4th ed. Dayton, Ohio: Morningside House, 1992.

————. *Stonewall Jackson at Cedar Mountain*. Chapel Hill: Univ. of North Carolina Press, 1990.

Livermore, Thomas L. *Days and Events, 1860–66*. Boston: Houghton Mifflin, 1920.

————. *Numbers and Losses in the Civil War in America, 1861–65*. 1901. Reprint, Dayton, Ohio: Press of Morningside House, 1986.

Longacre, Edward G. *The Cavalry at Gettysburg: A Tactical Study of Mounted Operations during the Civil War's Pivotal Campaign 9 June–14 July 1863*. Cranbury, NJ: Associated University Presses, 1986.

————. *Lincoln's Cavalrymen: A History of the Mounted Forces of the Army of the Potomac*. Mechanicsburg, Pa.: Stackpole Books, 2000.

Lowry, Thomas P. *Tarnished Eagles: The Courts -Martial of Fifty Union Colonels and Lieutenant Colonels*. Mechanicsburg, Pa.: Stackpole Books, 1997.

Malles, Ed, ed. *Bridge Building in Wartime: Colonel Wesley Brainerd's Memoir of the 50th New York Volunteer Engineers*. Knoxville: Univ. of Tennessee Press, 1997.

Marvel, William. *Burnside*. Chapel Hill: Univ. of North Carolina Press, 1991.

Marvin, William E. *The Fifth Regiment Connecticut Volunteers: A History Compiled from Diaries and Official Reports.* Hartford, Conn.: Press of Wiley, Waterman & Eaton, 1889.

Massachusetts Soldiers, Sailors and Marines in the Civil War. 8 vols. Norwood, Mass.: Norwood Press, 1931.

McClellan, George B. *McClellan's Own Story.* New York: Charles L. Webster, 1887.

McClellan, H. B. *The Life and Campaigns of Major General J. E. B. Stuart: Commander of the Calvary of the Army of Northern Virginia.* Boston: Houghton Mifflin, 1885.

McClenthen, Charles S. *A Sketch of the Campaign in Virginia and Maryland from Cedar Mountain to Antietam by a Soldier of the 26th N.Y.V.* Syracuse, N.Y.: Masters & Lee, 1862.

Meade, George. *The Life and Letters of George Gordon Meade, Major-General United States Army.* 2 vols. New York: Charles Scribner's Sons, 1913.

Milgram, James W., ed. "The Libby Prison Correspondence of Tattnall Paulding." *American Philatelist* 89, no. 12 (Dec. 1975): 1113–35.

Miller, Richard F., and Robert F. Mooney. "Across the River and into the Streets: The 20th Massachusetts Infantry and the Street Fight for Fredericksburg." *Civil War Regiments* 4 no. 4 (1995): 101–26.

Mills, J. Harrison. *Chronicles of the Twenty-First Regiment New York State Volunteers . . .* Buffalo: Gies, 1887.

Moore, Frank, ed. *The Rebellion Record: A Diary of American Events . . .* 12 vols. New York: G. P. Putnam and D. Van Nostrand, 1861–68.

Mundy, James H. *No Rich Men's Sons: The Sixth Maine Volunteer Infantry.* Cape Elizabeth, Maine: Harp Publications, 1994.

Murfin, James V. *The Gleam of Bayonets: The Battle of Antietam and the Maryland Campaign of 1862.* New York: Thomas Yoseloff, 1965.

Myer, Albert J. *A Manual of Signals.* New York: D. Van Nostrand, 1866.

Newcomer, C. Armour. *Cole's Cavalry; or, Three Years in the Saddle in the Shenandoah Valley.* Baltimore: Cushing, 1895.

Orr, Timothy J., ed. *Last to Leave the Field: The Life and Letters of First Sergeant Ambrose Henry Hayward, 28th Pennsylvania Volunteer Infantry.* Knoxville: Univ. of Tennessee Press, 2010.

Owen, Fred Wooster. *A Christmas Reminiscence of Fredericksburg, by Fred Wooster Owen, First Lieutenant and Signal Officer at the Battle of Fredericksburg.* Morristown, N.J.: N.p., 1895.

Phillips, Edward H. *The Lower Shenandoah Valley in the Civil War: The Impact of War upon the Civilian Population and Upon Civil Institutions.* Lynchburg, Va.: H. E. Howard, 1993.

Phisterer, Frederick. *New York in the War of the Rebellion, 1861–1865.* 3rd ed. 5 vols. Albany, N.Y.: J. B. Lyon, 1912.

Pride, Mike, and Mark Travis. *My Brave Boys: To War with Colonel Cross and the Fighting Fifth.* Hanover, N.H.: Univ. Press of New England, 2001.

Quaife, Milo M., ed. *From the Cannon's Mouth: The Civil War Letters of General Alpheus S. Williams.* Detroit: Wayne State Univ. Press, 1959.

Quint, Alonzo H. *The Potomac and the Rapidan: Army Notes from the Failure at Winchester to the Reenforcement of Rosecrans, 1861–3.* Boston: Crosby and Nichols, 1864.

————. *The Record of the Second Massachusetts Infantry, 1861–1865.* Boston: James P. Walker, 1867.

Raines, Rebecca Robbins. *Getting the Message Through: A Branch History of the U.S. Army Signal Corps.* Washington, D.C.: Center of Military History, United States Army, 1996.

Regimental Association. *History of the Eighteenth Regiment of Cavalry, Pennsylvania Volunteers (163rd Regiment of the Line), 1862–1865.* New York: Wynkoop Hallenbeck Crawford, 1909.

Report of the Adjutant General of the State of Maine for the Years 1864 and 1865. 2 vols. Augusta, Maine: Stevens and Sayward, 1866.

Reunions of the Signal Corps U.S.A. at Gettysburg, Pa. and Columbus, O., with a Roster of Members. N.p: n.p., 1888.

Robertson, James I., Jr., ed. *The Civil War Letters of General Robert McAllister.* New Brunswick, N.J.: Rutgers Univ. Press, 1965.

Robertson, John. *Michigan in the War.* Lansing: W. S. George, 1880.

Rowley, William W. "The Signal Corps of the Army During the Rebellion." In *War Papers: Being Papers Read Before the Commandery of the State of Wisconsin, Military Order of the Loyal Legion of the United States* 2:221–29. Milwaukee: Burdick, Armitage & Allen, 1896.

Sandburg, Carl. *Abraham Lincoln: The Prairie Years and the War Years.* One Volume edition. New York: Harcourt, Brace, 1954.

Scheips, Paul J. "Union Signal Communications: Innovation and Conflict." *Civil War History* 9, no. 4 (Dec. 1963): 399–421.

Schultz, Wallace J., and Walter N. Trenerry. *Abandoned by Lincoln: A Military Biography of General John Pope.* Urbana: Univ. of Illinois Press, 1990.

Sears, Stephen W. *Chancellorsville.* Boston: Houghton Mifflin, 1996.

————. *Controversies and Commanders: Dispatches from the Army of the Potomac.* Boston: Houghton Mifflin, 1999.

————. *George B. McClellan: The Young Napoleon.* New York: Ticknor & Fields, 1988.

————. *Landscape Turned Red: The Battle of Antietam.* New Haven, Conn.: Ticknor and Fields, 1983.

Sifakis, Stewart. *Who Was Who in the Civil War.* New York: Facts on File Publications, 1988.

Snell, Mark A. "Baptism of Fire: The 118th ('Corn Exchange') Pennsylvania Infantry at the Battle of Shepherdstown." *Civil War Regiments* 6, no. 2 (2000): 119–42.

Starr, George H. "In and Out of Confederate Prisons." In *Personal Recollections of the War of the Rebellion: Addresses Delivered Before the Commandery of the State of New York, Military Order of the Loyal Legion of the United States,* 2nd ser., 64–103. New York: G. P. Putnam's Sons, 1897.

Steiner, Jane B., ed. *George Washington Irwin: The Civil War Diary of a Pennsylvania Volunteer.* Lafayette, Calif.: Hunsaker, 1991.

Stevens, C. A. *Berdan's United States Sharpshooters in the Army of the Potomac, 1861–1865.* St. Paul: Price-McGill, 1892.

Stryker, William S. *Record of Officers and Men of New Jersey in the Civil War, 1861–1865.* 2 vols. Trenton, N.J.: John L. Murphy, 1876.

Styple, William B., ed. *Writing and Fighting the Civil War: Soldier Correspondence to the New York Sunday Mercury.* Kearny, N.J.: Belle Grove, 2000.

Survivors' Association. *History of the 118th Pennsylvania Volunteers Corn Exchange Regiment, from Their First Engagement at Antietam to Appomattox . . .* Philadelphia: J. L. Smith, 1905.

Tanner, Robert G. *Stonewall in the Valley: Thomas J. "Stonewall" Jackson's Shenandoah Valley Campaign, Spring 1862.* Mechanicsburg, Pa.: Stackpole Books, 1996.

Taylor, Frank H. *Philadelphia in the Civil War, 1861–1865.* Philadelphia: Published by the City, 1913.

Taylor, James E. *With Sheridan Up the Shenandoah Valley in 1864: Leaves from a Special Artist's Sketchbook and Diary.* Dayton, Ohio: Morningside House, 1989.

Thomas, Mary Warner, and Richard E. Sauers, eds. *The Civil War Letters of First Lieutenant James B. Thomas.* Baltimore: Butternut and Blue, 1995.

Thomson, O. R. Howard, and William H. Rauch. *History of the "Bucktails," Kane Rifle Regiment of the Pennsylvania Reserve Corps (13th Pennsylvania Reserves, 42nd of the Line)*. Philadelphia: Electric Light Printing, 1906.

Tobie, Edward P. *History of the First Maine Cavalry, 1861–1865*. Boston: Press of Emery & Hughes, 1887.

U.S. War Department, *The War of the Rebellion: A Compilation of the Official Records of the Union and Confederate Armies*, 70 vols. in 128 parts. Plus *Atlas*. Washington, D.C.: GPO, 1880–1901.

Wallber, Albert. "From Gettysburg to Libby Prison." In *War Papers Read Before the Commandery of the State of Wisconsin, Military Order of the Loyal Legion of the United States* 4:101–200. 1903. Reprint, Wilmington, N.C.: Broadfoot, 1993.

Walker, Francis Amasa. *History of the Second Army Corps in the Army of the Potomac*. New York: Charles Scribner's Sons, 1886.

Welker, David A. *Tempest at Ox Hill: The Battle of Chantilly*. Cambridge, Mass.: Da Capo Press, 2002.

Weld, Stephen Minot. *War Diary and Letters of Stephen Minot Weld, 1861–1865*. 2nd ed. Boston: Massachusetts Historical Society, 1979.

Wert, Jeffry. *The Sword of Lincoln: The Army of the Potomac*. New York: Simon & Shuster, 2005.

INDEX

Numbers in **boldface** refer to illustrations.

Hepburn, Lt. Leonard F., 5, 8, 11, 13, 14, 280n5

Hill, Maj. Gen. Ambrose Powell, 71, 78, 130, 136, 237, 238, 298n9, 313n21

Hill, Maj. Gen. Daniel Harvey, 129, 307n30, 310n8, 311n15, 333n30

Hill, Lt. George H., 205, 331n19

Hilt, Sgt. David B., 23–24, 286n25

Hogan, Martin E., 207, 209–10, 333n25

Holliday, Col. Jonas P., 49–50, 293nn20–21

Homer, Lt. Frederick, 124, 152, 155, 309n6

Hood, Brig. Gen. John Bell, 302n3, 311n15

Hood, Thomas, 196

Hooker, Maj. Gen. Joseph, 98, 126, 127, 129, 162, 164, 179, 188, 192, 196, 202, 203, 205, 212, 213, 219, 224–25, 226, 230, 232, 233–34, 237, 238, 239, 244, 247, 248, 310n9, 311n15, 327n15, 328n23, 330n13, 336n6, 337n13, 338n22, 340n3

Howard (civilian), 123–24

Howard, G., 207, **208**, 333n25

Howard, Maj. Gen. Oliver O., 174, 179, 203, 233, 324n4, 331n17, 338n20; Fortescue comments on, 204

Humphreys, Maj. Gen. Andrew A., 179, 323n1, 325n11

Hunt, Brig. Gen. Henry J., 173, 220, 324n3

Hyattstown, MD, 4, 5, 6

Imboden, Brig. Gen. John D., 270, 272, 273, 347n36

Indian Town, VA, 336n8

Indiana units, infantry: 16th, 281n9; 19th, 340n31

Iron Brigade, 304n16

Iron Springs-Maria Furnace Road, 343n19

Island No. 10, Battle of, 63

Jack's Mountain, 244, **250**, 257, 259, 260, 341n6, 342n8, 243nn19–20

Jack's Mountain Road, 343n19

Jackson, Lt. Gen. Thomas J., xxx, 29, 43, 47, 48, 51, 64, 72, 78, 81, 82, 83, 85–86, 95, 96, 98, 115, 124, 134, 136, 233, 234, 286n29, 300n25, 302nn2–3, 303nn10–11, 304nn16–17, 305n19, 307n31, 308n35, 313n22; Fortescue's comments on, 44–45

James City, VA, 298

James River, 64, 331n18

Janeway, Col. Hugh H., 247, 341n4

Jefferson, Thomas, 144

Jeffersonton, VA, 303n10

Jenkins, Brig. Gen. Micah, 315n28

Jerome, Lt. Aaron B., **8**, 124, **128**, 190, 222, 309n6

Jessie's Scouts, 162

Johnston, Lt. Gen. Joseph E., 22, 43

Jones, Brig. Gen. David R., 315n28

Jones, Capt. James Yancey, 293n18

Jones, Col. William E., 145, 317n6, 342n13

Kanawha Division, 126, 310n8,

Kane, Col. Dennis, 35, 144, 289n7

Kearny, Maj. Gen. Philip, Jr., 98, 158, 307n28; death of, 106

Kelly's Ford, 87, 91, 212, 214, 216, 225, 302n2, 303n11

Kelly's Ford, Battle of, 315–16, 333n30, 334nn31–32

Kendall, Capt. Charles S., 130, 144, 146, 150–51, 152, 156, 158, **159**, 161, 162, 167, 172, 173, 180, 184, 190, 199, 209, 216, 222, **223**, 226, 244, 250, 251, 257, 259, 261, 263, 266, 341n6, 342n9, 343n19, 344n22

Kernstown, VA, Battle of, xviii, 43, 45–46, 47, 56, 81

Kilpatrick, Brig. Gen. Judson, 257, 258, 260, 263, 265, 336n21, 344n21, 344n24, 345n26, 345n28

Kimball, Col. Nathan, 44, 45, 46, 47, 292n15

King and Queen County, 205

King George County, 205, 336n8

King, William S., Sr., 57, 294,27

Kirkwood House (hotel), 340n2

Knap, Capt. Joseph, 18, 27, 144, 148, 285n20

Knap's Battery. *See* Pennsylvania units, artillery, Independent Battery E

Knipe, Col. Joseph F., 64, 295n1

Knoxville, MD, 146, 149

Lacy House (Chatham), 162, 172–73, 174, 321n26

Larned, Lt. William C., 13, 18, 281n9

Lawton, Brig. Gen. Alexander, 302n5

Lee, Brig. Gen. Fitzhugh, 124, 145, 212, 214, 215, 309n4, 317n6

Lee, Gen. Robert E., xix, 64, 85–86, 104, 109, 112, 116, 125, 133, 138, 141, 146, 156, 169, 170, 183, 185, 188, 192, 202, 205, 209, 210, 211, 224–25, 230, 233, 234, 235, 237, 239, 242, 243, 247, 248, 258, 260, 265, 267, 268, 273, 302n6, 307nn33–34, 309n4, 313n22, 333n28, 336n10, 340n32, 343n16, 343n19, 344n24

Lee, Brig. Gen. William H. F., 317n6, 341n5

Leesburg Turnpike, 106

Leesburg, VA, 15–16, 34, 146, 284n16

Lentz. Maj. John D, 187, 327n16

Leppien, Capt. George, 300n25

Letford, Lt. William H., 4, 279n2

Lincoln, Abraham, xix, 25, 29, 36, 37, 47, 63, 75, 104, 122, 138, 139, 143–44, 156, 188,

192, 203, 220–21, 233, 234, 316n33, 318n11, 330nn12–13, 335n5

Lincoln, Mary, 220, 221, 335n5

Lincoln, Thomas (Tad), 220

Little River Turnpike, 306n23

Little Round Top, 253, 342n9, 343n14

Little Washington, VA, 65

Logan, Samuel, 25, 286n26

London, Lt. R. Horace, 6, 280n6

Long Bridge, 246

Long, Capt., 183–84

Long, Sans, 274

Long, William, 274

Longstreet, Lt. Gen. James, 85–86, 87, 95, 98, 235, 302n2, 303n12, 305n19, 313n21

Longworth, Mary C., xxxiii

Lord, Joe, 207, **208**

Loudoun County, 295n29

Loudoun Heights, VA, 34, 124

Loudoun Valley (VA), 14

Louisiana units

—artillery: Washington Artillery, 306n23

—infantry: Louisiana Tigers, 137, 315n28

Louisiana Tigers, 137, 315n28

Lovettsville, VA, 150

Lowe, Thaddeus, SC, 232, 235, 338n20, 339n25

Luray Valley, 48

Lyman, Lt. Col. Theodore, 335n4

Magee, (McGee), Sanford, 207, **208**, 333n25

Main Street (Richmond, VA), 274

Maine units

—artillery: 2nd Battery, 80, 300n25; 5th Battery, 80, 300n25

—cavalry: 1st, 81

—infantry: 6th, 229, 337n18

Major, Lt. W. N., 315n28

Manassas, Second Battle of, xxix, 96–99, 101, 104, 188, 234, 255, 318n15, 346n32

Manassas, Second, Campaign of, 86–104

Manassas Gap Railroad, 49

Manassas Junction, VA, 86, 96, 97, 304nn16–17

Manassas, VA, 30, 37, 38, 43, 95, 96

Mansfield, Maj. Gen. Joseph K. F., 129, 311n16

Marston, Lt. Frank W., 337n12

Martin, Pvt. James, 294n22

Martindale, Brig. Gen. John H., 314n25

Martinsburg, VA, 26, 37, 38, 60, 112, 269, 308n35, 315n31, 316n34, Unionism in, 286n29, 346n33

Marye's Heights, 181, 337, 338, 234, 237, 337n18, 338n23

Maryland Heights, 17, 26, 109, 115, 135, 144, 151, 278n10, 308n1; signal station on, **110**

"Maryland, My Maryland" (song), 160, 320n22

Marston, Lt. Frank W., 226, 337n12

Maryland Campaign (1862), xxix, 133, 211, 283n14, 307n34, 308n1

Mason-Dixon line, 243

Massachusetts units
—cavalry: 1st, 167
—infantry: 2nd, 51, 52–53, 55, 294n26; 12th, 6, 11; 16th, 176; 19th, 175; 20th, 175

Massanutten Mountains, 51, 55, 58

Massaponax Creek, 340n29

Mauch Chunk, PA, 23, 286n24

Maulsby, Col. William P., 113, 308n37

McCamick, George, 207, **208**, 333n25

McClellan, Maj. Gen. George B., xix, xxvi–xxvii, 16–17, 29, 30, 34, 35, 36, 43, 47, 64, 66, 67, 85, 95, 97, 104, 116, 122, 125, 126, 127, 129, 130, 132–33, 138, 139, 143–44, 145–46, 150, 154, 158, 169, 170, 172, 234, 312n19, 313nn20–21, 316n33, 318n11, 319n18, 323n1, 330n12; Fortescue's opinion of, xxv, 124, 155–56; relieved of command, 155–56

McDowell, Maj. Gen. Irvin, 47, 63, 65, 67, 72, 81, 87, 91, 94, 97, 98, 303n11, 304n16

McGill, Lt. James D., 144, 317n5

McIntosh, Col. John B., 213, 333n29

Meade, Maj. Gen, George G., 99, 126, 127, 129, 211, 244, 248, 252, 258, 260, 268, 305n19, 335n4, 342n9

Meagher, Brig. Gen. Thomas Francis, 216, 217, 334n33

Merritt, Brig. Gen. Wesley, 253, 342n12

Meterker family, 108

Metropolitan Hotel, 165

Michigan units, 33, 34, 59
—cavalry: 1st, 51, 289n3
—infantry: 7th, 175

Middle Bridge, 313n21

Middle Military Department, 308n35

Middleburg, PA, 118, 309n3

Middletown, MD, 126, 311n12

Miles, Col. Dixon S., 109, 111, 112–13, 124, 127, 247, 307n31, 308n35

Military Order of the Loyal Legion of the United States, xxxv

Millerstown Pike, 248, 253, 257, 258, 342n13

Milroy, Brig. Gen. Robert H., 305n19

Miner, Lt. Brinkerhoff N., 13, 18, 37, 38, 39, 46, 47, 48, 51, 53, 55, 69, 76, 87, 98, 195 109, 111–12, 124, 281n9, 299n17, 307n33

Minnesota units, infantry: 1st, 13, 71

Missionary Ridge, Battle of, 331n18

Mississippi River, 273

Taylor, Lt. Peter A., 164, 228, 229, 321n27

telegraph, xviii, 8, 30, 105, 274, 288n1, 322n30

Telegraph Road, 214, 229, 230

Thanksgiving, 25, 165

Thomas, Lt. Evan, 11, 17, 18, 281n8

Thomas, Maj. Gen. George H., xxviii

Thompson, Lt. H. H., 315n28

Thomson, James, 345n27

Thoroughfare Gap, 86, 95, 101, 303n10, 303n12

Thoroughfare Mountain, 69, 71, 72, 74, 298n10

Torbert, Col. Alfred T. A., 306n23

Tourison, Capt. Ashton S., 34, 289n4

Tower, Brig. Gen. Zealous B., 99, 305n19

Trenton, NJ, 155

Trimble, Brig. Gen. Isaac R., 302n3, 304n19

Tyler, Col. Erastus B., 44, 292n15

Turner's Gap, 125, 126, 310nn8–10

Tyler, Capt. Robert, 341n5

Tyler's Hill, 226

Tyndale, Maj. Hector, 25, 32, 286n28

Union Insurance Company, xxxiv

United States Ford, 329n7

United States units

—artillery: 4th, Battery F, 55, 76, 80, 202, 283n11

—cavalry: 6th, 253, 271, 342n13

—sharpshooters: 1st, 303n8; 2nd, 91, 303n8

U.S. Army Signal Corps, xvii, xxiii, xxxi, 30, 46, 82, 92, 107, 124, 141, 235, 236, 245, 279n17, 279n20, 312n18, 339n25; attitudes of U.S. officers to, xxvi, xxvii, 157; Civil War makeup of, 279n20; composition of detachments, xxi, 9; perception as

unreliable, xxvi–xvii; praise of, xxvi–xxviii, 46, 279n17, 292n17; promotion in, 278n9, 318n13; requirements for officers of, xv, 11, 277n5; role of, xxiii–xxiv; underappreciated, xvii, 292n17

U.S. Veteran Signal Corps Association, xxxv

Upton's Hill, 107

Valley Campaign (1862), 292n17

Valley Pike, 49, 55, 270

Vermont units, 104; cavalry: 1st, 49, 293w20

Vicksburg, MS, 243, 270, 273

Vienna Road, 105

Vincent, Pvt. Robert, 317n7

Virginia Central Railroad, 273

Virginia units

—cavalry: 12th, 301n31; 35th Battalion, 295n29

—infantry: 1st Battalion, 293n18; 12th, 83

Wadsworth, Brig. Gen. James S., 206, 332n22n, 336n10

Wagman, Mr., 251

Walker, Maj. Alvin, 203, 331n16

Walker, Brig. Gen. John G., 312n17

War Department, 30, 31, 43, 95, 113, 149, 189, 202, 236, 239, 244, 319n17, 343n16

Warren, Brig. Gen. Gouverneur K., 342n9

Warren Green Hotel, 64

Warrenton Turnpike, 92, 304n16, 305n19, 306n21, 306n23

Warrenton, VA, 64, 67, 81, 91, 94, 95, 157, 303nn9–11, 304n13

Washington, Adjutant, 263

Washington Chronicle, 178

Washington, D.C., xvii, xix, 11, 13, 22, 29, 35, 43, 48, 49, 61, 63, 65, 104–5, 111, 113, 116,